THE CACTUS THRONE
The Tragedy of Maximilian and Carlotta

Other books by Richard O'Connor

O. HENRY:
*The Legendary Life
of William S. Porter*

THE FIRST HURRAH

PACIFIC DESTINY

THE GERMAN-AMERICANS

AMBROSE BIERCE: *A Biography*

BRET HARTE: *A Biography*

JACK LONDON: *A Biography*

GOULD'S MILLIONS

BLACK JACK PERSHING

The

THE TRAGEDY

Cactus Throne

OF MAXIMILIAN AND CARLOTTA

by Richard O'Connor

G. P. Putnam's Sons, New York

Contents

6 CONTENTS

Illustrations appear after page 190

Prologue

WHAT a scheme it was. An unemployed Hapsburg princeling and his young wife, the daughter of the King of Belgium, would be placed on the throne of Mexico by a French emperor to guarantee the repayment of a fraudulent loan. They would be maintained amid the lost grandeur of the Aztecs behind a frieze of bayonets by the temporarily idle French Foreign Legion until the last peso had been wrung from the impoverished and resentful Mexican people. A Hapsburg/Bonaparte emperor would reign in Mexico City while Abraham Lincoln presided over the disunited states to the north. The paradox was that the Austrian archduke fancied himself as much a liberal humanitarian as the American President and that both would fall victim to gunfire directed at the ideas they lucklessly embodied.

Surely it must have seemed more like grand opera than a deliberate attempt to change history. From our viewpoint the actors on that stage appear as posturing anachronisms rather than great personages; a stranded company of players trouping in a Graustarkian drama which somehow ended its tour in the halls of Montezuma. Only in terms of nineteenth-century melodrama, complete with royal plotters, noble dupes, scheming bishops, self-dramatizing queens and gossipy courtiers, against a background of baroque palaces and crumbling plazas lighted by flamboyant Mexican sunsets, does the whole affair assume the credibility of something more than a harlequinade. The blood, after all, was real.

The tragedy of Maximilian and Carlotta, and that of the thousands who died or were bereft as a result of their venture in the New World, could have been the product only of a period phosphorescent with decay and delusion. Its rouged and corseted symbol was Napoleon III, pretender to the glory and accomplishment of his uncle; its capitals were the Paris of the Second Empire and the Vienna whose gorgeous soldiery waltzed better than they fought; its psychology was brilliantly illumined in the novels of Honoré de Balzac.

Balzac had worked himself to death by the time that his country experienced its second and final convulsion of Napoleonism, but in his novel *Père Goriot* he described its atmosphere precisely when the cynical Vicomtesse de Beauséant advises the thrusting young M. de Restignac on how to advance himself in Parisian life:

> The world is ignoble and nasty. As soon as one meets with misfortune, a friend always comes to tell of it and to twist a dagger in one's heart, and in the very moment of doing so asks one to admire the beauty of its hilt. . . .
>
> Well, Monsieur de Rastingnac, treat this world as it deserves. You want to succeed. I'll help you. You will discover how deeply corrupt women are, and you'll measure the enormous and wretched vanity of men. . . . the more coldly you calculate, the farther you'll climb. If you strike without pity, you will be feared. Use men and women only as horses for your coach, and by the time they've finished the stage they are to carry you, let them founder, and you will come to the very height of your desires. Note that you can achieve nothing here unless you have some woman who takes an interest in you. She must be young, rich and elegant. If you feel any genuine emotion, hide it like a treasure; don't ever let it be suspected, or you'd be ruined. . . . If women think you witty and gifted, men will believe them unless you show them their error. Then you can aim at anything; you will have an entry everywhere. And then you will find what the world is, a gathering of dupes and rogues. . . .

I. MIRAMAR

1. "A Gathering of Dupes and Rogues"

There are gentle natures in which ideas penetrate and carry destruction; but there are also tougher natures, skulls with ramparts of brass, against which the wills of others flatten out and fall as helpless as bullets before a strong wall. . . .

—Honoré de Balzac, *Père Goriot*

Bastard half brothers, rankled by shame and resentment, should be approached with caution. When that half brother is also the grandson of Prince Talleyrand and of the Empress Josephine, both persons of supple intelligence and nimble wit, his heredity alone makes him dangerous to befriend. Yet Napoleon III and the man officially known as the Duc de Morny became close friends and collaborators. And when the papier-mâché Second Empire was about to collapse in a rubble of nostalgic memories and called bluffs, Napoleon III still mourned his half brother's death for both sentimental and practical reasons. "Poor Morny, why did he die—the only man to whom I could talk," the ruined man meditated aloud to his physician. "He would have carried through the Mexican affair. He was a capable man—very capable. He warned me that Bismarck would make trouble. It has all come about as he foresaw. There would have been no war if Morny had lived; he would have seen through that Ems affair at once—that it was a trick."

It was too late to invoke the genius of Morny and probably
futile even if he were still alive. Even Morny's talent for inviting disaster, then avoiding the consequences, could not have
saved Napoleonic France from the Prussian armies. What was
significant about Napoleon III's touching tribute to his half
brother was that it testified to his faith in Morny and his own
misapprehension of what it had brought about. Thanks in
great part to Morny, he had been led down the sea road to Mexico, with all its disastrous consequences. The difference between the half brothers was that Napoleon III was part Bonaparte, while Morny was part Talleyrand—and it is the Talley-
rands of the world who survive.

The Duc de Morny was a master of the art of survival. He
had to be, considering the circumstances of his concealed birth
and the state of bastardy which was his inheritance. Illegitimacy ran in the family. His own father, the bastard son of
Talleyrand, would bewail the family tendency on the occasion
of the Duc de Morny's death: "It is strange," he said. "Here am
I—nearly seventy-four. My father Talleyrand—my son Morny.
I bury them both. And can call neither by name. No right
to say 'father;' no right to say 'son' when I bid them farewell. . . ."

That regretful man, son and father of bastardy, was Auguste
Charles Joseph de Flahaut—his mother's surname. His mother
was Adèle de Flahaut, an amiable woman who had acquired
the "protection" of the young priest Talleyrand, soon to be
Bishop of Autun and after being excommunicated still later to
be Prince Talleyrand and chief adviser to Napoleon I. One result of that protection was the son born to Adèle de Flahaut in
1785. With his unacknowledged father's assistance he became a
general at the age of twenty-four and a court favorite of Napoleon.

A handsome, dashing, witty young man, Charles de Flahaut
caught the eye of Hortense de Beauharnais, the daughter of the
Empress Josephine and stepdaughter of Napoleon, a plump
and passionate Creole who was married off with Corsican dispatch to Napoleon's brother Louis, the King of Holland, thus
becoming Napoleon's sister-in-law, as well as his stepdaughter.
King Louis was a dull dog, and Queen Hortense fell in love
with General Charles de Flahaut when he was serving as aide-

de-camp to the emperor. The young general was in love with a Polish lady but could not withstand the queen, who had Mother Josephine's amatory willfulness. Queens are not exempt from awkward pregnancy. In the fall of 1811 Hortense, accompanied only by a trusted woman servant, made a clandestine journey and took lodgings in Geneva under an assumed name. There a son was born to her on October 21, 1811. He would never frolic at Malmaison with another son, the legitimate issue of her marriage, Louis Napoleon, but they would eventually meet, without maternal sanction but with dire consequences to the French, Austrian and Mexican peoples.

The illegitimate son was in fact whisked away into temporary obscurity while his mother resumed her position as Queen of Holland. The grandson of Napoleon's consul for life and of Napoleon's first wife, the Empress Josephine, the son of the Queen of Holland and a general, was registered in the Third Arrondissement, Department of the Seine, as the son of a tradesman named Demorny. In gratitude to that shoemaker and tailor, who died three years after his birth, he later titled himself the Duc de Morny. At birth, however, he had been registered as Charles Auguste Louis Joseph Demorny.

His father married Margaret Elphinstone, Countess of Keith and Nairne, several years after the Napoleonic Wars had ended. Auguste Demorny was not abandoned. His paternal grandmother, now Mme. Flahaut-Souza, taking a lenient view of her son's indiscretion and its issue, assumed the responsibility for his upbringing. She and her family lived in London, a refugee household dedicated to Napoleonic memories. In 1820 they returned to France, and the nine-year-old Auguste Demorny was introduced to his natural grandfather, Prince Talleyrand. His natural father, too, returned to France and took an interest in the boy's education. Once, by accident, they met Queen Hortense, now the Duchesse de St. Leu, in Aix-la-Chapelle, and she made such a fuss over the uncomprehending child that he begged his father to ask the strange lady not to "paw" him.

With the Revolution of 1830 and the ascension of Louis Philippe, the social, political and economic climate warmed for all monarchist families. Auguste Demorny's father was appointed a lieutenant general of the royal army. The youth himself, now nineteen, manufactured a pedigree for himself with a stroke of

the pen, changing his name from Demorny to the more aristocratic De Morny, and it became known somehow that he was
not the son of a tailor but the grandson of Talleyrand and the
son of Queen Hortense. This provided him with social creden-
tials. A royal bastard gains in glamor what he loses in respect-
ability.

He entered the army as a dilettante sublieutenant in the First
Lancers and was often received by his grandfather, Talleyrand,
who once told him, from the depths of his own cynical wisdom,
"You and I, Auguste, we shall have our apologists a hundred
years from now. A man that is whitewashed at such a distance
of time must be gloriously black. . . . Black is not a color. It is
the symbol of invisibility—night, ebony, and the grave. Be
black, my dear boy, and you may accomplish anything beneath
the cloak . . . education, the franchise, liberty, democracy. Aye,
draw your sword! Brandish it in the name of democracy, work
for democracy. But under the cloak, always under the cloak of
blackness, of knavery. Otherwise your political life will be
snuffed out. . . ."

Talleyrand foresaw a Napoleonic restoration, and advised
Morny that when his half brother, Louis Napoleon, became
emperor to "stand by him" for his own selfish reasons. To prepare for that restoration, perhaps, he submerged himself in a
military career for the next half dozen years and accompanied
his regiment on the pacification campaigns in North Africa. An
English newspaper took note of his career some years later and
reported that Lieutenant Auguste de Morny "made the campaign of Mascara and of Constantine. Of the bravery, coolness
and energy of M. de Morny there can be no doubt whatever.
He was wounded under the walls of Constantine and was hon-
ourably mentioned in affairs, for which he received the reward dearest to a French soldier's heart—the *croix d'
honneur.*"

"Already," he wrote Grandfather Talleyrand, "I am
becoming Bonapartist in thought. Although my friends speak
of the ogrishness of the late Emperor, it seems to me that this
aspect is being forgotten . . . his name is being polished up for
the grandsons by the veterans of the neglected Grand Army. A
great champion of France will presently be in demand, and

anyone will be welcome who is against the profiteering of the existing dull government."

Morny resigned his commission and returned to France a hero. There was more to his ambition than an appetite for military glory. The speculators, the entrepreneurs, the stock promoters of the Bourse were the men who counted now, and Morny became one of them. Manufacturing beet sugar in the Auvergne may have lacked something in aristocratic grandeur, but it made Morny prosperous and gave him a leg up on a political career as well. As the *Times* of London summarized his career between leaving the army and taking up his "black" role as brother of Louis Napoleon: "The delegates of the sugar interest soon appointed him their Secretary with a view to defending the interests of the trade. The superior manner in which he explained and enforced their views in a clever pamphlet caused him to be ultimately elected president of the Society. In 1842, he first became a member of the Chamber of Deputies, and frequently spoke in a manner to excite attention, from his coolness and aplomb. But although a certain ability and energy cannot be denied to M. de Morny, no one supposed him to be specially cut out for a parliamentary life, or for a great minister of State. To every man acquainted with Parisian society in the five years from 1843 to 1848, it was well known that M. de Morny was more deeply engaged on the turf, at the Jockey Club and the gambling table, and in the foyer of the Opera, than in parliamentary business. . . ."

Morny was in fact a dandy, a boulevardier, a balding but still dashing pursuer of society women. His sugar factories in the Auvergne provided him with a mansion on the Champs-Élysées. One thing he had inherited from Talleyrand: the ability to manipulate other men and to survive the collapse of regimes. The Revolution of 1848 did not catch him in its rubble, nor did a stock-promotion scandal in which he made off with half a million francs.

Following his grandfather's advice, he cloaked himself in "blackness," invisibility, and while pretending to go along with the restoration of republican government, he had begun working underground for the elevation of his half brother, Louis Napoleon. Brother met brother one morning at the Hôtel du

Rhin with a cool handshake. There was little resemblance except for the sleepy Creole eyes and nothing to suggest that both were sons of the gushingly sentimental Hortense.

Their initial exchange was brief but revealing:

"You are an Orleanist, I am given to understand," Louis Napoleon said.

"I am anything the occasion requires," Morny replied.

Morny, bearing his grandfather's advice in mind, supported Louis Napoleon in the election of 1849, which placed the latter in the presidency. Thereafter he became his half brother's most ardent but calculating supporter and adviser. He made himself the steel rod in the vacillating, daydreaming Louis Napoleon's backbone. Without Morny, there could have been no *coup d'etat* of 1851, by which Louis Napoleon vaulted to the throne and proclaimed the Napoleonic restoration. Immediately appointed Minister of the Interior, Morny set about arresting and imprisoning all the more vociferous republicans and subduing the scattered uprisings; he gave the nation only two alternatives, Napoleon or anarchy. And he infused the newly minted Napoleon III with a sense of historical purpose.

"We are not rooted in power," he told Napoleon. "We are in the place of power, but we cannot remain against unpopularity. To retain popular imagination you must awake the old tradition. Wars will be necessary."

Napoleon demurred that he hated bloodshed, and besides, the country could not afford the costs of war.

"Wars are imperative," Morny replied. "They must be victorious, of course, and as bloodless and inexpensive as possible, but they must be, if there is to be any credit to the name of Napoleon. As for money, the people will pay for war with passionate eagerness when it is impossible to extract a two-centime tax for the decent operation of a peaceful government."

From the depths of his cynicism and his contempt for the masses, he prescribed "restricted political liberty" but increased freedom for the individual in the economic sphere. Napoleon went along with that prescription but differed with his chief adviser—or evil genius—on the necessity of forming a Franco-Russian alliance. Napoleon was pro-German and favored an alliance with Prussia, a fatal affection indeed. "With Morny originated the idea of an enduring and necessary alliance between France and Russia"—an idea carried out by a much later French government—as Maurice Paléologue wrote in his memoir of Eugénie, the consort of Napoleon III, in *The Tragic Empress.* "Morny spoke of the scheme in 1852. Though his dream was delayed, and, as it seemed, frustrated by the Crimean War, it is his great claim to the name of statesman. Because his nature was one of studied indifference, and because after originating a notable plan he permitted it to slide into hands more capable than his, he has not received credit for his soundest ideas." Obviously, if Prussia had been boxed in by a Franco-Russian alliance, the Second Empire might have survived.

Morny retired from the Interior Ministry after establishing order and flung himself into the wild speculations of the Bourse. Gambling on the stock market had become a national obsession, with even tradesmen and servants joining in the frantic speculation. Napoleon III wondered whether it shouldn't be checked by government intervention, but Morny, as one of the leading profiteers, an insider in both financial circles and the highest echelons of the government, firmly advised against it. "The fever of the Bourse," he soothingly explained to the new emperor, "is highly contagious and more difficult to control than the cholera. It must run its course. We must not make the mistake of the July Monarchy, which neglected the truism that riches are not so much a protection of the government in power as a challenge to the majority excluded from power by the barrier of wealth. Let everyone become rich—if he can."

For the richest of all, he nominated himself. From then on, he devoted himself increasingly to building up his fortune. If speculation was a fever, he was as stricken as any *midinette* gambling half her week's pay, and it was Morny the gambler, not Morny the statesman *manqué,* who would lead Napoleon into the Mexican morass for the sake of another spin of the wheel. Magic Morny he was called by those who watched him operating on the Bourse, his Auvergne sugar mills forgotten. But he was realistic enough to know it was all a game and that when it was over, the master thimblerigger himself would be blamed. "It is a house of cards," he said. "When it crashes they will say I blew it down."

Meanwhile, he used his position as imperial half brother, his seat in the Chamber of Deputies, his insider's knowledge of what was happening in the Quai d'Orsay to keep building that house of cards. "Who is there ignorant of 'those fortunate speculations' which lately signalize the stock exchange?" one of his fellow deputies demanded, glaring across the floor at Morny. "The news received in the evening and kept back till the following day, after time had been allowed for the transaction of important operations. The Chamber of Deputies, perfectly indifferent to the bounty on sugar, yet the bounty increased since 1830 from seven millions to nineteen, and singularly enough, nearly the third of this sum is divided between six large firms, including the houses of certain of your members whom you especially delight to honour and particularly that of a member of the Cabinet."

As of 1852, in fact, Napoleon III was still rather suspicious of his clever, epigrammatic half brother with his devilish smile, his casual manner, his supreme worldliness. He also suspected that a greater ambition burned in Morny than his careless attitude indicated, that Morny, having plotted on Napoleon's behalf to reestablish Napoleonism, might now be conspiring to take over the edifice as its proprietor rather than the doorkeeper. He was not yet reconciled to the fact that his sainted mother had actually provided him with an illegitimate half brother. Perhaps he also sensed that Morny's less protected youth had made him the stronger as well as the suppler of the two. "Louis Napoleon," wrote Morny's biographer, "was a mother-worshipper, and the affront of Morny's having been born at all was at the root of his dislike. Yet Hortense had served Louis Napoleon very badly and Morny very well. Morny had been disposed of and freed from her baleful influence while yet being watched over from a distance. Louis Napoleon had been tied to her erratic apron-strings until manhood, and, not content with that mischief, she had bequeathed to him, in 1837, a little black book full of bad advice."

In any case, Napoleon eventually realized that he was wrong in suspecting that his half brother wanted the throne for himself. That would have denied the Talleyrand, the kingmaker, the "invisible" exerciser of power, in Morny. His nature inclined him toward taking the cash and letting the credit (and the headaches of ruling the unruly French) go to someone else. "He was a pestiferous bee in the Bourse, lighting here and there to sting some rash speculator, and frightening everyone with his quiet, persistent buzzing," his biographer wrote. "For he knew some of everybody's secrets; he had his pockets full of secrets, from the circumstance that, in the eagerness for his advice, they all confided in him. And what he did not know, he soon guessed, from the formula that he was sure of nothing worse of himself than was generally true of his neighbors."

Morny reveled in his career as financial genius and industrial magnate. In addition to his sugar factories, he presided over a complex of farms, dye works, charcoal factories in Liège and zinc mines near Aix-la-Chapelle. Company promoters swarmed around him. If Morny was known to be "in" on a promotion, its stock immediately shot upward on the Bourse.

Daring enough in other matters, he waited until he was forty-five years old before getting married. It happened suddenly, in St. Petersburg, when he was dispatched as Napoleon's ambassador extraordinary to form a hasty alliance with Russia against the threat of a war with Austria late in 1856. His adoring valet reported the news in a letter to his wife in Paris: "Well, it is all over with my poor master. He has taken one of those Russian princesses for a wife. It is the Princess Sophie Troubetzkoi, one of the Tsarina's ladies. She got him at last and they were married this morning at the cathedral. It was a magnificent affair, with all Russia present." That occasion was marred only when the wedding procession left the cathedral and one of the capital's ubiquitous beggar-musicians, whom Morny for some reason loathed excessively, "came impudently close and began his plaint. The master turned quite green with rage." Morny took his religion lightly, and that worried his valet. "After taking a devout Catholic to wife any frightful thing may happen. There will either be a conversion or many scenes."

The Princess Sophie was as ornamental as she was devout. She and Morny got along well enough, and he even indulged her, on the return to Paris, by bringing along her menagerie of parrots, lizards, monkeys, a leopard and a tame wolf. "We are married to a circus, he and I," the valet, Henri, grumbled in a letter to his wife. The Mornys had four children. He is regarded in history as the No. 1 rakehell of the Second Empire, but at least he broke the chain of illegitimacy which began with the young priest Talleyrand.

For a year or two after his marriage, Morny retired to his château at Nades, near Clermont, where he ruled a 20-square-mile estate in a manner which suggested that the French Revolution had never happened. He returned to Paris when Napoleon, to the bitter disappointment of Empress Eugénie, appointed him regent while the emperor rode off with his armies for the forcible unification of Italy. It was a limited success. Morny's advice on Napoleon's return, which was hastened by a massing of Prussian armies on the Rhine, was to "liberalize" the government. "In concentrating upon our own affairs," Morny added in his sardonic fashion, "we must not neglect to bewilder Europe. We are weak in the military sense; our navy is laughable; therefore, we have only bewilderment as a weapon." Morny believed that France could be governed only with the gambler's insouciance which characterized his own operations on the Bourse; he also knew better than anyone else that France was not in any material or spiritual way equipped for large-scale adventures abroad. There was an illusion of prosperity; Paris itself was being rebuilt by Baron Haussmann and others, but it was all a façade. Morny saw that his country could only bluff and bewilder for the time being and hope that other nations did not realize how poor she was in spirit.

Yet it was the clever Morny who arranged for his country's prestige to be involved in an overseas venture and a French army to be committed to the Mexican deserts and the French nation, as a result, to be weakened that much more just when she needed all her strength to confront Bismarck's Prussia.

That disastrous intervention began one day in 1859 just after Morny had surrendered his regency. A man named Jean Baptiste Jecker, a Swiss national who had been living in Mexico, came to see him at his mansion on the Champs-Élysées. Such unbidden visitors were always received during the two morning hours which the elegant Morny devoted to preparing himself to face the world. Between nine and eleven his valet, Henri, shaved his master, ministered to his complexion with massage and ointments, and waxed his skewerlike mustachios.

In that heavily scented dressing room the plump and nervous

M. Jecker explained his situation to Morny. Until recently he had headed the banking house of Jecker, Torre and Company in Mexico City. He had arranged a 3,000,000-franc loan for the Mexican government on issuance of Mexican State Bonds which would mature at a value of 75,000,000 francs. The deal was so usuriously outrageous that even Morny must have been shocked. At that, only part of the loan had been paid into the Mexican treasury. Jecker was bankrupt and could not conclude the transaction. He had come to Paris to settle down and wanted to become a naturalized French citizen.

Everyone said, Jecker went on, that the Duc de Morny was the one man clever and influential enough to rescue him from his dilemma. So he had a proposition for Morny: He would sell his Mexican State Bond issue for 10 percent of the loan to Morny, who would also see to it that Jecker became a French citizen. A juicy proposition indeed, especially since the Jecker loan carried with it the right to explore Sonora and Baja California for mineral concessions.

Morny promptly formed a syndicate to take the Mexican State Bonds off Jecker's hands and began investigating the possibilities of collecting on them. The prospects, at the moment, were rather dim. The French minister to Mexico City, Count Dubois de Saligny, was a friend and collaborator of Morny's and supplied him with the necessary information.

Morny immersed himself in a study of recent Mexican history. It was a study in political and social turbulence. During the long and intermittent reign of General Antonio López de Santa Anna over Mexican affairs, the country had engaged in a disastrous war with the United States, which a dozen years earlier had detached the territories of Texas, New Mexico, Arizona and California. The country now had two presidents, General Miguel Miramón, the Conservative who was supported by the privileged classes, the landowners, the Catholic hierarchy, the Spanish aristocracy and most of the mestizos, and Benito Juárez, a full-blooded Indian, head of the Liberal Party and hope of the Indian masses. Miramón sat in Mexico City's National Palace at the moment while his better-equipped troops harried Juárez and his followers from place to place. Yet the fugitive president, Juárez, had been recognized by the United States, partly because the European powers favored Miramón and partly because Juárez had signed the McLane-Ocampo Treaty which, in exchange for $2,000,000 to keep his army in the field, provided that the United States was granted two rights in perpetuity: the right of transit across the Isthmus of Tehuantepec and the option of sending American troops onto Mexican soil to protect endangered American property.

It was obvious that General Miramón deserved French support, or at least Morny's. He was manageable or corruptible, it was apparent from Dubois de Saligny's dispatches. Juárez, during a brief term in power, had passed the Reform Laws which abolished all titles of nobility, proposed to break up the great haciendas, granted freedom of the press and the right of assembly. Even more drastically, Juárez's doctrine, not yet placed into effect except in territory under his military control, called for confiscation of all church property, closed down all monasteries, convents and seminaries, and prohibited priests and nuns from appearing on the streets in their clerical robes. To Morny's sensitive nostrils there was more than a whiff of Jacobinism about Benito Juárez. Miramón, on the other hand, had signed the agreement with Jecker, Torre and Company for the minuscule loan backed by Mexican State Bonds.

The Mexican balance sheet made very depressing reading for Morny. The Jecker loan was only a tiny fraction of Mexican indebtedness, and France itself was the least of Mexico's creditors. The claims against Mexico included England's $69,311,657, Spain's $9,461,986 and France's $2,860,762 (excluding the Jecker loan). Against all those claims, greatly inflated as they were, the annual income of the Mexican government totaled only 12,000,000 pesos; not enough to pay the interest, let alone reduce the principal.

Unless some sort of drastic action were taken, it was apparent that Mexico would never be willing or able to pay off her foreign obligations. The possibility that the silver and other minerals of Sonora, conceded to Jecker under the loan agreement with General Miramón, might be more profitable than the Mexican national treasury naturally occurred to Morny. The Sonora concession probably was what persuaded Morny to take over the Mexican bond issue with his syndicate.

A rapid turn of events, a shuffling of presidential occupants of the National Palace, soon queered that calculation. President-General Miramón was proving to be something of a disappointment to his European supporters. In desperate need of money to pay his mercenaries, he had broken the British legation's seals on the house of an English financial agent and helped himself to the 600,000 pesos deposited there to cover payments on an English loan. A few weeks later Miramón scuttled the Conservative cause, for the time being, and fled into Cuban exile. He was immediately replaced by Juárez, who began instituting his radical reform program.

With Juárez as president, it was obvious that Morny's syndicate would never be able to recoup on the Jecker loan. Among his first pronouncements from the National Palace were a "postponement" of payments on all foreign loans, which Juárez contended were fraudulent to begin with and should not be a burden on the Mexican people, and a cancellation of the Jecker concession to exploit the Sonora silver mines.

About the same time Abraham Lincoln was elected President of the United States and instructed his appointee as U.S. Minister to Mexico City, "Be just, frank and magnanimous. Gain the confidence of the people, and show that your mission is earnestly American, in the continental sense of that word, and fraternal in no affected or mere diplomatic meaning." The new American President obviously was going to befriend Juárez—and the Seine was a lot farther from Mexico City than the Rio Grande.

Morny's problem was how to unseat Juárez and install as president a man more sympathetic to the claims of foreign bondholders, without offending the United States and its sacred Monroe Doctrine and possibly provoking a counterintervention. That was solved, of course, when the South seceded from the Union and Washington was fully occupied with fighting a civil war. The cause of Benito Juárez would have to wait until Washington put down the secession. The cause of the foreign bondholders could now be advanced.

And with Morny in command of the French syndicate, collaborating with the English and Spanish bondholders, that cause would be advanced vigorously. The matter of Mexican indebtedness was transferred from the Bourse to the Tuileries, where Napoleon and Eugénie were seized with the fever dream of an overseas empire, a massive resurgence of French influence over the New World, a twin capital of Napoleonic splendor built on the ruins of the Aztec civilization. Skeptical though he was of such adventures, of overextending the diminished energies of the French nation, Morny evidently did little or nothing to discourage such ambitions or dissipate the grandiose vapors which had begun to envelop his half brother.

Morny himself was preoccupied with the ceremonies attendant on his elevation to a dukedom. All through the countryside surrounding his country estate, with Clermont-Ferrand as the center of the festivities, the Auvergnats decked out their houses with flags and flowers for the occasion. Napoleon and Eugénie came down by railway, and there was a vast assemblage in Clermont when Auguste de Morny was proclaimed the Duc de Morny. A rainstorm suddenly descended on the crowded square, but no one took it as a bad omen.

Once that seal was affixed to the clouded lineage of the man who had been given a tailor's name at birth, the brothers could turn their attention to the possibilities of taking a more forceful interest in Mexican affairs. It was even whispered that the Duc de Morny might be elevated still further to Emperor of Mexico, but he was too realistic to place much actuarial confidence in such a regime.

To an admirer who mentioned such rumors he replied, "My dear sir, if I depart from France, neither I nor my brother would be an Emperor in six months time. . . . The Great American Empire shall be accomplished only if it have an engineer as well as an Emperor. I choose the more concealed position."

He still followed the advice on "invisibility" promulgated in his youth by his cagey Grandfather Talleyrand. The "concealed position" was not only safest but the most profitable. The role of "engineer" suited him to the waxed spikes of his mustachios. Already the quest for a Mexican emperor was well under way, not in Mexico but in Europe, and a suitable candidate had been selected in the Austrian realms to the east.

2. A Prince for Herr Biedermeier

Authority was a brazen tablet with these indestructible words engraved upon it: "No concessions, no constitution, no innovations." It stood above a prostrate living organism called the state, its limbs bound in chains.

—MATTHIAS KOCH

VIENNA, Paris's twin capital of imperial illusion, would provide the highly varnished figurehead for the new French empire overseas. If the Second Empire took its march step from the frenetic tunes of Offenbach, the Austrian regime of Franz Josef moved to the swirling rhythms of the Strauss waltzes toward the industrial, social and political revolution sweeping mid-century Europe. Looking back through old memoirs and political tracts, however, one realizes it was only superficially a time of chocolate soldiers, waltzing archdukes, strutting dandies and coffeehouse intellectuals.

More than such manifestations of the Viennese spirit, the Austrian captial was governed by the appetites and attitudes of Herr Biedermeier, who never existed except in a writer's imagination. Biedermeier symbolized the epoch as Colonel Blimp stood for a certain English class before World War II and George F. Babbitt represented the Middle America of the 1920's. He was the semicomic creation of a writer named

Ludwig Pfau, for whom he represented the typical, conventional, respectful, middle-class Viennese. Herr Biedermeier valued comfort, security, *gemütlichkeit* above everything else; he was different from the bourgeoisie of other lands only in the enthusiasm for music and the theater which qualified and partly concealed his philistinism. He wanted order imposed from above, as it had always been, and closed his ears to the clamor for change and progress.

To the outsider Beidermeier's Vienna was the most charming capital in the world. "The whole aspect of the city and its surroundings," as Goethe's friend Karl Varnhagen von Ense wrote, "has something rich, pleasurable and gay of heart about it. People here seem healthier and happier than elsewhere; the dark spirits which dog mankind, which harass us unremittingly, find it hard to breathe in this air, and seldom have tried to lodge here. Such an appearance has something uncommonly agreeable; it exerts a power for peace on every temperament, every humour, and promotes the feeling that thus should it be for every man among us; for everybody such an atmosphere is the right and natural one. And even if it is only an appearance, the appearance is not in vain."

But that was only a well-bred German tourist's view of Vienna. To the rebellious Viennese writer Franz Schuselka, who had to have his work published in Hamburg, his fellow citizens were light-headed creatures unworthy of their heritage and incapable of making something better of it. "The people of Vienna," he declared, "seem to any serious observer to be revelling in an everlasting state of intoxication. Eat, drink and be merry are the three cardinal virtues and pleasures of the Viennese. It is always Sunday, always Carnival time for them. There is music everywhere. The innumerable inns are full of roisterers night and day. Everywhere there are droves of fops and fashionable dolls. Everywhere, in daily life, in art, and in literature, there prevails that delicate and witty jesting. For the Viennese the only point of anything, of the most important event in the world, is that they can make a joke about it."

Yet amid all the frivolity set to three-quarter time, underlying the jesting, buttressing the foppery, and paying for the revelry, was the fact of empire. The vast family estate of the Hapsburgs stretched from the archduchy of Austria and encompassed Bohemia, Moravia, Hungary, Illyria and part of Galicia—or in more modern terms the present nations of Austria, Hungary, Czechoslovakia, Yugoslavia and part of Poland —from the Alps to the mountains of Transylvania. And the seat of the empire, retrieved and held together by the temporizing genius of Prince Metternich after the downfall of the first Napoleon, was mindless, music-loving, wine-bibbing Vienna. Its centerpiece was the Hapsburg emperors, archdukes and archduchesses and their satellite courtiers, chamberlains, ministers and peers of the realm; their summer and winter palaces in Vienna and their hunting lodges (one called Mayerling) in the surrounding countryside; their gilded state coaches and Hungarian Guards and Gobelin tapestries and baroque fantasies of colored marble, gleaming crystal and alabaster—a world that seemed to be created for the Hapsburgs out of marzipan and whipped cream.

It was the world which an archduke, born in the summer palace but destined to die before a Mexican firing squad, inherited as a birthright in those Biedermeier years between the Congress of Vienna, which preserved his world, and the Revolution of 1848, which almost shattered it. For royalty, a lovely world remote both from the Biedermeiers and the slum-dwelling lower classes of his native Vienna, even more remote from the experiment in democracy being conducted in the Americas.

The traveler from the west approached Vienna along a road through the low hilly woods. Short of the scattered suburbs of the capital he would come to a short avenue leading to the cream-colored palace of Schönbrunn. If the court was not in residence, he might be permitted to tour the state rooms, all cream and gilt, porcelain and crimson silk, and glimpse through tall windows the marble alleys populated by statues and leading to the pillared hilltop overlooking the formal gardens. In the summer, however, Schönbrunn really came to life, and the sunlight glittered on the silver-and-red Hungarian Guards with tiger skins draped over their shoulders and Prince Esterhazy at their head, on the imperial suite strolling in the gardens among the collection of Alpine plants or joining the ladies of the court at the Tyrolean chalet.

The traveler from the west would enter the city through the Josefstadt Gate and proceed to the center of Vienna. He would find himself in a world little changed from the past century, a maze of dark, narrow streets and tiny squares in which light penetrated only through the attic windows, a capital that was still a collection of Middle European villages, while in Paris light and air were being introduced through wide boulevards. This was where the thousands of Biedermeiers lived in their tall, narrow houses, ventured out on cobbled streets thronged by a polyglot people whose mixture of tongues alone testified to the fact, otherwise not strikingly apparent, that this was an imperial city, the Byzantium of the Teutonic world. The Hofburg, or imperial palace, was grimly ornate, heavily Teutonic. The vast state rooms, with their acreage of tapestry, their tons of crystal chandeliers, their delicate porcelain stoves, had not been redecorated since the time of Maria Theresa, and even the private apartments were dank, airless and threadbare.

What Vienna offered the world in those years was already anachronistic but nonetheless admirable. "It provided," as one expert on the period observed, "a momentary suspension of history—a breathing-space before the great industrial struggle of the mid-century, in which men and women of different classes, religions, nations, showed themselves perfectly at home in a strongly hierarchical society, perfectly disposed to innocent amusements, and singularly free from the warping rancours which disfigured the more liberal countries of western Europe. . . . For if the Viennese were not happy they were nothing. The paternalism of the state took away much of their responsibility for their own welfare, the barriers established by a strict censorship between Austria and the rest of the world (not least the rest of Germany) gave them an unusual intellectual self-sufficiency. The empire could feed, amuse and (between economic slumps) employ them. They lived, therefore, in almost a private world, moved by internal stresses but secured, for a whole generation, from the disturbing touch of the unexpected."

It was this superficially cozy world, during that generation in which everything seemed predictable and ordained, which saw the birth of the Archduke Ferdinand Maximilian in the palace of Schönbrunn on July 6, 1832. He was the second son of the Archduke Karl and the Archduchess Sophie. His elder brother was Franz Josef, who was to ascend the Hapsburg throne and rule until World War I. The male side of his house, until his brother Franz Josef came along, had produced an alarming number of dimwits. Ferdinand I, his uncle, was feebleminded and had to turn over the administration of the empire to a three-man council headed by Prince Metternich. His father was also an amiably dim fellow whose main interest in life was consuming bowls of dumplings drenched in gravy. But his mother, a member of the Bavarian house of Wittelsbach, was the stuff of imperial Roman matrons, a tall, bony, iron-willed woman, one of six imperious sisters who married their way into princely or kingly houses. She was determined to be the mother, if not the wife, of an emperor.

Historians have depicted her as a she-dragon; Rebecca West in *Black Lamb and Gray Falcon* summed her up with more pith than compassion as the sort of woman all-male committees choose to be the matron of a hospital. The tenderest moments of life had come long before she assumed the matriarchy, before life in the Hofburg desiccated a warm and lively spirit. She had been forced to marry the Archduke Karl despite her protests that he was an "imbecile." On taking leave of her royal parents, she defiantly told them, "I have resolved to be happy, and I am going to be."

For a half dozen childless years she was happy enough, not with her amiably fuddled husband but because of Vienna's most glamorous resident, or prisoner, the only legitimate child of Napoleon and his Austrian second wife, variously known as Napoleon II (to Bonapartists only), the Duke of Reichstadt (to the Austrians), l'Aiglon, the Eaglet, the King of Rome.

They formed a curious alliance, the Bavarian bride, the ugly duckling, and the beautiful, lonely youth who was being "systematically coddled to death," as one historian put it, in Austrian captivity. Neglected by his vain and beautiful mother, Marie Louise, whose time was taken up by her morganatic husband in the Duchy of Parma, the young duke was regarded as a pawn in power politics who must not be permitted to leave Austria and preside over a Napoleonic restoration in France. So he was kept under constant surveillance by Austrian secret police and by the French embassy in Vienna. The French ambassador kept a close watch over his growth and reported to Paris: "The young Duke of Reichstadt is beginning to develop. He has an attractive face and entertains the whole court by his liveliness and wit, that stand in singular contrast to the habitual gravity of all others in the Imperial family. The Emperor often scolds him; but the Empress, the Archdukes and Archduchesses cannot resist the charm of his manners. He knows that and takes advantage of it to obtain whatever he desires. But one cannot help wondering what is going to happen when he comes to understand all that has happened and to grasp the role he was born to play in the future of Europe. It is difficult to foresee what effects these modern ideas are to have on a wideawake mind which personal interests may chance to excite still further and which a position in itself too prominent will have prepared for the planting of seeds of ambition which will be only too easily made to bear fruit. . . ."

The least impervious of all to the duke's fascination—the inheritance of his mother's beauty, at least a measure of his father's enormous intelligence—was the Archduchess Sophie. They spent hours together daily in her apartment in the Hofburg. Sophie was six years older, but they were drawn together by a mutual passion for poetry and the theater. Their intimacy continued in the summertime at Schönbrunn, where, according to backstairs gossip, there was a connecting staircase between her apartment and his, which was on the floor above.

Undoubtedly she felt a deeper affection for him than anyone in her life then or later. It became most fervent, according to various chroniclers of the Hapsburg court, during the summer of 1831, after the birth of Sophie's first son, the future Emperor Franz Josef. Sophie was then twenty-six, the duke twenty, but no one could or would say how far their intimacy had developed. Few of her notes and letters to the duke can be found in the court archives; the supposition is that she later destroyed them, but one surviving note reads in part, "I kiss you with all my heart," and was signed: "She who loves you deeply." Certainly the duke, golden-haired and spectacularly handsome in the green-and-silver uniform of the Hungarian Grenadiers, could have found plenty of other young women among the celebrated beauties of Vienna, yet he preferred the awkward and sentimental Sophie.

Late in 1831 l'Aiglon learned that he had tuberculosis. When he became too ill to stand parade with his regiment and was ordered to his bed, Sophie was at his side constantly, talking and reading to him. By the summer of 1832, when Sophie gave birth to her second son, Maximilian, who so closely resembled the dying duke in golden-boy looks and winsome personality, in a similar tendency toward escapism and poetic dreaming, it appeared that he had only days or weeks to live. Platonic or not, the bond between Sophie and Napoleon's only son was the most precious thing in their young lives. When it snapped, with l'Aiglon's death, everything that was romantic and sentimental in Sophie vanished and was replaced by an ironbound sense of dynastic duty.

The duke died on July 22, sixteen days after Maximilian's birth, and a dry-eyed Sophie, her voice harsh with suppressed emotion, delivered the funeral oration: "It is true that it is sad, very sad to die young, before being able to enjoy the pleasures of life, but with these passing pleasures he would have come to know great bitterness, for he was not young in spirit but serious and thoughtful, and he did not see the world as young people see it—adorned with illusion and hope—but in all its sorry reality. Oh, no, I knew him too well not to feel that he is better off, much better off up there than he would have been on earth."

Whether the young Napoleon was actually the father of Maximilian could only be the subject of fascinating conjecture, something for courtiers and servants to gossip about on the long winter nights in the Hofburg. As one of l'Aiglon's biographers (Octave Aubry) remarked, "Was he [Maximilian] of Napoleon's lineage? How decide such a question today? If the frail Archduke who was born during those stifling July days was the son of the King of Rome, he was to have a destiny worthy in its tragedy of his father and his grandfather."

The Archduchess Sophie was left with her sons, with her feelings of imperial responsibility. As the sister-in-law of a dim-witted emperor and the wife of his near-dotard brother, she conceived it her mission to hold the House of Hapsburg together single-handedly and ensure that her eldest son would rule, that Maximilian and two younger brothers would stand in ready succession. She became a kingmaker because there was no one else among the slack and sybaritic Hapsburgs to do the job. In the years following l'Aiglon's death she became a fanatic on

two subjects: her devotion to the church and her determination
that her sons should be trained and educated to rule the Austrian empire.

Of those four sons Franz Josef, as the emperor-designate, was
fittingly the handsomest, the most intelligent, the firmest in
character, more of a Wittelsbach, perhaps, in his mother's esti-
mation—he had not inherited the drooping lower lip of the
Hapsburgs which afflicted his younger brothers. Yet it was his
brother Maximilian, with his wit and gaiety, his golden hair,
his striking blue eyes and his princely height, which early attracted the Viennese. He looked like a Hapsburg princeling,
while there was something dourly non-Austrian about Franz
Josef. He was a prince for the Biedermeiers.

The nursery of the Hofburg, under Archduchess Sophie's
stern management, was to be the forcing bed of rulership rather
than a royal playpen. Both Franz Josef and Maximilian were
placed in the charge of a French tutor, Count Heinrich Bombelles, with instructions to teach them both that destiny had appointed them to imperial tasks. If Maximilian was only the
second son, like his father, he would not be turned into another
dumpling fancier, but would be prepared for some other monarchial seat than Vienna—a throne could always be found for
a Hapsburg with his wits about him. Both boys spent most of
their waking hours under Count Bombelles' tutelage, learning
languages, the sciences, history, and above all what was expected of a Hapsburg prince. They were required to master a
bewildering variety of subjects, a curriculum which grew more
exacting every year. In addition to a perpetual cram course,
they were subjected to physical training and encouraged to take
up the more rugged outdoor sports.

To those close enough to the imperial court to know or care
about such matters, it appeared that in other ways than looks
Maximilian was more the true Hapsburg princeling than his
older brother. Horsemanship was highly regarded as a kingly
attribute in a capital where the Spanish Riding Academy was
one of the showplaces. In that activity Maximilian easily out-
shown his older brother. Franz Josef was always reluctant to
mount a horse while Maximilian vaulted into the saddle and
rode like a captain of dragoons. He was an expert but reckless
horseman who felt he had to win every race and take every

jump. "To walk one's horse," as he observed in his aphoristic memoir (*Aus meinem Leben,* published shortly after his death), "is death. To trot is life. To gallop is bliss. It is not given to me to ride slowly." He looked forward to the day when men could soar above the earth. "It is from flying alone that I look for extraordinary experiences; and if ever the theories about the air-balloon become a reality, I shall take to flying, and certainly find the greatest concentrated pleasure in it."

Early in his youth he showed a talent for artistic pursuits, writing, painting, modeling in clay, that his more earthbound older brother lacked. They were, he wrote, "an inexhaustible source of consolation." That, too, pleased the artistic Viennese. And while Franz Josef even in his youth was self-contained, aloof, coldly reserved in manner, Maximilian was much more pleasing to the imperial court as well as the Biedermeiers because of his engaging personality, his cordiality, his eagerness to achieve popularity. Maximilian was a true Viennese, with that admixture of Slav and Latin diluting the Teutonic, while the emperor-to-be was more rigid, repressed and Germanic by temperament.

He was a romantic while his older brother was a realist. To Count Egon Caesar Corti, who as his official biographer had exclusive access to the Hapsburg archives, Maximilian was a "charming figure of a young man, instinct with a gentle and almost feminine quality. . . . The heart played a great part with him. . . . His pride in his Habsburg descent had developed his sense of honour to the highest degree; he grew to manhood full of ardent ambition. . . . In other respects his whole temperament was a little superficial, with something of the easy-going, light-hearted Austrian character. . . . The Archduke Max, as he was called for short, was a typical Viennese, with all the qualities and defects of one. Among his intimates, or in circles where the object was to please, he often displayed a merry wit which won him success in the salons. . . .

"On the other hand, there were also extremes in his nature. If he once gave his confidence to anybody, he always went too far. He would lay bare his whole heart and pour out all his ideas to his confidant, but he was often mistaken in people, and so fell into complete dependence on them. This love of confiding in people was a result of his good-heartedness, and his innate conviction—which seemed to him self-evident—that every-body was like himself, and could only think, feel, and act like a thorough gentleman."

His private code of conduct, partly derived from consulta-tions with Count Bombelles and his religious instructors, was written down on a card which he always carried with him. Though he did not always abide by it, that card tells much of what he hoped and wanted to be. "Never a false word, not even out of necessity or vanity. . . . Be kindly to everybody. . . . Justice in all things whatsoever. . . . Not to answer without reflection. . . . Take it coolly. [This was written in English, the other injunctions in German.] . . . Never joke with one's infe-iors, never converse with the servants. . . . Listen to all; trust few. . . . Never scoff at religion or authority. . . . No exaggeration but moderation in all things. . . . Never let one-self be carried away by the first impression. . . . In judging other's fault remember one's own. . . . Two hours' exercise daily. . . . When unwell, cut oneself off entirely from the world. . . ."

The memorandum reflected the sense of moral purpose which both the Archduchess Sophie and Count Bombelles regarded as a necessary attribute for the ruler of a Germanic people; how well they would serve in the turbulence of Mexico was beyond their calculations. Maximilian, like his brothers, was brought up to believe that if Hapsburgs ruled by divine right, they also had a divine duty to be more exalted, more selfless than ordinary people.

Such beliefs were called into question in 1848, the year of revolution for Paris, Vienna, Berlin and other Western capitals. Maximilian was then sixteen years old, and with his upbring-ing in the theory that the House of Hapsburg was as solid as the Rock of Gibraltar, that it was adored by the Austrian people, he must have been thoroughly bewildered at the red flags and dissident mobs raging through the streets of the capital.

Not only God but the people, it appeared, could topple a dy-nasty. Incredible news was received that the Bourbon-Orléans firm had gone bankrupt in France and been forced to liquidate, that the Hohenzollerns were forced to promise democratic re-forms in Prussia and the German states. Hungary was pro-claiming itself an independent republic under Lajos Kossuth, and the Hapsburgs had to appeal to Czar Nicholas I of Russia for help in quelling the insurrection. The Hungarians were subdued only after the most rigorous campaigning by the Austrian and Russian armies.

Even in Vienna it was touch and go. Metternich, the real ruler of Austria, succumbed to panic, renounced his title, and fled to England under the alias of Herr Meier. The imperial court, a small city within the capital, was forced to abandon Vienna and move to Innsbruck while a counterinsurgency effort of the greatest severity was mounted.

Field Marshals Alfred Windischgratz and Joseph Radetzky preserved the monarchy with blasts of grapeshot and mass arrests. When it was all over, on December 2, 1848, Emperor Ferdinand abdicated, and his brother the Archduke Karl renounced his right of succession. The eighteen-year-old Franz Josef became emperor. When he thanked his uncle for the crown and scepter, Ferdinand amiably replied, "Don't mention it, Franzl, it was a real pleasure." Prince Metternich was unceremoniously retired but shed his cognomen of Herr Meier and returned to Vienna as a prince again, with Prince Felix Schwarzenberg replacing him as Prime Minister.

By then the imperial court had returned to Vienna and resettled itself at the Hofburg, but without ex-Emperor Ferdinand ("Goodinand the Finished," as the wits of the Vienna coffeehouses called him) and the Archduke Karl, uncle and father of Franz Josef and his brothers, both of them retiring to the Hradčary Castle in Prague to live many more years in comfortable vegetation. Archduchess Sophie did not accompany her husband; her hopes were centered on their four sons; her energies were to be expended on establishing a matriarchy.

Once the specter of revolution was banished, she ordained a livelier atmosphere at the court. Her sons were growing into young manhood, and if they did not meet eligible young women under her supervision, at dancing parties in the Hofburg, they would find them on midnight excursions to the cabarets, wine gardens and public dance halls beyond the palace walls. The daughters of the court and of the diplomatic corps were invited, and the musty old Hofburg was enlivened by the strains of the waltz.

Only recently had Archduchess Sophie decided that the

waltz, mainly violent exercise on the polished parquet, after all, was respectable enough for the imperial court. And while the young people swirled around the ballroom, in a kaleiodoscope of multicolored uniforms and bare white shoulders, a hundred couples at a time, their elders watched from the rows of gilt chairs placed along the walls. The parties lasted from eight in the evening until five in the morning, but Sophie sat bolt upright in her chair throughout, always vigilant, eying her sons and their partners through a jeweled lorgnette. The *Kapell-meister* of the court orchestra was Johann Strauss himself.

Franz Josef and his brothers wore the white uniforms of the Austrian guard regiments and distinguished themselves, like the cavalry officers from the Spanish Riding School who also attended, as exponents of the waltz. No one, amid all the gaiety, reflected that the Austrian archdukes and the Austrian officers might be more skilled at the ballroom graces than ruling a country or leading a successful cavalry charge.

Archduke Maximilian fell in love for the first time at one of his mother's dancing parties. The girl was a pretty little brunette, the fifteen-year-old Countess Paula von Lindon, daughter of the ambassador from Württemberg. There was a mini-scandal when Maximilian, without consulting his imperial brother, his mother or his tutor, sent Countess Paula a corsage of orange blossoms.

Any hopes of marriage were quickly dashed; the young prince's bride would have to be of royal blood; mere nobility would not suffice. This was sternly impressed on Maximilian by his tutor and moral preceptor, Count Bombelles. But Maximilian rebelled and followed up the orange blossoms by sending Countess Paula a huge bouquet of roses.

It was evident that sterner measures would have to be taken, or the House of Hapsburg might inadvertently acquire an unwanted infusion of nonroyal blood. Since the best known cure for infatuation was distance, preferably over the seas, Maximilian was hastily consigned to apprenticeship for a naval career. It was brief but not undistinguished. From 1850 to 1854 he spent most of his time aboard one or the other of the Austrian navy's warships, always surrounded by aides, protectors and preceptors. In 1854, at the age of twenty-two, he was promoted to vice admiral and commander in chief. But it was a Gilbert and Sullivan sort of navy, a flotilla of antiquated gunboats, frigates and sail-driven cruisers. Its principal function was firing salutes and cruising around the eastern Mediterranean paying courtesy calls and being snickered at by the French and British navies.

His first cruise in 1850, designed to take his mind off the Württemberg nymphet, took him through the Aegean to ports of call in Greece and Asia Minor. He kept a diary which, for an eighteen-year-old, showed considerable powers of perception and observation. It was mandatory to make a tour of Greece and visit the local royalty because King Otto, who had ruled since the Greek War of Independence, was one of his Bavarian cousins. Family loyalty did not restrain him from observing that Cousin Otto was amiably slack in the performance of his duties. In Greece Maximilian was able to study conditions which would become even more painfully apparent during his later stewardship in Mexico. "As all men who fought in the War of Independence have the right to bear arms, robbery becomes especially easy to them. Banditti in Greece," he observed in the diary which became part of his published *Recollections,* "are an understood thing. It appears that the morality of the Greeks is not raised by the ideas of King, fatherland, and brotherly love. Their own advantage is their guiding star. Even the marriages are not from affection, but in most cases bargains of convenience; and the reflection that you are committing a wrong upon another vanishes with them before the pleasure of filling their own pockets." Even King Otto's Chamberlain, General Griva, was supposed to have been a bandit in his prime, with "a gloomy, somewhat lowering countenance" that made the rumors credible.

Ottoman Turkey, however, delighted him from his first glimpse of the Anatolian coast. "Before us lay the East with its wealth, its vegetation, its thousand dazzling appeals to the senses. . . . our long-cherished dreams were realized." He was almost drowned when a Turkish pasha's barge, on which he was a guest, made a stormy passage of the Bosporus. But there were other dangers, those of flesh and spirit, confronting the young naval person. His ship called in at Smyrna (now Izmir), and Maximilian visited the slave market with his aides while Berber, Circassian and Nubian beauties—blonde, brown and black—were being auctioned off.

Evidently, for a fleeting moment, he regretted not having been born to the House of Osman. "The sight of a naked woman frightens me," he later confided to his diary, but it was the true Viennese who promptly added, "I am made to realize that sin is unbearably attractive." Later the cruise proceeded toward less permissive shores. A gloomy piety had enveloped him when the squadron visited Spain. His aides, for some reason, tried to dissuade him from journeying to Granada, where the tombs of the Spanish branch of the Hapsburgs were located. He refused to listen to them, explaining in his journal, "However stubborn people may be, and however hard to persuade to anything, I am still more obstinate and stubborn." He was deeply affected when he was shown the insignia of King Ferdinand. "Proudly, longingly, and yet sadly, I grasped the golden circlet and the once mighty sword. What a lovely glittering dream for a nephew of the Spanish Hapsburgs to wield the latter in order to win the former!" Such dreams, he would learn, could also glitter with danger.

He returned to Vienna in 1854 when Franz Josef married Princess Elizabeth of Bavaria. The new empress, then only a girl of sixteen, was red-haired, proud and independent of spirit and, judging from her photographs, the most beautiful queen since Helen of Troy. She and the Archduchess Sophie, though both Wittlesbachs, were as different as though they had been born on separate planets. To the matriarch of the Hofburg, her spirit long congealed in the iron mold of imperial duty, Empress Elizabeth was a girl who must be converted immediately from the customs of a bucolic Bavarian court to the intricate and long-established traditions of a Hapsburg court. For the next several years whatever family life was allowed by etiquette to Franz Josef, Elizabeth, and the young archdukes would be shadowed by the struggle between the lovely and high-spirited Elizabeth and her mother-in-law.

The impressionable Maximilian fell in love with Elizabeth at first sight—platonically, of necessity—and thought it deplorable that Sisi should be married off to such a stodgy fellow as his older brother. She should have been his bride, he believed. They both loved nature, horses, poetry, everything but duty; they both liked to gallop their horses and take reckless jumps. Elizabeth was even more daring on horseback than Maximilian.

To the secret resentment of his older brother for claiming more of their mother's attention was now added an understandable envy of Franz Josef for having acquired, unearned, such a prize as Sisi. His bitterness was only increased by the fact that Franz Josef treated Elizabeth so casually, as if unaware of her rare beauty, insensitive to the qualities that set her apart, unwilling (it seemed to Maximilian) to accept her as much more than another broodmare for the Hapsburgs.

From such considerations Maximilian was diverted by the demands of his naval career, which progressed at a royal pace. A lieutenant at eighteen, he was given command of the corvette *Minerva* three years later. His first independent mission aboard the *Minerva* was to show the flag in Albanian ports. Recently Albania had wrenched itself away from the Ottoman Empire, though many of its citizens had been converted to Mohammedanism, and Vienna had decided that a show of naval power might persuade the Albanians to accept Austrian guidance. Judging from his diary, portions of which were incorporated in his *Recollections*, Captain Archduke Maximilian was dubious about the possibility of Austrian-Albanian friendship. Albania was a heathen wilderness, he observed. "In its woody confines, Turks, boars and many Catholic Christians live in contention and strife, chasing each other in wild pursuit. . . . Although near in the point of distance Albania is separated from our country by a chasm as wide as an ocean, for it is situated within the territory of the decaying Crescent, where civilization has not yet found an entrance and where all is abandoned to the despotism of the Pashas and their hordes."

His instructions from Vienna were to provide "moral support" for the Albanian Catholics and conduct a reconnaissance without stirring up the religious hornet's nest. Any remaining Turkish authority was to be uncontested, since a naval landing party would not be able to fight its way into or out of the interior. The *Minerva* first displayed its ensign in the port of Antivari (now Bar, Yugoslavia), where it was promptly fired upon from the customshouse. All a misunderstanding. The local Albanians had mistaken the *Minerva* for a Turkish warship. Later she dropped anchor up the coast near Cape Rodoni while her officers and crew, led by Maximilian in a white burnous given him by Algerian friends the year before, went ashore for a try at boarhunting.

The boar hunt through the Rodoni woods proceeded splendidly for several days until a band of armed and mounted police sent by the governor of the province appeared on the scene to investigate reports that foreigners had landed without permission and were making themselves free with the local game. Maximilian displayed a certain flair for naval diplomacy. He received the police with as much ceremony as he could muster, inviting their officers to his tent and bringing out the hubble-bubble pipes. Without saying so, actually, he indicated that he and his companions were coreligionists of theirs. The Albanian police were invited aboard the *Minerva,* given food, wine and coffee. "When they were fairly crammed," Maximilian recorded in his journal, "they were taken ashore in a boat, whilst . . . making 'salaam alaiks' as if zealously performing our religious duties. The Moslems were most edified by our devoutness and waved a friendly farewell. . . ."

Learning of the *Minerva*'s hospitality and the friendly disposition of her commander, the Pasha of Tirana, the Albanian capital, sent word that he too would like to visit the Austrian warship. An invitation was extended. The pasha arrived, and the splendor of the occasion was only a little dimmed when that dignitary let it slip that he had never heard of the Austrians or their ancient empire. The meeting of archduke and pasha was described by Maximilian with a spirited humor: "At half-past nine a.m. one of the corvette's boats brought the formidable but now tamed Bimbashi on board. Like all Osmanli aristocrats, the lion of Tirana was a fat, delicate little mannikin with bandy legs, a quivering paunch, and a thin pagoda-like countenance. He wore a fez on his round shaven head, a dressing-gown about his panting body, and dirty pantaloons covered his shanks.

"A lazy nod from me told him that he might be seated, and we offered him watermelons and champagne to refresh his soul, if by chance the infidel had one. Some meaningless hollow phrases and a somewhat stern admonition from me in regard to

Christians formed the subjects of our diplomatic conversation, while his unintelligible roaring or rather grunting nearly made me laugh openly in the face of this bloodthirsty tyrant. When His Highness had refreshed himself he was dismissed with a few bottles of stale champagne and was honoured with a salute from our thirty-two pounders which rather shook his nerves."

Concern with the Moslems' treatment of the Christian minority took up most of the remaining time of the Albanian expedition. *Minerva* sailed on to the chief port, Durazzo, where Maximilian was informed that the local bishop had been imprisoned in his house for the past six months. He sent an armed landing party to the bishop's home and freed him. Along the southern coast he dropped in on the Bey of Avlona, a worldly young man who had disbanded his harem and taken as his mistress "the wife of a Frenchman who does not object, as by this means his position here is greatly enhanced."

The expedition was regarded as a success in Vienna, and a year later, in 1854, Maximilian was promoted over the heads of his seniors to be vice admiral and commander in chief of the Austrian navy. Although only twenty-two, he apparently took his career seriously and applied himself to a study of modern navies, which just about then were undergoing a technological revolution. Aside from establishing a hydrographic institute and a naval museum, he concerned himself with modernizing the Austrian fleet and using his influence to obtain a larger share of the available defense funds. Naval actions in the Crimean War dictated armor plate for warships if they hoped to survive the fire of land batteries or come to grips with modern enemy vessels; the age of the ironclads had begun. It was informally inaugurated when a Turkish squadron was almost wiped out by Russian batteries on the Crimean shore. Late in 1855, however, a squadron of French and British ironclads not only engaged the Russian shore batteries, surviving heavy fire with scarcely a dent in their hulls, but forced the Russian garrison ashore to run up the white flag.

The significance of those two actions did not escape Admiral Archduke Maximilian. He obtained the funds to build a new shipyard and arsenal at the Adriatic port of Pola and begin construction of several modern new warships, not only armored but steam-driven. Under his supervision the keel was laid for the battleship *Kaiser,* with ninety-one guns, and two large frigates and two corvettes, all with $4\frac{1}{2}$-inch iron plating around their hulls.

At twenty-three, a man of some accomplishment, Maximilian had begun to hope that his horizons would widen beyond the Adriatic seascape, if only Franz Josef could be convinced that he needed a sort of assistant emperor to help administer the increasingly complex affairs of his realm. He went to the Hofburg to advance this ambition, but was rather coldly received. Franz Josef refrained from pointing out that the Ottoman emperors traditionally disposed of their younger brothers by having them strangled and thrown into the Bosporus. He agreed that the naval burden might be laid down, now that the new navy was well under way, but politely rejected Maximilian's offer to help shoulder the actual responsibility of administering the empire. "In all friendliness," Count Corti observed, "but beneath it all, full of courteous denial, he refused his brother the collaboration which he desired. He did not wish to have any second person near him, especially not such a near relation. Maximilian's repeated hints met with a rebuff. This hurt him, for he saw quite well that all they were ready to assign to him was a merely subordinate and ornamental sphere of activity—one, at any rate, which would keep him at a distance from the capital, and hence from all possibility of directly influencing the business of government. . . ."

For the next several years Maximilian served as a sort of commercial traveler or goodwill ambassador for the House of Hapsburg. Employment was found for his charm and looks— his erect bearing, golden hair and sincere blue eyes—if not his brains. Maximilian was no literary, political or military genius, but his letters back to Vienna from his tours of European capitals demonstrate a fine eye for significant detail, a talent for expressing himself vividly and pungently that would have made him a first-rate journalist. In Spain, he noted that the queen used smoked binoculars when attending the bullfights so she wouldn't see the blood. In Lisbon, he excitedly reported on a balloon ascension, one of his dreams come true, though his position forbade his becoming an aeronaut himself. And from the Vatican came a witty and irreverent dispatch describing an extended audience with the Pope, Pius IX, who a decade later would be visited by Maximilian's wife on a much more desperate mission. "You must know," Maximilian wrote Franz Josef, "that I found His Holiness as jolly as a cricket and looking more fit than two years ago. . . . After a bite of breakfast, which we enjoyed *entre nous*, the Order of Pius was conferred upon me with apologies for its modest value which might be offset by the fact that the Holy Father's blessing rendered any trifle a *cosa santa*. . . .

"Next, Pio Nono invited me to drive (in an ancient vehicle with patched harness and the most theatrical liveries imaginable) to the cathedral for mass. Throughout the service I was disturbed by the nonchalance of the lesser clergy who engaged in a constant gabble while they exchanged various brands of snuff. After high mass I continued my interview with the Holy Father until, around one o'clock, we were joined by four cardinals. . . . The cardinals knew some rakish tales which presently launched a most incredible *conversation gaillarde*. Then the Pope ordered dinner which turned out to be pretty dreadful but since it was served by monsignori of the papal household the hilarious chatter between the portly brethren continued.

"Everyone was in such good spirits by the time the ices and coffee came around that the Pope decided to do the serving in person. This caused more pleasantries, until at last, realizing that I had been on parade with the riband and collar of my order from seven in the morning through four in the afternoon, I begged to be excused. It was necessary to genuflect and kiss the Pope's foot before I could climb half-dead into my carriage and speed away."

The lively correspondence through which Maximilian acted as his reigning brother's reporter on the political and social atmosphere of the other European capitals, which Franz Josef found both enlightening and amusing, continued when Maximilian was sent to Paris in May, 1856, to sound out French attitudes and size up the newest crop of Napoleons, which in the past had caused so much trouble for the Hapsburgs.

Whatever their military achievements, the Bonaparte clan had always struck more established royalties as Corsican upstarts. Maximilian's first acquaintance with the new lot, who were to be the patrons of his own imperial career, was disillusioning. He was met at the station by Prince Napoleon, more familiarly known as Plon-Plon, Napoleon III's cousin, in a "cold, stiff manner."

They traveled out to St.-Cloud by carriage, and Maximilian was received by the emperor on the palace steps. "His short, unimposing stature, his exterior, which is utterly lacking in nobility, his shuffling gait, his ugly hands, the sly, inquiring glance of his lustreless eyes, all these things made up a whole which was not calculated to correct my first unfavorable impression."

Nor was Eugénie much more impressive. "I found the Empress, whom I visited immediately afterwards, in a state of great weakness and lassitude; she took extraordinary pains to be nice, but was at the same time uncommonly embarrassed. Her beauty, which is undeniably great, though it owes a great deal to art, reveals no trace of the Spanish type. She is quite thoroughbred, but essentially lacking in the august quality of an empress; and the impression produced in me by her appearance was dimmed by imperial memories. [by which he meant the incomparable beauty of his sister-in-law, Empress Elizabeth]. . . . The dinner was badly served, everything was lacking. At the table the Emperor was so ill at ease that the conversation was never entertaining, and it was all I could do to infuse a little life into it."

The next morning he and Napoleon strolled in the palace gardens, and the conversation turned to matters of state. On that subject Napoleon was more interesting. France and Britain had just collaborated with Ottoman Turkey in defeating the Russians in the Crimea, and Napoleon complained about the Austrians' refusal to join in that more or less holy crusade. Maximilian was astonished when his host suggested that the time had come to "partition" Turkey, his recent ally, "in which case Austria could enlarge her borders by annexing Albania and Herzegovina. I replied that the right time for such a partition did not seem to me to have arrived, especially since Turkey had displayed far more vitality in the course of the war than she had generally been credited with. The Emperor then changed to a half-laughing tone and said that, after all, it was a sorry business to have to bolster up the Turks, the stupidest people in the world." Maximilian was equally appalled by Napoleon's brutal pragmatism and his lack of discretion. But it was the bulbous Prince Plon-Plon who drew his unkindliest attention: "He has absolutely the look of a worn-out *basso* from some obscure Italian opera-house."

Paris itself seemed to lack the qualities of an imperial city, but he was astonished at the vigor with which Napoleon was transforming his capital. "New streets, new boulevards, countless new buildings, all of gigantic dimensions, have sprung up under the present Government." Maximilian shrewdly noted, however, that the changes had been made with military—that is, counterinsurgency—purposes in mind. "Witness the Palace of Industry, which he [Napoleon] himself pointed out to me as a splendid rallying-place for troops; witness the Rue de Rivoli, which leads to the Caserne Napoleon [barracks]; witness the macadamized roads which . . . have the advantage of doing away with what used to be the material for barricades; witness the squares, which are intended to provide open spaces for the troops, in which they can move freely. Witness the filling up of the trenches, which makes attacks by cavalry possible; witness, in short, all the main lines constructed or projected—the whole arrangement of which is mainly dictated by military aims."

In his reportage to Franz Josef, now preserved in the Austrian State Archives, Maximilian admitted that daily meetings with the emperor and empress modified his first impressions to some extent, but there was a tawdry air of opportunism about their court. "Napoleon is one of those men whose personality has nothing winning about it at first sight, but ends by producing a favorable impression owing to his great calm and noble simplicity of character. The reckless way in which he speaks in the presence of his servants is more remarkable; he often lets fall the most incredible statements before them; this seems to be typical of a parvenu, utterly lacking in that esprit de corps which makes one careful not to expose oneself before those in subordinate positions. The Empress's gaiety and naïve vivacity do not always seem to please her imperial husband, who sometimes casts reproving glances at her. . . . The whole impression is, so to speak, that of a make-believe court, the various offices of which are occupied by amateurs who are not very sure of their parts. There can be no question of a good or bad tone here, for this Court is absolutely lacking in tone."

On May 22 a state ball took place in the palace at St.-Cloud, and Maximilian appeared in the procession with Eugénie on his arm. That occasion seemed to the Austrian guest of honor to have attracted all the well-placed riffraff in France. "The society was inconceivably mixed, and distinguished for its disgusting dress and tactless behaviour. Adventurers swarmed, which is a leading characteristic of this Court. Among them I reckon a certain Countess Castiglione, who is lovely, but reminds one, not only by her costume and coiffure, but also by her free and impudent bearing, of some dancer of the Regency period come to life again. This person may prove dangerous to the domestic happiness of the Emperor and Empress. The courtiers are already vying with one another in paying court to her; Princess Mathilde and the Countless Hatzfeldt spoke to me indignantly, and with a characteristically French lack of reticence, about her lack of decency in choosing this precise moment for supplanting the Empress. The Emperor's assiduity with all pretty women is unpleasantly conspicuous, and detracts greatly from his sovereign dignity."

Maximilian was quite right about the "danger" posed by the beautiful Countess Virginia di Castiglione but could not have known how much a threat she was not only to Eugénie's self-esteem but to Austria's hold over its Italian provinces. She was a Botticelli type of Lombardian beauty with red-gold hair, green eyes and the body of a "nymph sculptured of pink marble," as the otherwise hostile wife of the Austrian ambassador described her. Her mission was to seduce and influence Emperor Napoleon as an agent of the Italianissimi, the movement to unite Italy under King Victor Emmanuel and Prime Minister Camillo Cavour.

Countess di Castiglione's role was to persuade Napoleon to provide French support for a scheme to drive the Austrians off the Italian peninsula. Separated from her spendthrift husband, she was Cavour's mistress until he decided that her bewitching personality and red-haired beauty must be shared with Napoleon, who had a demonstrable weakness for redheads and who often excused his lechery on the grounds that he had a lot of "catching up" to do because of his years of imprisonment at Ham. "If we did for ourselves what we do for our country," as Count Cavour sighed to his biographers in explaining the loan of the Countess di Castiglione's pink body, "what rascals we should be." At any rate, as Maximilian would learn to his later sorrow, the countess's mission was entirely successful.

Perhaps those impressions of his twelve-day visit to France and of the unreliable quality of its regime would have remained fresh, more premonitory a half dozen years later when Napoleon and Eugénie would reappear in his life as fairy godmothers; but it had been decided in Vienna that it was time for Maximilian to marry, and he was now preoccupied with that summons to duty. It was an affair of state as much as or more than an affair of the heart. The decision was made for dynastic reasons by his mother. The Archduchess Sophie was determined that her second son marry into a suitable royal house. Naturally Maximilian's feelings in selecting the woman who would share the rest of his life would not be of the utmost importance.

The first prospective bride, No. 1 on his list, was Princess Maria Amelia, a member of the Portuguese royal house. As a Braganza, her standing in Debrett's and other studbooks was top-drawer. She was twenty years old and described as strikingly beautiful, if exceedingly frail. When he was still a vice admiral, Maximilian had visited Portugal and had been presented to Princess Maria Amelia. Though not yet marriage-minded, he was favorably impressed and considered her "a perfect Princess such as one rarely meets."

At his urging Archduchess Sophie entered preliminary negotiations with the House of Braganza. A tentative marriage contract was drawn up, disregarding the fact that Princess Maria Amelia was tubercular and her father, Dom Pedro of Brazil, had died of the disease. Before Maximilian could journey to Lisbon and seal the bargain, in fact, she suddenly died.

So the matrimonial search had to be resumed later in 1856, when he set out on a tour of European capitals surrounded by a sentimental aura, not entirely valid, of deeply mourning a girl he had met only once.

The purpose of the tour was to look over the available supply of eligible princesses, which was not good. If he found one that seemed suitable from the dynastic viewpoint as well as one meeting his own exacting tastes in style and pulchritude, it would be decided by his mother, his elder brother and their counselors whether the marriage would enhance the prospects of the House of Hapsburg. On this mission Maximilian visited Spain and found no one eligible from any viewpoint; France was out of the question, since no Hapsburg in his right mind would marry one of those swarming, swarthy Bonaparte upstarts; so he went on to Belgium. Here, too, there was a question of opportunism. The kingdom of Belgium had been established for only twenty-seven years, following the breakaway from the Netherlands, and its first and only king was a German import, Leopold I of the House of Saxe-Coburg-Gotha.

Now sixty-six years old, Leopold had gained a considerable reputation for his craftiness. He prided himself on being the reincarnation of Machiavelli, or at least a Machiavellian prince, but in other capitals was known as the "shopkeeper king" for his niggling parsimony and his delight in tortuous negotiations. He had a real vocation, however, for marrying off Coburgs and extending his influence through the boudoir and the nursery. In his role of royal matchmaker he had married off his nephew Prince Albert of Saxe-Coburg-Gotha to the future Queen Victoria of England. He had also supervised the elevation of another Coburg to the Portuguese throne. In his own case he had miscalculated. He had married the daughter of Louis Philippe, only to watch the Orléans dynasty displaced, driven into exile, by the Bonapartes, whom he accordingly detested.

Naturally Maximilian, known to be looking for a wife, was greeted by dazzling smiles when he arrived in Belgium. He was greeted by the Duke of Brabant, Leopold's eldest son and successor-to-be, and escorted in style to the royal palace at Laeken outside Brussels. The Belgian king's head was buzzing with schemes: He had a sixteen-year-old daughter named Charlotte for whom he would soon have to find a husband. What better one than Archduke Maximilian, who was the right age, who carried himself well, and who had now grown a splendid, downright kingly golden beard to conceal that depressing Hapsburg jaw?

In his report to Vienna, Maximilian took a cool, objective view of Leopold, his family, his court and country. Laeken was a "delightful residence" but "has not even stone staircases."

King Leopold was something of a bore who "involved me in an interminable political conversation, to which might have been prefaced the motto, 'Wash my fur, but don't wet me'; his discourses were like articles from the *Independence* and the *Debats.* . . . The King repeated several times the hackneyed phrase that he was the Nestor among monarchs and that all of them might learn from him. He also promised to come and see me the following day and give me a lecture upon political science and the balance of Europe; an offer which I received yawning in spirit."

As for the crown prince, the Duke of Brabant, he was a sly fellow who "under the guise of overwhelming friendliness never let me out of his sight during the whole of my travels about the young kingdom, in order by his ceaseless presence to see to it that the homage of the inhabitants, which might otherwise have been too marked, should not go beyond the limits of a fitting cordiality."

Maximilian did not mention meeting Princess Charlotte in his letter to Vienna, perhaps because he hadn't made up his mind about her. The girl was pretty enough, with striking dark-brown eyes, a round face with delicate features, a slender neck and a promising figure, to lend credence to her father's boast that "I think she will be the most beautiful princess in Europe—if only it will bring her happiness!" Maximilian did not rise to the bait. Greatly offending Leopold, he pointed out that his schedule called for visits to the courts of Holland and Hanover in his search for a bride. It did not help that he had to talk to Charlotte in French because she did not then speak German, or that she was eight years younger, or even that she was greatly attracted, as her father claimed, to Maximilian.

Princess Charlotte was born on June 7, 1840, German on her father's side, French on her mother's. Her mother, Queen Louise, was the daughter of King Louis Philippe and Queen Marie Amélie, who still occupied the French throne when Charlotte was born. She was a serious child, able to follow the prayers in church at the age of five, when an intense schooling in the duties of a princess began. The rigors of her education were reflected in a letter she wrote at the age of eight to her cousin Victoria of England, who had been subjected to the same sort of duty-bound childhood: "I have received the beautiful dolls' house you have been so kind as to send me, and I thank you very much for it. I am delighted with it; every morning I dress my doll and give her a good breakfast; and the day after her arrival she gave a great rout at which all my dolls were invited. . . ."

Queen Louise died when her only daughter was ten years old. She caught the whooping cough from Charlotte just about the time she received the news that her father, deposed two years earlier, had died in English exile. A combination of whooping cough, more severe in an adult, and mental depression sent her into a fatal decline, and Charlotte was left to be raised by her pedantic father. It must have been a dreary childhood listening to the sonorous voice of King Leopold instructing her in how royalty must cling to its privileges in a changing world. "The position of what is generally called great people has of late become extremely difficult," he gravely informed the child. "They are more attacked and calumniated and judged with less indulgence than private individuals. What they have lost in this way, they have not by any means regained in any other. Ever since the revolution of 1790, they are much less secure than they used to be, and the transition from sovereign power to *absolute want* has been as frequent as sudden. It becomes, therefore, necessary that the character should be formed so as not to be intoxicated by greatness and success, nor cast down by misfortune. . . ."

Charlotte, as her later career demonstrated, totally absorbed the lessons learned at her father's knee, particularly his dictum that "absolute want" awaited any princess who did not take herself seriously. At thirteen she claimed Plutarch as her favorite author and wrote her governess, Countess Hulst, the same year Maximilian was appointed commander of the Austrian navy, "I studied my history and drawing lessons and practiced the piano, which I like better now. I know all the Kings of England and their dates without a single mistake and, most remarkable of all, my arithmetic is progressing well; I do as many as three problems in a day sometimes, and they are not easy problems. The languages are not progressing too badly either. I hope that when you return you will find me completely changed both physically and mentally, since I am now working better and have grown a great deal and am less awkward than before."

Her social life in the early teens was tightly circumscribed. Only partners of royal blood were allowed to dance with her, and only her brothers to embrace and lead her in the waltz. Although she was only sixteen when trotted out for Maximilian's inspection, she had already been under matrimonial consideration, one candidate being Prince George of Saxony, the other the nineteen-year-old King Pedro V, who had just assumed the throne of Portugal. Pedro was still in the running when Maximilian presented himself at the Belgian court and was the favorite of Queen Victoria, who declared that Pedro was "*the* most distinguished young Prince there is . . . good, excellent and steady. . . ." For Portugal, she added, "an *amiable* well-educated Queen would be an immense blessing for there *never* has been one. I am sure," she wrote Leopold, "you would be more likely to secure Charlotte's happiness if you gave her to Pedro than to one of those innumerable Archdukes or to Prince George of Saxony."

Pedro, however, had not made an impressive appearance when he showed up in Brussels shortly before Maximilian's visit. Charlotte liked neither him nor the idea of having to live in Portugal but was fascinated by Maximilian's golden beard and gallant bearing. Her former governess, Countess Hulst, supported this choice and told her, "The Portuguese are only orang-utangs. They have no resources, not even a priest capable of understanding you."

For a time it appeared that Charlotte might not have a choice. Maximilian had gone on his way to inspect the current crop of princesses at the Dutch and Hanoverian courts. His own feelings about Charlotte had not been revealed, but it was possible that he was put off by her one visible flaw—a habit of squinting, because she was nearsighted—or considered her too provincial for a sophisticated, well-traveled Viennese. Nothing suitable or attractive met Maximilian's eye on the remainder of his wife-hunting expedition, however, and when he returned to Vienna, he found that Archduchess Sophie had decided that Princess Charlotte was the best choice.

The tortuous negotiations preceding a royal marriage now began. Haggling might be a better word for it. In December, accompanied by his friend and go-between Baron Alfons de Pont, Maximilian returned to Brussels and made a formal proposal of marriage, not to Charlotte, of course, but her father. King Leopold rubbed his hands in a shopkeeper's glee over a good matrimonial bargain. Princess Charlotte considered herself fortunate to be married off to a Hapsburg rather than a Braganza or, worse yet, some doddering specimen from a Balkan court.

And while Maximilian and Charlotte got to know each other as best they could in a swarm of chaperones, strolling through the gardens or riding through the wet woods at Laeken, the practical aspects of their marriage were being discussed by Baron de Pont, on behalf of Maximilian, and Count Conway, Leopold's financial adviser (little though he needed one). The Belgians were advised that the Austrians considered that a sizable dowry would be necessary to maintain the couple in princely style. No dot, replied King Leopold through his representative; he didn't believe in such medieval nonsense; Charlotte would bring to her marriage the jewels she inherited from her mother and a small stipend, not quite the size of a clothing allowance, recently voted by the Belgian Parliament.

Both sides were adamant, and finally Maximilian took a hand himself. "This insuperable tenacity," he wrote Franz Josef, "prompted me, two days before my departure, to remind the king of his own words, 'how necessary it is that the princely household should be comfortably established.'" He also pointed out to his future father-in-law, he said, "that it could arouse none but the worst impression in Austria if it were to become known that the King could not bring himself to put his hand in his own pocket for the benefit of his beloved daughter."

Before he could escape from dowdy, parsimonious Belgium, he was forced to attend the New Year ceremony at which the nation's twenty-fifth anniversary was celebrated, an occasion, he biliously reported to Franz Josef, for the "most pompous self-glorification." One speech was so ridiculous that the crown princess, the Duchess of Brabant, née Archduchess Henriette of

Austria, burst into giggles "only half concealed by her gigantic bouquet. . . . A contrast was provided by the Cicero of the civic guard, a colossus who stammered out his harangue in stentorian tones, faltering over the words and accenting them in a way so comically destructive of sense that nobody had an idea of the meaning of what he was reading."

A "constitutional" court ball, which was supposed to testify to the democratic nature of the regime, was another comedy as viewed by a Viennese sophisticate. "The higher nobility of the land rubs shoulders with its own tailors and cobblers; all the English shopkeepers who have retired to Brussels on grounds of economy have access to the ball with their respective families. . . . The state officials and diplomatic representatives with their wives were truly a pitiful sight, being doomed to sit for five mortal hours tied to the same spot, in a semi-circle to the right and left of the royal dais, with no resource save to groan a word of lamentation first to one neighbor and then to the other. . . . Anyone accustomed to the old court ceremonial must be unpleasantly struck by the ill-bred haste with which most of the guests went away after supper, even before the royal family had left the hall."

Before he left Belgium, he managed to extract from Leopold the promise of a marriage settlement. "You have no idea," he reported to Franz Josef, "what sport it was to wring from the old miser something of that which is dearest to his heart."

In return for a sketchy dowry, Leopold demanded that Franz Josef provide Maximilian and Charlotte with a position worthy of them. Reluctant though he was to share even the semblance of power with one of his brothers, particularly the thrusting Maximilian, Franz Josef finally agreed to appoint him governor-general of the provinces of Lombardy and Venetia. Lombardy had been ceded to Austria in 1714 at the end of the War of the Spanish Succession, while Venice had been handed over to Austria as lagniappe when Napoleon I used the palace of Schönbrunn as his headquarters for the invasion of Russia. Both provinces were restive. Turning over viceregal powers in northern Italy to Maximilian was not the finest imaginable wedding present, as Franz Josef well knew. Early in 1857 Franz Josef, with Empress Elizabeth at his side, had toured the provinces, and despite the efforts of the Austrian occupation forces, they had been sullenly received in Trieste, Milan and Venice. Shortly after his return Franz Josef announced that Maximilian, who was to be married to Princess Charlotte that summer, would be his viceroy in the troubled provinces.

In boyhood and youth, Franz Josef and Maximilian had been very close, but something verging on estrangement had occurred when Maximilian urged that he be given a share of imperial responsibilities. From then on Franz Josef was a less than zealous guardian of his brother's interests.

The wedding of Archduke Maximilian and Princess Charlotte took place in Brussels on July 27, 1857, in the Church of Ste. Gudule. They made a beautiful couple, perhaps the most attractive among European royalty, Maximilian tall and blond, Charlotte small and brunette and vibrant. He was twenty-five; she was seventeen. They were not then in love—it was no more a love match than the marriage of a peasant boy and girl whose fathers wanted to combine two farms—but it was the European belief that love could just as well follow marriage as precede it. In the case of Maximilian and Charlotte, from all accounts, that theory was proved out.

Their honeymoon, such as it was, was spent on the journey to Italy and the assumption of their duties at a *palazzo* in Milan. Charlotte at first was enchanted with Italy and announced that she was changing her name to Carlotta (by which she will henceforth be referred to), a Coburg princess destined to share the responsibilities of ruling over resentful Latin and Indian peoples. For a few months their beauty and charm and youth— and the goodwill they radiated—provided a honeymoon period with the northern Italian people. Their carriage was cheered when it appeared in the streets and square of Milan; Carlotta went shopping in the fruit and vegetable markets like any young Milanese housewife (except for the military escort). But politics, especially revolutionary politics, cannot abide sugary sentiment for long, and those who agitated against "Austrian tyranny," of which Maximilian and Carlotta were the official and visible symbols, were soon successful in reminding the populace that it was a patriotic duty to detest the viceregal couple, no matter how pretty they looked in their costumes. Soon even the Italian nobility was finding it discreet to refuse invitations to the palace.

Even when Franz Josef loosened the bonds slightly and made concessions to Lombardy and Venice on taxes, the position of Maximilian and Carlotta was not improved, and demonstrations against them gathered force in the northern cities. Every concession, in fact, weakened their position. The Italians simply wanted the Austrians out and would not be appeased.

Less than a year after he had been appointed viceroy, Maximilian was writing his mother: "If it were not for my religious duties, I should long since have left this land of misery, where one is doubly depressed by having to act as the representative of an inactive government with no ideas, which one's judgment tries in vain to defend. It was with a feeling of profound shame that I recently entered Milan, doubly weighed down and depressed by a friendly manner, full of goodwill, in which we were both personally received, as it were, like respectable private persons. This private friendliness, combined with public repudiation, is what shows me most how clearly things stand; it shows how powerless I am, but also shows how irresponsibly the Government trifles with the goodwill of the masses.

"One thing has been achieved at Vienna; if that was the aim, then we have displayed a statesmanlike spirit. . . . Only one voice is now heard, that of indignation and disapproval; it pervades the whole country, and before it I stand alone and impotent; I am not afraid, for that is not the way of the Hapsburgs, but I am silent and ashamed. . . . If things continue to grow serious at the same rate as they have done, I shall soon begin to think of sending Charlotte back to her father at Brussels; for I have no mind to let her be sacrificed to weakness and irresolution. . . . I am accordingly beginning to ask myself whether my conscience will allow me blindly to follow instructions from Vienna. . . ."

Indirectly, of course, Maximilian was attacking his older brother, and one wonders if the Archduchess Sophie showed his letters to Franz Josef. If she did, it could not have improved relations between the two brothers.

The political chaos increased, as Maximilian foresaw, and during the winter of 1858–59 he did send Carlotta back to her father for several months. Late in January, 1859, he wrote his mother that he was "lonely as a hermit in the great palace at Milan" while "before me dances and whirls the carnival. . . . In my apartments it is as silent as Lent, and the old Countess Lützow takes the place of the mistress of the house at table." A short time later he complained of being "hemmed in by hostile parties, never to be sure whether one will be approved by the vacillating center [Vienna], in constant fear of hearing that one's innocent wife has been insulted or injured, never to be sure that one will not be hissed at the theater, or whether one will return alive from one's promenades."

And now the tricky Napoleon III was taking a hand in the game. He had decided to ally himself with the forces led by Count Cavour, who aspired to unite Italy under Sardinian rule. The issue would be decided not in the riotous streets of the northern cities but on the battlefield; Napoleon would pit his army against the Austrian cavaliers, so beautifully clad it was a shame to riddle their ranks with musketry and massed batteries. Bravely but foolishly led, the Austrian cavalry in their white and gold uniforms, equitation experts to a man, were routed by the French at Magenta and Solferino. A peace was hastily concluded between France and Austria—what with Prussians menacingly concentrating on the Rhine to discourage any further Napoleonic maneuvers—and the Austrians sullenly withdrew from the northern Italian provinces. Maximilian was an unemployed viceroy, forced to flee Milan and join his wife briefly in Belgium. To his father-in-law, he wrote of how "wretched" it was to "see our fine and once powerful monarchy sinking lower and lower through incompetence, misunderstanding and conduct difficult to explain." His role, as he saw it, had been that of the prophet scorned.

Unemployment rests as heavily, if without the physical privations, on the princely head as on any other. The main function of royalty, after all, was to find and keep employment wherever people were docile enough to accept the principle that certain men were divinely appointed to rule over them. Doubtless Maximilian hoped that Franz Josef would summon him to Vienna and provide him with duties suitable for a second oldest brother. Maximilian was no longer second in line of succession.

In the summer of 1858 Empress Elizabeth had given birth to a son, Crown Prince Rudolf, making it unlikely that Maximilian would ever ascend the throne of the Hapsburgs.*

The occupation to which Maximilian and Carlotta devoted themselves after the flight from Milan was castle building. Traditionally it was a job for dreamers, and Maximilian surpassed himself in the role of master builder. He would leave behind him several masterpieces of nineteenth-century architecture which expressed his ability to find poetry in stone, harmony in land and water.

Even before he had been relieved of his viceregal duties, he had started construction of a summer castle on a rocky promontory extending into the Adriatic and overlooking the harbor of Trieste. Now it would be his refuge from an unfeeling and unappreciative world as well as a summer retreat.

Miramar—view of the sea—a small white palace as lovely and melancholy as its name. It was built of dazzling white limestone and Carrara marble. Its flanks rise from the sea, and from Trieste the castle appears to have been built on an island. With little else to occupy them, Maximilian and Carlotta supervised every detail of its construction, its exterior and interior decoration. The granite for the terraces was quarried in the Tatra Mountains. Sphinxes were brought from Egypt to enhance the terraces. Rich soil was transported to the rocky headland, in which oleanders, myrtles, olives and laurels were planted. Oranges, figs and pomegranates were grown in the gardens for the palace table.

Since Maximilian considered himself an old sea dog, the interior, except for Carlotta's domain, was decorated in a naval motif. The walls of the various salons were covered with a blue damask threaded with anchors. Maximilian's private apartments were a replica of his headquarters, as vice admiral of the Austrian navy, aboard the frigate *Novara*; sextants and charts strewn around as though Miramar were about to be launched into the Adriatic at any moment. And there was a throne room, high-vaulted with a balcony running around the sides, ready

---

* Yet it could have happened, if events had taken a different course. Crown Prince Rudolf killed himself—apparently—in 1889. Emperor Franz Josef lived until 1916 and would have been succeeded by Maximilian if the latter had survived to his eighty-fourth year.

and waiting for occasions of vast import. Shimmering in the sun, with its broad terraces and gardens running down to the sea, Miramar was not only the residence of an ex-viceroy and an ex-admiral but the capital of a dream. Its builder was still convinced that great events were in store for him. He had always known that he was more popular with the people of Vienna than his rather dour brother; the Biedermeiers had not forgotten him, and probably he sustained himself in what amounted to exile with the possibility that he would be called to the Hofburg as emperor.

Meanwhile, he would be patient, observant, preparing himself for great tasks. Patience was a part of greatness. So he occupied himself with reading, writing travel sketches, memoirs and aphorisms, and studying botany. He would spend whole days with an Austrian botanist, both armed with butterfly nets, chasing specimens across the countryside.

Besides those avocations, he sustained himself with the belief that only he saw things clearly, that only he could rescue the monarchy, if only the summons would come from Vienna. In the spring of 1860 he made a brief visit to the capital and with gloomy relish recited in a letter to his father-in-law just how badly things were going months after the Austrian defeat. "I found the condition of our poor country, as I expected, tangled and gloomy," he wrote Leopold I. "Corruption on the one hand and unrest on the other are growing stronger and more disquieting every day. As in the days of Louis XVI, irresolution and inaction prevail; men do not and will not grasp the situation; there is storm and stress on every side, but in the face of it all, men close their eyes and ears more and more. Perhaps I see things in too gloomy a light, but in my private life I am making all preparations for a crisis."

That visit had been an unhappy one all around. Carlotta had accompanied him and was puzzled by the coldness of their reception, the inimical atmosphere of the dank old Hofburg. To solve some of the monarchy's problems, it had been suggested that Maximilian be placed on an autonomous throne in Hungary and that country be granted a measure of independence before she was detached like Lombardy and Venice. Franz Josef was only irked the more when unwanted advice to this effect came from Britain, where Maximilian was now regarded with affection by Queen Victoria and Prince Albert.

In addition, the atmosphere of the Hofburg was thunderous with the feuding of the Wittelsbach ladies. Archduchess Sophie had ordained that Empress Elizabeth's children, Crown Prince Rudolf and his sisters, be cared for and brought up, as well as educated, by the imperial tutors and governesses. Elizabeth was putting up a spirited resistance to this dictum; she could not see why she should be barred from the nursery, nor could she be convinced that Count Bombelles and his colleagues had done such a splendid job with the archdukes. Young mother and matriarch battled it out, with Franz Josef acting as referee and finally ruling in favor of his mother. To cap it all, Archduchess Sophie's spies informed her that Sisi smoked cigarettes in her boudoir, a highly unconventional habit for any lady in 1860 and unspeakable for a Hapsburg empress. Sisi defiantly informed her mother-in-law and husband that she not only smoked but was a chain smoker.

Maximilian and Carlotta stayed in Vienna just long enough to absorb the sultry atmosphere and join in sitting for a family portrait. It was a strange and awkward gathering, the first and last time the whole tragic family would be grouped together. They posed for Raoul Korty, the court photographer, with little more animation than waxworks dummies. Empress Elizabeth, with a daughter on her lap and Crown Prince Rudolf standing at her knee, shows her lovely profile. Sitting next to her on the huge baroque sofa is Archduchess Sophie staring straight into the lens and looking rather wistful for a change. Her husband, Archduke Karl, had come down from Prague for the occasion and wearing a stovepipe hat, with his hands resting on the arms of his chair, looks as though he cannot wait to spring up and catch the next train back to Prague. Behind them stood Franz Joseph, slim and dashing in a wasp-waisted tunic; then Maximilian, staring down at his equally ill-fated nephew Rudolf, who resembled him more than Franz Josef in temperament; Carlotta, standing behind Archduchess Sophie and looking very demure; finally the chinless archdukes, Maximilian's brothers, Ludwig and Karl.

Before they left Vienna, Maximilian and Carlotta also posed

for a separate photograph for Korty: Maximilian a tall and handsome figure standing beside his wife's chair, Carlotta (seen closer up than in the family portrait) displaying in the straight line of her mouth some of the firmness that even then was placing her in a dominant position over her husband and an odd, faraway look in her dark eyes.

They returned to Miramar glad to be away from the tensions of the Hofburg, yet finding themselves more discontented than ever with the idleness of their seaside retreat, the necessity to find something to occupy themselves. Maximilian practiced the pipe organ and chased butterflies. Carlotta busied herself with embroidery and supervising the work of the gardeners. But it was an empty life for a vigorous young man of twenty-eight and a young woman of twenty, both of them trained since infancy to expect greater tasks and responsibilities. Both wondered whether they would live out the rest of their lives in this barren magnificence, this sterile splendor of the white palace by the sea.

Maximilian alone, always ready to give himself up to daydreaming, might have found the place tolerable, might have accepted the slow shriveling of his ambitions. But it was Maximilian's destiny to be goaded by women of stronger spirit: first his mother, now his wife. He would not find himself as a man until the last few months of his life, when he was separated from those strong-willed women by the Atlantic Ocean and half of Europe.

The trip to Vienna had only made Carlotta more dissatisfied with the elegant stagnation of Miramar. "Her desires and complaints increased the Archduke's discontent," wrote Count Corti, "all the more so since she did not find the imperial family very congenial, and in particular did not get on very well with the Empress Elizabeth. She, too, was characterized by a boundless longing for action, intensified by the ambition inherited from her father, and the Orléans pride, her mother's heritage."

Months went by with no important visitors, with nothing but the echoes of great events far from the Adriatic coast, with nothing but bucolic pursuits, plans for providing Miramar with more distractions, to occupy them. The world seemed to have forgotten them. Not even their royal relatives made the long journey across Europe, through the northern provinces of Italy to the head of the Adriatic.

It was a year after their visit to Vienna, in fact, before their household was enlivened by news that Franz Josef and Elizabeth, fortunately unaccompanied by the Archduchess Sophie, were coming to stay with them. Carlotta suffered spasms of jealousy over Maximilian's obvious affection for his sister-in-law. Just as obviously it was reciprocated. But Sisi, Carlotta also saw, was no coquette; she even seemed to be unaware of the effect she had on men. Empress Elizabeth, in fact, was one of those rare beauties with the ability to fascinate equally men, women, children, dumb animals, and even desiccated historians; she was simply a work of art to be judged by other than human standards. Carlotta thawed out when she saw that Elizabeth was no home wrecker, and the two brothers and their wives, away from the pomp and intrigue of the Hofburg, enjoyed themselves thoroughly. They spent the days wandering over the estate, admiring Carlotta's flowers and Maximilian's groves of cypress, date palms and pomegranate trees. At night they sat for hours on the loggia, with the lights of Trieste across the black velvety water, while the two brothers discussed imperial affairs and grew closer than they had been since youth. Carlotta listened raptly to Elizabeth's account of her recent stay on the island of Madeira, to which she had fled for six months' respite from the incessant struggle with the Archduchess Sophie, listened so attentively, in fact, that she later wrote a memoir of her sister-in-law's adventures, having none of her own to recount in the eternal quiet of Miramar.

Then Franz Josef and Elizabeth left. The long, lovely summer beside the shimmering Adriatic stretched ahead of Maximilian and Carlotta—an infinity of idleness, dawdling and boredom—and they could only wonder if they would ever be recalled to the great world.

A civil war had broken out in America; there was a rustle of opportunism in certain European capitals where the loss of American territories had never been entirely forgotten or forgiven. Very soon now the master and mistress of Miramar would be sought out for the roles they were destined to play.

3. The Invasion of America

To a Zouave, of course, it was natural to pass joyfully from continent to continent. . . . When bugles echo, a feverish trembling flows in our veins. We are exalted by the thunder of the cannon. The odor of powder awakens in us those warlike instincts which sleep in our breasts. We fill our lungs with the hot breath of battle and throw ourselves with fury—indescribable fury—into the combat. . . .

—Captain Louis Noir, *Campaign of Mexico* (Paris, 1867)

The plans for an establishment of European power on the American continent, once again, were well under way by the time that the Union and Confederate armies were grappling at Bull Run. It looked like a long war, with the outcome uncertain, with even the possibility that the Confederacy might win its struggle for secession. In that case, with Jefferson Davis said to view European intervention in Mexico with a tolerant eye, the Monroe Doctrine would be a dead issue and Washington would be able to do little about its enforcement except protest; its support of Juárez would be meaningless and futile, and the European powers—France, Spain and Britain—could proceed to collect on their questionable loans to past Mexican governments and exploit that country's mineral wealth without hindrance from the north.

An English statesman remarked that Napoleon III's mind

"seems to be as full of schemes as a warren is full of rabbits." True enough, but in the past decade Louis Napoleon had managed to pull off a number of coups, first of all in his own country, then the joint victory over Russia in the Crimean War and the victory over Austria in 1859. Those, too, had been schemes, but they had enhanced the glory of the Second Empire. In the light of the subsequent collapse of that empire, he has been judged by history as a shallow, vain, inept marplot, with the mentality of a riverboat gambler and the moral outlook of a confidence man. Yet in the context of his own time his plans for extending the Second Empire to Mexico were not entirely ridiculous. The concept was a gamble largely based on the hope of a Confederate victory, but history is a series of gambles. Its center was not so much the ancient Aztec throne as an old ambition of Louis Napoleon's to build a transisthmian canal. (This had first arisen when he was imprisoned in the Belgian Château of Ham after the failure of his first attempt at a *coup d'état*. A group of Nicaraguans visited him there with elaborate plans for the construction of the *Canale Napoleone* across the narrow waist of Nicaragua. For years afterward he kept going over the sketches and reviving the dream of such a project.)

So his idea of building an overseas empire was more grandiose than a mere debt-collecting expedition to Mexico. He envisioned a latter-day Byzantium, built around the Napoleon Canal, lying halfway between Europe and the Orient and acting as an interchange on the world's trade routes. Mexico would be its northern bulwark, with its stability restored by foreign occupation forces and maintained by a handpicked sovereign. After all, Brazil, the largest state in South America, was ruled by a Portuguese, the Emperor Dom Pedro. Furthermore, his European alliances would be strengthened in the process. The choice of an Austrian archduke for Emperor of Mexico would make Austria beholden to him, and a Franco-Austrian alliance would make his the strongest power in Europe. Checkmate to the growing menace of Prussia.

Around him Napoleon could see a France being restored to the vigor it had shown under his great-uncle. Despite the forebodings of his half brother, the Duc de Morny, that France lacked the strength and morale for imperial adventures, Napoleon, reading dispatches from his soldiers and diplomats, saw evidence of a resurgent conquering spirit. Beyond the parochial borders of France itself, which so obsessed his half brother, French troops had pacified North Africa, more recently had stormed the Taku forts guarding Canton and marched to Peking, had mounted a successful expedition to the Levant and pacified Syria. Paris was again the City of Light, the center of the civilized world, the cultural standard-bearer, from which other nations took their style in dress and literature and city building. Now "under a mounting sun," as Philip Guedalla has written, "the Empire moved towards high noon. In the blaze of it were French victories, an heir, a smiling Empress, and the world seemed waiting for Napoleon to remake it."

And Napoleon was not unwilling, with Mexico as the first giant step toward recasting the world order. Everything seemed to conspire toward that end. There was the matter of the Jecker bonds, which would be so profitable to the Duc de Morny and his friends. There were large-scale commercial ventures to be undertaken across the Atlantic. There was Louis Napoleon's ambition to exceed the empire building of his uncle and restore the glory of France, far from the constricting influence of Prussia and other rivals. Not least there was the urging of the Empress Eugénie, who, having fallen under the influence of aristocratic emigrés from Mexico and being a devout daughter of the church, yearned to see a Catholic empire dominant in the Americas, superior even to the more secular United States.

The last invasion of the Americas from Europe was considerably motivated by the great ladies, no longer content with setting fashions, raising heirs to the throne or managing their households, who felt they had to urge on their royal menfolk to greater deeds. Strong-willed feminism was on the march in the Tuileries, the Hofburg and Miramar. Without the devout hopes of Empress Eugénie, the matriarchal drives of Archduchess Sophie and the restless ambition of Carlotta, the American invasion might never have been launched. Not at all invisibly they were the props under Napoleon, Franz Josef and Maximilian.

Eugénie de Montijo, like her husband, was descended from a colorful lineage, and like Napoleon III, she felt the necessity to sanctify it with her own accomplishments. One grandfather was a Scottish wine merchant and tavernkeeper named Kirkpatrick, who had settled in Spain and from whom she had inherited her red-gold hair and pale-blue eyes. Her voluptuous and carefree mother had once posed in the nude for Goya ("The Naked Maja"). Her father was an elderly cuckold who had ennobled the tavernkeeper's daughter through marriage and then faded from the domestic scene after providing her with two daughters. Eugénie herself was born in a garden tent during an earthquake in Granada—the omen of a very active career.

She and her sister trailed along after their scandalous mother, banished from the court of Isabella II for her misconduct, elegantly exiled in London, Paris, the Riviera. Both sisters were courted by the Duke of Berwick and Alba, who chose Francesca over Eugénie when their mother insisted on his making a choice. Eugénie, always a self-dramatist, promptly swallowed poison, but the dosage apparently was insufficient for anything but the purpose of creating a scene. Her mother took her to Paris in 1848, when she was twenty-one, to find a husband. One night at the Élysées she was presented to Louis Napoleon, then President of France, and caught his somewhat lecherous eye with her red hair, white shoulders and ripe figure. Napoleon discarded his English fiancée and in 1853 married Eugénie.

Emotionally the marriage was not a happy one. Napoleon's heavy-lidded eyes roved continually over her ladies-in-waiting, and his empress' most intense preoccupation—until she schooled herself to ignore his infidelities—was discovering which of her ladies was currently betraying her.

On learning to live with the knowledge that her husband was afflicted with a fairly virulent case of satyriasis (it was the Bonaparte curse, hypersexuality, like hemophilia with another royal family), the Empress Eugénie channeled her volatile energies into more historical matters. She plunged into a study of the lives of such predecessors as Marie Antoinette and Empress Josephine and the more successful Elizabeth of England, Catherine the Great, Maria Theresa of Austria and the lethal Medicis of Italy. Intellectually she was ready to add her name to that list—Eugénie the Devout, certainly, and Eugénie the Great if possible.

The aspiration was given focus and intensity one summer

afternoon when she was being driven in her carriage from the summer villa at Biarritz to Bayonne, where she intended to watch the bullfights. Along the way she met José Manuel Hidalgo, a slender, foppish, licorice-eyed young man who was traveling from Madrid to Paris to take up his new post as secretary of the Mexican legation. He was also the leader of a group of Mexican émigrés who were plotting in various European capitals to obtain support for an intervention that would rid Mexico of republicanism. Eugénie had met him years before in Madrid and asked him to ride along to Bayonne in her landau.

Hidalgo was an agile fellow and seized the opportunity to urge his faction's case on the Empress Eugénie. The power and glory of France must be exercised to save his homeland from anarchy and atheism; it was the duty of her rulers to "build a French empire beyond the Atlantic, to save Catholicism, as well as the Latin races, from being engulfed by uncouth Anglo-Saxons and their mercenary culture." Eugénie was impressed; might this not be the historic role she felt was waiting for her?

Perhaps partly, too, to distract Napoleon from his attentions to the Countess di Castiglione, the Countess Walewska (wife of Napoleon I's illegitimate son) and the Countess de Labedoyere and other ladies mentioned in the memoirs of the time, Eugénie introduced Hidalgo into the most intimate circle of their court. He was closer to Eugénie than to her husband at first, but in the autumn of 1861, with things looking so badly for the United States and even worse for Mexican aristocrats, with Juárez seemingly solidifying himself in power, Hidalgo delivered a most persuasive argument for intervention to Napoleon while a guest at the Biarritz summer villa. Until now Napoleon had resisted him by claiming that France could not intervene without the active collaboration of Britain. That argument, Hidalgo informed the emperor, was no longer valid.

Displaying letters from other émigré groups, as he related in a memorandum later deposited in Vienna as proof of his leading role in bringing about intervention, he told Napoleon that "England, together with France and Spain, is now irritated by Juárez's policy, and they are all going to order warships to our [Mexican] ports. And so, Your Majesty, we have what we needed: English intervention. France will not be acting alone, which Your Majesty always wished to avoid. Spain has long been prepared; General [José Gutiérrez de la] Concha told me not long ago that he had left six thousand men in Havana, ready to land at Vera Cruz, but that the Cabinet of Madrid prefers to proceed hand in hand with France and, if possible, England. And so the French, English and Spanish naval squadrons might be dispatched to Vera Cruz and land these six thousand Spaniards.

"In view of the three combined flags, Mexico would recognize the full strength and superiority of the alliance, and the overwhelming majority in the country could rely on the support of the intervening powers, annihilate the demagogues, and proclaim a monarchy, which alone can save the country. The United States are in the throes of war; they will not move. Besides, they would never oppose the three united powers together. Let the allied flag once show itself, sir, and I can assure Your Majesty that the country will rise as one man and rally to the support of this beneficent intervention."

Napoleon, naïvely taking the assurances of an intriguing émigré, immediately agreed that if France and Spain were ready to invade Mexico, "I will also join them, but I will send only warships, no landing-troops . . . I will lend a hand. . . ."

Empress Eugénie joined the two men, and the conversation turned to who might be picked as Emperor of Mexico to preside over the Latin resurgence in the Americas. Not a Latin; the Spanish had already announced they had no candidate, and the Duc de Morny, the logical French draftee, had made it known that he would not allow so weighty an honor to fall on his cynical head. One of the unemployed Austrian archdukes seemed to the three conferees the best possibility. A seriocomic exchange, again as reported by Hidalgo, then took place.

EUGÉNIE: "But which archduke?"

HIDALGO: "I believe that the Archduke Rainer [a cousin of Maximilian's] was spoken of."

EUGÉNIE: "Yes, for the Archduke Maximilian would not be willing."

HIDALGO: "Oh, no, he would not accept."

NAPOLEON: "Oh, no, he would not be willing."

EUGÉNIE (as if suddenly inspired): "Well! I have a presentiment that tells me he *will* accept."

HIDALGO: "We can but try, and I might write to Gutiérrez de

Estrada [the son-in-law of Countess Lützow, a member of Maximilian's court] to go to Vienna and sound his Imperial Highness."

So Gutiérrez, along with Hidalgo and General Juan Almonte, a leader of the Mexican émigrés living in Europe and plotting for the day when they could return to their homeland and recover their confiscated estates, journeyed to Vienna and broached the matter of Archduke Maximilian's appointment. Franz Josef listened to the offer, then sent Count Johann Bernhard Rechberg to Miramar to outline the proposition to Maximilian and Carlotta. There it was received, according to Count Corti, with measured rejoicing. "The whole trend of Archduke's disposition, reinforced by the influence of his wife, who had too little distraction for her loneliness at Miramar and was ripe for a grave folly, disposed him to listen to the offer. The Emperor, on the other hand, appeared in a sense glad of the possibility that his restless, critical, 'free-thinking' brother, who was always causing him embarrassment and anxiety, but was at the same time extraordinarily beloved in the whole country, should find a sphere of activity which should at once be grandiose, promise fame, and be worthy of the house of Hapsburg."

Maximilian gave no definite promise that he would accept, but the understanding was that he could be counted on when the time came. First Mexico would have to be pacified, Juárez kicked out of Mexico City, and as much of the country as possible brought under the control of foreign troops. Then serious negotiations could begin on the terms under which Maximilian and Carlotta would become Emperor and Empress of Mexico. There was the question of costs—setting up a new imperium would not come cheaply—of the composition of occupation forces, of repayment of Mexico's foreign debt, of all the measures that would have to be taken to guarantee that the new rulers could be maintained, as well as installed, on the throne of Montezuma. That process would, in fact, take more than two years.

Meanwhile, the diplomatic and military steps toward intervention were being taken in Paris, Madrid and London. The clauses of President Monroe's doctrine, issued in 1823, were studied, interpreted and reinterpreted, particularly the clause to the effect that "any attempt on their part [the European powers] to extend their system to any portion of this hemisphere as dangerous to our peace and safety. . . . Nor would such extension be regarded with indifference. . . ." But times had changed, and the United States would have all it could do to preserve the Union. There was no need to anguish over the Monroe Doctrine. Before the year 1861 ended, the forces of intervention, largely naval, would be encroaching on the American continent and initiating what was jocularly known as the bondholders' war.

Yet there were sobering moments, soon forgotten, such as the Empress Eugénie's curt conversation with William Lewis Dayton, the American minister in Paris, at a New Year's reception.

"Madame," Dayton told her, "the North is going to win. France must abandon her project or there is trouble ahead."

Eugénie's pale face was flushed with anger. "Permit me to assure you," she almost hissed, "that if Mexico were not so distant, and my son not a mere baby, I myself would place him at the head of the French army, in order to write with his sword one of the most shining pages in the history of this century."

"Madame," Dayton calmly replied, "you had better thank God that Mexico is so far away, and that your son is still swinging a toy saber."

The bondholders, undismayed by warnings from Washington, plunged into preparations for their adventure. Spain would send warships and a brigade of infantry under General Juan Prim; France, a landing force of marines and zouaves under an admiral, and Britain, more marines and sailors under a commodore. Compared to the Spanish contingent of 6,000 troops, the French would land 2,000 marines and 600 zouaves, England a mere 800 marines, being the least interested party to the intervention (Prince Albert and, therefore, Queen Victoria felt a certain sympathy for the North in the American Civil War).

The zouaves, a crack regiment seasoned under North African suns, were dispatched at the pleading of Eugénie and her friend Hidalgo. They marched through Oran and down to the harbor of Mers-el-Kebir eager—or so their officers claimed—for a fresh field of battle. Their standards bore the honors won in the campaigning in Italy and the Crimea in recent years, and at

least one of their officers, Captain Louis Noir, was brimming
with Napoleonic sentiments.

"Descendants of the Gauls," he thundered at his company,
unmindful of the fact that many in the ranks were Africans and
Egyptians, "when the bugles echo, a feverish trembling flows in
our veins. We are exalted by the thunder of cannon. The odor
of powder awakens in us those warlike instincts which sleep in
our breasts. We fill our lungs with the hot breath of battle and
throw ourselves with fury—indescribable fury—into the combat. It is thus that our infantry make their terrible charges
. . . wild and furious as the sea in a tempest, terrible and
thunderous like avalanches in the Alps. . . . Oh, in action we
are transfigured! Then, when the victory is ours, we become
simple and modest fellows."

No one, the fire-eating zouave captain recalled in his two-
volume memoir of the expedition, knew exactly why the regiment was being shipped to Mexico, or cared. Any enemy would
do. They were professionals, though dressed more for a costume party in baggy crimson trousers with white gaiters and
turbans trailing scarlet tassels than for the sober business of war
on another continent. "Certainly," Captain Noir gloated on
board the ship that carried them to Mexico, "our troops are the
most picturesque on earth. The turbans of the Algerian jan-
issaries, added to the rich uniform of the French soldier, gives
our fierce African regiments a poetic cachet." They also made a
beautiful target for Mexican guerrillas, as Louis Noir and his
comrades would learn.

The initial stages of the invasion, unopposed except by the
humid coastal climate and the endemic yellow fever, went off
smoothly enough. Better, in fact, than such a combined, multi-
lingual operation had any reason to anticipate. The Spanish,
with their expeditionary force waiting in Cuban waters, landed
first. A few weeks later the English flotilla rounded the reef outside the roadstead of Veracruz and joined the Spanish ashore.
Days later the French warships and transports landed their regiments under the command of Vice Admiral Jean Pierre de la
Gravière.

Soon enough the Anglo-Franco-Spanish forces learned why
there were no coastal defenses around Veracruz. It lay in the
yellow fever zone, surrounded by swamp and jungle, and the in-

vaders, quartered in dank barracks, warehouses and abandoned convents, began succumbing to the "black vomit." Well into the new year (1862) there had been no overt reaction from the Mexican republican army. What had all these troops been gathered for, to die of yellow fever or teach the Mexicans a lesson? The allied commanders, aware of their forces' restiveness over the inaction, decided to send a message to President Juárez suggesting negotiations. They were willing to confer with Juárez's representatives if the president agreed to allow the allies to transfer their forces from the fever coast to the temperate zone. Orizaba, a little less than halfway up the Sierra to Mexico City, was the chosen point of concentration. Needing time and unable to muster the forces necessary to drive the invaders back into the Gulf of Mexico, President Juárez agreed.

Time, it appeared, was on the side of the patient Indian. The allies had begun quarreling among themselves. The Spanish General Prim, who somehow had got the idea that he might be appointed viceroy of Mexico, heard from exiled Mexican generals recently arrived from Europe that the French were proposing that Archduke Maximilian of Austria be crowned Emperor of Mexico. Prim had not come to this ghastly country to fight for an Austrian princeling. He wrote Napoleon directly that he and his troops would not contribute toward such an effort. "Moreover, sire, is it my profound conviction that in this country monarchial ideas find few supporters. . . . The neighborhood of the United States, and the severe strictness of those republicans against monarchial institutions, have greatly contributed to create here a positive hatred against them. It will be easy for Your Majesty to conduct Prince Maximilian to the capital, and to have him crowned a king, but that monarch will find no one to support him should your help fail him. . . . Leaders of the conservative party just landed at Vera Cruz say that it will be sufficient to consult the upper classes, and this excites apprehensions and inspires a dread, lest violence may be done the nation's will." General Prim was immediately informed by the French that whatever his reservations, a Mexican empire was going to be established under French protection—and their allies could do what they pleased about that.

The Spanish were outraged, the British dumbfounded. The commodore commanding the British expeditionary force, declaiming that London had joined in the excursion as a gesture of friendship, nothing more, announced his marines would retire to their ships in Veracruz Harbor rather than join the movement to Orizaba. The Spanish let it be known that they hadn't joined the intervention simply to place a French puppet, of Austrian design, on the Mexican throne.

Napoleon's response to his associates was high-handed: They could pull out if they wished, now that they had helped France establish a foothold. He ordered an additional 4,500 troops sent to Mexico and placed the whole French corps under the command of Brigadier General Count de Lorencez. The switch in command from an admiral to a general indicated Napoleon's intention of changing that force from a sea to a land animal—and penetrating farther into the interior. On hearing that the French were sending reinforcements of that size, realizing that intervention had become a Napoleonic rather than an allied venture, the Spanish marched back down the road from Orizaba to Veracruz, and shortly both they and the British forces sailed away and abandoned the project of Mexican debt collecting.

The French were overjoyed; now they'd have Mexico to themselves. Thousands of French citizens would be transplanted to the new colony. The shipping house of Pereire formed the Compagnie Transatlantique and announced a regular steamship service to Veracruz. In April, 1862, about the time the French were breaking off negotiations with President Juárez and announcing their intention of marching to Mexico City, the new line's steamship *Louisiane* inaugurated that service. A special train carried its passengers and a delegation of notables to St.-Nazaire for the embarkation.

Among them was a fifteen-year-old American girl, Sara Yorke, who was being educated in Paris while her family lived in Mexico City. Tragic news had just come from Mexico City. Her brother Ogden had been carrying dispatches for Thomas Corwin, the U.S. minister to Mexico, and his stagecoach had been attacked by bandits on the road to Veracruz. The young man had been killed, and the Yorkes wrote Sara asking her to join them. Her guardian, M. Achille Jubinal, a historian and Liberal member of the Chamber of Deputies, escorted her to St.-Nazaire.

At the inaugural banquet she listened to speeches proclaiming the prosperity awaiting the colonists bound for Mexico and toasts to the new wing of the empire, which would be acquired without bloodshed because everyone knew the Mexican hordes wouldn't dare to stand up against French bayonets, and besides, all decent Mexicans welcomed the chance to become part of the Second Empire. The observant Sara, whose published recollections of her years in Mexico during and after the Maximilian-Carlotta period would be among the most clear-sighted and compassionate toward all factions, noticed that only a few of the celebrities who toasted the glorious Mexican future actually boarded the *Louisiane,* while the rest hastened back to Paris to sell bonds and make their fortunes, at safe remove, on the transatlantic extension of the empire.

Years later she would remember how bewildered and depressed she was that night when the *Louisiane* steamed out from St.-Nazaire. Until now she had believed anything that adults told her. Now, going out on the deck of the "dark hulk of the old ship," she heard two young men standing at the rail nearby discussing their own reasons for going to Mexico. They were surgeons being sent to the French military hospital just established at Veracruz. Then Sara realized that despite all the fine speeches she had heard, the Mexicans were not throwing flowers at the feet of Napoleon's troops, and ever afterward would remember the "loneliness of that night in the Bay of Biscay . . . it was my first serious disillusion. . . ."

At Miramar, too, there was a measure of disillusionment over the progress of the intervention. The task of persuading Maximilian to take up the Mexican crown had been left largely to Gutiérrez de Estrada, whose mother-in-law, Countess Lützow, had long been a member of Maximilian's suite. Gutiérrez had managed to convince Maximilian, and even more so Carlotta, that the whole Mexican people, not just the émigré aristocrats, yearned to be ruled by him. Gutiérrez could not stay at Miramar the whole time, however, and when his near-hypnotic presence, his eloquent assurances were removed, Maximilian, like a certain legendary Danish prince, was whipsawed by doubt.

One thing he insisted on was that the Mexicans, or at least the majority of them, would accept him as emperor, but now he was beginning to wonder whether puppet strings might not run from the Tuileries to the National Palace in Mexico City, whether he would be an independent sovereign or the creature of Napoleon. The fact that he could expect anything else testified to the flattery and cajolery which had been lavished on him. "In my opinion," he wrote Count Rechberg in Vienna, the latter one of Franz Josef's chief advisers, "the Emperor Napoleon wants to be master in Mexico, without directly seeming so in the eyes of Europe. To this end he proposed a Prince upon whose entire devotion he thinks he can reckon, and whom he can in any case keep under constant pressure, owing to the fact that he will find in France the sole support of his throne."

This letter was dated February 28, 1862, before the French expeditionary force, now abandoned by the English and Spanish, suffered any setbacks. It shows that Maximilian saw clearly what Napoleon was up to. He was further dismayed by the fact that under the agreement with the French all military forces except "five hundred life-guards" protecting the palace would be controlled from Paris, so "the future ruler of Mexico should not be able to dispense with his [Napoleon's] tutelage." For that reason Maximilian had insisted that other powers besides France be part of the intervention. He also wrote Count Rechberg that he had no faith in a throne with an underpinning of French bayonets, that the new Mexican regime must have "a moral foundation: namely, the conviction and devotion of the people."

Yet he could not say no, once and for all, to the proposals that he become Emperor of Mexico. He knew that his elder brother and his mother wanted to see him under a crown of his own, and the restless ambitions of Carlotta, pacing the salons and terraces in the mocking quiet of Miramar, were even more imperative.

Mexico was to be the graveyard of French military reputations, as well as the actual graveyard of thousands of young French, Belgian, Austrian, German, Swiss and North African men who fought under the tricolor in a thousand skirmishes, ambushes, razzias, and an occasional pitched battle.

First came the minor disaster which provided the Republic of Mexico with the Cinco de Mayo, its version of the Fourth of July. Shortly after the French occupation forces were left to their own devices by their former allies, General Lorencez with his 7,000 troops started the march on Mexico City, though when they occupied Orizaba during the negotiations with President Juárez they had agreed to return to Veracruz if the negotiations failed. Breaking that agreement, Lorencez on May 4, 1862, advanced on the fortified town of Puebla, apparently unaware that the Mexican republican General Ignacio Zaragoza had collected 4,000 volunteers there to beat them off and send them reeling back to their ships. Lorencez's assault was dashed to pieces on the outer works of Puebla's defenses. He considered that he did not have sufficient force to take a stoutly defended town, though it was astride the route to Mexico City and must be captured or the whole project of intervention abandoned, and fell back to conduct a siege.

The French War Ministry, on receiving the news of that setback, decided that General Lorencez must be replaced and his successor provided with the necessary force. General Élie Frédéric Forey, a conscientious soldier with a long and distinguished record of colonial and European campaigning, was appointed to take over supreme command. His forces would be raised to 28,000 troops, divided into two divisions, one commanded by General François Achille Bazaine and the other by General Félix Douay. The new commanders and their reinforcements sailed almost immediately from Cherbourg.

Of those new paladins General Bazaine was to become the outstanding figure, his career beginning as a hard-bitten ranker and ending as marshal of France. Born in 1811 in the town of Versailles, François Bazaine came of a middle-class family and was more or less deserted by both parents early in his childhood. He was brought up by a guardian, who was understandably disappointed when the stocky, taciturn youth failed to pass the examinations for the École Polytechnique; that meant any possibility of a professional or academic career was foreclosed.

Young Bazaine was not greatly disappointed because he yearned for a life of action and adventure. At the age of nineteen he enlisted as a private of the Thirty-seventh regiment of the Line; two years later he was a sergeant, and in 1832 he volunteered for the newly formed French Foreign Legion, which, composed of Germans, Swiss, Poles, Italians and Spaniards, as well as French noncoms and officers, was to undertake the pacification of Algeria. His aptitude for colonial warfare and especially the fact that he was French propelled him out of the ranks and into a commission as *sous-lieutenant*. Lieutenant Bazaine became an adept at the type of operation called a razzia, in which a legion company or battalion descended on hostile villages, shot them up, seized cattle, and generally made the Algerians feel the weight of French displeasure. He fought in campaigns against the Arab rebel Abd-el-Kader, rose to captain, and learned Spanish when the legion was sent to Spain during the Carlist revolt.

And he continued his methodical rise as the army of occupation in Algeria expanded and blossomed with such colorful formations as the green-turbaned zouaves, the chasseurs d'Afrique in sky-blue tunics, the spahis and the turcos. It was all very picturesque, even romantic in a way that certain fiction writers would capitalize on, but Bazaine was a down-to-earth fellow, a professional, the antithesis of the adventurers who volunteered for duty in the North African regiments. The Bureau Arabe, part military government, part intelligence service, was established, and Bazaine was appointed chief of the bureau's branch at Tlemcen. This hot dusty little Algerian town was Bazaine's university in learning the art of ruling a subject people; everything he learned there—and not a great deal more—would be applied thirty years later in Mexico. A chunky man of thirty-one with heavy-lidded eyes, practical, hardheaded and ambitious, he "became the channel through which the French authorities imposed their will upon the population and the difficulties of unruly Kaids [native chiefs] were transmitted to their masters," as one of Bazaine's biographers noted. "Interpreter, judge, tax-collector, and policeman, he administered extensive territories. . . . His intelligence reports on local temper and affairs helped to form policy; his attitude to local worthies controlled their rise and fall. . . ."

By 1850 Bazaine had advanced to colonel despite a scandal over his determination to marry a very young Spanish girl. Very young Spanish girls, in fact, were to be a continuing weakness. There was further disgruntlement among his colleagues when Colonel Bazaine insisted on bringing his bride and her pianoforte to Constantinople during the French involvement in the Crimean War, in which—armed only with a little cane which he would always carry into battle—he distinguished himself by leading his troops in the victorious assault on Sevastopol. Bazaine was promoted to general and commanded a division with striking success at Solferino, after which he wrote his family, "This great battle was really grand! But when the excitement of the fight is over," he piously added, "what a dismal sight is the battlefield covered with dead and wounded. In these days war is really an evil, and the men who drive nations to it are very guilty."

In his momentary distress over the mangled corpses of Solferino General Bazaine did not, however, break his little cane over his knee, tear off his epaulettes, or resign his commission. A seasoned, shrewd and ambitious soldier of fifty-one, he was eagerly available when new commanders were needed for Mexico. He spoke the language, he knew how to maneuver a division in battle (at least against Austrian cavaliers), and he was experienced in dealing with dissident natives. The razzia could easily be adapted to Mexican conditions. Bazaine was confident that his military reputation would only be enhanced by the campaigning in Mexico.

Late in 1862, with Napoleon's directive to smash their way to Mexico City before the year was out, the new divisions from France were unloaded from their transports, formed into marching battalions and led upcountry to Puebla and the siege line. On the march up from the coastal fever swamps, however, their ranks were decimated by malaria and yellow fever; one regiment alone lost 900 of its 1,800 effectives. It was obvious that the French army would have two enemies, the Mexicans and the Mexican diseases.

As the siege ring tightened around Puebla in April, 1863, French morale rose despite the fact that the town was now defended by 18,000 Juaristas. Bazaine, with his division organized like an Algerian flying column into four battalions, three cavalry squadrons and a battery of mountain howitzers, was assigned to guard the siege line against attack from a relieving army.

General Forey's main force spent weeks hammering away at the citadel of Puebla, but the Mexican resistance was so stubborn that Forey began bringing up the possibility of bypassing the town and slipping around the left to march on Mexico City instead. He was dissuaded when his staff pointed out that a thorn that size could not be left in the line of communications. The savage pressure maintained by the French began to have its effect on the defenders. French assault columns were driving closer to the inner works and fighting house to house on the outskirts. The citizens of the town were reduced to eating their house pets and whatever small animals they could trap.

To relieve the town, a Mexican column of 5,000 troops under General Ignacio Comonfort marched to attack the French from the rear. This provided Bazaine with his first opportunity. He had organized many such counterstrokes in Algeria. Advised of the direction of Comonfort's advance by spies, he took the Mexicans by surprise, marching all night to the heights of San Lorenzo and then launching his attack shortly before dawn.

The Mexican relief column was routed, Bazaine and his division of 3,500 men taking 1,000 prisoners, eight field guns and large quantities of food and ammunition Comonfort had been transporting to the starving garrison of Puebla. Bazaine had won the first striking victory of the Mexican campaign, given sustenance to the illusion that a French expeditionary force could somehow subdue and control the vast bewildering country from the Yucatán jungles of the south to the Sonora mountains of the north.

In mid-May General Forey threw the full force of his army against Puebla, whose defenders naturally had been disheartened by the news of the rout at San Lorenzo. The French broke through a wall of the citadel and fought at bayonet point for the inner defenses of the town.

The fire-eating Captain Louis Noir, waving his sword then, brandishing his rhetoric later in the two blood-drenched volumes of his history of that campaign, led his company of zouaves in the vanguard of the assault. "The garrison took flight throwing themselves into subterranean stables of what had been a factory," he recalled. "Our Zouaves seeing the enemy disappear as if by magic were for a moment stupefied. But Zouaves are men who would pursue an enemy, though it led them into the very depths of hell. They followed, throwing themselves against masses of humanity, piled one upon the other in the narrow passages. The crush was such that the Juaristas were suffocated, unable to advance. When they felt the bayonets their struggles were violent. Ah, it was a scene! The passages echoed with angry curses, with heart-rending pleas, with blasphemies, with hoarse sighs, and with the choking death rattle. The massacre was hideous. . . . But of us, few were wounded."

General Jesús González Ortega, commanding the Mexican garrison, ran up the white flag and asked for terms. General Forey demanded an unconditional surrender, and the Mexicans had no choice but to comply. Twelve thousand surrendered; among them were twenty-five generals, many of whom were sent back to France as prisoners. Some of the glory of the occasion evaporated for the French soldiers when the gaunt and starving civilians caught in the siege staggered out and some of the children stole corn from the fodder bags of the French cavalry mounts. But the road to Mexico City was open. . . .

And then there was Camerone, that blood-red-letter day in the annals of the French Foreign Legion (still celebrated with an extra ration of rum and a sounding of bugles at the legion's last outpost on Corsica). If the sunrise attack at San Lorenzo and the capture of Puebla proved that the French could win pitched battles and were experts at siege warfare, Camerone showed that they were not invincible or invulnerable, no matter how heroic.

In the continuing reinforcement of the army in Mexico, two battalions of the legion landed at Veracruz on March 31, 1863, with a third disembarking a short time later. Altogether they formed a brigade of 4,000 men—fewer than half of whom would ever return to their cantonments in Algeria.

Colonel René Jeanningros, their commander, and the men of the battalions were outraged when they were assigned to guard the supply route up from the swamps of Veracruz to the forward positions at Puebla. It seemed to the legionnaires that they were no more highly regarded by General Forey than such sorry outfits as the Egyptian Legion, who wore fezzes and fell on their knees to Mecca and who were guarding the stores down on the quays of Veracruz. Instead of joining in the assault on Puebla, they were broken up into small detachments and stationed at posts along the mountain road which had been taken by all of Mexico's conquerors from Cortez to General Winfield Scott and his American army in 1846.

On April 29, the Third Company of the First Battalion, normally 112 men and 3 officers, was ordered to convoy a supply caravan of 60 carts and 150 mules from Veracruz to Puebla. The company had been riddled by fever, however, and none of its officers and only 62 of its enlisted men were available for duty. Colonel Jeanningros asked for volunteers among his battalion staff to take over the command, and Captain Danjou, battalion adjutant major, stepped forward, followed by the paymaster, Vilain, and Lieutenant Maudet of the First Company. The colonel offered to reinforce the Third Company, but Captain Danjou was certain that 62 legionnaires could handle any number of Mexican bandits or guerrillas they might meet on the road to Puebla.

Jeanningros was worried by the fact that the caravan, in addition to munitions, would carry 3,000,000 francs in gold bullion to pay the troops at Puebla and that the guerrillas were known to have an excellent spy system, but he accepted Captain Danjou's assurances.

The following morning, April 30, the Third Company marched out in advance of the caravan to scout the road ahead. About 7 A.M. the company, in a double file on each side of the road, passed through the ruined and deserted hamlet of Camerone. About all that was left standing, as Danjou observed, was a farmhouse with a few collapsed outbuildings. The column continued for about a mile through the rolling brush-covered countryside until Captain Danjou called a halt for breakfast. They had just started their cook fires when a swarm of mounted Mexicans appeared on the ridges above them. Heavily outnumbered, as Danjou could see at a glance, their only hope was to conduct a fighting retreat to the ruins of Camerone. It was a maneuver they had often performed in Algeria under attack from tribesmen just as fierce—but seldom against such heavy odds. The enemy force consisted of 800 Juarista cavalry supported by 1,200 militia on foot; worse yet, it had learned of the gold bullion the Third Company was assigned to protect.

Danjou formed his company into a rectangle and retreated through undergrowth so thick they could not be charged by the

Juarista cavalry. Despite the skill with which this maneuver was conducted, the understrength company lost 16 men, who were captured during the retreat to Camerone. They made a dash for the farmhouse, and were bitterly surprised when gunfire blazed out of the upper windows and wounded several men.

Captain Danjou, who had lost a hand during some previous campaign and now wore a wooden one encased in a white glove, flourished his sword in his good left hand and started to lead a charge on the farmhouse when they were suddenly attacked by the Mexican cavalry from the other side. They were forced to take shelter behind a broken wall and around a tumbled-down outbuilding, but managed to repulse the cavalry charge.

Their situation was desperate. Closely surrounded, they could not reach the well for water, nor could they send to headquarters for help. The pack mules with extra rations and ammunition had been driven off by the Mexicans. And they were outnumbered by 50 to 1.

After about an hour of fighting in the swirling dust of the farmyard, with a number of legionnaires dead, wounded or dying behind the stone wall, the Mexican colonel in command rode forward under a white flag and called out in Spanish: "I ask you to surrender. You are surrounded by two thousand soldiers. Surrender and you will be fairly treated."

"We'll die before we surrender," Danjou replied. That was the legion doctrine; the lives of its men were forfeit the moment they were committed to battle.

For the rest of the morning and into the afternoon the Battle of Camerone continued. The Mexicans attacked the French position repeatedly in a series of rushes but failed to overrun it; each time, however, they left another legionnaire or two wounded or dead. Danjou kept warning his men to make every shot count and use the bayonet whenever possible.

In midafternoon, he was just reassuring the surviving members of Third Company that "aid will come" when he was killed by a sniper on the roof of the farmhouse. Two of the other three officers were also cut down. By five o'clock in the afternoon there were only Lieutenant Maudet and twelve enlisted men still on their feet. They were surrounded by the dead and dying piled in grotesque heaps. The Mexicans had tightened the ring around them and when night fell would surely overrun the surviving legionnaires.

An hour later only Lieutenant Maudet and five rankers were still standing—Corporal Maine, a Frenchman, and Privates Wenzel (German), Katau (Polish), Constantin (Austrian), and Leonhart (Swiss), a fair representation of the makeup of the legion. Although they had stripped the dead of their ammunition, they each had only one round left. To a legion officer there was only one possible tactic: a suicidal charge.

"Reload," Lieutenant Maudet ordered the survivors. "Fire on command. Then follow me through the breach. We'll end this with our bayonets."

On command, they fired their last round, then followed the lieutenant in possibly the most hopeless charge in military history. Hacking away with their bayonets, they plunged into a mass of Mexican militiamen. During the melee Colonel Milan, the Mexican commander, rode up and whacked his troops with the flat of his sword to prevent them from finishing off the survivors of Third Company. Corporal Maine and Private Katau were taken alive and along with several other wounded legionnaires were removed to a hospital fifty miles away.

Third Company, First Battalion, was wiped out, but its fight at Camerone saved the supply train, which had turned back on hearing the sounds of battle.

At dawn the day after the battle Colonel Jeanningros marched into Camerone at the head of a relief column, just twelve hours too late to do anything but bury the dead. Captain Danjou's body could not be found—only his wooden hand, the white glove stained with blood. Colonel Jeanningros picked up the hand and sent it back to legion headquarters at Sidi-bel-abbès. The wooden hand of Captain Danjou is still the legion's most sacred relic, the stark symbol of one of its most gallant actions.

To the French commanders in Mexico it should have symbolized something else. Camerone was fought just before the glorious victories at San Lorenzo and Puebla, far to the rear on the army's line of communications. Forey, however, was a soldier of the old hollow-square, fire-by-volleys school and did not comprehend the significance of Camerone. In Mexico there would be no front lines, no secure communications, no neat echelon or order of battle extending from headquarters to rear areas to forward positions, no safe roads, no gentlemanly combat or rules of war. It would be a death grapple, a campaign of extermination. Sun-cured legionnaires like General Bazaine understood that; the conditions of Algeria and Morocco had been transferred to Mexico, with certain bewildering and frustrating alterations.

In any event the French commanders were too exalted by success to consider the meaning of a deplorable skirmish like Camerone; it was only one little pawn on the chessboard. Their eyes were fixed on Mexico City. The capital, from the reports they received, was waiting for its newest conqueror.

President Juárez and his ragtag government obliged them by taking flight with his remaining troops and settling down, once again a government on the run, at San Luis Potosí, 300 miles northwest of Mexico City. In one night the Juaristas vanished from the capital. The young American girl Sara Yorke had rejoined her family by then. From the windows of their house on the Calle de San Francisco, she watched the republican army marching silently in the moonlight, "a strange weird sight," as she later recorded, "men whose equipment consisted of a musket and a cartridge-box slung over their white shirts," followed by their wives, children and camp-followers. An anxious day followed; no one knew for certain then whether Juárez might be marching out to defend the capital; members of the foreign colony organized a patrol to protect their families and properties. Everyone sat up the next night; the city was hushed with expectancy. Then, at her window, Sara Yorke heard "a distant but strangely familiar sound . . . but never did the finest harmony of Wagner's genius so fill a soul with ecstasy. There was no mistaking it; it was a French bugle. The French were entering Mexico. We were safe, and now might go to bed."

That bugle sounded the advance of Bazaine's division. By June 11, 1863, the French took possession of the Mexicans' capital. Rockets soared, bands played triumphant marches; bells clamored in every cathedral (the church celebrating a victory over its own people); flowers were strewn in the path of the incoming chasseurs, zouaves and spahis. Mexican beauties in ball dresses stood on balconies and pelted the French columns with magnolia blossoms. A *Te Deum* was celebrated in the cathedral, and French generals slept in the bug-infested National Palace that night.

The rejoicing in Paris and other European capitals was even more fervent, if anything. Emperor Napoleon wept for joy; for months he had anguished over the possibility that his gamble had failed, that an unheard-of place called Puebla might be the rock on which his hopes were finally dashed. Now the French flag rippled over a vast, rich new domain, gold, silver, the Seven Cities of Cíbola. To Louis Napoleon and most Europeans it seemed simple enough: Once you took the enemy's capital the war was over, and you settled down to enjoy the fruits of victory. Now all that remained to be done was to persuade Maximilian and Carlotta to stop dithering and take up their duties as his proxies on the throne of Montezuma.

4. A Ship of Fools Westbound

What a lot of cannon shots will be necessary to set up an emperor in a foreign land. . . .

—Prince Richard Metternich

Following the occupation of Mexico City, there was a long lull in the proceedings which were to provide the Mexicans with an emperor chosen for them in Paris and Vienna. It almost seemed as though the promoters of that project were pausing on the edge of a precipice, having second thoughts, brooding over their premonitions. Was it possible that Mexico City, so quickly surrendered while the bitterest resistance was offered at inconsequential Puebla, was only the bait in a trap being prepared by the Mexican republicans?

Saligny, the French minister in Mexico City, friend of Morny and fervent advocate of intervention, seemed to be encouraging that view when he wrote, "Reactionaries, *Puros, Liberales,* are all alike. The former are brigands, the latter are robbers. Everywhere venality, corruption, incompetence. The Republic no longer exists except in name. The other states pay no more attention to what happens in the City of Mexico than if it were China or Japan." It might be gathered from that dispatch that the Mexicans would not be disheartened by the occupation of their capital but would go on fighting in the vast hinterland.

Ordinarily Louis Napoleon paid little attention to the powerless Liberal opposition in the *corps législatif,* but unwanted advice was offered from the floor of those chambers by a former Premier, Adolphe Thiers, who had come out of retirement to bolster the Liberal cause. He warned Napoleon: "Above all, do not engage in an attempt of monarchial restoration [in Mexico], for even without taking a formal engagement, you would be morally bound to the man you placed on the throne. And you, my colleagues, after encouraging the government in its designs, you will be in a poor position to refuse him later the troops, the sailors, the millions which he will demand to complete the mad operation that you have undertaken."

Prince Richard Metternich, son of the former chancellor and Austrian ambassador to Paris, was asked for his opinion of the Mexican venture by Empress Eugénie and bluntly replied, "What a lot of cannon shots will be necessary to set up an emperor in a foreign land, and what a lot more to maintain him there." Minister-President Calderón Collantes of Spain offered the opinion that "it would be impossible to found anything durable in Mexico." The Austrian ambassador to Washington advised his government that the Union would triumph over the Confederacy sooner or later and warned against sending Archduke Maximilian to Mexico in the strongest terms. "It would be unpardonable," declared Ritter von Hulsemann, "for the name and person of the Archduke, our Emperor's brother, to become entangled in this dangerous affair and exposed to its inevitable failure. And moreover, it is unthinkable that the fate of His Serene Highness, our Prince, should depend entirely upon the good or ill will of a randomly picked French bodyguard." But Hulsemann was regarded in his chancellery in Vienna as an alarmist where the Americans were concerned; perhaps he had been posted to Washington too long. During the 1848 Revolution, the United States had sent a warship to Turkey to bring the fugitive rebel Kossuth to America, and Hulsemann had duly protested. Secretary of State Daniel Webster starchily replied that compared to the United States "the possessions of the House of Hapsburg are but as a patch on the earth's surface." Hulsemann, it was believed in Vienna, had never quite recovered from the shock.

Early in the negotiations Leopold of Belgium was also inclined to be cautious in counseling his son-in-law. In a letter addressed to "my dear son," he placed considerable weight on obtaining the support of Great Britain, which he believed should "provide a support for the monarchical-aristocratic principle in the Southern states." Another question to be resolved: "Will the [Mexican] Conservatives have the courage to undertake the necessary steps? They might be encouraged by the approaching help of Europe. On the other hand, I heard that the mob might massacre the Conservatives should it be faced with such an expedition. Thus, the ultimate decision depends on what the country *itself* would do. . . ."

Leopold, however, was hopeful that the Mexicans as a whole would see virtue in the intervention. "Had the secession not taken place in the United States, Mexico would have been seriously threatened from that quarter, since the idea of entirely absorbing her had taken firm root in the United States; but irrespective of the outcome of the war, there can be no longer any thought of conquest south of the border. . . . You must insist on your *freedom of action* without, however, declining the offer."

Bored as she was with embroidery and listening to Maximilian's organ recitals, the twenty-three-year-old Carlotta was having her own second thoughts about the venture being urged on her husband. She wrote her father that there ought to be an "impartial exposé" of Mexican public opinion conducted by someone with no real connection with the intervention. The only reports received at Miramar regarding conditions in Mexico, she complained, were "passed through the channel of Mexicans in Paris," an émigré group too small and self-interested to represent a nation of 8,000,000 people.

Yet her choice of the man to provide that "impartial" survey was M. Bourdillon, a former correspondent for the *Times* of London, who had been expelled from Mexico by President Juárez for openly siding with the reactionaries. On returning to Paris M. Bourdillon had expressed the opinion that it should take no longer than four or five months to establish a monarchy in Mexico. Furthermore, he had been recommended as an objective observer by Gutiérrez de Estrada, the émigré leader whose interests were entirely subjective.

"For the rest," Carlotta added, "we are not, thank God, bound by any sort of engagement in this affair, and however things turn out, we shall be able to withdraw in time."

Carlotta underestimated the tensile strength of the gossamer web of intrigue, flattery and self-interest being woven around the two innocents of Miramar. From the spring of 1863 to fall of that year a stream of emissaries made the journey from Paris, Vienna and Brussels to Trieste and the white castle overlooking its harbor. One of the first was the same M. Bourdillon who had been expelled from Mexico, a journalist more persuasive than most, possibly because he had acquired a financial interest in some Mexican mines. He appeared at Miramar after visiting Brussels and having long interviews with King Leopold, who recommended to his daughter that he be given a most attentive hearing.

M. Bourdillon stayed at Miramar for three days, which were filled mostly by the sound of the correspondent's voice reciting the glorious possibilities of a Mexican empire. Carlotta herself wrote a lengthy memorandum of what he had to say. The whole of Mexico, M. Bourdillon declared, was populated by thieves whom it would be a Christian duty to reform and civilize. The worst thieves of all were the politicians, particularly the nationalists and liberals. All you had to do to make one of them change his attitude, he said, was to take him into another room and tell him, "Here are five hundred pesos, now unsay all that you said in the other room." Not only were the Mexicans astonishingly ignorant, but they could be saved from themselves only by a wholesale infusion of European blood. Frankly, Bourdillon informed Maximilian and Carlotta, they were "too good" for the people they were destined to rule. All this went down well with Maximilian, particularly, with his conception of himself as an idealistic and modern-minded sovereign-to-be who would rescue a nation from barbarism.

His sponsors, Napoleon and Eugénie, meanwhile were occupying themselves with designing tropical uniforms for the French army in Mexico, ordering tons of mosquito netting to be sent overseas, and planning the extension of a railroad from Veracruz up the plateau to Mexico City. They were not visibly distressed by dissension among their representatives in Mexico;

now that they had won their great victory at Puebla the French characteristically fell to quarreling among themselves. The French minister, Saligny, was not getting along with the commander in chief, General Forey, or with General Douay, the commander of one of Forey's two divisions, and was plotting to have General Bazaine given the supreme command. He wrote Hidalgo, who was expected to pass the word along to Napoleon, that Forey was inept and fainthearted, that he should have captured Puebla before the Mexicans had a chance to fortify the place (it had been fortified even before Forey's predecessor, General Lorencez, was flung back from its ramparts). As for General Douay—Saligny tattled to Hidalgo—he had declared the town to be "impregnable" and was heard to state that the whole expedition was an absurdity "born of a woman's whim" —that is, Eugénie's. Bazaine, on the other hand, was a "true general," utterly loyal to the emperor. Saligny then made it clear that he wanted viceregal, instead of merely diplomatic, powers for himself, which he hoped to achieve with Bazaine as the military chieftain and the stubborn Forey recalled to France. "I have good hopes," he added with an artless immodesty, "if only things are left to me."

Hidalgo lost no time in showing Saligny's backbiting letter to Napoleon and Eugénie. The trouble with General Forey, from the Mexican émigrés' standpoint, was that despite his victory at Puebla he saw that conquering Mexico with a small expeditionary force would be an impossibility and that the French could prevail in the long run only by taking in a wider spectrum of Mexican political forces than that represented by the refugee aristocrats, who had more influence in Paris than in Monterrey or Hermosillo. In a letter to Baron de Pont, Maximilian's confidant, Hidalgo boasted that he had engineered the replacement of General Lorencez by General Forey, and the latter would similarly be recalled, but that would take time because of the brilliance of Forey's victory at Puebla.

Evidently referring to the Duc de Morny, he declared that "the person who is working in Their Majesties' entourage and I have hopes of success, all allowance being made for the delicate position in which events have placed us. If Forey is created a marshal, things will be much easier for us, since in that case there would not be enough troops in Mexico for such a high rank. As for General Douay, things are moving faster; it is noteworthy that General Bazaine is as much beloved by the French as by the Mexicans; expressions of the highest praise are indulged with regard to his abilities as a soldier and statesman. It is he whom we should like to see at the head of the army. Shall we succeed? God will decide."

These, however, were mere crosscurrents of individual ambition and intrigue, eddying around the mainstream of the effort to place a pliant and attractive pair of figureheads on the Mexican throne. Other candidates had been considered: an elderly Spanish duke who was too frail for such ardors and several German princelings who were Protestant and would not convert to Catholicism as part of the employment contract. It almost had to be Maximilian and Carlotta, though it was regrettable that they were now in a position to haggle over terms.

The mechanics of supplying a formal invitation to the master and mistress of Miramar were now given priority over equally pressing matters. It could not be said that the process was tinged with much regard for the wishes of the Mexican people. General Forey, as the interim ruler of the country, nominated a governing junta of thirty-five members, largely contributed by the Conservatives with a sprinkling of Liberals willing to collaborate with the French. The junta elected a provisional regency consisting of General Juan Almonte, who had been Mexican minister to Paris before Juárez's presidency; the ultrareactionary Bishop Pelagio Labastida of Puebla; and General Mariano Salas. With admirable dispatch they proceeded to form an Assembly of Notables, mostly citizens of Mexico City and all impeccably Conservative, who would be convened to proclaim a monarchy. This was done instantly. On July 11, 1863—just one month after the French army occupied Mexico City—the Assembly of Notables issued the following proclamation:

"1. The Mexican nation adopts as its form of government a moderate hereditary monarchy under a Catholic Prince. 2. The sovereign will take the title of Emperor of Mexico. 3. The Imperial Crown of Mexico is offered to his Imperial and Royal Highness Fernando Maximiliano, Archduke of Austria, for himself and his descendants. 4. If, owing to circumstances, impossible to be foreseen, Fernando Maximiliano should decline the throne offered to him, the Mexican Nation will appeal to the wisdom of His Majesty Napoleon, Emperor of the French, begging him to designate some other Catholic Prince."

A commission of eight members, including José Hidalgo and Gutiérrez de Estrada, was appointed to journey to Miramar and formally to present the offer to Maximilian. It would arrive late in August.

Thus began months of dithering in Miramar, of impatience in Paris, of anguished rumination in Vienna and Brussels.

Essentially Maximilian, with his liberal leanings, wanted an unobtainable assurance that the Mexican people really would accept him as their ruler. As for the others, Napoleon was eager to have the matter settled without expense to his depleted treasury; the quicker Mexico was pacified, the sooner he could begin withdrawing his expensive army of occupation. Franz Josef and the rest of the Hapsburgs wanted to see "Maxl" worthily employed again. King Leopold of Belgium hoped that his son-in-law would provide an imperial diadem for his daughter.

Carlotta, her own doubts about the venture dissipated, was so determined to reach for the ermine that she wrote her father that she was distressed by Maximilian's inability to make up his mind and accept the Mexican offer and urged him to write Maximilian. Always proud of his astute management of royal affairs, King Leopold advised his son-in-law to accept but to be extremely businesslike about the conditions of acceptance. Maximilian's reluctance could work in his favor, could be used to extract the best possible terms from his French sponsors, not forgetting the importance of the financial arrangement. "Without money," he wrote Maximilian, "your participation in the Mexican scheme is impossible. Why, in 1830 each of the three powers, England, France and Russia, offered me a guaranty of twenty million francs [to assume the throne of Belgium]. They did this with extreme reluctance and only because I forced them to it by declaring that I wanted no crown.

"In regard to military support, even if you were to provide your own Austrian suite, the Emperor Napoleon is quite capable of recalling his troops from Mexico if anything goes wrong, in order to exonerate himself. Therefore, you ought to have something definite in writing, a document as binding as a treaty. Insist upon having clear stipulations in reference to the period during which the French forces will remain in the country—the longer the better. Remember, they constitute your main support! The Foreign Legion is of course excellent but care should be exercised in recruiting and selecting volunteers for it, lest too much riffraff be included.

"To sum up it is folly to let yourself be confounded by polite phrases. One must guard against illusions. Besides, no one can be expected to do the impossible. This is all the more vital since all blame for a failure (due to inadequate resources) will fall upon the one who undertakes the enterprise. Without money, without some sort of contract, I would not budge. They are in your power—you are not in theirs. The whole thing is of the utmost importance to the Emperor Napoleon, for he has got himself into it, whereas you are still free from any entanglement. . . ."

It was sound advice, and so was that of Maximilian's old friend and adviser Baron de Pont, who pointed out that there should be a firmer foundation for the establishment of a monarchy in Mexico than the expressed will of 215 "notables" out of a population of 8,000,000, that such a mockery of a plebiscite would "produce nothing but a phantom monarchy."

Maximilian in the late summer and fall of 1863 was a man beset by pressures of loyalty, of appeal to his sense of honor, of well-intentioned and ill-intentioned advice from all quarters. There was a rather menacing note from the United States consul at Trieste, Richard Hildreth, who warned Maximilian that the Mexican masses would never accept an emperor, that the United States would drive out the French if necessary, and that "anyone aspiring to the throne of Mexico, if he really attains it, ought to be extraordinarily happy if he escapes with his life." Maximilian could disregard that warning as representing the jealous interest of Mexico's northern neighbor, but there was the more temperate advice offered by Sir Charles Wyke, the former British chargé d'affaires in Mexico City, that Maximilian would be "sticking his head into a hornet's nest" if he accepted the throne with only the backing of the clerical and Conservative elements. And from Maximilian's aged father and uncle, the dumpling eaters of Prague, also came warnings against becoming involved in the Mexican venture.

But all these promptings could hardly be balanced by Carlotta's almost frantic insistence that they accept. The thought that the interminably quiet and peaceful days at Miramar, beside the shimmering sea, surrounded by their flowers and trees and birds and Maxl's butterfly collections, might continue indefinitely was intolerable to the young archduchess.

Both their hopes were raised when Napoleon forwarded a memorandum stating the conditions under which the French would maintain Maximilian and Carlotta on the throne of Mexico. The lengthy document was conveyed by Napoleon's special envoy, M. d'Herbet, and provided that the French army of occupation would be kept at a level of 25,000 troops, including the Foreign Legion, for the time being. It would be gradually withdrawn when Maximilian found native replacements. However, the Foreign Legion, totaling 8,000 men, "shall nevertheless continue service in Mexico for another six years, even after all other French forces have been recalled."

All that was most satisfactory. There was an addendum composed by Achille Fould, the Minister of Finance, which should have chilled Maximilian to the marrow. Mexico would be required to indemnify France for the costs of the occupation thus far—270,000,000 francs—that is, Mexico would be required to pay for the pleasure of being invaded, subjugated and occupied by a foreign power invited in by an infinitesimal fraction of its citizenry. From the summer of 1864 onward the Mexican treasury would be required to pay 1,000 francs annually to each French soldier remaining in Mexico. Just as incredibly, the French ships bringing mail and provisions for the army would be paid for by the Mexicans at the rate of 400,000 francs per voyage. Another 25,000,000 francs would be required as damages for Frenchmen living in Mexico for "wrongs" done them. And there was the matter of the Jecker bonds: 75,000,000 francs to be recovered for their retirement even though the Miramón government had received only 3,000,000 francs of the loan on which the bond issue was based. Those terms alone would justify any number of volcanic upheavals in the country on which they were imposed.

Maximilian's eyes seemingly glazed over that array of de-

mands—he wasn't very good at finances and such boring matters—but his blue eyes glinted with satisfaction when they
came to the clause detailing the amounts to be paid him and
Carlotta. The job of Emperor of Mexico would pay 125,000
pesos, while the Empress would receive 16,667 pesos, both
monthly. The combined income would come to almost
1,700,000 pesos a year. The archduke did not bother his golden
head with such calculations, but they would be receiving just
about one-seventh of the Mexican treasury's annual receipts.

Maximilian was so exhilarated by the offer, which he did not
pause to reflect was made by the French, not the people from
whom the tax and customs receipts would be wrung, that he
clapped M. d'Herbet on the back, then bounded up the staircase to an upper hallway. He galloped along the corridor until
he came to Carlotta's boudoir, where her lady-in-waiting,
Countess Paula Kollonitz, was arranging the archduchess' hair.

He burst into the boudoir, as Countess Paula would recall in
her memoir, shouting like any clerk with a pay raise, "Carla, we
are rich! They are giving us a throne and a fortune as well!"

His mood was still on the upswing on October 2, 1863, when
the delegation from the Assembly of Notables headed by Hidalgo and Gutiérrez, one young in years but both old in intrigue, appeared at Miramar to offer the Mexican throne.

The Mexicans were somewhat taken aback when Maximilian
replied to the flowery phrases of their offer by saying he would
accept conditionally, that there must be a popular referendum
to ratify the Assembly of Notables' choice. "A Hapsburg," he
remarked with what his guests considered an excessive priggish-
ness, "never usurps a throne." He also pointed out that since
the French army controlled only a small part of the country—a
corridor from Veracruz to the capital and a few outlying points
—he "could not expose himself to the risk that the majority of
the population might declare for the Republic while he was in
the country."

With a flood of rhetoric the Mexican delegates overwhelmed
Maximilian's doubts. The archduke would be Mexico's savior.
The people had nowhere else to turn. All his doubts were dissolved in the flattery which Gutiérrez de Estrada knew so well
how to fabricate expressly for the idealistic Maximilian. The

day following the arrival of the delegation it was formally announced that Maximilian and Carlotta would accept, conditional only on the working out of financial, military and dynastic questions with Paris and Vienna.

Maximilian's psychic barometer continued to register fair weather for several months. It always ranged between deep melancholy and high euphoria, with few stops in between. In his euphoric mood, now, he was seized with the proposal that his younger brother, the Archduke Ludwig, who so far had given promise of being no more than Vienna's leading playboy, be married off to one of the daughters of Dom Pedro II, the Emperor of Brazil. Dom Pedro had no sons, and Ludwig thus could hope to found a new Hapsburg dynasty in the largest country of South America. Brazil and Mexico together, as Hapsburgian provinces, could dominate all the Americas south of the Rio Grande. Maximilian intoxicated himself for weeks on that dazzling vision of empire building.

Less than three weeks after conditionally accepting the Mexican throne, he hurried off to Salzburg, where his brother Ludwig was resting from his exertions in Viennese night life. Archduke Ludwig was weak and self-indulgent, but balky as a mule when Maximilian appeared in the guise of a matchmaker.

"My conversation with Ludwig showed me clearly that he is anything but pleased with the idea," Maximilian wrote their brother Franz Josef. "He cannot imagine an existence for himself beyond the ocean, is afraid he will suffer from homesickness, and so on. Meanwhile I have, however, accomplished this much: he told me he would obey a formal command from Your Majesty, though only, as he expressed it, 'as a martyr.'"

In his enthusiasm for a Hapsburg American empire, Maximilian was so carried away that, forgetting his own youthful resentment of dynastic necessities, he urged that his brother be ordered to marry a Brazilian princess he had never seen. "Owing to Ludwig's nature," Maximilian sternly explained, "it is just such an order that would be most suitable; it is not to be expected that he should of his own accord tear himself away from his surroundings in Vienna, which are so harmful to him. It would take a powerful initiative, an authority such as is possessed by Your Majesty alone, to prompt him to such a resolution. . . . I know the Emperor of Brazil, and believe him to be the man who will be able by his intelligently directed energy to lead Ludwig into serious, sane, and active ways. . . ."

On the same subject Maximilian wrote Count Rechberg in Vienna, hoping to forge an iron collar around his waltzing brother and spirit him off to Brazil as his imperial collaborator, that there were respectable precedents for such more or less forced marriages as Marie Louise's to Napoleon I. "All who know my brother well must desire that he should be removed from the aimless existence which he has led hitherto in the atmosphere of Vienna, which is not good for him, and be made a man of. . . ."

That character-building effort failed, however, when Franz Josef replied that he could not and would not order their brother to marry. Maximilian did not give up on the idea of extending a Hapsburg empire in America, however; it would be revived later, not at Miramar but in Chapultepec, and he would prove his right to the somewhat scornful title of the Dreamer of Caserta.

Maximilian's euphoric mood was sustained that winter while negotiations for his removal to Latin America proceeded and his spirits were kept soaring by such letters as Gutiérrez de Estrada's from Rome: "All classes of society, without distinction of sex or age, all Mexicans, wherever they may be, on one continent or the other, call upon God for that sovereign whom God has bestowed upon them, and no other. . . . For how could a reproach of ambition or rashness rise so high as Your Imperial Highness, a prince so well known and admired in Europe for his youthful but profound wisdom, his high courage and purity of heart?"

He might have been less cheerful if he had been kept aware of the vigorous measures the French were being forced to take in Mexico to make that country safe for its designated ruler. To ensure that such operations were conducted with ruthless persistence, General Forey had been promoted to marshal of France and recalled, with the hard-eyed Bazaine as his successor. Saligny, to the dismay of the Mexican émigrés and the Duc de Morny, had also been recalled, and Bazaine thus became, in effect, the French viceroy. He proceeded on wholesale search-and-destroy operations against the Mexican republican and guerrilla forces wherever they could be pinned down and brought to battle, deploying his 40,000 French troops (their numbers steadily increased since the victory of Puebla), his 13,000 Mexican auxiliaries (unreliable even with French officers), and a "counterguerrilla force" commanded by a desperado, Colonel Jean Charles Dupin, who had once been cashiered from the French army. Dupin's terror squads, specializing in murder, robbery and torture, operated much like the Black and Tans during the later Irish insurrection.

Bazaine's columns struck north, west, south; drove Juárez and his government from San Luis Potosí to Saltillo and finally into the northern deserts; easily defeated the enemy, whom they outnumbered by three to one, at all points of the compass. Shortly after the New Year the French army and its Mexican auxiliaries formed a curving shield around the capital on an immense arc to the north and east. His labors skillfully, if bloodily, accomplished, General Bazaine left the field command to General Douay and returned to Mexico City to receive the congratulations of his Mexican supporters and Napoleon.

Napoleon and Eugénie were eager now to propel Maximilian and Carlotta on their way to Mexico and rather pointedly sent such gifts to Miramar as the uniform of a Mexican field marshal—a purely imaginary rank in a nonexistent army—and a carton of elegant stationery bearing the crest of the Hapsburgs superimposed on the Aztec eagle. The traditional Aztec serpent was tactfully omitted.

The practical details of that stately movement were, however, proving tiresome.

Just before Maximilian and Carlotta set out on a round of farewell visits to the European courts, he received a memorandum from the Hofburg, countersigned by Franz Josef, suggesting that it would be necessary for Maximilian to renounce his rights of succession to the Austrian throne before he ascended the Mexican one. It struck Miramar like a thunderbolt. Until now Franz Josef had been most agreeable, providing Maximilian's old flagship, the *Novara,* for the journey, recruiting an Austrian volunteer force of 1,000 men for duty in Mex-

ico (while Leopold did the same in Belgium), and establishing
a fund of 200,000 gulden to set him up in impressive style. Now
it appeared to Maximilian that his brother's solicitude was all
part of a scheme designed to turn him into a Mexican by fiat
and cut him off from his rightful inheritance as a Hapsburg.

The memorandum, Franz Josef further informed him, would
be followed by a contract which provided that Maximilian resign all his rights as a Hapsburg. Franz Josef pointed out that
in the event of his death Maximilian would be ill prepared,
after years in Mexico, to act as regent for Crown Prince Rudolf
or, if Rudolf died, to rule the Austrian empire himself. No,
Maximilian must dedicate himself to Mexico and its suffering
masses; he would prove his devotion to the Mexican people by
cutting himself off from Europe.

Now began a long period of melancholia for Maximilian. For
weeks before he and Carlotta finally sailed for Mexico, it appeared that he was on the verge of a nervous breakdown. Once
again he was assailed by premonitions and second thoughts,
which were only reinforced by Franz Josef's unfeeling, un-
brotherly insistence on sticking to the letter of dynastic law.

Intermittently, of course, he was cheered by the enthusiasm
of their reception in the capitals of western Europe. Their first
stop was Paris, where he and Carlotta were received with full
honors, with gala performances in the theaters, entertainments
at the Tuileries, receptions at the embassies (from which the
United States ambassador absented himself on orders from
Washington). But negotiating the nuts-and-bolts issues of setting up a new regime in Mexico proved to be more difficult and
vexing than he had expected. Napoleon's Finance Minister
would not consider reducing the 270,000,000-franc levy on
Mexico for the costs of intervention. Floating a loan to get the
Mexican economy back on its feet was another sticky problem.
Maximilian at first hesitated over borrowing money for a country whose rule he had not yet formally accepted but finally was
led into negotiations with French and English financiers for a
loan of 201,600,000 francs at 6 percent interest.

On the evening of March 12, 1864, Maximilian and Napoleon signed the convention providing for their collaboration in
administering Mexico. About the only concession Maximilian
had managed to extract from the hardheaded bargainers in

Paris was a codicil providing that "However events in Europe might turn out, the assistance of France should never fail the new empire."

Maximilian and Carlotta left to continue their rounds and receive the blessings of other royalties, practically all of them relatives near or distant, after Eugénie presented Maximilian with a gold medallion of the Madonna, which she assured him would bring luck. It became apparent that Eugénie considered herself the chief architect of Mexican intervention when she firmly ruled against their visiting Madrid on their farewell tour. Spain was balking at providing a naval escort for the voyage to Mexico, and as Eugénie put it, "No frigate as escort, no visit!" So they went on to London while the Austrian ambassador, Prince Richard Metternich, wrote his superiors in Vienna that despite all jubilation in Paris about the "colossal undertaking," he remained gloomy about its prospects. "The nearer we get to the great ordeal, the more rooted become the doubts even of those in favor of the 'Monarchizing' of Mexico. The destiny held out to the young Prince and the high-spirited Princess appears to be surrounded by so many clouds that even Eugénie is a prey to feverish excitement, which may be attributed to the responsibility which she feels weighing upon her."

In London their reception among royalty was warm and familial, that of Whitehall more than a trifle wary and dubious. Bearing in mind Sir Charles Wyke's witticism that Maximilian had been "elected" to the throne by "a majority vote from places inhabited by two Indians and a monkey," the Prime Minister, Lord Palmerston, warned them against overexpectations. Maximilian retorted that several Bourbon princes were offering themselves for the imperial role in Mexico; perhaps Britain would prefer one of them? Palmerston roared with laughter and said, "A Bourbon? There's not one of them worth a fig." However, Queen Victoria beamed on them and called them "my dear children."

A duty visit was also paid to Claremont, where Queen Marie Amélie, the widow of King Louis Philippe, who had been deposed and exiled by Napoleon III, was living with her embittered memories. She was also Carlotta's grandmother. Obviously Queen Marie Amélie could not be pleased by the fact that her granddaughter was being made Empress of Mexico by the man who had driven her and her husband off the French throne.

To the visitors' consternation, the queen in exile implored them to give up the Mexican venture while her daughter, the long-nosed Princess Clementine, clicked away at the beads of her rosary.

As they left, the old lady suddenly rose from her chair and shrieked, "They will be murdered," as if suddenly afflicted by a vision. Queen Marie Amélie then collapsed in the arms of her attendants. Her parting words would stay with Maximilian and Carlotta for a long time. A few weeks later, in fact, Carlotta wrote her grandmother from Miramar trying to assure her that they would make a success of the Mexican venture, that "Maxl" had a genius for governing and would bring the Mexican people around to his side.

On to Brussels, where the streets were decorated in their honor and the populace turned out to cheer. King Leopold and Carlotta's two brothers, the Duke of Brabant (the future Leopold II) and the Count of Flanders, awaited them in a glow of family pride. The occasion was marred for Maximilian only by a pompous welcoming address from the Duke of Brabant, who had inherited the square root of all his father's bad qualities. "The Hapsburgs, when joined with the Coburgs," brayed the Duke of Brabant, "find ever new opportunities to indulge their legitimate passion for doing good to the most different peoples." As Leopold II, his own "legitimate" passion would be exerted on the wretched natives of the Congo, where he established the most brutal and profitable of all the African colonial regimes.

In Vienna, too, they were paid imperial honors with a reception and state dinner in the Hofburg. That was on the evening of March 21. On the morning of March 22 came the dash of cold water—a document titled the Family Pact which Franz Josef required his brother to sign. Thereby Maximilian would renounce his rights of succession. With it was a letter from Franz Josef beginning "Sir, my dear brother, Archduke Ferdinand Maximilian," and reading:

"Since, according to information I have received, you are disposed to accept the throne of Mexico which has been offered to you, and to found an empire there, God helping you, I find myself compelled, as Supreme Head of the House of Austria, and after the most mature and earnest consideration of the duties which are incumbent upon me as sovereign, to notify you that I can consent to this grave and momentous act of state only on condition that you previously draw up and solemnly confirm the deed of which I enclose a copy. . . . Should you be unable to consent to this, and prefer to refuse the crown of Mexico which is offered to you, I would take it upon myself to notify foreign countries of your refusal, and in particular the Imperial Court of France."

Maximilian sent a bitter reply to Franz Josef protesting that when he accepted the Mexican throne, "I was entirely unaware of any such condition as you have now imposed upon me" and threatening to withdraw from the overseas venture.

He and Carlotta then returned to Miramar, determined to back out if the Family Pact were not withdrawn. At Miramar there was deep melancholy: in Carlotta because she saw her diadem disappearing in a fog of family bickering, in Maximilian because he felt betrayed. In Paris and Vienna there was uproar. Napoleon and Franz Josef, for different reasons, were eager to see Maximilian and Carlotta safely on their way to Mexico. It was, in fact, too late for any withdrawal; all plans had been laid on for their ceremonial departure from Trieste early in April— only a few days away!

Franz Josef begged Napoleon to intercede. Empress Eugénie was having hysterics and sent a message at midnight on March 27 to Prince Metternich which she concluded "in a most justifiable ill temper" and which read in part, "I say nothing of the appalling scandal which this will cause to the House of Austria, but, as regards ourselves, you must admit that there can be no excuse, whatever may be the obstacles which have arisen in various quarters. The fact remains that you had time to consider everything and weigh it well, and you cannot, at the very moment when the arrangements for the loan have been concluded, and the conventions signed, put forward a family matter of no importance compared with the confusion into which you throw the whole world . . ."

Meanwhile, Napoleon was groaning in the Tuileries, "I must say I have no luck with Austria; it looks as though I were being purposely left in the lurch at the last moment."

The next morning Napoleon pulled himself together and telegraphed Maximilian at Miramar: FAMILY QUARRELS CANNOT PREVENT YOUR IMPERIAL HIGHNESS FROM FULFILLING MORE EXALTED TASKS ELSEWHERE. ONLY THINK OF YOUR OWN REPUTATION. A REFUSAL NOW SEEMS TO ME IMPOSSIBLE.

The same morning he wrote an urgent letter which his aide-de-camp, General Charles Auguste Frossard, hastened to deliver at Miramar. Its shrewdest passages were directed at Maximilian's delicate sense of honor, his conception of himself as a Christian knight anachronistically cast up in a world being transformed by the railroads, the telegraph, the steamship, the steel cannon and the machine gun.

Napoleon wrote of his agitation over the news just received from Vienna that Maximilian was balking at renouncing the Hapsburg succession, and informed him that "Your Imperial Highness has entered into engagements which you are no longer free to break. *What would you really think of me, if, when Your Imperial Highness had already reached Mexico, I were suddenly to say that I can no longer fulfill the conditions to which I have set my signature!* [The agitated italics are Napoleon's.] No, it is impossible for you to give up going to Mexico, and admit before the whole world that family interests compel you to disappoint all the hopes that France and Mexico have reposed in you. In your own interests and those of your family the matter must be settled, for the honor of the House of Hapsburg is in question."

Miramar was serene no longer. Its halls and salons were filled with turmoil and recrimination; Maximilian paced his study among the sextants and stared for hours out its tall windows; wailing Mexicans from the delegation waiting in Trieste for the departure ceremony arrived to add their voluble protests; emissaries arrived from Brussels, Paris, Vienna and Rome. The "shopkeeper king" of Belgium counseled his daughter to hold out until the last possible moment for better terms in the Hapsburg Family Pact, having in mind the futures of any grandchildren who might be born to Maximilian and Carlotta. Carlotta herself was torn between the Coburg bargaining instinct and the imperative to reign which she inherited from her French mother's side. If only Maxl would keep his nerve, they might save both the cake (Mexico) and the frosting (the Austrian succession).

Characteristically, while Miramar seethed, Maximilian withdrew into his melancholic depths and eased internal pressures by expressing himself in weepy verse which told more about that tormented prince in his thirty-second year than all the bales of state papers in the Austrian State Archives:

"Must I forever be separated from my dear native land? . . . You would seduce me with a crown . . . But must I listen to your sweet siren's song? . . . You speak to me of a scepter and power. . . . Ah, let me follow in peace my tranquil way! My obscure path among the myrtles! . . . Believe me, work and science, and the arts, are sweeter than the glitter of a diadem. . . . Ah, let me follow in peace my tranquil way!"

His brooding and versifying were interrupted by the arrival of an emissary from Vienna, the Archduke Leopold, a cousin, who bore several codicils to the Family Pact. The emperor had decided to relent rather than have the most ambitious of his brothers on his hands. One article promised that a volunteer corps of 6,000 troops, instead of a 1,000-man bodyguard, would be raised and sent to Mexico, another that his rights as an Austrian archduke would be protected to a certain extent. This article read:

". . . In the event of the Archduke Ferdinand Max's either voluntarily renouncing the throne of Mexico or being deprived of it, he [Franz Josef] will allow the [Family Pact] to lapse and reinstate the Archduke to his former rights. His Majesty likewise promises the Archduke's widow and children, in case they have to give up their position in Mexico, shall be reinstated in all the rights appertaining to the Austrian archdukes."

Maximilian saw that he still had to renounce the succession and in return would receive a *promise* that his "former rights" would be restored if the Mexican venture failed. He realized, however, that his stubborn brother would yield no further.

Hesitantly, still dubious about the whole affair, he signified that he and Carlotta would go to Mexico. The news of his acceptance ran through Miramar like an electric shock; everyone joined in the cheers and congratulations, and from there tidings spread to Trieste, where the Mexicans exploded with joy, and over the telegraph to Vienna, Paris, Brussels, London, Madrid. Even to Berlin—which unfortunately had been left out of all the calculations but which would profit more than any of the contracting parties—where Prince Bismarck permitted himself a tigerish smile.

The stately business of transporting Maximilian and Carlotta from the Adriatic seaside to the Mexican shore was now set in motion. First there would be a Hapsburg family reunion, then Maximilian would formally accept the crown, and finally the imperial couple with their suite would sail on April 11. In between Miramar, for the first and last time in its bucolic history, would be crowded with visitors, would blaze nightly with light from every chandelier, would gently vibrate to music for dancing, and would tremble momentarily with the rumble of history making.

With daunted smile, hollow eyes and trembling hands, Maximilian as the centerpiece of all this trumpery, the focus of all the ritual and celebration, moved through his performance like a sleepwalker. His mind was in limbo, looking neither forward to the promised glories of Mexico nor backward to Vienna and the illusions of his youth. He felt more like a man condemned to the gallows than one elevated to an ancient throne.

And Carlotta meanwhile, her expectations finally coming true, blossomed into her imperial role. Her dark eyes flashed with joy and triumph, not only as an empress but as a woman. The last few days had shown her that she would be dominant, more than a mere consort. Maxl needed her strength and determination. He was a dreamer, but she was a doer. Mexico would be her fulfillment.

On April 9, Maximilian's three brothers arrived by railway from Vienna to make their farewells. Maximilian and Franz Josef were closeted for hours that day in the library, and when they came out, it appeared to those watching that it had been an emotional and rancorous session. They rejoined their two brothers, both lucky enough never to be summoned to greater responsibilities than leading a promenade in the ballroom of the Hofburg, and others who had come down from Vienna— Prince Esterházy as representative of the Hungarian realm, Field Marshal Ludwig von Benedek, Count Rechberg, and other dignitaries.

The fraternal reunion—the last—was brief. The next morning Franz Josef boarded the imperial train. At the last moment the icy reserve, the encrustations of duty and responsibility, broke as they would break only twice again, when he learned of the suicide of Crown Prince Rudolf and the assassination of the Empress Elizabeth.

Franz Josef had just started to mount the steps to his car after bidding Maximilian a stiff and formal good-bye. Then he turned, came back down, and hurried over to his brother. He held out his arms; the brothers embraced and kissed each other.

"Max," he murmured, "dynastic law compels us to do terrible things."

The rest of that day, April 10, was filled with pageantry. In the marble-walled ballroom Maximilian and Carlotta sat under the canopy on gilded chairs and received the Mexicans. Grouped around them were many of the dignitaries who had come down from Vienna with Franz Josef, as well as representatives from Paris and Brussels. Maximilian wore the white uniform of a vice admiral with the Order of the Golden Fleece and the Grand Cross of St. Stephen blazing on his tunic. Carlotta was radiant in a crimson robe trimmed with Brussels lace, with an archducal coronet on her mass of dark hair, diamond necklace and bracelets, and the Order of Malta crisscrossing her bosom with its black ribbon.

Outside the palace windows a spectacular sunset flamed across the blue-green waters, but it was outmatched by Mexican oratory. Two émigré lawyers expanded on how gratefully the Mexican people would welcome their new rulers. Their blandishments were easily exceeded by Gutiérrez de Estrada, who assured them of the "unending love and unshakable fidelity" of their new subjects. Ironic echos chased one another around the high-ceilinged room. The speeches went on into the twilight and might have gone through the night except that the *Novara* was supposed to sail the next morning.

Finally the crown was formally offered, and Maximilian formally replied, "It can only be flattering to our house that at the first mention of the word 'Monarchy' the eyes of your countrymen were at once turned to the race of Charles V. I am ready to accept the throne, supported by the acquiescence of the high chief of my family and confiding in the protection of the Almighty."

Gutiérrez de Estrada knelt and paid homage, the assemblage cried out in unison "Long live Emperor Maximilian! Long live Empress Charlotte!" and the oath of allegiance was administered by the Abbot of Lacroma. From the organ in the chapel, at which Maximilian had spent many soulful hours during the long golden afternoons, which he would remember with nostalgia, Carlotta with exasperation, there pealed out the majestic chords of the *Te Deum,* and Maximilian and Carlotta led the assemblage in a procession from the ballroom.

That night, a few hours after becoming emperor, Maximilian finally cracked. He had held himself together for days, almost as though hoping it were all a bad dream and he would be able to go back to pottering around his groves of palm and oleander, but now reality crashed in on him. That crown was real. Those bearded mouths shouting their *vivas* were real. And the frigate *Novara* down in the harbor getting up steam, the ship on which he had been a relatively carefree cadet and a touristic vice admiral, was the most ironclad reality of all.

To spend another day at Miramar seemed the most precious thing in the world.

Conveniently—or psychosomatically, as a much later generation would put it—he came down with an illness that night. An overwhelming weakness struck him as he was preparing for bed. Dr. Anton Jilek, his physician, was hastily summoned to the chamber. He noted that Maximilian was suffering from a fever, that he was visibly unstrung, eyes rolling, breath coming in gasps, all of which Dr. Jilek took to be the symptoms of an incipient nervous and physical breakdown. The physician ordered that the journey be postponed for several days.

The departure was now set for April 14. Carlotta assured the swarm of interested parties, both in person and by telegraph, that Maxl would be ready to leave on the new sailing date. For forty-eight hours Maximilian stayed in his chambers, gripped by melancholia, seeing no one but his physician.

Certainly his gloom had more to feed on than Carlotta's elation. The majordomo of Miramar had committed suicide rather than accompany the imperial suite to Mexico, and Maximilian had received a letter from an Italian poet advising him to "renounce the rotten throne of Montezuma." And Maximilian secretly was convinced that poets knew more than statesmen; besides, they weren't governed by self-interest. He was also deeply affected by a telegram from Vienna signed by the Archduchess Sophie: FAREWELL. OUR BLESSING—PAPA'S AND MINE—OUR PRAYERS AND TEARS ACCOMPANY YOU; MAY GOD PROTECT AND GUIDE YOU. FAREWELL FOR THE LAST TIME ON YOUR NATIVE SOIL, WHERE ALAS! WE MAY SEE YOU NO MORE. WE BLESS YOU AGAIN AND AGAIN FROM OUR DEEPLY SORROWING HEARTS. That must have bemused him. Hadn't his mother trained him from childhood to be a ruler, drilled into him the sacred obligation of all Hapsburgs to find a suitable throne? Then why the "deeply sorrowing hearts" when at last he had found employment?

April 14 inevitably dawned, Maximilian made a farewell tour of his beloved groves and gardens; then he and Carlotta were driven in a coach from Miramar to Trieste and its cheering throngs. The Molo, stretching into the harbor, was strewn with flowers. Maximilian and Carlotta stepped into the launch of the *Novara,* waved, smiled to the crowd on the Molo, and were rowed away. Out in the harbor the frigate *Novara* and its escort vessels, the French warship *Themis* and the Austrain gunboat *Bellona,* were decked with flags from bow to stern. As they boarded the *Novara,* the municipal band on the Molo played the newly composed Mexican national anthem, then thundered into "Gott erhalte, Gott beschütze," the Austrian imperial anthem.

Standing at the railings behind and alongside Maximilian and Carlotta were the members of the imperial suite, a cosmopolitan group including Count Franz Zichy, grand master of the imperial household; Countess Melanie Zichy and Countess Paula Kollonitz, ladies-in-waiting; Marquis Corio and Count Charles de Bombelles (the son of his tutor and a friend of Maximilian's since boyhood), gentlemen-in-waiting; M. Sebastian de Schertzenlechner, counselor of state; M. Angel Iglesias, undersecretary of state; Herr Jacob von Kuhacsevich, treasurer of the Crown; M. Felix Eloin, private secretary; M. Joaquín

Velásquez de León, minister of state; General Adrian Woll, first aide-de-camp; and others.

The Mexican ensign fluttered up to the masthead while shore batteries fired a final salute. *Novara* and her escort ships weighed anchor, turned their bows, and headed out to sea on the long voyage to Veracruz.

Carlotta and the ladies and gentlemen of the suite laughed and chattered in their elation at finally starting on the glory road to Mexico.

The new Emperor Maximilian stood apart from the others at the railing, staring across the waters at Miramar, gleaming white as a wedding cake on the Adriatic shore. His mind was fixed, not on the promised triumphs ahead, but on the contentment and security of the past. Miramar was his creation, a miniature masterpiece of stone and landscaping, a tiny realm but an undisputed one. He had clamored for larger responsibilities while ignoring an inner voice that pleaded for a quieter, more contemplative life. Now he could only wonder whether ambition had not driven him into a bad bargain; vast unruly Mexico for the small perfection of Miramar. Would he ever walk in its gardens again, ever look out over its terraces at another dawn gilding the waters surrounding it?

Miramar receded inexorably, and he was almost suffocated by homesickness.

Carlotta glanced over at him, then nudged her lady-in-waiting, Countess Zichy, and said, "Look at poor Maxl . . ."

The Emperor of Mexico was weeping.

II. CHAPULTEPEC

5. Welcome to the Fever Coast

I'm not exactly skeered, but I don't like the looks of the thing. Napoleon has taken advantage of our weakness in our time of trouble. . . . If we get out of our present difficulties and restore the Union, I propose to notify Louis Napoleon that it is about time to take his army out of Mexico. . . .

—President Abraham Lincoln

AFTER a leisurely and roundabout voyage of six weeks, the *Novara* and its escort stood off the roads at Veracruz on May 28, 1864. Emperor Maximilian had been somewhat revived by the sea air, by the naval atmosphere and the opportunity of wearing his vice admiral's uniform on the bridge of a warship. Possibly he had time to reflect that all his troubles had begun when he had allowed himself to be lured ashore and appointed viceroy over northern Italy.

Certainly he suffered several sinking spells when his morale had to be propped up by Carlotta, and members of their entourage heard her murmur to him, as they stood at the rail, "There is nothing to fear, Max."

Novara had sailed along the coast of Italy to the ancient Roman port of Civitavecchia, where the imperial suite was landed for a stopover in Rome and an audience at the Vatican with Pius IX. The most fervent papal blessings were conferred on the new Emperor and Empress of Mexico, who were expected to restore the church to its former position in Mexico and nullify the decrees of the excommunicated and execrated President Juárez. As he gave holy communion to the kneeling Maximilian, Pope Pius gently reminded him that "Although the rights of nations are great and must be respected, those of religion are much greater and holier."

Maximilian, who regarded himself as a liberal humanitarian as well as a Catholic, did not quite agree. Nor was his reply to the Pope entirely satisfactory: "While honestly endeavoring to fulfill my Christian duties, I have been called to rule a state whose interests I must primarily protect."

A slight frost developed. The Pope must have realized then that he had overestimated Maximilian's fealty to the church and its temporal aspirations; he had not done sufficient research into the young Hapsburg's background. Some of Maximilian's early writings would have revealed to Pius IX more than a few traces of sentimental and romantic liberalism. As a student of those youthful writings had noted, "A Liberal Catholic, a parliamentary monarchist, a sentimental rationalist, his thought is shot through with borrowed French revolutionary sophistry. He presents us with a series of maxims on how the enlightened prince should govern . . . once more proving that philosophers may be kings but kings can rarely be philosophers."

The Pope, however, decided that Mexico would knock much of the nonsense out of Maximilian's head, once he experienced its political and social realities. Just before they left Rome, he paid Maximilian and Carlotta the unusual honor of calling on them at the Palazzo Marescotti, where they were quartered, and bestowing his farewell blessings on them. "The Pope," observed a German historian then living in Rome, "never blessed any prince with such emotion."

Even as the imperial party departed from Rome by train for the port of Civitavecchia, however, the Roman intellectuals were shaking their heads and warning of disaster. One of them, who wrote under the pseudonym of Pasquin, remarked that the French knew what they were doing when they closed off the streets around the Palazzo Marescotti and kept the party under close guard, because "they would not find anyone else to accept the crown of Mexico in a hurry." Pasquin distilled his forebodings in a six-line stanza:

> Beware, Maximilian!
> Return at once to Miramar.
> The frail throne of Montezuma
> Is a Gallic snare, a cup of froth.
> He who does not remember the *timeo Danaos*
> Shall instead of purple find a halter.

From the port of Civitavecchia the imperial party sailed down to Naples for an exchange of royal courtesies with Victor Emmanuel II and his Sardinian brood, then continued through the Mediterranean with a side glance at Corsica, the island cradle of the Bonapartes, and on through the Strait of Gibraltar. A pleasant surprise, wreathed in gunsmoke, awaited them when they passed through the strait and the British forts, on orders from Queen Victoria, saluted *Novara* and its personages.

The *Novara* was designed for Mediterranean cruises, not for the rougher and stormier Atlantic. As it headed westward, many of the passengers grew violently seasick and were confined to their cabins. It somewhat revived Maximilian's spirits to find almost everyone laid low except himself and the other professional sailors.

When they reached the calmer waters of the South Atlantic, he began holding daily meetings with his advisers. One result of the shipboard deliberations was a document signed by Maximilian and Carlotta which formalized their objections and attempted to nullify the Family Pact. "We were made to sign this act," they affirmed, "without having previously read it, and subject to the most notorious moral pressure brought to bear up to the last moment and by all possible means, a pressure admitted and established by a number of exalted personages in Austria, France, Belgium and Mexico, and to exert which advantage was taken of the complicated situation prevailing at the time between France, Austria and ourselves. . . . We declare upon oath that we had never read the document, nor heard it read. . . . Should the occasion arise, we solemnly protest as from today against this attempted usurpation."

The declaration was not only disingenuous, since Maximilian had been told the terms of the Family Pact before it was presented for his signature, but indiscreet. Word of its contents soon leaked out through his gossipy suite, reached Vienna, and resulted in further strain on the relations between him and Franz Josef. Undoubtedly it was mostly Carlotta's doing. The original copy was in her handwriting, and she had been constantly prodded by her father to hold out against any renunciation of their rights of succession for themselves or their putative children.

Otherwise Maximilian and his councilors busied themselves with matters of administration and protocol. There was some displeasure when M. Eloin, a Belgian, was appointed chief of the Civil Cabinet over Herr Schertzenlechner, who had once served as Maximilian's valet and who believed that he was entitled to the post. Eloin, furthermore, was suspected by the Austrians of acting as King Leopold's informant and go-between.

During the voyage Maximilian also composed a memorandum expressing concern over his lack of a personal military force to deploy as he chose; all the outward forms of authority obsessed him to the exclusion of such boring and incomprehensible matters as financing Mexico's economic recovery and repairing the damage of years of intermittent revolution. "As ruler of Mexico," he declared, "I ought to command an armed force of my own which would enable me to exact respect from a nation possibly less prone to accept authority without military backing. It would therefore be advisable to take with me a detachment of troops recruited in Europe but wearing the Mexican cockade and carrying Mexico's flag. In time these men will ask to be relieved. There will be vacancies which should gradually be filled by Mexicans, establishing the nucleus of a native army." The *Themis*, in fact, was carrying a contingent of Europeans who had volunteered to serve under his colors. Every day they drilled on the *Themis'* main deck while Maximilian watched through field glasses and delivered a critique on their maneuvers by semaphore from the bridge of the *Novara*.

Aside from such diversions he could also brood over an anonymous note which had been included in the mailbag picked up during the passage of the Strait of Gibraltar. The note threatened his assassination "as soon as you reach American shores" and denounced him as a "usurper" and "tyrant." Maximilian, who still suffered under the delusion that a ruler must be loved, was upset by the anonymous note to the extent that he solemnly examined his conscience for his real and true reasons for accepting the Mexican throne. "In all circumstances of my life," he wrote for his own edification, "I shall be only too happy to make every sacrifice, no matter how great, for Austria and the future of my house. Throughout the centuries every dynasty in Europe has adhered to the prudent practice of appointing cadet sons to conspicuous posts where they may further the interests of their mother country. This policy has been known to embrace diplomatic and political as well as commercial fields. . . . Owing to the accelerated pressure of modern conditions the power of our family has diminished. While the adaptable Coburgs take throne after throne, our ancient house has in recent times forfeited two sovereignties [the province of Tuscany in 1859, the seat of Austria-Este in Modena during 1860]. In view of these misfortunes I have become convinced that it is the sacred duty and desire of every Hapsburg to wipe out this stain. I cannot but believe that a good impression will be made upon the world, and especially upon our weakened Austria, if the Mexican enterprise attains success."

Maximilian had sat down at his desk to answer in his own mind the charge of that anonymous correspondent that he was usurping the Mexican throne and establishing a tyranny behind a hedge of French bayonets. Instead of answering the charge—and this was a fair indication of how his mind worked, sideslipping, dodging the logical conclusion, falling back on abstractions like honor and destiny—he explained to himself the "sacred" responsibility of a Hapsburg as though it existed in a lofty vacuum. He believed himself to be the very model of a modern prince, yet at thirty-two he was as antiquated as the courts of love.

A bushel of documents has survived that voyage of the *Novara*, some of them meticulously defining the duties of a master of ceremonies and a Lord Chamberlain (somehow recalling how the great minds of Byzantium were disputing over how many angels could stand on a pinhead while the Turks were thundering at their gates), but there is no scrap of paper to show that Maximilian and his brain trust gave a moment's consideration to how the United States and the rest of the world were viewing what Maximilian called "the Mexican enterprise." Yet Maximilian's success depended greatly on North American forbearance. Only ten days before the *Novara* sailed from Trieste the U.S. House of Representatives had unanimously adopted a resolution declaring itself opposed to the establishment of a monarchy in Mexico, no matter which or how many European nations sponsored it. And by the spring of 1864 the Civil War was slowly but unmistakably turning in favor of the North, which had captured Vicksburg and beat back the Confederates at Gettysburg the summer before and was now advancing southward on all fronts.

The American attitude had been most pungently and accurately expressed by President Lincoln when General John M. Thayer asked him, "Mr. President, how about the French army in Mexico?"

"I'm not exactly skeered," the President drawled, "but I don't like the looks of the thing. Napoleon has taken advantage of our weakness in our time of trouble, and has attempted to found a monarchy on the soil of Mexico in utter disregard of the Monroe doctrine. My policy is, attend to only one trouble at a time. If we get well out of our present difficulties and restore the Union, I propose to notify Louis Napoleon that it is about time to take his army out of Mexico. When that army is gone, the Mexicans will take care of Maximilian."

In the last tropical stages of the voyage that prince and his party might have been on a pleasure cruise rather than a journey to a land rumbling with revolutionary volcanoes. They sailed into the harbor of Martinique, where Countess Paula Kollonitz recorded in her journal how "hundreds of negroes in very deficient costume" resupplied the *Novara* and *Themis* with coal, fresh water and food. On May 21 they dropped anchor at Jamaica (the day Washington notified Paris that it was recalling its minister to Mexico), went sight-seeing and drank tea with Admiral Sir James Hope and the military governor of that British colony.

Two days later the two warships set their course for Veracruz. Maximilian had begun work on what was to become a 600-page volume detailing the etiquette, ceremonial details, costuming and order of precedence of his court. The Mexican people must be as impressed by the pomp and elegance of their new empire as they were overawed by the French battalions which had established and would sustain it. Both he and Carlotta were busy scriveners. The latter was writing long letters to her grandmother, the slightly senile but sibyline Queen Marie Amélie, who had predicted their deaths. Not to worry, Carlotta was assuring her grandmother; the journey had been smooth and carefree; she dreamed of butterflies and hummingbirds every night; and looking through a porthole, she could see Max "gazing quietly and cheerfully into the distance." In a few hours "we shall stand upon the soil of our new country, after a most happy voyage."

So on May 28 the *Novara* steamed into the roads off Veracruz with the guns emplaced at the fortress of San Juan de Ulúa firing the imperial salute and the French warships in the harbor providing a naval counterpoint.

From that moment on, everything seemed to go wrong. There was no sign of welcome from the city of Veracruz itself, where the streets seemed to be deserted and only a cold silence emanated. No welcoming committee of Mexicans rowed out from the quays. The *Novara* might have been a rusty tramp dropping anchor to unload a cargo of guano for all the attention it received from the shore.

A short time later the liverish Rear Admiral Bosse, commanding the French flotilla in the harbor, was rowed over from his flagship. He came over the side "in a very bad temper," as Countess Paula Kollonitz observed, because *Novara* had not anchored closer to his ships; whether for protection or out of consideration for some vague point of naval etiquette, Admiral Bosse did not say. After scorching the Austrian navy, especially as represented by the frigate *Novara,* he stomped off to be rowed ashore and find out where the devil the Mexican reception committee was keeping itself.

Formally welcoming Maximilian and Carlotta was the responsibility of General Almonte, the arrogant president of the regency, and the French admiral learned ashore that he had not even arrived in the port city. Almonte had sent word that he was hastening down from Orizaba, high above the fever zone. The vain and ambitious general had also delayed his departure because he had been appointed Grand Marshal of the Imperial

Household, a purely ceremonial function instead of the high political or military office he had expected as a leading member of the junta which had summoned Maximilian to the Mexican throne.

All day Maximilian and his followers paced the decks of the *Novara,* staring across the leaden waters at the ominously silent city. Their apprehension was only increased when Admiral Bosse mentioned reports that guerrilla bands were lying in wait in the hills about Veracruz to capture the emperor and his party. As for the city itself, Admiral Bosse explained, it was notoriously a hotbed of liberalism and had sullenly, if passively, opposed the intervention.

Sunset was guttering out on the waters of the harbor when General Almonte and his reception committee finally arrived on board the *Novara* with profuse apologies for their late arrival. He did not bother to explain to Maximilian that there are two kinds of time in Mexico; Standard Time, by which foreigners set their watches, and Mexican Time, which is dreamily elastic and cannot be measured by the hands of a clock. That evening all the French ships were illuminated, and rockets were fired from both the ships and installations ashore.

A feeling of dread enveloped the imperial suite that night. Fear was mirrored even in the dauntless dark eyes of Empress Carlotta. Something of the strangeness of that dark land, its implacable hostility, the Indian patience in resisting a long series of interlopers, the fetid odors of the swampy jungle extending up and down the coast, seemed to be wafted on the heavy tropical night.

Most of those aboard were too excited or fearful to sleep that night, but at 4:30 A.M. they assembled on deck in the darkness and attended mass by lantern light. At dawn they proceeded ashore in launches. It was a strange moment when Emperor Maximilian and Empress Carlotta set foot on the stones of the quay. The armed French sailors guarding the landing place sent up a few halfhearted *vivas* on command.

Veracruz had always been the beachhead of invasions from Europe and North America. It was the most gloomy and Iberian of all Mexican cities, a place where windows looked inward on courtyards and the streets were lined by blank walls. "It is Cádiz," as the Countess Paula Kollonitz later wrote, "but a little more Oriental." Certainly the civic reception of Veracruz was inscrutably Oriental.

A procession of open carriages awaited Maximilian and his party. With an escort of French and Mexican imperial troops they clip-clopped through silent streets and plazas. Not a Veracruzano could be glimpsed; the whole population stayed indoors, as though mourning its lost freedoms. The only welcoming sound came from the *zopilotes,* the huge black vultures waddling officiously everywhere in their function as the Veracruz Sanitation Department.

As they were driven to the railroad station, Carlotta gasped at the sight of a dozen of the *zopilotes* outlined against the morning sky as they squatted on the cross of the cathedral and stared down in ominous meditation on the newcomers. Carlotta asked Admiral Bosse why they weren't destroyed.

"Madame," the admiral replied, "they are protected by law because the carelessness and indifference of the inhabitants to sanitary matters makes them a necessity." And he added, even more sardonically, "It's an evil place for Europeans. There's a graveyard full of them."

At the tiny railroad station the imperial party boarded a dusty battered train, no imperial state coaches laid on, for the 45-mile journey into the uplands to the railhead at La Soledad. There they waited while the 85 persons and 500 pieces of luggage constituting the imperial party were offloaded from the train to a cavalcade of mail coaches which would carry them over the mountains to the capital. No French troops were in sight. A villainous-looking native escort, mounted under the command of Colonel Miguel López, would ride with them. Another ill omen: López was a man of shaky loyalties who had once been dismissed from the army for treason. His future role was equally sinister.

But something much more depressing than the anomalous presence of Colonel López, of which Maximilian could not have been aware, occurred during the wait at La Soledad station. A message from President Juárez was waiting when the train arrived; it had been carried by a hundred nameless couriers down from Juárez's transient headquarters.

For a moment Maximilian's hopes bounded upward. Secretly he had based much of his confidence in the "Mexican enter-

prise" on somehow reaching an agreement with Juárez. Secretly, too, as a man of liberal instincts he rather sympathized
with Juárez's objectives. Maximilian's dream, which he kept to
himself, was that he would be enabled to rule justly and peace-
fully, not by means of French military force, but through the
acquiescence of Juárez and the republicans, once the latter understood that Maximilian was a man of goodwill. It would take
a long time for him to realize that the Mexicans wanted no part
of any European ruler imposed on them, regardless of his high-
minded intentions.

That dream was shattered, at least for the moment, by Juárez's message: "It is given a man, sir, to attack the rights of others, seize their goods, assault the lives of those who defend their
nationality, make of their virtues crimes, and one's own vices a
virtue, but there is one thing beyond the reach of such perversity—the tremendous judgment of history."

The judgment of history—it was the sort of abstraction calculated to strike deeply, painfully, into the sensibility of a man
like Maximilian, whose whole life had been guided by romantic abstractions.

Sadly bemused, he joined Carlotta in one of the cumbersome
mail coaches, and the long caravan began its journey over the
mountains. Travel by a Mexican diligence was twice as risky as
a stagecoach in the American West; not only were they constantly menaced by bandits but the coaches rarely, if ever, completed a run without tipping over. The operators of the route
offered a bonus of 100 pesos to any driver who made the journey without capsizing; the reward had never been collected
since the formation of the company. A later traveler on that
route, Princess Salm-Salm, who would attempt a rescue of
Maximilian in the style of the Graustarkian fiction soon to become popular, wrote in her memoirs that it was difficult to tell
whether a Mexican mail coach or the road on which it traveled
was more "wondrous." As she described the journey, "The
coachman keeps up a perpetual conversation with his mules,
which he calls by their names, animating them by all kinds of
extraordinary sounds. His eloquence alone, however, would
scarcely succeed in persuading them to do their duty, if not
supported by an assistant, a boy as active as a monkey. The latter runs along the road collecting stones with which he clam-

bers up beside his chief for the purpose of peppering the recalci-
trant beasts with emergency volleys."

The rainy season had just begun, and that made the journey,
crisscrossed by swollen rivers, all the more perilous. They were
supposed to reach Orizaba, in the healthy, fever-free uplands,
early that evening but the welcome arranged by the French garrison there would have to wait. In a letter to Empress Eugénie
written two weeks later, Carlotta described how their coaches
passed through a countryside seemingly rich in fruit, vegetables
and other products, with the inhabitants living in sizable haciendas surrounded by gardens and orchards (the adobe huts in
which the Indian laborers and their families lived were not visible from the road). Then the aspect suddenly darkened. A
cloudburst descended as they made their way through a dense
rain forest. Night had fallen by the time they reached the
flooded banks of the Chiquihiute River, upon which their
conveyance suddenly collapsed under a broken wheel. Emperor
and empress had to change coaches. "The journey," as Carlotta
wrote Eugénie, "has supplied me with ineradicable recollections. The Mexicans kept apologizing for the roads—we had
lumbered through half a dozen ravines by that time, some of
them hemmed in by rocks several meters in length. Of course
we insisted that we didn't mind in the least, but as matter of
fact it was all beyond words. We needed every ounce of nerve
and good humor to pull us through without damage to life or
limb. However," she bravely added, though not quite truth-
fully, "let me assure you that the roads are the only detail
which I have found rather worse than I anticipated."

When they arrived in Córdoba, at two o'clock in the morning,
they found the town waiting for them with a banquet, which
they had to attend with strained royal smiles. A few hours'
sleep and they jolted off again on the climbing road to Orizaba.
A large barouche carrying Minister of State Velásquez de
Léon and five other Mexican gentlemen tipped over, and its
occupants had to be hauled out one by one, with only their
dignities injured, before the caravan could proceed. From then
on, as they grew closer to Puebla and Mexico City and into the
ring of French garrisons, their reception was warmer. Indian
townsmen were turned out, perhaps with the jab of a French
bayonet or two, to cheer and throw flowers. Orizaba reminded

Carlotta of a mountain town in the southern Tyrol; Puebla (aside from towers, roofs and walls punched out by French artillery during the siege) on its surrounding plain looked like Lombardy. They passed under triumphal arches bearing the legends "Long live Napoleon III" and "Long live Maximilian I," and Maximilian made little speeches in Spanish.

General René Brincourt, the commander of the French garrison at Puebla, welcomed them and was awarded the first Grand Cross of the Order of Guadalupe the following year because Maximilian and Carlotta were so impressed by his gallant bearing. "Of all the capable officers here," Carlotta wrote Eugénie, "he is, to my mind, the most remarkable in courage, energy and tact, for he understands and humors the Mexicans better than anybody."

Now on the last lap of their journey, with the snow peaks of Popocatepetl and the volcanic smokes of Ixtacíhuatl looming before them, they paused devoutly at Cholula to hear mass celebrated in what had been an Aztec temple, before an altar on which feather-cloaked priests had once made human sacrifices. Nearby was the shrine of Our Blessed Lady of Guadalupe, the holiest Catholic place in Mexico and the scene of a miracle, to which they also made a ceremonial visit.* It all made a pious mural for the inspiration of the Mexican masses, whose faith was regarded in Rome as a variable quality. Carlotta was puzzled by the brownish Indian features of the Blessed Lady, but then reflected that German paintings of the Virgin Mary tended to be blondly Teutonic and Italian ones equally brunette and Latin.

When the imperial group left the basilica, they found a large assemblage in the square outside, Mexican gentlemen on horseback but formally attired, carriages crowded with their womenfolk in brilliant finery, and beyond them General Bazaine, the new French minister to Mexico City, the Marquis de Montholon, and the Austrian chargé d'affaires—all come out from the capital to accompany Maximilian and Carlotta on their triumphal entry the next day.

On June 12 they crossed the poplar-lined causeway which led

---

* Catholic tradition has it that in 1531, not long after the Cortez conquest, an Indian convert saw the Virgin Mary, surrounded by a rainbow, and that she ordered him to build a shrine to her on the spot. It was done.

to the capital and found it ostensibly transformed by joy at
their appearance. Flowers were strewn in their path (for which
the French duly billed the Mexican treasury). Every church
bell in the city shed its own bronze petals of sound over the occasion. Arches of flowers spanned the main avenues, and a forest of flags had sprung up overnight. Maximilian and Carlotta
were totally deceived by the artificial warmth of their reception. Not so the seventeen-year-old American girl Sara Yorke,
who watched the procession and noted in her diary later that
Bazaine and the French military had spent days planning for
the event and turning out a huge and enthusiastic throng. Also
in the crowd was a young educated Mexican named José Luis
Blasio, who would soon be closely associated with Maximilian.
Blasio did not realize, apparently, that the welcome had been
stage-managed by the French and was awed by its magnificence.
"The principal streets of the city appeared more like the halls
of a great palace with triumphal arches made of flowers, enormous mirrors, carpeted walks, and Mexican and foreign flags.

"In the vanguard of His Majesty's retinue came the regiment
of Mexican lancers under the command of Colonel López.
After them rode the French regiment of Chasseurs of Africa
and the Hussars preceding the state coach. On both sides of
Their Majesties, riding on magnificent horses, were Generals
Bazaine and Neigre escorted by their staffs; sixty coaches occupied by the dignitaries of the Empire followed the imperial carriage. . . .

"It was then, almost within touching distance of him, that I
could for the first time look closely at the man to whom later I
should become debtor for countless benefits. I saw him pass, arrogant, majestic, and well proportioned. Above all I was impressed by the mildness of his expression which later it was my
privilege to contemplate so many times. His long golden beard,
parted in the center, gave him such an aspect of majesty that it
was impossible to see him without immediately being attracted
and fascinated."

As they crossed the Plaza Mayor toward the cathedral,
Countess Paula Kollonitz was surprised by the exaltation which
transfigured Carlotta's face: This was the culmination of all her
girlhood dreams in dreary Laeken Castle in gloomy Belgium.
"The Empress, especially, was very much charmed," Countess

Paula noted, "and in a state of enthusiasm, of which I never could have imagined so quiet a person capable."

After a day of ceremony and an evening of banqueting, they were escorted to the National Palace, a rambling and barracks-like structure of more than a thousand rooms, which had been decaying steadily ever since the last Spanish viceroys had departed. The suite set aside for them looked like similiar quarters in a Montparnasse hotel or slightly worse. There was a smell of rotting plush, dust and mice droppings throughout their rooms. Worse yet, the beds were crawling with vermin which were no respecters of royal skins. In the middle of the night they got up to find another place to sleep. The Emperor and Empress of Mexico slept that first night in their capital on a billiards table.

6. The Building of Miramar West

The building operations quite frighten one. The Emperor's passion is well known! I should at least have waited till the honeymoon was over, for one cannot say how this marriage will turn out.

—JACOB VON KUHACSEVICH,
treasurer of the crown

SOCIALLY the new regime was inaugurated with a magnificent ball given by General Bazaine at his general headquarters in the Palace of San Cosme. One night shortly after their arrival Maximilian and Carlotta were the guests of honor at the splendidly, lavishly arranged occasion for which the palace's huge patio was roofed and floored to provide a ballroom. After all, the Mexicans were paying for the French to welcome the Austrian archduke and his Belgian consort; under those terms no expense must be spared.

The bright-eyed American teen-ager Sara Yorke was one of General Bazaine's guests and was dazzled by the pomp and splendor as well as the great personages. "In the middle of the huge improvised ballroom the great fountain played, and its sparkling waters were seen through masses of tropical vegetation. Here and there warlike trophies reminded the spectator that he was the guest of a great army. The artillery had supplied groups of heavy cannon, stacked on end, and huge piles of cannon-balls, while at intervals trophies of flags and drums, of guns and bayonets, tastefully grouped about the French and Mexican coats of arms, broke with striking effect the expanse of wall above the arcades."

The ball opened with the *quadrille d'honneur* danced by Maximilian and Carlotta, General Bazaine and his more distinguished guests, after which the bulky commander escorted the emperor and empress to a dais under a canopy of crimson velvet, where they spent the rest of the evening on display.

"They were so young and handsome in their imperial pomp!" it seemed to Sara Yorke. "By them stood Princess Zichy, tall and distinguished, in a simple white tulle gown and natural flowers, with a wealth of such diamonds as are seldom seen on one person—a homely woman, but interesting to us as the daughter of the Metternichs. Her husband, Prince Zichy, was the most striking figure in the imperial party. He wore the full state costume of a Hungarian Magyar; and his many orders, hanging around his neck and upon his breast, as well as the marvelous hilt, belt and jeweled sheath of his ancestral sword, stood out finely upon his black-velvet costume and made him a conspicuous figure even in an assemblage where the ordinary evening dress was almost unseen."

General Bazaine's inaugural ball was more than a social amenity; it was designed to symbolize to the country the deceptive initial prosperity the French occupation had brought. "The glitter of all this court life," as Sara Yorke later wrote, "the revival of trade, the abundance of money so freely brought and spent in the country, dazzled the people, and a golden dust was thrown in the eyes of all, which for a brief period prevented them from seeing the true drift of political events. Indeed, the brilliancy of the scene was not entirely due to flash-light. The revenues derived from the customs of Tampico and Vera Cruz were at this time materially increasing."

The golden dust—a good part of it money he had brought from Franz Josef's share-out of the Austrian privy purse—blinded Maximilian as much as any of his new subjects. One thing seemed certain to his retinue: No great sea change had come over him on the journey from Trieste; he was still the master builder of Miramar rather than the emperor of a deeply troubled land.

Even the similarly bedazzled Carlotta recognized the urgency of simultaneously taking firm control of the country and beginning its reconstruction. In her first letter to Eugénie from Mexico City, after describing the mishaps and triumphs of their journey from Veracruz, she emphasized the need for building from the ground up after forty years of the most wretched misgovernment. The state had maintained its existence only through the stolid but unrewarded efforts of its Indian and mestizo population, on whose bent backs the aristocracy, the clergy and the military had long been riding. "Everything in this country calls for reconstruction; nothing is to be found, either physical or moral, but what Nature provides. . . . Things will go on here, if Your Majesties will stand by us, since they must go on, and we mean them to go on; but it is an appalling task, for when a country has spent forty years of its existence in destroying all that it possessed in the way of resources and government, everything cannot be set right in a day. . . ."

It was apparent that Carlotta grasped the seriousness of the challenge, realized that governing Mexico would take both immense efforts and the time in which to undertake them. She tried to supply the practical outlook, to keep her husband's mind focused on the realities of administration, on the dangers that confronted them if they did not take themselves seriously.

Her sense of realism, however, was opposed by Maximilian's obsession with the outward forms of monarchy, with style rather than substance. Before anything else was done, he insisted, a proper Hapsburg atmosphere must be created. Instead of lifting his eyes to the mountains that girdled his capital and seeing beyond them the whole country in its confusion and despair or recognizing that his regime was stitched together only by French bayonets, he concerned himself with establishing a court and ordaining a fitting pomp and ceremony.

His initial decisions involved a change of residence from the verminous and depressing National Palace to the summer castle of Chapultepec, acquainting himself with the Mexican members of his court (including fourteen ladies-in-waiting "a little fierce and swarthy in their fashionable crinolines"), and overseeing the palace guard commanded by an Austrian count, gorgeous in gold lace and aiguilettes and wearing a splendid helmet, who looked as though he were going to burst into an aria from *Lohengrin*.

The emperor had, in fact, turned once more to his favorite occupation of castle building; Chapultepec would be Miramar West, and a swarm of workmen was recruited, and building supplies were gathered immediately to make it a showplace of the Western world. The National Palace, which would serve as an administrative center, was also to be rehabilitated. The French and Austrian funds which might have been channeled into easing some of the burdens on his people were diverted to these purposes at a rate alarming to his personal treasurer, Jacob von Kuhacsevich, who wrote the wife of the prefect of Miramar: "The building operations in the palace in Mexico [City] and at Chapultepec quite frighten one. The Emperor's passion is well known! I should at least have waited until the honeymoon was over, for one cannot yet say how this marriage will turn out." He meant the "marriage" of Maximilian to Mexico.

And while Carlotta was writing to Eugénie of practical matters, her husband was relaying one of his travelogues to his brother the Archduke Karl and referring already to Chapultepec as the "the Schönbrunn of Mexico, a fascinating country residence on a basalt crag, surrounded by Montezuma's famous giant trees and offering a prospect the like of which for beauty I have seen perhaps only at Sorrento."

From the tone of his letter he might have been vacationing in Mexico. ". . . The Mexican's only enjoyment is to ride about his beautiful country on his fine horse and go to the theatre frequently; I too naturally treat myself to the latter. Moreover, there is excellent Italian opera at the chief theater, one of the finest in the world. Balls are rare, but when they do take place they are very fine and animated, and the elegant and rich society of this place is passionately fond of the national dance, which is the most fascinating one could see, and which the Countess Melanie Zichy says she wants to introduce in Vienna. . . . The stables are directed by Bombelles and fall into two sections, the European for town and ceremonial use, and the real national stables for country use.

"You would be much amused to see us in our Mexican equipage, a little, quite open carriage, as light as a feather, the famous Mexican state coachman on the box, with his gigantic white hat and full, white linen trousers, with his poncho of three colors round his shoulders, beside him a copper-colored Indian lad in a similar costume, driving a team of six cream-colored mules with zebra hoofs, two of them harnessed in the shaft, the other four harnessed in a row in front; an outrider on a cream-colored horse, with rich silver-mounted Mexican harness; and the whole turnout racing madly about as swift as an arrow."

But his ruling passion of the moment was rebuilding and renovating the Castle of Chapultepec, then on the outskirts of the city, and re-creating the terraces, gardens and groves of Miramar around it. Chapultepec was laden with historical significance. Montezuma's palace had once stood on its basalt outcropping. On that site the Spanish viceroys, between 1783 and 1785, had built their summer palace overlooking the capital and the volcanic smokes of the Valley of Mexico. In 1847 the "little heroes" of the military academy had refused to surrender to the American invaders on its ramparts and had jumped to their deaths from the northeastern tower.

The castle was massively constructed, with an eye toward the defense of its viceregal occupants, and was surrounded by giant cypresses, some of them 200 feet high and 40 to 50 feet in circumference, in whose shadow Montezuma was supposed to have strolled. Flowering creepers were twined through their branches, and the ruined gardens were alive with butterflies and hummingbirds.

A Mexican architect, Rodríguez Arrangoitia, was engaged to renovate Chapultepec in the Tuscan style. The Alcázar Wing was turned into a royal compound with some degree of privacy, while the West Wing housed the palace guard. A closed garden, or loggia, was built on the upper terrace just off the Alcázar Wing at Carlotta's request. Roadways were cut through the rock from the carriage house and guardhouse at the base of Chapultepec Hill, and a magnificent avenue bordered by eucalyptus was built from the palace to the center of the city below. Later an elevator was installed in the Alcázar Wing to allow easy access to the private apartments and Maximilian's study in the tower. A tangle of forest behind the castle was cleared for sweeping gardens, lawns and balustraded terraces. Tons of furnishings—ornate furniture, coronation gifts, bric-a-brac donated by Queen Victoria and Czar Alexander II, acres of tapestry, a museum collection of majolica, crystal and silver— had been transported aboard the *Novara* and hauled over the mountains from Veracruz on mule trains.

Nor was the matter of plumbing neglected as it was in European palaces. Versailles, the Hofburg, Schönbrunn and other such establishments relied on the thunder mug and assorted crockery, concealed behind elegant screens, for their sanitation facilities. Maximilian, however, was modern enough to insist on a certain amount of indoor plumbing, since water was available through an aqueduct of 904 arches which tapped the springs below.

Thus an Italianate Eden was constructed before Maximilian devoted any serious thought to administering his new empire. He and Carlotta busied themselves in their hothouse and spent hours deciding where to place the court portraits, the gilded bedchamber coronas, the ormolu furniture, the Sèvres services, the paintings, and the six-ton golden state coach manufactured in Milan. They supervised the work of scores of artisans furnishing the state dining room with new gilt and carvings and did not worry overmuch when the 200,000 gulden bestowed by Franz Josef slipped through their fingers. Maximilian's theory was that his new subjects had to be impressed by these trappings, that monarchy could not be expected to function properly until it was elegantly and comfortably placed in its rightful setting.

During his first months in Mexico, in whatever time he had free from his building projects, riding with his suite and attending the opera, Maximilian happily occupied himself with his masterwork, the *Reglamento de la Corte*, a 600-page volume bound in green and stamped with the gold imperial crown, which instructed the court in its duties to the last minute detail. It was illustrated with precise diagrams showing where everyone should stand in the throne room for the reception of a visiting diplomat or a cardinal or the presentation of Mexico City's debutantes. There was an inventory of all members of his suite and an outline of their duties and privileges, their costume at any given time of day or night.

All the ceremony and ritual of the Hofburg, in fact, were to be transplanted to Chapultepec. Etiquette was laid down for balls, concerts, birthday parties, holidays, dinner parties, gala performances. Three classes of banquets were established and lists provided for those guests who were to receive written invitations and those downgraded to printed ones. The conduct of everyone connected with the court was precisely defined, whether for vespers in the palace chapel or a third-class dinner in the fever belt. There were even six final regulations dealing with how the emperor was to be mourned in the event that an assassin's bullet or yellow fever ended his reign prematurely.

By the time all these seating arrangements, wine lists and orders of precedence had been drawn up, of course, Maximilian had ventured far enough out of his royal vacuum to see something of the countryside, if only on his daily rides. He was impressionable enough to understand what a strange, forbidding country he had come to rule, its immense barrens where nothing but cactus would grow, its silent, enigmatic Indian masses under their sombreros and serapes, its stained and crumbling cathedrals where the Aztec gods had not been entirely displaced by the Holy Trinity, its dust-blown plazas with the black buzzards lurching around like drunken undertakers.

As one bemused student of the *Reglamento de la Corte* wrote, Maximilian and Carlotta, aside from their busy nest building, "could see quite well, if they could see at all, that this was not Vienna, that the splendid edifice of Hapsburg etiquette was somehow out of place in the clear light of the New World. . . . Yet they deliberately reproduced it in a handbook that bore no relation to reality. It might have been composed for Offenbach's delicious *Grand-Duchesse de Gerolstein*. For there was not the slightest hint of Mexico anywhere in its crowded pages; and though careful charts told everyone where to stand on all occasions with meticulous distinctions between their respective magnitude that strained the typographical resources of a local printer, there was no provision in their majestic fairyland for a French general."

L'Affaire Countess Paula, however, showed that they were willing to make some accommodation for local sensibilities. Countess Paula Kollonitz had come over as Carlotta's closest confidante among the ladies imported from Miramar, yet less than six months after their arrival was sent packing back to

Austria. Judging from her memoir, the Countess Paula, despite the handicap of her upbringing as a royal satellite, a professional handmaiden to the Hapsburgs, was a young woman of acute perception. The immediate reason for her dismissal was her scorn of the Mexican ladies recruited for the court and her undisguised resentment of the French. Since the reign of Maximilian I could exist only on the sufferance of the Mexicans and with the constant support of the French, her bristling attitude alone would have made repatriation necessary. To this was added a defeatist attitude toward the whole future of the intervention.

Countess Paula believed that Maximilian and Carlotta were being fed on illusion by the French, who were proposing that troop withdrawals could begin soon. She knew that the French military, on that subject, was divided. Bazaine was willing to propose a reduction in the French forces because he knew that was what Napoleon wanted done as soon as possible, but General Douay, his second-in-command, was saying in private communications to France that any thought of withdrawal was insane. To Countess Paula it was also apparent that pacification was not succeeding, that bandit and guerrilla bands were becoming "every day more audacious, more confident, and the high-roads daily more dangerous. Daring burglaries and assassinations are committed in the very neighborhood of the capital."

The mere arrival of an emperor, the construction of an imperial façade were not overawing the Mexicans, who knew all about conquerors and how to send them reeling back to their homelands. Even Maximilian and Carlotta, in their cocoon of isolation from the turmoil around them, should have quickly become aware that the French and other foreign forces, with their Mexican levies, had not succeeded in imposing order. "The Empress was obliged to curtail her rides, and even the roads had to be swept beforehand by French troops, all of which was a source of great sorrow to Her Majesty, who had cherished an almost poetical idea of her future life, and with an entire absence of fear had put her trust in the love and protection of the people."

The bulletins of French victories in outlying districts, she believed, were largely meaningless. "By the time one town is freed

from the insurgents and opens its gates with joy—by the time
that dispatches have been written, and messages of victory
broadcast far and wide—the guerillas have mastered some other
important place, and the troops leave the conquered town to
hunt them from their new acquisition. But scarcely are the
troops out of sight when one hears the ring of the guerilla cavalry, which surrounds the deserted town."

Napoleon was a "much-praised friend" at the moment but
would scuttle the Mexican intervention at "the veto of
America." And Juárez was a much underestimated enemy,
whose intelligence and character could not be denigrated by
"even his greatest detractors." The penalty—or reward—of
Countess Paula's clarity of vision was a trip back to Trieste on
the *Louisiane,* which had just brought a contingent of the Belgian Legion to Veracruz.

Maximilian saw himself as a liberal emperor pitting himself
against a fugitive liberal president. One way of imprinting this
image of himself on the people's minds was to grant them the
right of petition. Every Sunday, on the way to mass at the cathedral below, he would hold an informal audience for people
with grievances, protests, appeals.

One of the more desperate petitioners was young José Luis
Blasio, who was to become Maximilian's private secretary. His
fifteen-year-old brother had run away from their Mexico City
home and joined the Juaristas. The French had captured him
and were holding him in the Martinica Prison, with the possibility that he would be executed. Blasio and his mother drew up
a petition and had it signed by family friends who had some influence with the new government. One Sunday they posted
themselves outside Chapultepec and waited for the imperial carriage to appear. "Soon two outriders who preceded the French
carriage in which Maximilian and Carlotta rode trotted into
sight. The vehicle halted in front of the group of petitioners.
The Emperor, after courteously saluting everyone, took the
papers that were handed him and placed them on the seat in
front of him. . . . A few days later my brother came home.
Thus my family contracted the first debt of gratitude. . . ." A
short time later Blasio heard there was a vacancy in the emperor's secretariat for someone to act as interpreter for the

French-speaking M. Eloin, the chief of Maximilian's Civil Cabinet, and he was accepted; later he served as Maximilian's private secretary.

Such acts of clemency were a matter of cynical amusement to the narrow-eyed professional soldier who really ruled Mexico. Though he wore the gold-braided kepi of a full general instead of a crown, that man was General Achille Bazaine. Royalty might take the bows, plead successfully—but still plead—for the liberation of 250 prisoners of war, and endow hospitals and foundling asylums, as Maximilian and Carlotta did during their first few months on the throne, but the ex-sergeant of the Foreign Legion knew who really wielded the power. His hard-headedness was visible in the succinct reports he sent Paris (as differentiated from the optimistic bulletins he forwarded to Maximilian). "It would be a military blunder to extend our line, which is already lengthened by the necessity of covering our base [Mexico City]," as one report to the French War Ministry read. "We cannot have our right at Vera Cruz and our left on the Pacific. We are confronted in the north by troop concentrations, and they must be dealt with first. . . ."

Already Bazaine had sacrificed much to place Maximilian and Carlotta on their puppet stage. While engaged in the campaign to clear the countryside around Mexico City of rebel bands and make the capital safe for their coming, Bazaine had consoled himself in the field with the thought that his young and beautiful Spanish wife would soon be joining him in Mexico. Unknown to her husband, Mme. Marie Bazaine had become infatuated with an actor at the Comédie Française. She had written the man letters, which his wife found. The jealous wife not only sent Marie's letters to Bazaine's headquarters in Mexico, but told Marie what she had done. On learning that her husband would find out about her affair, Marie Bazaine went home and killed herself.

Fortunately for Bazaine's peace of mind, and his tender memories of the beautiful young woman who had accompanied him to Italy and the Crimea, the letters were intercepted by a captain who had long served on Bazaine's staff. The captain destroyed the letters, also a communication from Paris giving the details of Mme. Bazaine's death, and several days later told the general that his wife had died after a long illness. Bazaine was prostrate with grief for days but finally got hold of himself. Nevertheless, the fact that he regarded his wife as a sacrifice to the intervention which placed an Austrian archduke and a Belgian princess on the French-built throne grimly colored Bazaine's attitude toward those newly minted sovereigns.

He was wise enough to know that royalty does not live in the real world, and he always presented a cheerful and optimistic face when he appeared at Chapultepec. He also understood that it was his job, as a French officer, to distinguish French interests from Mexican, Austrian or Belgian ones. Thus it was necessary to present the cheering aspects of the situation, military or otherwise, so that his forces could be sent home as soon as Emperor Napoleon wanted them back.

But that did not mean he had to lie or pretend to himself, and he was brutally realistic in dispatches to Paris on the failure of the new regime to make an impact on the Mexican people. "There has been no indication on the part of the Government," he wrote, "that the Emperor has taken any step with regard to the grave questions by which the country is disturbed. No order, no decree has yet been issued to announce the Sovereign's intentions and to reassure opinion as to the future.

"So I observe a sort of uneasiness and general discontent, indicated by an attitude of increasing reserve and a tendency of the Liberals to draw closer to the reactionaries for opposing, but equally thwarted, purposes.

"The Liberals will make use of their rivals to overturn the edifice that has been so laboriously constructed, and it is undeniable that energy and intelligence are on their side. . . . Everywhere there is a sort of indifference that I can only attribute to the cause which I have mentioned; the absence of any decision on the great questions which divide the country.

"Confidence is only established under the influence of French bayonets, by which safety is insured, and under the authority of French commanders, by whom public and private interests are protected. But it is impossible to leave garrisons everywhere; and I do my best to convince everybody that, when a country desires to save itself, it must help itself and make its own contribution to the work of regeneration."

After several months in the country Maximilian, not an insensitive man despite his sheltered life, became aware of that massive indifference noted by General Bazaine. He began to bestir himself, investigate conditions, and poke under the crust of the national life. The emperor in the guise of a social worker sometimes stumbled into low comedy. One night, after making a surprise descent on the city prison, walking through the cell-blocks and exhorting the prisoners to rehabilitate themselves, he decided to investigate reports that workers in the bakeries were being treated like slaves.

Accompanied only by José Blasio (who told the story) and an aide named Feliciano Rodríguez, and wearing a black coat and sombrero, Maximilian slipped into the street where a number of bakeries were located. They knocked at several doors, but they were kept barred, apparently, in fear of bandits. At one Maximilian pounded on the door and thundered a command that it be opened in the name of the emperor.

"Emperor the devil!" a voice inside roared back. "Go amuse yourselves somewhere else or we'll call the police, and you and the Emperor will sleep in jail."

They finally succeeded in persuading the proprietor to open up, and Maximilian trotted around inspecting the premises. The workers told him they had no complaints, and he gave each of them a peso.

Despite the earnestness of his intentions as displayed on the nocturnal visitations, according to Blasio, most people considered them ridiculous and said: "What kind of ruler is this, who wants to find out everything for himself, instead of sending some subaltern to do it for him? Doesn't this prove how little confidence he has in his subordinates? Doesn't it make a fool of him, to be treated as he was at some of the bakeries?" Obviously Maximilian would find it hard to please the Mexicans. If he shut himself up in his palaces, he was criticized for being too aloof and unfeeling. If he went into the streets, he was accused of lacking imperial dignity.

Late in August, 1864, after he had been in Mexico for about three months, he left Carlotta behind at Chapultepec (with full powers to reign in his absence, confirming the suspicion of many at the court that she was not so much an empress as a co-emperor) and undertook a tour of the provinces which had been carefully "swept" by the French army, mostly those to the north of the capital. His reception was enthusiastic, though they may have owed much to the local French commanders in turning out the citizenry to cheer and throw flowers. For days he traveled on horseback at the head of a cavalcade which visited Cuernavaca, Morelia, León, Dolores, a rigorous journey in the middle of the rainy season.

He was perceptive enough to know that much of the enthusiasm was manufactured, and later wrote a maliciously amusing account of his provincial tour for his brother Archduke Karl. At León he was the guest of honor at two lavish balls, and from that place he wrote Gutiérrez de Estrada in a much soberer vein than that of the letter to his brother. It was obvious from his observations, he said, that "the whole administration must be placed upon a new footing."

There was so much incompetence and corruption among the ruling classes, he informed Gutiérrez, that it would take years to build a new system from the ground up. "There are three classes which are the worst thing I have found in the country so far, the judicial functionaries, the army officers, and the greater part of the clergy. None of them know their duties and they live for money alone. The judges are corrupt, the officers have no sense of honor, and the clergy are lacking in Christian morality and charity. But all this does not make me lose hope for the future. A commission is already at work on judicial reorganization of the army. As regards the clergy, if they are to be improved, what is necessary is a good concordat, and a [papal] nuncio with a good Christian heart and an iron will. Only thus will the clergy be reorganized, made Catholic (which they are not at present), and acquire the good influence which they have hitherto not possessed. . . ." This was Maximilian in one of his periods of intellectual vigor, of perception and concern, when he was shaken out of himself and his training as a Hapsburg. The trouble was that they did not last long enough, and the youthful viceroy who had been called the Dreamer of Caserta would soon lapse into the Sleepwalker of Chapultepec.

On that provincial tour, for which opponents of the regime called him a *lavavava* (featherhead) because he undertook it in the rainy season, he demonstrated a kingly courage on at least one occasion. He arrived at the town of Dolores on September 16, which was a national holiday. In that town, on September

16, 1810, the rebel priest Father Miguel Hidalgo had proclaimed the first movement for independence: "Long live the
Americas and death to bad government!" Bad government then
was represented by the Spanish. Now an Austrian interloper appeared in the town where Father Hidalgo had uttered his
defiant cry, and he proposed to be the centerpiece of the patriotic celebration.

Dark masses of the peasantry moved into the town that evening for the ceremonial firing of cannon at eleven o'clock,
when Father Hidalgo was supposed to have issued his call for
independence. A more discreet man might have avoided the occasion. Maximilian, however, was determined to show himself
on the principle that a ruler who is afraid of facing his own
people is not fit to rule. At the sacred moment, just after the
cannon boomed and bells rang, he stepped into a balcony, by
the light of torches, an easy mark for any assassin. The crowd
fell silent. It was said that many of the peasants, glimpsing his
tall frame and golden head above them, were superstitiously reminded of the ancient fair-haired Aztec god Quetzalcoatl; but
this seems unlikely, since the Mexicans had been disillusioned
long ago by mistaking Cortez for the same god, and blond conquerors were in bad repute.

Maximilian stepped forward and made a graceful tribute to
Father Hidalgo. "You can imagine," he wrote his brother later,
"how embarrassed I was before a tightly packed, silent mass of
people. It went off well, thank God, and the enthusiasm was indescribable."

He was indeed showered with *vivas*. Later that night his own
enthusiasm matched that of the crowd's. He received dispatches
from General Bazaine stating that the *pantalons rouges* of the
French army had been strikingly successful in clearing the
country farther to the north. Bazaine's strategy of the moment
was to ignore the republican army commanded by Porfirio Díaz
in the south, around Oaxaca, as the lesser of two dangers. Instead he concentrated on harassing Juárez and the republican
forces to the north. A column of zouaves stormed into the town
of Ortega, and the important northern city of Monterrey was
captured. President Juárez was forced to flee from Monterrey
into the deserts of Chihuahua again.

That news persuaded Maximilian that he should extend his

tour, and the next morning he and his mounted escort galloped northward toward Monterrey. Along the way they ran into a heavy rainstorm, and Maximilian came down with a bad cold. He was so ill, in fact, that he had to rest for several days at a wayside inn. One of his chief advisers, Schertzenlechner, the ex-valet who contemptuously referred to Mexicans as *la race cuivrée,* convinced Maximilian that he should turn back to Mexico City, that a proper emperor ruled from a palace, not from horseback. So the cavalcade, with its sneezing leader, returned to the capital.

And once returned to the palatial atmosphere, again out of touch with the realities represented by the dark faces huddled under the balcony at Dolores, he submitted to the autointoxication of his daydreams. The military successes to the north encouraged him—and the more practical Carlotta as well—to believe that Mexico would soon be pacified completely, that they would be able to turn away from domestic problems (which they had as yet confronted only in the most glancing way), that they could look beyond the present horizons to a more splendid future. Mexico was three times the size of France, but so much of it was desert scrub, as he had noted on his tour. It should be merely the base of a mighty empire stretching far to the south.

Incredible as it would have seemed to the more realistic French, if they had known about it, Maximilian and Carlotta, less than five months on the throne, were secretly plotting an extension of their largely ephemeral empire. The French learned about it only after the scheme began to develop. Its inception cannot be traced, but on recovering from his cold, Maximilian felt charged with energy and expanding hopes. "Work," he wrote one of his brothers at the time, "was and always is my joy, especially when one counts upon success."

Thus it was in a self-confident mood that he began angling for support of his scheme to expand the Mexican empire; it was difficult to tell whether Maximilian was more dangerous to himself when sunk in melancholia or afflicted by euphoric delusions. With Carlotta's eager assistance, since they both were children of the royal belief that territorial expansion was the first business of a ruler, Maximilian delegated Count Ollivier Resseguier, with whom he had served in the Austrian navy, to undertake a secret, sounding-out mission to Central America.

Count Ollivier was to observe political conditions in the tiny countries to the south and find out whether they might be annexed without too much opposition. He hurried off to Guatemala in mid-October, shortly after a dictatorial general, Rafael Carrera, had overthrown the previous regime. Guatemala, lying on Mexico's southern border, was essential to the development of Maximilian's plan. Among those Count Ollivier talked to was Tallien de Cabarrús, the French consul general in Guatemala. Possibly that was an indiscretion, but naval officers were not noted for their diplomatic skills. In the strictest confidence Count Ollivier informed the French consul that there was a possibility of "annexing Central America to the Empire of Mexico in the more or less remote future." No doubt Cabarrús was taken aback; there was a possibility of conflict between Napoleon's and Maximilian's ambitions in these isthmian jungles, the former having long nourished the idea of a Central American colony.

Tactfully enough, Cabarrús suggested that before annexing any states to the south, Mexico should settle its long-standing border dispute with Guatemala. Then perhaps France and Mexico together could work on the consolidation of all Central America. His report on the conversations with Maximilian's agent must have made amusing reading back in the Tuileries.

Count Ollivier returned to Mexico City without gathering any encouragement from the Guatemalans, the Hondurans, Salvadorans or Nicaraguans.

Maximilian refused to be disheartened. As he told General Bazaine about that time, "The present is gloomy but the future will be splendid."

7. An Ill-Will Embassy from Rome

*To expect this country—burning with resentment
against theocracies—to return the enormous holdings
of the clergy would be not only blind and irrational,
but silly beyond compare.*

—CARLOTTA TO EUGÉNIE

For months Maximilian and Carlotta had been awaiting, with
both dread and hope, the arrival of a papal nuncio designated
by Pope Pius IX to settle the dispute over church property in
Mexico and other outstanding issues between church and state.
Soon after his arrival they were beginning to compare Monsignor Meglia, the Pope's emissary, with one of the black vultures visible in every Mexican town.

They hoped that by nationalizing church property—"a splendid stroke of business" for the state treasury, as Maximilian
expressed it—and by granting freedom of worship they could
bring the Mexican masses to their side. Half a year in the country convinced them that an American state could survive only
under a liberal government, whether it was directed by an emperor or a president. "This continent," Maximilian wrote his
brother Archduke Karl, "is very progressive in a political sense, more so by far than European states with their ex-
aggerated self-esteem. What we know in the Old World as
mandarinism, with all its ridiculous bathos, is utterly incongruous here. All the stilted trumpery with which we so stupidly en-

cumber ourselves in Europe, and shall continue encumbering ourselves for centuries, has been discarded over here." Maximilian might have old-fashioned monarchial ideas of absorbing more territory, but he realized that absolutism of any kind was doomed to shrivel in the more astringent air of the Americas. And he now viewed himself, oddly, pathetically, considering his real position as an anachronism fabricated by European intrigue, a citizen of the New World.

If the Catholic hierarchy could make an exception of Mexico, if it were wise enough and flexible enough to comprehend that the Mexicans would not put up with dictates from the Vatican, then European "mandarinism" would be defeated and the new empire would have a chance of survival. Mexico's differences with the church could be settled in "an entirely Catholic, but also perfectly liberal sense," he hoped and believed. But that depended on a lenient attitude in the Holy See and a pliancy in the papal nuncio it had dispatched.

However, instead of sending a delegate to negotiate its dispute with Mexico, the Vatican had dispatched Monsignor Meglia with a virtual ultimatum that required the clock to be turned back to the Spanish conquest. The Reform Laws passed by the Juárez government were to be nullified; it would not hear of giving up church property, nor would it consider Maximilian's plan to allow freedom of worship by all creeds while simultaneously proclaiming that the Catholic faith was the state religion, a compromise by which Maximilian hoped to pacify both the Juaristas and the clerical-conservative elements which had summoned him to the throne.

Monsignor Meglia brought with him a letter from the Pope —whom Maximilian could remember all too well from their first meeting years before disporting himself with his "rakish" cardinals—which demanded the annulment of the Reform Laws, the establishment of the Catholic Church "to the exclusion of all other creeds," complete freedom of the bishops in the exercise of their official functions, the restoration of the religious orders, clerical supervision of both public and private education, the removal of all restrictions which had made the church dependent on the state.

Somewhat angrily, Maximilian, on reading the Pope's letter, replied that he was determined to maintain religious freedom and to nationalize church property, in return for which the state treasury would be responsible for the clergy's salaries. Monsignor Meglia stared at him as though confronted by the Antichrist. He then hastened from Chapultepec and began urgent consultations with Archbishop Labastida and other members of the Mexican hierarchy.

For two days Maximilian and Carlotta heard nothing from Monsignor Meglia, and finally they sent a representative to ask whether their counterproposals had been considered.

No, came the reply. The Pope's letter would have to be obeyed to the last comma. There could be no negotiations.

Maximilian and Carlotta were outraged, convinced they could not rule Mexico unless the religious laws were liberalized. The church, they believed, had betrayed them. Carlotta was especially furious and in an interview with General Bazaine cried out that he "ought to throw the papal nuncio out the window." But that was not a part of the responsibilities of a commander in chief.

Carlotta relieved some of her feelings in a letter to Empress Eugénie, whom she had come to regard as a long-distance confidante. "Really, to assert that the country, which is steeped in hatred for the theocracy, wishes this property to be restored to the clergy, bears witness to a weakmindedness, a blindness, and a stubbornness beyond compare. It is just as if someone were to come up to one in blazing sunlight and allege that it was night, but unfortunately—I must admit this fact though it is difficult for Catholics of our age—such is the stuff of which the Church of Rome is made."

Maximilian summoned a meeting of the Ministerial Council to decide on what could be done. They had to walk a knife-edge, they knew, between the people and the hierarchy. If the crown sided with popular opinion, it would probably lose the support of the clerical-conservative faction, numerically a flimsy political prop. On the other hand, the clerical-conservative party had no alternative to Maximilian; if he fell, they were also ruined. Even if he defied the Pope, however, he probably could not gain any wide support among the masses, who could not easily be weaned from republicanism. Still there was a chance of demonstrating to the people that he was on their side against the blackest of the reactionary forces.

The Ministerial Council, after deliberating for hours, decided that if the papal nuncio did not offer a compromise, a proclamation would be issued in which the Juárez Reform Laws would substantially be affirmed.

Then Maximilian decided to attempt a last-minute reconciliation with the hierarchy. He told Carlotta he could not trust himself to keep his temper, and asked her to plead with Monsignor Meglia. The interview was arranged for December 23 in hopes that the advent of Christmas might soften his adamant stand. Carlotta, however, found the Pope's delegate in a mood as hard as the obsidian from which Aztec sacrificial knives were made. After two hours with Monsignor Meglia, she left him white-faced and shaking with rage and frustration. A graphic letter to Eugénie described that ordeal:

"I can tell Your Majesty that nothing has given me a better idea of hell than that interview, for hell is no more or less than a blind alley with no way out. To try to convince someone, knowing that it is love's labor lost, that one might as well be talking Greek, since one side sees things black and the other white, is a labor fit for the damned.

"Everything slid off the nuncio as if from polished marble. At last he said to me that the clergy had set up the Empire. 'One moment,' I replied. 'It was not the clergy; it was the Emperor, who did so on the day of his arrival.'

"I made every possible representation to him in every possible tone, grave, gay, weighty, and almost prophetic, for it seemed to me that the situation might be followed by developments, perhaps even by a break with the Holy See, to the great detriment of religion. It was no use, he brushed my arguments aside like dust, but produced nothing in their place and seemed to be quite at home in the void which he created around him and in his utter denial of all light.

"By way of an ultimatum, I brought forward the Emperor's letter and said to him, as I rose: 'Monsignor, whatever happens, I shall take the liberty of recalling this conversation to you; we are not responsible for the consequences; we have done everything to prevent what will now happen, but if the Church will not help us, we shall serve her against her will.' "

Again the Ministerial Council was summoned, this time with Carlotta in attendance. Maximilian declared it was time to issue his proclamation, since the papal nuncio could not be swayed. Several members argued for less drastic action on this occasion, but on December 27 he published the decree nation-alizing church property, establishing freedom of worship, and placing the clergy on the government's payroll.

Now clerical passions flamed. Monsignor Meglia forwarded an angry letter to Maximilian declaring that he had made the church a "slave" of the Mexican government. It was sent to the imperial chancellery and was opened by Minister of Justice Pedro Escudero, who took it upon himself to declare that "this insolent letter" violated all the polite usages of diplomacy and should not be submitted to the emperor. It was returned to the papal nuncio. On January 7, Maximilian hardened his position by issuing another decree which declared that papal bulls were not to be placed in effect without sanction from the throne.

This was only the beginning of a long struggle between Max-imilian and the church, which was outraged that a Catholic prince should defy its absolute powers. The Mexican émigrés who had just begun drifting back to Mexico City from Parisian and Roman exile were appalled; they believed that restoration of the church's position was essential to reestablishing the order and decorum of the prerevolutionary years; the Indian hordes had to be kept in check by a combination of military power and ecclesiastical domination. Some of the capital's more prominent families now refused to appear at court.

Nor were the Liberals, the Juaristas, appeased by Maximi-lian's defiance. Opposition newspapers gloated that Juárez, though a fugitive, had triumphed in absentia. In the capital's cafés the witticism was that "Juarism without Juárez" had been achieved.

Again Carlotta confided in Empress Eugénie, writing in the first week of the new year: "The situation is very strained, as much so, thanks to the nuncio and the clergy, as is possible, in this country at any rate. There is indeed nothing to be uneasy about for the future; it is perhaps better that the storm should break at last, but it is an unpleasant quarter of an hour to live through. This state of affairs has now lasted for a week, and for my own part I could wish it was over.

"The bishops are drawing up petitions which are respectful, at any rate, in form; the nuncio, unseemly notes; ladies are making unseemly representations; in short, all passions are let loose; the extremist newspapers are at daggers drawn; the more extreme Liberals are exclaiming that the ideas of Juárez have triumphed, and exulting maliciously over the defeat of their adversaries; the Conservatives, on the other hand, imagine themselves to be the temporal subjects of the Pope and are fools enough—pray excuse this word—to believe that religion consists in the tithe and the rights of property.

"It is evident enough that behind all the doings of the nuncio, who is a mere puppet, is concealed the figure of Archbishop Labastida, whose bad Italian I know so well that I can recognize it in every line."

The enmity between church and throne would deepen, but for the moment neither side could take any drastic action. Obviously, the matter should have been thrashed out before Maximilian and Carlotta left for Mexico.

Among those greatly alarmed by the schism was Gutiérrez de Estrada, the elegant *doyen* of the Roman colony of expatriates, who regarded himself as the chief sponsor and architect of the new empire. His vehement patriotism, his vicarious devotion to the throne which he believed he had created had not yet propelled him back to Mexico. Gutiérrez was also a cautious man, who wanted to be sure of the durability of his creation. On learning of the break between Maximilian and the hierarchy, he took the part of the church. Ancient privilege could be maintained only by an alliance of military and clerical power. When he received a letter from Maximilian complaining of the corruption of the Mexican clergy, he replied that reforms might be necessary, but first the convents and monasteries had to be reopened, the Jesuits recalled, the membership of the various religious orders increased.

Gutiérrez, in making himself a defender of the faith, was involved in a scandalous postscript to the break between Maximilian and the church. Late in 1865 the Abbé Alleau, identified as a secret agent of the Vatican, was arrested in Mexico. A number of papers were found on his person. One was a pamphlet he had evidently been distributing to stir up the lower-ranking members of the clergy against Maximilian. Another was a letter from Gutiérrez expressing hope for the success of Abbé Alleau's mission in Mexico, the exact nature of which was never learned.

Also among the abbé's papers was a memorandum declaring that Empress Carlotta was causing trouble through her restless activity because she had no children to take up her time. The empress was not barren, the memorandum stated, but the emperor was sterile because he had been infected by a venereal disease during his brief naval career. Maximilian insisted on being shown the papers found on the Abbé Alleau, and his bitterness toward the church was hardly alleviated. Childlessness after seven years of marriage had become a very sensitive subject at Chapultepec; one duty of a dynasty, after all, was to perpetuate itself.

Shortly after New Year's, 1865, Maximilian and Carlotta took steps to ease the disaffection of the aristocracy. With abandon, and a measure of cynical amusement, they created orders, awarded decorations, made court appointments, and held lavish entertainments at Chapultepec. All this designed to take the aristocratic minds off that troublesome guerrilla war being waged between Maximilian and the church.

He was soon swamped with petitions for court appointments which listed the petitioner's often imaginary and remote connection with a viscount or marquis who had sojourned in Mexico three or four centuries earlier.

Maximilian laughed over these vainglorious documents— being a Hapsburg, he could afford to—and told José Blasio, his young private secretary: "It is a great pity that we haven't a factory here for turning out parchments and family trees, for we could make a lot of money by it. These gentlemen seem to believe that the blood of nobility is blue, and forget that much noble blood ran during the French Revolution and that it was as red as that of the lowest plebeian. . . . To the real nobility of France—the émigrés—when they returned to their country —were added adventurers, new-made nobles, the dukes, counts and marquises created by Napoleon; almost all of them were as plebeian as the humblest bourgeois."

During what Blasio called "this craze to demonstrate noble descent," the Countess del Valle became the mother of triplets.

"When the news was communicated to the Emperor," Blasio recalled in his memoir, "he remarked that his Grand Chamberlain, the Count, was to be congratulated, not only for having three members added to his family, but also for having provided the Empire with three new subjects of proved, ancient, and legitimate nobility. [They were descendants of Hernando Cortez.]"

Before January was out, Maximilian announced that he had created the Order of the Mexican Eagle, of which he was to be the grand master, as the first of the folderols to be bestowed on his restive followers. It was a gorgeous bauble: a spread eagle holding a serpent in its beak, above which was the imperial crown, with a blue ribbon attached and bearing the inscription "Equality with Justice," a motto which some of its recipients might have found repellent. Five classes would form the Order of the Mexican Eagle: 200 officers, 100 commanders, 25 grand crosses, 12 grand crosses with collar, and an unlimited number of knights.

With all the fighting going on, it seemed wise to revive two of the military orders, in addition, the European-styled *Pour le mérite* and the Cross of Constancy, which President-General Antonio López de Santa Anna had initiated, though constancy —military or civil—was in desperately short supply. The *Pour le mérite* would be issued in gold, silver and bronze medals. Maximilian also revived the Order of Guadalupe, which had been established by an unfortunate predecessor, the Emperor Agustín de Iturbide, with five classes ordained from officers to knights.

Nor was Carlotta forgotten in this whirl of medal pinning and ribbon fastening. In honor of her patron saint and of the empress herself, the Imperial Order of San Carlos was established, with grand cross and small cross, both to be awarded on the saint's day and on Carlotta's birthday. Competition for the order among the Mexican ladies became so heated and was attended by so much jealousy and recrimination that Carlotta had to pass out crosses big and little almost indiscriminately.

Creole society never gorged itself so completely and repeatedly as during the early months of 1865, when night after night the state dining room at Chapultepec was thrown open to the feasting. State dinners began at 3:30 P.M. and ended five or six hours later. The wine bill alone for Chapultepec in 1865 amounted to more than 100,000 pesos, with whole regiments of French, Rhenish and Hungarian wines being brought up from the cellar and expended against the Mexican thirst. The finest vintages flowed at all meals, as José Blasio recalled. "His Imperial Majesty was a refined gastronome and his cooks did their best not to disappoint him. The cuisine was French, modified to some extent by the culinary art of Vienna. The finest wines were served at the imperial table; at breakfast sherry, bordeaux, burgundy, and wine of Hungary; at dinner Rhine wine and champagne, as well as those mentioned before."

A menu dated March 29, 1865, the work of the court printer, survives to indicate the extent of Maximilian's hospitality and the reason eyes brightened among Creole society and the diplomatic corps at the arrival of an invitation from the palace. This was the dinner served in honor of Bazaine's promotion to marshal of France:

Potage Brunoise, Potage tapioca.

RELEVÉS: Bouchées aux huitres, poisson aux fines herbes, filet braisé, sauce Richelieu.

ENTRÉES: Côtelettes jardinière, vol-au-vent financière, saumon à la Tartare, cailles Périgeuex.

Punch à la Romaine.

Rôts, dinde au cresson, selle d'agneau.

ENTREMÉTS: Pois à la Française, asperges hollandaise, gelée au marasquin, gâteau d'abricots, pudding diplomate, glace à la vanille.

Afterward there was music to snore by, provided by the court orchestra, with the more elderly guests dozing in their chairs, the ladies gossiping and passing boxes of chocolate bonbons. The emperor smoked a cigar, helped himself to the cognac, and then withdrew to his own quarters at eight o'clock sharp. He presided over the feasting with a jaded eye, judging from a report to his brother Archduke Karl. "Every Monday Charlotte gives a ball, which is always a great success and very animated, and at which a bevy of the loveliest women join in the dance. The diplomatists are arriving one after the other, which gives us boring receptions and dinners. Thanks to great efforts, our cuisine at least is one of the best that exists at present, and so are the imperial cellars. The diplomatists gorge and swill to such an extent that as a rule after dinner they can only mumble inarticulate sounds."

Another social report, this one less blasé, was forwarded by Carlotta to Eugénie, advising the French empress that she was giving evening parties "exactly like Your Majesty's. . . . The guests put on their best finery and really look presentable. There are many types of beauty hereabouts, suggestive of Your Majesty's homeland. One Spanish lady, the wife of a doctor named Solís, is exquisite; at the masked reception of the Bourse quite recently she had powdered her hair and woven a poppy-colored ribbon about it. The effect was dashing—a perfect Sappho of the classic age. Another handsome woman is Madame Sánchez-Navarro, one of my attendant ladies. Hers is the face of a Murillo Madonna, with the black brows and long eyelashes of an Oriental. To offset so much dark beauty she wears a string of enormous pearls from the Pacific Ocean (which reminds me that I must have some fished for in the spring—that seems to be the proper season)."

Evidently Carlotta's dancing parties grew livelier after the emperor retired. "My soirees end after one o'clock. Next Monday will be the sixth. I usually whirl through several quadrilles, one of these with General d'Herillier. In time I hope to invite all the French officers, even the paymasters, who we have been told are very anxious to dance. . . . At the finish there is a loud cornet signal, whereupon we all start into a *galop* which goes so fast that somebody always ends by falling down." The empress, after all, was only twenty-four.

Young Sara Yorke attended one of the balls at Chapultepec and this time was a little less impressed by the two rulers. With shrewd insight, she sized up Carlotta as by far the stronger and more intelligent. Maximilian was handsome enough, but "the whole expression of his face revealed weakness and indecision. He looked, and was, a gentleman. His dignity was without hauteur . . . he had the faculty of making you feel at ease; and he possessed far more personal magnetism than did the Empress."

Carlotta impressed the young American as the "better equipped of the two to cope intelligently with the difficulties of practical life. . . . Hers was a strong, intelligent face, the lines of which were somewhat hard at times. . . . It is probable that, had she been alone, she might have made a better attempt at solving the problems than did Maximilian; at least such was Marshal Bazaine's opinion, as expressed before me on one occasion, during her brief regency, when she had shown special firmness and clear judgment in dealing with certain complicated state affairs. . . . She was, however, reserved, somewhat lacking in tact and adaptability; and a certain haughtiness of manner, a dignity too conscious of itself, at first repelled many who were disposed to feel kindly toward her. It is more than likely that under this proud mien she concealed a suffering spirit, or, at least the consciousness of a superiority that must efface itself."

During the early months of 1865 it seemed to Carlotta and Maximilian that their defiance of Mother Rome was having the desired effect. They were not even greatly alarmed when Marshal Bazaine reduced the expeditionary force, under pressure from Paris, by sending home General Douay's division; it seemed an indication that the country was under control, though the French command knew better. Maximilian wrote Dr. Jilek, the physician at Miramar, the kind of optimistic letter many a humbler immigrant might send home after making good in the New World. "Though here I no longer have the breezes of the Adriatic or the air of Lacroma, I am living in a free country, among a free people, where principles prevail of which you at home cannot dream. I am no longer cramped by any fetters, and here I may openly say that I desire what is good.

"Though Mexico may be retrograde in many respects, and lacks material prosperity and development, in social questions, which are the most important in my opinion, we are far in advance of Europe and especially of Austria. A healthier democracy prevails among us here, free from the morbid, fantastical character of that prevailing in Europe, but with a strength and conviction such as will perhaps not develop among you till after a hard struggle lasting fifty years. European judgments with regard to this country are almost universally false, Europeans cannot and will not understand conditions out here, they are too proud to admit that we Americans are a long way ahead in essentials."

We Americans. Until the day he stood against a hillside at

Querétaro, he would regard himself—this was not a public pose but a private fantasy—as just one of many young *Wandervögel* from Europe who had packed up and sought freedom and opportunity in the Americas.

He was utterly confident in the letter to Dr. Jilek that he had put the clergy in their place. "All that has been said about the clericals and their overwhelming influence is utterly false, the Blacks are bad and weak, and the enormous majority is liberal and desires progress in the fullest sense of the word. If you were to know my new ministers and hear them talk, my excellent Doctor, you would see all the more clearly that your great and far-famed minister is really no more than an obscurantist and a Jesuit."

Carlotta was also convinced that their program of appealing to the Liberal majority by curbing the temporal powers and some of the religious primacy of the Catholic Church, combined with buttering up the native aristocracy, was working. Not only the Liberals, she wrote Eugénie, but "I think even a few French immigrants are coming over to us, since their rights of possession have been recognized." However, she was worried about the withdrawal of General Douay and his troops. Instead of reducing the French forces, Carlotta wrote, they should be increased by 40,000. Both Generals Douay and D'Herillier agreed with her that the army of occupation was spread too thin to hold the country down if there was a determined and coordinated effort by the Juaristas. "*We* might, in certain circumstances, survive a blow, nobody would be surprised; but the French army could not. *We* might, in case of necessity, retire to a remote province, like Juárez; we could go back to where we came from, but France cannot dispense with a triumph. . . ."

A little more effort by the French, she emphasized, and the empire could get on with what she now revealed was its principal aim, a project of breathtaking audacity. If her subjects had ever got wind of it, certainly, they would have risen en masse. Her plan—and presumably Maximilian's—was to flood the country with European immigrants. That would ensure stability and the continuity of the empire. The United States had moved forward only after enough Europeans had arrived to subdue and replace the Indians. The same program, though more gently applied, would save Mexico from itself and from what she defined as the Mexican spirit of "nothingness," which was "more powerful than the spirit of man . . . only God can bend it."

To vanquish that invisible resistance to progress, it was necessary to thin out the Mexican (Indian) blood by a wholesale infusion of European stock. As she bluntly explained to Eugénie: "Our mission is slowly, in all friendliness, but none the less surely to bring about the immigration into Mexico of a population which shall absorb the one previously existing, for nothing can be done with the present elements. I should say it quite openly if I did not fear that it would be reported here. I reckon upon the immigration from Europe, which will perhaps set in in the course of this year, and if I were not convinced that it would be considerable, I should have to admit to Your Majesty that all we are doing is absolutely to no purpose."

The letter showed how different were the attitudes of Maximilian and Carlotta. He saw himself as an American; she knew herself to be a European. Maximilian delighted in putting on a sombrero and mingling with the people or at least placing himself on view, convinced that he could make himself loved. Carlotta regarded Chapultepec as a fortress, a haven of enlightenment, surrounded by forces equally ignorant and menacing. Maximilian felt that he could convince the Mexican people through democratic means that he was best equipped to govern them; their consent was all-important. But Carlotta believed that their subjects could only be ruled, that once repressive force was withdrawn, the empire was lost.

Early in 1865, while Chapultepec was brilliant with gala nights and the lively strains of a Viennese orchestra urged on a whirl of dancers on the polished parquet of its ballroom, grimmer business was getting under way far beyond the capital. Bazaine had decided it was time to earn his new marshal's baton. He was always conscious that a sergeant's stripes had once graced his brawny arm, that the officers' corps looked down on him as a crude and pushing outsider. "I cannot deny my humble origin," he wrote his sister, "and no doubt it is because I have risen from the common people and the ranks that the envious pursue me, especially since my promotion to be Marshal;

the officers who came from the special schools cannot forgive me." The inferiority that dogged him for not having graduated from St.-Cyr impelled him to prove that he was worthy of his supreme rank.

Not merely to ensure the stability of Maximilian's regime but for the glory of French arms and not least for the enhancement of his own career, he undertook a vigorous campaign in the south. Juárez was pushed up against the American border, and further action there would only enrage the North Americans; now that the Confederacy was being squeezed into extinction on all fronts, Bazaine had to keep one eye on the Juaristas and the other on the Union armies, which might soon be released for other duties. This left him some freedom of activity to the south, around Oaxaca, where there were strong republican forces somewhat vainly styled the Army of the East, actually a collection of militia and guerrilla bands which could be severely damaged by a concentrated effort.

Bazaine took personal command of the operation against Oaxaca and its crude fortifications. His opposite number among the enemy was Porfirio Díaz, the boldest and most skillful of the republican military leaders, and a man with a temperament much like Bazaine's. Smashing Díaz would be a genuine triumph.

He directed a brisk and competent campaign at the head of 5,500 troops. First he enveloped Oaxaca; then he pounded it steadily with his artillery for a week—the commander of an overseas expedition cannot risk many casualties. Oaxaca was forced to surrender, yielding up 8,000 troops and 60 guns at a cost of only 50 casualties to the French. Among those who surrendered was General Díaz, who was promptly imprisoned under what was hoped were maximum security conditions. Within a few months, however, Díaz had made his escape and continued his career as the most dangerous and enterprising of the republican generals.

Meanwhile, the interallied forces in Mexico had been considerably augmented by the arrival of the Austrian and Belgian forces. General Count Franz Thun had arrived at the head of 6,000 troops recuited under the terms of Emperor Franz Josef's agreement with Maximilian, and a Belgian Legion—romantically inspired by King Leopold's offer of an opportunity to

serve as liegemen of a Belgian princess—had also marched up
the road from Veracruz, 1,200 strong, with Lieutenant Colonel
Paul van der Smissen in command. The Belgians were untried
troops and content to place themselves at Marshal Bazaine's disposal, but the Austrians were a different matter, having their
own long, if checkered, military tradition.

Count Thun immediately proposed to Bazaine that since
each commanded the forces of allied powers, they were to be on
an equal footing. Bazaine heartily disagreed; the footling Austrian contingent was too small and probably too inefficient
(judging by memories of Magenta and Solferino) to operate in-
dependently. He believed that there was too much division of
authority among the occupying powers as it was. It was all he
could do to hold his own with those who preceded Count
Thun. "The Arabs have a saying," Bazaine was fond of saying.
" 'When two are on the road, mistrust your fellow traveller;
when there are three, choose a leader.' Here there are four of us
—the Commander-in-chief, His Majesty's aide de camp, the
French minister, and the head of the financial mission, each
with his own instructions and his own point of view!" Making
Count Thun his equal would only further dilute his authority.

While the French and Austrian commanders were embroiled
on that question, the Belgian Legion was preening itself in
front of Maximilian and "our Carlotta." All the Belgians were
young, few of them over twenty-five, and none of them had ever
smelled gunpowder. Their devotion and enthusiasm, their in
nocent and untried gallantry were touching. Maximilian and
Carlotta reviewed them in front of the National Palace, then
invited all the officers to a banquet that evening. Carlotta
talked to each of them, including Captain Chazal, the son of
the Belgian Minister of War, and asked about their birthplaces
and families.

Then late in March the Belgian Legion moved away from
the delights of their capital and marched south into the hostile
and forbidding hinterland. There was more fighting in the interior than they had been led to believe. In Mexico City everyone was talking about Bazaine's glorious victory at Oaxaca; at
the field headquarters of the French army they were a lot busier
trying to keep the insurgent forces under control. Fresh troops
were so badly needed, in fact, that the Belgians were hurled

into action immediately. On arrival at Michoacán they were ordered to reinforce the Eighty-first French Regiment.

A report came to French headquarters that the republican General Corona Regules, with 3,000 men, was marching to attack the French garrison in Morelia, the capital of the state. Colonel Van der Smissen was then ordered to send a mere 300 of his force to the village of Tacámbaro under Major Tigdal to confront an enemy which outnumbered them by 10 to 1.

Major Tigdal and what may well have been the flower of Belgian youth dug trenches around Tacámbaro and eagerly awaited the chance to prove the superiority of Europeans. On April 11 they were surrounded on all sides and almost overwhelmed. Three times they left their trenches to counterattack, and each sally with the bayonet left them weaker. Finally, four hours after the battle began at sunrise, they retreated to the plaza and barricaded themselves inside the church. By this time all the officers had been killed or wounded, with Major Tigdal, Captain Chazal and three lieutenants among the dead. Of the 300 men who had occupied Tacámbaro the day before, only 190 were still alive.

The enemy set fire to the church, and the Belgians were forced to surrender. Just then a General Arteaga arrived to supersede General Regules among the victorious Mexicans, and over Regules' protests he ordered all the surviving Belgians lined up against the church walls and shot. This was done. Weeks later the Franco-Belgian forces in Morelia avenged that slaughter, when Colonel Van der Smissen led his own diminished force, plus 600 French zouaves and several thousand Mexican imperial troops, to retake Tacámbaro and capture the republican infantry trying to defend the place.

The news of the massacre at Tacámbaro had greatly shocked Maximilian and Carlotta, particularly the latter, because her own countrymen were involved. "Carlotta," the emperor's secretary, José Luis Blasio, recorded, "upbraided De Portier [the French commander at Michoacán] for sending out a little detachment of three hundred new soldiers, knowing that a greater force would attack them." But the news from Tacámbaro came as an even greater shock to Belgium, where it was charged that Marshal Bazaine was sacrificing Belgian troops to protect his own. The whole intervention, no matter how flattering it was to have a Belgian princess enthroned in Mexico City, now seemed a ridiculous business to the stolid burghers. Their opinion of dying for Carlotta was expressed by a deputy in a newspaper article published shortly after news of Tacámbaro reached Brussels: "The French Emperor cannot tolerate freedom or independence anywhere. His aim is to strangle liberty, even beyond the oceans. He has sent an army to crush the Mexican people, imposing an emperor by force. Mexico languishes today under the yoke of foreign domination and Belgium is expected to go to war for the simple reason that our Princess is married to the despot who rules that land."

Just about that time Maximilian was learning that far from his being a despot, his scepter was more ornamental than a symbol of real power.

That reality was financial, as the stage managers of intervention back in Paris well knew. A jerk on the purse strings controlled Maximilian's every movement. His proclamations were greeted by the French in Mexico or in France with a tolerant smile.

Shortly after the celebrated victory of Oaxaca he learned that the Mexican treasury was bare and his own personal one close to depletion. Kuhacsevich, his personal treasurer, plucked up the courage to inform his master that the French had not been forwarding the 125,000 pesos monthly he had been promised, that the 200,000 gulden given him by his brother was almost exhausted. Maximilian immediately summoned his Ministerial Council, and though figures and statistics of any kind produced a severe headache and fatigue, he listened to his advisers spelling out the financial facts of life. A total of 336,000 pesos had been spent on various émigrés and immigrants who had to be induced to join him in Mexico, on 100,000 pesos' worth of improvements on the National Palace, on renovating and refurnishing Chapultepec, and on the Mexico City reception. Not only that, but the Mexican treasury was being charged 1,000 francs a year for each member of the French occupation forces.

Shortly after that lugubrious session over the growing deficit came word that Paris was sending one M. Bonnefond, an inspector of finance, to take over "provisional control" of the Mexican Ministry of Finance, though he was not even a member of the Mexican civil service. Such niceties were not to be wasted on Mexicans. Simply put, Bonnefond would collect at the source for the French. Since the only fruitful source of Mexican revenue was the duty on imports and exports, Bonnefond's agents immediately took over all customshouses on the Atlantic and Pacific. In effect, therefore, France would be taking over the Mexican treasury. Maximilian was informed that if he needed any modest sums for the government, he would have to apply to Marshal Bazaine.

In addition, at immense profit to the operators on the Paris Bourse, a new Mexican State loan would be floated for 250,-000,000 francs—of which Mexico would see only 110,000,000 francs. Even after announcing that immensely usurious deal to his protégé in Mexico City, Napoleon had the gall to write Maximilian that his financial troubles were due to the fact that the Mexican treasury—empty as it was—was being looted from within. "Mexico owes its independence and its present government to France." Napoleon bluntly reminded Maximilian, "yet it seems as though some mysterious influence were constantly at work to prevent the French officials from devoting themselves to the welfare of the country; even our just claims are not always treated with consideration."

A few French bankers enormously enriched themselves on the proceeds of the new loan, while Maximilian was unsuccessfully trying to persuade his unwanted "adviser," M. Bonnefond, to draw up a budget. Meanwhile, with Napoleon's approval, the Hidalgo and Gutiérrez families, both of which preferred to remain expatriated and live lavishly off the people they endlessly plotted against, were presenting claims for millions of pesos for property alleged to have been confiscated by Juárez.

The matter of mineral-rich Sonora had also cropped up again. France was demanding that she be ceded the state for ten years, during which her mines would be exploited to the utmost, as a means of paying off Mexico's obligations. Maximilian saw this demand in a blindingly clear light: A large Mexican state would be annexed by France in return for the favor of being conquered. Maximilian bluntly refused to accede to this demand.

His refusal only heightened tension between him and his patron, just at the time, mid-April, 1865, that the Confederacy's main army was surrendering at Appomattox, and he could expect greatly increased diplomatic (if not also military) pressure from the north.

The final spurt of good feeling between Maximilian and his French patrons came during the festivities attending the wedding of Marshal Bazaine to Señorita Josefa Peña Azcárate. For some months the court had been whispering and giggling over the Marshal's infatuation. He was a grizzled fifty-four. The *señorita* was seventeen. The marshal, two years a widower, could never resist the large dark eyes of a Spanish type, and "Pepita" Peña came of a good family, an uncle having once been President of Mexico.

At first Carlotta witnessed the infatuation with disgust, particularly when watching the bulky marshal gallop through a habanera with the slender young girl. "He reminds me of a huge, lazy fly, gloating over that child-like fiancée of his," she waspishly remarked. "Now I sense Bazaine's character. Why do men of his type look so demoniacal when they are in love?"

Then, flatteringly, Marshal Bazaine asked Carlotta to intercede for him in obtaining permission from Napoleon and Eugénie for him to marry the girl. Carlotta the realist, at least in matters of power, agreed to undertake that chore because Bazaine, with his regiments, was the real ruler of Mexico; she and Maximilian were his dependents. So she wrote Eugénie: "Dona Josefa Peña is seventeen years old; she has a pretty face, extraordinary grace and simplicity, beautiful black hair, and a very expressive Spanish type of countenance. She is an only daughter; her mother is a widow; she belongs, they say, to a very good family, and is very well educated.

"She speaks French with a pure accent, and it is to her credit that, although she is the object of a Marshal's attentions, and hence of those of the whole French army, she has not lost her naturalness for a moment. She did not seem to notice either the admiration of which she was the center, or the great future opening before her, though she seemed most enchanted when her future husband was at her side, which still further increased her enthusiasm; to tell the truth there is a very decided attraction, for the Marshal has even begun to dance again, and gave us to understand that he had not missed a single habanera."

When news reached him that Paris beamed on Bazaine's matrimonial venture, Maximilian had just entered Puebla on a tour of the pacified eastern provinces. He had taken a more indulgent, but still ironic view of Bazaine's romance; perhaps his feelings on the subject would have been stronger if he had realized that Bazaine was conducting his courtship just when he should have been taking the field against the increasing level of insurgency. The impatient Bazaine was determined on an immediate marriage, and it had to be made an occasion of state, so Maximilian was required to hurry back to the capital. Overwhelmingly cordial and generous as he would behave toward the marshal in a few days, Maximilian wrote the Archduke Karl on June 20, 1865, that "we have, *alas*, yet another great state entertainment at the palace in Mexico, the wedding between Marshal Bazaine and a charming girl of seventeen, who will do us credit in Europe by her beauty and amiability. In spite of his fifty-four years, the marshal is perfectly infatuated; may this hazardous conjugal happiness agree with him."

Much as he detested all such ceremonial occasions, Maximilian presided over Bazaine's wedding with a well-schooled Hapsburgian grace. It took place on June 26 at Chapultepec before a select assemblage of the country's notables. The civil ceremony was held in one of the larger salons, the religious in the palace's chapel.

A wedding breakfast, with lashings of champagne, was laid on at noon in the state dining room, with Maximilian seated next to the bride, Carlotta beside the groom, who must have reminded her more than ever of a blowfly as he swelled and buzzed in anticipation of finally engorging that seventeen-year-old limpid-eyed morsel.

After dessert was served, the emperor manfully rose to his duty, lifted his glass and announced: "We drink to the health of our dear Marshal and Señora Bazaine. May God bless the union."

Carlotta went over and embraced the bride, doubtless with more pity than enthusiasm.

Maximilian then handed Marshal Bazaine a note which conveyed to the latter possession of a palace which, strictly speaking, it was not Maximilian's to give. "Desiring," the note read, "to provide a proof of friendship, as well as of appreciation for the personal services which you have extended to our country, and taking advantage of the occasion of your marriage, we present the Palace of Buena Vista, including the gardens and furniture, on condition that when you return to Europe, or if for any reason you do not desire to retain possession of the palace, the nation will receive it, and then the government shall be obligated to give her [Madame Bazaine], as a *dot,* the sum of one hundred thousand pesos."

The marshal, who had studied the art of pillage on razzias with the legion in Algeria, received the stolen property without flinching. He did not enjoy the use of his wedding present for long, and not many years later the palace was converted into a cigarette factory.

While the French commander in chief honeymooned, the Mexican empire's situation internally and externally deteriorated. Guerrilla activity increased in all directions from the capital, keeping pace with encouraging developments in the outside world. Further bad news came from Washington when President Lincoln was assassinated. Lincoln was inclined to take a tolerant, if not exactly indulgent, view of the French adventurism in Mexico and believed the empire would collapse under the burden of its own follies. His successor, Andrew Johnson, was being urged to take a sterner attitude by his military chiefs and the leaders of the dominant political party in the North. Washington, too, had its counterpart of the Mexican *émigrés* in Paris and Rome who had instigated the intervention; it was floating loans, gathering arms and making propaganda for a counterintervention from the United States. Secretary of State William Seward referred to Maximilian as "that Austrian fellow" in his dispatches, and there was a rising clamor for enforcement of the Monroe Doctrine.

A cogent argument against the sanctity of that doctrine as it affected Europe was entered by Jerome David, an influential member of the French *corps législatif:* "There is much talk of the Monroe Doctrine. Since when has a 'doctrine' enunciated in a message to one nation assumed the category of 'law' for foreign nations? The Monroe Doctrine happens to be a paragraph in a political speech, foisted upon Latin America without a 'by your leave.' We could understand the United States becoming alarmed over an aggressive neighbor, or one jeopardizing the institutions of the Union. But simply because the government at Washington happens to be republican in form, it cannot be contended that monarchies have no place in the New World."

French logic, however, had less force than the old witticism: "Poor Mexico, so far from God, so near the United States."

Maximilian and Carlotta could reflect on their first year in the country with less satisfaction than concern. A rumble of protest had arisen over the wedding gift of the Palace of Buena Vista to Mexico's conqueror, and the country was flooded with pamphlets charging that Maximilian was giving away the nation's few treasures, that he was a monster of lechery, that Carlotta's dancing parties at Chapultepec were orgies on a scale rivaling a Roman saturnalia.

In the continuing correspondence between Maximilian's rear echelon at Miramar and his entourage at Chapultepec, Frau von Kuhacsevich, the wife of his treasurer, wrote in near hysteria to a friend back at the home base of the tension and fear in which they all lived even in the "occupied zone." The Austrians of the palace guard were constantly on the alert. "The clergy are rabid at the emperor's Four Articles, they are conspiring, a general has escaped from Mexico City and is six leagues from here with a thousand men, our sentinels are doubled! Bombelles arrived this morning from Vercruz, they drove from Veracruz under escort, were fallen upon and robbed at Río Frío and had to pay ransom. If they had known Bombelles" —perhaps Maximilian's closest personal friend—"they would have dragged him off too. . . . They say a couple of bishops will have to be hanged. I am more afraid of them than of the guerrillas, especially as regards poison." The fear of being poisoned or otherwise done in by clerical plotters was almost as prevalent among Maximilian's courtiers as in Italy under the Borgias.

At night sometimes they could hear artillery fire as the occupation forces skirmished with a marauding guerrilla band. The palace guard was reinforced and artillery hauled up to Chapultepec against the possibility of a really determined assault. A signal system was set up to summon troops from the barracks in the city below. An atmosphere of siege and suspicion had begun to envelop the seat of Maximilian's empire. From now on he would be made to know that he sat on a cactus throne.

8. Uneasy Lie the Heads...

These people of Mexico are strange. For anyone who does not know them and who is foolish, their ovations and flatteries are intoxicating; they sweep him off his feet and destroy him; and if he is weak their curses also drag him down and destroy him.

—BENITO JUÁREZ

INCREASINGLY as the long summer of 1865 went by and Mexico shimmered in a heat haze that distorted everything, as in a defective mirror, Maximilian was obsessed with trying to learn what people really thought of him and his regime. After more than a year in the country, was he still regarded as an interloper? Did the people understand what he was trying to do? If only they could comprehend the purity of his intentions, the nobility of the visions he had of a peaceful and prospering Mexico. . . .

His obsession was not really as ridiculous as it may seem; at least he realized that he was there on sufferance, that nothing is so easily removed as a crown, unless it is the wearer's head.

Once on their morning ride from Chapultepec to the imperial offices in the National Palace, he rather wistfully told his secretary, José Luis Blasio: "You probably hear a good deal of talk about me, and although knowing your position, persons in your presence always speak well of me, there may not lack gratuitous enemies of mine who, to annoy you, say unpleasant things about me. If they do, don't fail to tell me what you hear them say about my acts or myself, favorable or unfavorable, so that I can prevent the evils or abuses. I do not ask that you tell me the names of those who criticize my acts, or to take the part of a spy; I only want to know what they criticize in my government."

With the candor of his twenty years, Blasio replied that even Mexicans favorably disposed toward Maximilian were disturbed by the fact that the French not only dominated military affairs but had taken many of the posts in the civil administration that could have been filled by Mexicans. He cited the case of M. Langlais, a minister without portfolio who "received the enormous salary of one hundred thousand francs a year, with fifty thousand for expenses, and at the end of three years a gratification of two hundred thousand. . . . The disgust caused the Mexicans by the arrival of this Minister-of-Everything may be understood. . . ."

Maximilian, as Blasio recalled, often chafed under the social and administrative routine, the incessant ceremonial surrounding his life. He was intelligent enough to realize that he was existing in a vacuum, that he was out of touch with reality. At times, too, his sense of humor was irrepressible, and he saw himself clearly as an anachronism. Occasionally Blasio would try to avoid accompanying the emperor on his early-morning rides and suggest that he stay in his room and work if His Majesty permitted. "No, sir," Maximilian replied, "My Majesty will *not* permit you to stay here, for something might occur to me while we are riding that I should want you to note down."

The daily routine began shortly after dawn at Chapultepec. Maximilian, by preference, went to bed as early and rose as early as any peon on a hacienda. As soon as he awakened, he pushed an electric bell at his bedside which summoned Blasio. His secretary would find him in his embroidered nightshirt, staring out the tall windows across the gardens of Chapultepec with their marble avenues, statuary and urns. He gloried in that landscaping, never more gorgeous than by dawn light. Once he remarked as Blasio entered, "Do you think that this should be called Miravella [view of the valley] as my castle at Trieste is called Miramar [view of the sea]?"

They would go over the papers in Blasio's portfolio while two valets dressed the emperor in his riding costume. By seven o'clock they were ready for the morning ride. Maximilian's white Arab charger, a military aide and the grooms were waiting in the patio. For the next two hours the emperor and his companions would ride along the roads surrounding the palace. He and Blasio breakfasted together, then donned the morning clothes prescribed by the court regulations: light trousers, a black coat with tails, and a tall gray hat. Then they rode to the National Palace over the Veronica causeway or the aqueduct.

Some days Maximilian conferred with his Council of State; on others he granted audiences. Carlotta also presided over an office in the National Palace, where she directed the work of various charitable enterprises, including a maternity hospital, which she had endowed. In midafternoon they returned to Chapultepec for a stately and often boring dinner. "There were usually twenty at the table," as Blasio recorded, "including the aides, the ladies in waiting and the chamberlain for the day, and me, with such other ladies and gentlemen as had been invited the day before by notes despatched them by the master of ceremonies. Agreeable topics were discussed, all unconnected with politics. Their Majesties spoke Spanish to everyone at the table, and if anyone chanced to be there who did not understand the language, one of them translated the principal points of the conversation."

When dinner had ended, the empress and the ladies retired to her apartments while Maximilian led the gentlemen to the smoking room. He was an inveterate cigar smoker and had humidors scattered around the palace. By eight o'clock, no matter what the occasion, he had retired to his own quarters. "Before retiring at night," as Blasio recalled, "the Emperor would turn over to me the late letters that had been received and if some of them were in cipher I would hurry to my room for the code and decipher them. If a letter was to be sent in cipher, Maximilian would dictate its contents to me, and I would put it in cipher. Sometimes as I was busy at this, he would smile and say jestingly, although there was a serious meaning in his words, 'Señor, if at any time any of these matters in cipher should be divulged, instead of the future to which you are looking forward, you would go to prison for the rest of your life."

Maximilian regarded his public duties, ceremonial and otherwise, as coming to an end at eight o'clock sharp. Even on the

celebration of his thirty-third birthday, July 6, 1865, he withdrew from public view while an evening reception in his honor
was held at Chapultepec, followed by a fireworks display and a
serenade. He broke his own rule only infrequently when his
presence was required after hours—but never long after—at
the balls in which Mexico City society delighted. His slightly
fatigued smile, masking an earnest desire to be smoking one of
his long cigars, fluttered out over the assemblage. He and Carlotta would mount the throne at the end of the ballroom,
which was canopied in crimson velvet and surmounted by an
imperial crown. Beside them stood two palace guards wearing
helmets and parade uniforms and armed with halberds. Under
the impassive gaze of the halberdiers, each guest was presented
to Maximilian and Carlotta by the master of ceremonies.

A quadrille of honor opened the festivities, with Maximilian
and Señora Bazaine leading and Carlotta and Marshal Bazaine
next in line. The emperor would wear the tricolored band of
the Order of the Mexican Eagle across his chest. The empress
often appeared in a gown of yellow silk, with the ribbon of the
Order of San Carlos running from shoulder to waist and a
heavy brooch representing the leaves of a water plant, made of
emeralds with diamonds set below to resemble dewdrops, on
her bosom. After the first quadrille, the empress would listen to
the chattering of the ladies while Maximilian circulated among
the diplomatic corps and the high-ranking French officers.

For such affairs Maximilian, according to his secretary, reserved his powers of observation, viewing the social opportunism and polite jostling for position with a sardonic eye. On
mornings after one of those balls which kept him out of bed
until what he regarded as an unreasonable hour, midnight or
after, he was "prolific with comment. He was a close observer;
little escaped his notice—the costumes of the ladies, the comical
—to him—gravity of the elderly gentlemen who, he said, would
have been more comfortable and happy in bed. Either at the
breakfast table or in the smoking room, when surrounded only
by his intimates, he would give rein to his sarcasm and gibes.
His wit was pungent and cutting. Of a young and personable
army officer who was married to a woman old enough to be his
mother, he remarked that he did not see how anyone could

have married that mummy whose fine clothes and jewels hid nothing but bones and parchment.

"One of the court officials and his wife were parents of a dozen children. Maximilian said that it was obvious that they made excellent use of their time and toiled so patriotically to increase the population of the Empire that he would take care never to permit the official to accompany him on any of his journeys, and thus compel him to lose precious hours which might be employed more agreeably and profitably. Of certain ladies he said that he could see their ardor in their eyes and that they ought to be formidable women to love."

But when young Blasio fell in love with one of those ardent females attached to the court and asked Maximilian's permission to marry her, the emperor was only grimly amused. "What!" Maximilian protested. "You are scarcely twenty years old and you want to marry? It would be not your fault, but mine, if I gave you permission. Do you think I want you to be like a rabbit? By the time you are thirty you will have ten children and then farewell to work, to judgment, to rising at four in the morning. Wait eight or ten years and I will arrange a suitable match for you."

The boredom of his ceremonial functions several times during the summer of 1865 impelled him to take any opportunity of escape. Once when he was dressed for one of the court balls he detested, there was a wreck on the railroad that ran in through valley below Chapultepec. Hurriedly Maximilian sent word to Carlotta that she would have to stand in for him that evening, dressed in rougher clothing, and hurried first to the scene of the train wreck, then to the Hospital de Jesús to oversee the treatment of the eight or ten persons who had been seriously injured.

Rubbing elbows with the citizenry seemed to revive his spirits, and after such experiences "with his customary optimism saw everything in a more rosy light." Yet the necessary circumstances of an imperial descent on the populace often negated whatever benefits might have issued from them; a barrier of epaulettes and plumed hats isolated him from the ordinary people. On August 24, for instance, he decided to tour the countryside across the lake from Mexico City.

It started out as a canoe trip, but in a style that emulated Montezuma's. "There was a large canoe for the Emperor, richly carpeted, with divans and cushions," one of his companions recorded. "Supper was served at midnight by the indispensable Venisch [one of his valets]. Besides champagne, it occurred to some one to bring pulque which, mixed with the champagne, naturally produced a deplorable effect upon the heads of some of the members of the party. This, together with the cold of the early morning, kept the Emperor from sleeping until five o'clock."

With some royally aching heads, the party left their canoes at Texcoco, where the cheers of the townspeople greatly enthused Maximilian, a reception which made it impossible for him to believe that "outside of the sympathetic crowds surrounding him there, he was detested and regarded as a usurper and an adventurer. . . ." And Maximilian and his entourage were quickly whisked away from the proletariat, driven in carriages to the nearby hacienda of one of his chamberlains. In the next few days he visited the pre-Aztec pyramids, stayed on haciendas, and bestowed decorations with a liberal hand. Given a long enough reign, it appeared, he would see to it that every other citizen was beribboned with the Order of the Mexican Eagle or emblazoned with the Cross of Constancy. On one of the lordlier estates he spent hours talking about literature with the Spanish poet José Zorrilla. In the town of Pachuca he insisted on inspecting the schools, the jail and the hospital.

His considerable charm, when exerted in man-to-man encounters, could work wonders. An ardent follower of Juárez, Dr. José María Bandera, was in charge of the hospital and had refused to attend the reception. Maximilian, however, sought him out at the hospital and won him over in a few minutes (according to Blasio) by announcing that the institution badly needed more funds. He donated 1,500 pesos on the spot, for which, he told Dr. Bandera, the physician was "responsible only to himself." Afterward they dined together, and Maximilian convinced the doctor, at least for the moment, that he was as sincere as Juárez in wanting to better the living conditions of the Mexican people.

Such bracing encounters, as Blasio observed, convinced him that he could displace Juárez in the people's affections, "being

what he was—inherently more of an idealist and a dreamer
than a politician. . . . He believed that it would be easy to end
civil war and party division, by calling to his side Liberals who
were willing to serve him. . . ."

On his return to Mexico City from the two-week journey
around the countryside, Maximilian devoted himself to other
efforts at closing the gap between himself and his subjects.
Sometimes he walked back to Chapultepec instead of riding,
dropped in at offices along the way, and talked with clerks. He
also tried to extend his influence as an arbiter of Mexican
culture and visited the Academy of San Carlos, where "the Emperor praised the work of the Mexican artist, Reboull, the
sculptor Norena and the architect Rodríguez," as his companion noted, "and expressed a desire to extend his patronage to
them. He commissioned Reboull to paint portraits of him, one
on horseback and the other, garbed as a Mexican general, with
the imperial mantle over his shoulders, and Norena to fashion
bronze busts of himself and the Empress." Evidently he also recalled how Napoleon III had won public favor by rebuilding
Paris but did not reflect that the French treasury was able to
withstand such expenditures while the Mexican was bankrupt.
"He summoned Rodríguez to the palace and discussed with
him at length various projects for embellishing the capital, one
of the most ambitious ones being that for an independence
monument in the main plaza. . . . Maximilian also contemplated a reconstruction of the façade of the palace after the
style of the Tuileries. . . ."

Such grandiose fancies should, in fact, have been quenched
by a conversation he had with General Douay, who had returned to Mexico City for reassignment after accompanying the
division of French troops back to their homeland. Douay was
ambitious, junior to Marshal Bazaine in age, rank and achievement, but did not scruple to intrigue against his superior.
Whether he hoped to supplant Bazaine or to be given
command of the separate Mexican army there was talk of raising, he obviously was hoping to use Maximilian's and Carlotta's
favor to achieve greater power for himself than a subordinate
command in the interior. This he hoped to bring about by telling them what they wanted to hear, by impressing them that he
was more devoted to their interests than Marshal Bazaine.

At the interview with General Douay, Carlotta acted as her husband's confidential secretary and recorded the talk in her own handwriting. Douay told them at the outset of his report on the trip to Paris that he had been informed by the Minister of War, Count Jacques Randon, that it was Bazaine's idea, not Napoleon's or Randon's, to send the division home. (This was untrue; Napoleon had ordered the withdrawal.) Douay wanted to know whether the 6,000 Austrians and 2,000 Belgians were serving as adequate replacements for the battle-hardened French.

Maximilian shook his head. "They march very well," he told Douay, "they have made great efforts, they have taken part in a number of engagements and are beginning to settle down. As to the Belgians, the mistake was made of sending beardless boys, who were disheartened from the first, and nobody made any attempt to raise their morale; in the mean time they were killed like flies, but in time it will be possible to make something of them, for their nature is not very different from that of the French."

Douay then indicated that the continued and increasing unrest in Mexico was due to Marshal Bazaine's lack of skill and determination. Bazaine, according to Douay (but not any other sources), had entered the campaigning the previous year full of false hopes and had declared that Juárez's insurrection would be smashed before the end of 1864.

"At the beginning of his expedition into the interior," Douay told the sovereigns, "he [Bazaine] told me that the decisive point would be San Juan del Río; later it was to be Querétaro; once scattered, the Juarista troops would never form again, and the business would be at an end; he had no doubt of that. I know Americans [by which Douay meant Mexicans] better than he does, and so I never shared his illusions. This was what made me seem opposed to the expedition at first, for I took it seriously. This, it seems to me, is why the Marshal will not admit that he has been wrong from the very beginning, and started on the wrong course. Moreover, he has the good fortune to be the only person to write reports on the situation, which have almost the force of law in France, and he naturally represents things in his own way. On the other hand, he does not like the idea of going home before the mission entrusted to him is at an end, and since he has always said that it is a mere trifle, he is afraid that at any moment the truth may be revealed."

A wiser man than Maximilian, a woman more experienced in dealing with people than Carlotta would have pulled back in alarm. They would have questioned Douay's motives in talking against his superior officer. They would have asked themselves: How much can you trust a man who is disloyal to his commander? What right did they have to meddle in a French military intrigue? How could dissension between the commanding general and his second-in-command do anything but weaken the forces protecting them?

Instead, with startling indiscretion, Maximilian told Douay he wished that Douay could take Bazaine's place, apparently not realizing that—Chapultepec being an echo chamber in which every whisper became court gossip before nightfall—Bazaine was certain to learn how he was being undercut.

Thus encouraged, Douay expressed the opinion that not only should Maximilian assume dictatorial powers, but the French commander in chief should be subordinate to and take orders from Maximilian rather than his own government. "The Emperor must have large military forces, in order to compel the Mexicans to make sacrifices which they would not make voluntarily," Douay explained. "The French commander-in-chief must be subordinate to the Emperor, and not vice versa, and he must be prepared to cooperate in Your Majesty's projects and serve you in all things."

This was the sort of talk Maximilian liked to hear. One day he pictured himself as the idol of the masses, the next as their iron-fisted ruler.

"Since we have no secrets from each other," he told Douay, "you must know the Marshal always opposes all attempts to organize an army. Did Napoleon tell you this? He has thwarted everything we have wanted to do. The older Mexican generals have been astonished; they think I do not want an army. Whereas it is the Marshal who will not give me anybody to organize it. D'Herillier was spoken of, but the Marshal gave me the worst possible account of him; I next asked him for a younger man, Lajaille, but he would not consent. . . . You know that I first thought of Loysel, whom I made a brigadier-general. When he returned from the interior, where he had accompanied me on my tour, the Marshal began to treat him like a dog. Later on I had some trouble in getting him transferred to me as chief of my military cabinet. I chose him so that France might get the straightforwardness of my policy. . . ."

General Douay agreed that there was "discord" between Bazaine and his generals. If Maximilian had known a little more about military history and a little less about butterflies, he would not have been greatly impressed by this bit of news. French generals, including the fraternity whom the first Napoleon had gathered around him and maneuvered like a stage manager with a surplus of jealous tenors on his hands, had always fought among themselves.

Douay had other complaints about Bazaine. Each district should be thoroughly pacified before French forces moved on to another, so that taxes could be wrung out of the controlled areas. Instead Bazaine had made spectacular marches to the north, then had fought the set piece Battle of Oaxaca to enhance his military reputation, even though the siege had cost more than the objective was worth. Furthermore, "the distances which the troops are made to cover are simply insane. My division has travelled 19,000 miles in seventeen months, and the 81st Regiment of Infantry, which I have just inspected, has not had a moment's rest."

Douay also urged that Maximilian would not be able to enforce such measures as "colonization and sequestration of undeveloped lands" unless he assumed dictatorial as well as imperial powers.

In that conversation Maximilian disclosed that he had learned how he had been used as cat's-paw in collecting the Jecker loan for France. "Another affair that we have settled," he informed General Douay, "was the Jecker business. When Dano [the new French minister] arrived, he said: 'Good heavens, did Your Majesty lend yourself to that business?' 'Yes,' I replied, 'it was your predecessor, Montholon, who desired it.' "

Frenchmen, General Douay remarked, believed that "the whole object of the expedition was to help Jecker get his money."

That cozy chat with Douay was costly to Maximilian and Carlotta, although they congratulated themselves on having won so loyal an officer to their side. Bazaine was now openly regarded as an opponent. Yet it was Bazaine, not Douay, who had the power to help them in persuading Napoleon to keep the French forces in Mexico. They were even more indiscreet in writing Napoleon and Eugénie how impressed they were with Douay and the other anti-Bazaine partisan, General d'Herillier. It should have been obvious that Napoleon would insist that the commander in Mexico be his man, not Maximilian's.

That Marshal Bazaine realized he was being plotted against at Chapultepec was evident from his subsequent actions. He rarely appeared, either officially or socially, at the palace again. General Douay was dispatched to the interior, far away from the capital and its intrigues, and the dashing General d'Herillier, Carlotta's favorite dancing partner, was recalled to France. Regarding Douay, Carlotta wrote Eugénie that "we parted from him with a heavy heart, and he from us. . . . The Emperor and he have an absolutely electrical effect upon each other, and are like two friends, or even brothers." Eugénie pointedly replied that she and Napoleon regarded Bazaine as their most capable field commander, who "had confidence in the existing order of things" and whose recall "would have the disadvantage of making people believe that interest is slackening, if the person left in command is of inferior rank."

The anti-Bazaine intrigue subsided with the departure of Generals d'Herillier and Douay, but within a few weeks, almost as though waiting in the wings for the stage to be cleared of those persuasive military personalities, another marplot made his appearance. This one, wearing the Roman collar, was to exercise the most fateful influence on Maximilian. Of all the grotesque aspects of the reign of Maximilian and Carlotta, none was so bizarre as the fact that a former Texas ranch hand could suddenly become the ruling influence over a son of the House of Hapsburg. Only history can get away with such tricks; the most skillful dramatist or novelist would not have dared invent Father Augustin Fischer.

He is the mystery man of the regime. His background is as shadowy as his motives. His almost immediate acceptance at the court of Maximilian and Carlotta is also hard to believe, except that he blandly proposed instant solutions to some of their most pressing problems. A quack is often clutched at with desperate hope when one's condition appears to be terminal.

The man who would play the role of Maximilian's Rasputin —though without the sinister beard and glaring eyes of the Russian "holy" man—was German-born. Some time during the 1840's he had migrated to the United States or had been brought there by his parents. In his early youth Augustin Fischer, a Protestant, worked on Texas ranches as a cowhand or farm laborer. When gold was discovered in California, he joined the rush but failed to make his fortune. Possibly it was a Spanish priest out in California who converted him to Catholicism. Later he was accepted into the Jesuit order, was sent to Mexico, and for some years served as chaplain to the Bishop of Durango. He lost that post, according to one source, because of "various unpleasant incidents." There were more than a few hints from those who knew him later in Mexico City that he had not abandoned all worldliness as a member of the Society of Jesus. After the empire was established, he turned up in the capital as the favorite confessor—possibly because of his tolerant views—of the more fashionable ladies.

Soon he managed to insinuate himself, with his cleverness, his command of Spanish, German and English, into the inner circle of Maximilian's court. Always eager for information on what was really happening in the country, Maximilian asked Father Fischer to write a report on the political and psychological climate of Mexico. Father Fischer's treatise was brilliantly executed, it was said, and presumably it told Maximilian what he wanted to hear.

Father Fischer was not one of those blue-jawed, morbid-eyed Spanish Jesuits or a member of the hierarchic cabal which condemned Maximilian and Carlotta for defying the dictates of Rome, but a handsome, hearty fellow who spread cheer and confidence at a time when they were in short supply around Chapultepec. "The priest was tall, with a clear, ruddy complexion," as one member of Maximilian's entourage described him, "he had an agreeable personality, he was always jolly, and had the faculty of promptly creating a favorable impression because of his geniality upon those with whom he came into contact."

Aside from his intellectual powers and his considerable charm, Father Fischer made himself a welcome figure at Chapultepec by proposing quick and easy remedies for two currently pressing problems: closing the breach with the Vatican and assuring a dynastic continuity. The latter, of course, was of more importance to Maximilian and Carlotta than to their indifferent subjects.

Father Fischer was the first entirely sympathetic churchman whom Maximilian had talked to in months. He asked the Jesuit, whose connections with the hierarchy were all but nonexistent since his dismissal by the Bishop of Durango, whether a new concordat with the Vatican could not be arranged. Yes, replied Father Fischer, if Maximilian was willing to compromise on various matters. The only issue on which he could not yield, Maximilian told him, was freedom of worship for all creeds. Something, Father Fischer assured him, though he certainly could not speak for the Mexican hierarchy or even less for the Vatican, could be worked out. On September 21, 1865, he was appointed honorary court chaplain and for several weeks busied himself drawing up the terms of a new concordat which he would take to Rome, via New York, and discuss with the Pope. Before departing on that mission, late in October, he was given a letter from Maximilian to the Pope introducing him, with pardonable exaggeration, as "one of the most distinguished members of the Mexican clergy," a claim the Bishop of Durango would have gladly contradicted, and expressing the hope that a peace could be arranged between Chapultepec and the Vatican.

Before leaving on that errand, however, Father Fischer had also turned his hand to assuring Maximilian's succession. As tactfully as possible, he pointed out that Maximilian and Carlotta had been married for eight years and since they were still childless, it would appear that there would be no natural heir to the throne. Then why not adopt as crown prince-designate one of the grandsons of the Emperor Agustín de Iturbide? The Iturbide regime had come to a sorry end forty years before, and its survivors lived in the crumbling Palacio Iturbide on the Avenida San Francisco. Thus, at Father Fischer's urging, a secret agreement was reached with the Iturbides by which Maximilian and the Princess Josefa, the boy's aunt, would become guardians of the youngest grandson, Agustín, who was three

years old, with the understanding that he would be Maximilian's successor. The rest of the Iturbide family was given an
annuity of 150,000 pesos and packed off to European exile.

Carlotta accepted that decision reluctantly but with dignity.
She did not allow her feelings to show except in a letter to her
aged grandmother, Queen Marie Amélie, who had prophesied
a tragic end to the Mexican enterprise. Only twenty-five years
old, she felt twice that, in despair and disillusion, when she
wrote her grandmother: "Today I am aging; if not in the eyes
of others, in my own eyes I grow old, and my thoughts and sentiments are indeed far from what outwardly appears."

She explained the adoption of Agustín de Iturbide as a matter
of dynastic necessity, as an "act of justice" by which they were
taking under their protection the offspring of a previous
regime.

Carlotta further unburdened herself: "People say that I have
influence and that I use it in this or that matter. But Max is so
much my superior that I cannot see how I might influence him
in anything, and moreover I am too loyal to attempt it. I try to
help where I can. It seems natural to me, in our position, that a
wife who is not the mother of a family, should devote herself to
assisting her husband. And I do it because Max wishes it—and
for my love of useful occupation. I have not two grains of personal ambition. Among laborers, the wife contributes to the
tilling of the field. There is here a great field of fallow land.
The task is not too much for two who have no child, and nothing better to do.

"And all this I tell you, dear grandmother, that you may
judge for yourself the truth of those criticisms of me which
have been carried to Rome. They take me for a kind of virago,
when I am absolutely as you have always known me. . . .
Ambition to do good, perhaps I have that, but it is only as Maximilian's wife."

The story of Maximilian and Carlotta has been converted
into a romantic legend; they are usually depicted as partners in
one of the great love stories of all time, rivals of Héloïse and
Abélard, Romeo and Juliet, Tristan and Isolde. But what was
the truth of their relationship? By the time they jointly ascended the Mexican throne, from all accounts, theirs was a

working partnership. The great love story was a fraud, at least in the sexual sense.

Their marriage had been arranged by dynastic promoters. Love, apparently, came after marriage—and that can be the most durable kind, as Europeans know. The memoirs describing their life at Miramar hymn their devotion to each other; Carlotta's initial jealousy of her beautiful sister-in-law, the Empress Elizabeth, might be cited as a symptom of Carlotta's feelings about Maximilian. And Maximilian felt deeply enough about her to allow himself to be dominated.

A modern searching for the fatal flaw in their marriage might seize on that domination as an indication that Maximilian had thereby been "emasculated," but Carlotta maintained that in public and in private she considered Maximilian the superior partner.

Something undoubtedly happened during the Miramar years that ruptured the emotional fabric of their marriage. By the time they reached Mexico the situation between them could be summed up in two words: "separate beds." For the reasons behind that estrangement, one can only consult that compendium of malice, hearsay and guesswork generically titled backstairs gossip. Even royalty cannot hide from their servants, who see all and sometimes publish all.

With a Latin's curiosity about such matters—or perhaps it is only a wider human trait, but more noticeable among a people whose first principle is *machismo*—young José Luis Blasio, from his intimate vantage point, candidly observed the relationship, which had puzzled him from the beginning of his employment as Maximilian's secretary. Shortly after taking that post he had accompanied the emperor and empress on a visit to Puebla, where the first revelatory incident took place. "After breakfasting," Blasio recorded, "Maximilian visited the rooms which had been prepared for the Empress and manifested his satisfaction at seeing the magnificent double bed, with its canopy of fine lace and silken ribbons, which was waiting for the imperial pair. But as soon as the host was out of the way His Majesty ordered the servants to find a room at a distance from the bedchamber and set up his traveling cot there. *He did this almost angrily*. Being completely new to the court, and not having confidence in any of the servants, I was unable to let any of them know how strange Maximilian's conduct seemed to me."

Blasio asked himself: "What conjugal drama was concealed by the Emperor's action? Why was it that two young married persons, who in public seemed to love each other, at the age of vigor shared no marital life, and the husband appeared irritated at the prospect of sleeping in the same bed with his wife?" Certainly, to Blasio's eye, Carlotta was an attractive young woman with her only possible flaw the fact that she was nearsighted and when addressing someone narrowed her eyes to see him better. Blasio's first speculations were that the estrangement may have been created "because of reasons of state, because of the Emperor's infidelity or because of some organic defect in Maximilian." He was inclined to favor the theory that Maximilian had been caught in some moment of infidelity, which Carlotta could not forgive because she had "the pride of a beautiful woman."

As Blasio later observed, the emperor's blue eyes were likely to light up with the greatest enthusiasm, not over some infrequent political or military success, but at the sight of a beautiful young woman. And the evidence mounted that aside from his sad-eyed wife, Maximilian was neither a eunuch nor a monk. Blasio heard rumors of Casanova-like activity on the part of the emperor, but could find nothing to substantiate them. "Nevertheless," he noted, "it escaped no one's attention that he cast desirous eyes upon various beautiful women about the court, and when discreet mention was made of topics of gallantry the Empress would smile with a sadness that we all observed."

Blasio pursued the matter even after the collapse of Maximilian's empire. He and Maximilian's Viennese valet, Grill, were traveling to Mexico City in the rear guard of the republican army as it advanced on Mexico City when Blasio took the opportunity of questioning the valet about the reasons for the "separation of the beds." "Grill, who had been in close contact with the sovereigns since their residence at Miramar, said that there they had seemed to be still enamoured and were always together, but that afterward, during a trip to Vienna, something had happened which alienated them from each other. [Grill apparently referred to the unhappy "family reunion" of the spring of 1860.] From that time, although their mutual attitude before the world remained affectionate and loving, privately there was no such affection or confidence. . . . As I had imagined from the beginning, some infidelity of the Emperor had become known to the Empress. This having wounded her pride as a sovereign and a beautiful woman, she had decided to adopt the attitude toward her husband which I had observed all the time they were in Mexico, naturally without seeking to create a public scandal."

His curiosity still unsatisfied, Blasio pressed on his questioning of Grill as they trudged through the dust of the victorious Juarista army.

"I never observed the least sign of amorous adventure [on Maximilian's part]," Blasio said. "Did you?"

"You may have seen nothing," Grill replied, "but I saw a good deal. The Emperor's bedroom was visited many times by ladies of the court, who slipped in and out so mysteriously that only I saw them, and frequently without knowing who they were. How many of them—whom no one would believe capable of it—yielded to His Majesty's desires!"

Grill was adamant in refusing to name any of the ladies who lay their virtue at the emperor's feet, or at least on his canopied bed, but it was apparent to Blasio that there was a double meaning to the term "ladies-in-waiting."

"Such things," he remarked, "were easy enough in Mexico City, at the [National] palace, for any of the ladies to whom you refer; there were secret doors there, to let them in and out at night. But at Chapultepec and Cuernavaca [a later vacation residence of Maximilian and Carlotta]?"

Grill laughingly explained, "At Cuernavaca the guards were so stationed that they might not have seen a woman going in or coming out. Did you never observe in the garden wall a narrow door, scarcely wide enough to let one person through? It was always closed, but that door could tell you many curious things about the persons who used it. I can assure you, though, that a woman never entered the Emperor's rooms at Chapultepec."

There was a deeper and subtler tragedy to the reign of Maximilian and Carlotta seldom, if ever, touched upon in the various documentary, fictional and cinematic recapitulations of their joint career. Most chroniclers have accepted the romantic public image they projected, the affection they openly displayed: one of history's great love stories. Actually it was a love story with human flaws, that of a prince to whom casual infidelity was a princely privilege and a princess whose intense pride would not allow her to grant it. That monogamy had never been held in the highest esteem by the Hapsburgs, that their estrangement was part of the domestic history of the house—Archduchess Sophie voluntarily separated from her doltish husband by the distance between Vienna and Prague, Franz Josef from Empress Elizabeth during most of their married life—could hardly have been any consolation to Carlotta as she faced a year of mounting crisis.

9. The View from Abroad

It required the patience of Job to abide the slow and poky methods of our State Department . . . it was often very difficult to restrain officers and men from crossing the Rio Grande with hostile purposes.

—GENERAL PHILIP H. SHERIDAN

DURING the fall of 1865 Maximilian busied himself with an assortment of projects, none of which had any critical bearing on the preservation of his empire. He drew up elaborate plans for a Mexican imperial navy which would dominate the Caribbean; he and architects from the Academy of San Carlos spent hours laboring over plans for a monastery to be established in the Holy Land; he renewed his campaign to marry off one of his younger brothers to one of the daughters of Dom Pedro II of Brazil; he built a pleasure dome outside Mexico City to escape even farther from reality. And Carlotta, always in closer touch with reality, wrote of the "spontaneous generation" of guerrilla bands which had begun operating closer to Mexico City and the other population centers.

From capitals to the north and across the Atlantic, it appeared that Maximilian's empire, sooner or later, would be cut off like some night-blooming vine whose scent had become cloyingly obnoxious even in places where it had once been so hopefully nurtured.

Paris was hectic with gaiety and despair. In the closing phases of the Second Empire there was a fever flush on politics, society, literature, music, the theater, "all were racing with the outgoing tide of imperial glory." The wild rhythm and frenetic scoring of Jacques Offenbach's *The Orphans of the Storm,* the title of which was said to epitomize Napoleon III's ministers, provided the tempo. Newspapers sprang up overnight, until the kiosks were festooned with scores of them, each offering their centime's worth of distorted current history. The capital was awash in journalistic advice; almost hourly the press, in one journal or another, declared that each of Napoleon's ministers was a hero or a dastard, frivolous or deeply concerned, a savior of his country or a lunatic leading it to destruction.

Earlier in the year, on March 10, the Duc de Morny died with only his adoring valet at his side. The originator and prime mover of the Mexican intervention had been ill for several years and had submitted himself to the treatments of a Dr. Olliffe, a society quack whose "magic pearls"—arsenic and opiates—were supposed to work miracles. Morny died well doped, not long after his last scheme—buying Cuba from Spain for $3,000,000 and adding it to the Mexican empire—had fallen through.

The writer of his obituary in one of the Paris weeklies suggested that "Lucky" Morny was fortunate indeed to have died when he did.

Some of that sense of foreboding was conveyed in a speech by the eminent politician Jules Favre, who demanded, "Since Maximilian is established; since Maximilian is the Messiah announced in all time past; since he is really the man both for the Indians and the Spaniards, who receive him with acclamation; since he meets on his passage only with bouquets from the señoritas—let our soldiers return. What have they to do in Mexico?" Yet he voiced suspicions that France was not hearing the truth, cited rumors of widespread fighting in Mexico, of the shooting of prisoners of war, of a recent action in which French troops had destroyed the town of San Sebastián, in Sinaloa, as an example to those who resisted the army of occupation. "Why," he asked, "this discrepancy between the official statements as to the pacification of Mexico, the unanimous consent to Maximilian's elevation to the throne, and the facts; that is, the country under martial law, and the French army, marching, torch in hand, protecting one party and punishing the other by the wholesale destruction of life and property?"

It was a troubled autumn in Paris, with Prussia reportedly planning to upset the military balance in central Europe, with Washington becoming almost daily more exasperated with the presence of French troops in Mexico. There was alarm and outrage, more of the former than the latter, at the Tuileries when a note was received from the U.S. State Department which practically ordered the French expeditionary force out of Mexico. Unknown to Maximilian and Carlotta, Napoleon had been promising increased withdrawals to the Americans, but now they were digging a sharp elbow in his ribs.

"Our Government," wrote Secretary of State Seward to the U.S. minister in Paris, "is astonished and distressed at the announcement, now made for the first time, that the promised withdrawal of French troops from Mexico, which ought to have taken place in November (this month), has been put off by the Emperor. You will inform the Emperor's Government that the President desires and sincerely hopes that the evacuation of Mexico will be accomplished in conformity with the existing arrangement. Instructions will be sent to the military forces of the United States, which have been placed in a spot of observation, and are awaiting the special orders of the President; this will be done with the confidence that the telegraph or the courier will bring us intelligence of a satisfactory resolution on the part of the Emperor in reply to this note. You will assure the French Government that the United States, in wishing to free Mexico, have nothing so much at heart as preserving peace and friendship with France."

Napoleon rather weakly replied that he didn't have sufficient transports to speed the withdrawal. Meanwhile, the Paris press and politicians were charging Napoleon with the duty of standing firm against the importunate Yankees. Even the Liberal statesman Émile Ollivier implored Napoleon not to desert Maximilian or discredit French honor, to risk a revolution in France rather than withdraw Bazaine's expeditionary forces. And a Paris newspaper advised him: "The United States tracked French policy step by step; never before has the French Government been subjected to such dictatorship. During America's civil strife France spoke boldly to Ambassador Drayton—'Do you want peace or war?'—Today our foothold in Mexico is challenged by Washington and the Emperor Maximilian will fall because our Government allows its conduct to be dictated by American arrogance." On the other hand, Napoleon was warned by a spokesman of the Radicals that if he did not end "this wild dream of foreign empire that is no more than an additional burden on the French working-man," the emperor would have a revolution on his hands.

Napoleon by then was thoroughly disillusioned with the whole venture. "The Emperor Maximilian," he wrote Bazaine, "must understand that we cannot stay in Mexico forever. . . . He ought to realize that a Government that has done nothing to enable it to live on its own resources will be more easily abandoned than supported through thick and thin." But he revealed little or nothing of this attitude in his letters to Maximilian. When the French pullout came, Napoleon wanted it done without any outcries from Mexico City.

In Vienna, the mood was even more somber. Austrian relations with Prussia had taken a turn for the worse, and war was only a matter of months in the offing. Franz Josef necessarily was more concerned with the security of his own borders than with the health of his brother's Mexican enterprise. Furthermore, he was still irked with Maximilian for trying to evade the terms of the Family Pact and for maneuvering to secure his own succession to the throne. From Vienna to Mexico City, henceforth, there would go no more troops, no more gulden from the imperial treasury, but only what sympathy Franz Josef could spare for his brother's plight.

Brussels was on the verge of national mourning, not only for its youth dying in Mexico, but for King Leopold I. He had always suffered from a defective gallbladder, but now his forty-year reign was coming to an end. In November 12, shortly before his death, he had sent a last exhortation to his son-in-law: "Success is the only thing that counts in America. Everything else is poetic twaddle and a waste of money. God bless you, my boy, for I am unable to write more—"

Both his sons, the Duke of Brabant and the Count of Flanders, were opposed to supporting the Mexican venture. His heir, the Duke of Brabant, who became Leopold II on December 10, had inherited all of his father's acquisitive traits, raised to a geometric degree, and he could see no profit for himself in keeping his sister on the Mexican throne.

One of his first moves, after the death of his father, was to padlock all the recruiting offices in Belgium which had forwarded the sturdy Flemish and Walloons to the Belgian Legion in Mexico. Hereafter Belgium would devote itself to exploiting the rubber plantations of the Congo, where the natives were less capable of resistance.

In Washington a young Mexican competed with victorious Union generals for public favor and attention. He was Matías Romero, envoy extraordinary and minister plenipotentiary of the Juárez rebel government, which of course did not regard itself as rebellious but a legitimate entity which happened to have been driven from its capital by foreign troops. Romero, at thirty-two, was a remarkable young man who had won the confidence of many of the Union's leading citizens, including Presidents Lincoln and Johnson and General Ulysses S. Grant. He had also vigorously spread propaganda on behalf of his cause all during the Civil War and made certain that once the Confederacy was beaten, Washington would turn its attention to the Mexican intervention. The importance of influencing American public opinion had also belatedly been grasped by Maximilian, who sent an agent to New York and tried to buy James Gordon Bennett's *Herald,* which had been fairly sympathetic to his cause; his most trusted emissary, Count Ollivier Ressequier, had also been dispatched to New York to interest capitalists in promoting a joint venture for steamship and railway lines between Mexico and the United States.

But none of Maximilian's representatives could really compete with Matías Romero, because American sympathy was all on the side of the Juaristas. The rudimentary Eastern Establishment was entirely on his side. That was testified to by the guest list at a banquet given in his honor at Delmonico's in New York City. Among those who joined him over oysters, truffles, plovers, snipe, canvasback duck and various roasted meats, sluiced down by vintage wines, were James Beekman, the toastmaster, who was vice-president of the Union League Club; William Cullen Bryant, the editor of the New York *Post*; William Aspinwall, founder of the Pacific Steamship Company and one of the builders of the Panama Railway; John Jacob Astor; the eminent historian George Bancroft; and Charles King, the president of Columbia College.

Toasts were proposed to Juárez, "a man of the Indian race, striving to see his country free," which hypocritically ignored the struggle of the American Indian against a far more devastating juggernaut than the French army of occupation. William E. Dodge, Jr., announced that he was present as a spokesman for young America—evidently self-appointed—and "I assure our guest of honor that the French invasion of this continent is to youth a direct insult. . . . There will not be a city, nor a town, nor a village which will not immediately arm a company of soldiers to fly to the aid of our sister Republic, now making so glorious a fight." It could hardly have escaped Romero that Americans had recently been all too eager to fly at the throat of the Mexican republic, nor can he have been unaware of the fact that Juárez was determined not to exchange the French expeditionary force for an American one, which would have been even more difficult to dislodge.

All that, of course, was vinous rhetoric. Romero listened politely, but it was President Lincoln's attitude that concerned him. Lincoln, who had never been the favorite of the Eastern club men or such semi-imperialistic interests as those which built the railroad across Panama, temporized on the Mexican situation because the Union was fully occupied with subduing the Confederacy; anyway he believed that the Mexicans themselves would unseat their imported monarch. His definitive statement on the intervention came on March 3, 1862, in a note delivered to Napoleon by his ambassador in Paris. In Lincoln's opinion, "No monarchical government which could be founded in Mexico, in the presence of foreign navies and armies in the waters and upon the soil of Mexico, would have any prospect of security or permanence. Secondly, that the instability of such a monarchy there would be enhanced if the throne should be assigned to any person not of Mexican nativity. That under such circumstances the new government must speedily fall, unless it could draw into its support European alliances, which, relating back to the first invasion would in fact make it the beginning of a permanent policy of armed European monarchical intervention, injurious and practically hostile to the most general system of government on the continent of America, and this would be the beginning rather than the ending of revolution in Mexico. . . ."

He also warned that it was improbable that "European nations could steadily agree upon a policy favorable to such a counter revolution."

In one of his last speeches he indicated, however, that he was opposed to the use of armed force in encouraging the French army to leave Mexico, when he said: "I do not know what the nation wants. All I know is that there will be no more wars under my presidency."

Both his successor and the Union generals were more pliable. President Johnson was being persuaded that it might be necessary to use military force to get the French out of Mexico. Elsewhere, too, the pressure was building for an American intervention below the Rio Grande. In New York there was an organization called the Mexican Patriots Club, and in New Orleans the Defenders of the Monroe Doctrine was sending men and arms to the Juarista forces. That a large number of ex-Confederates had recently crossed the border, prepared to take up arms on behalf of Maximilian, only increased the pressure.

Romero's greatest influence, however, was exerted on General in Chief Grant, who regarded Romero as one of his closest personal friends. Grant had been a Mexicanophile ever since participating in the American invasion of Mexico in 1846-47; he fell in love with the country he was helping conquer as a young lieutenant and ever since had felt guilty about that war. Partly in expiation, partly out of his friendship with Romero, and partly out of hatred for the whole idea of Napoleonism being planted on the American continent, he was determined to expel the French forces. Despite his enormous prestige, he had to move cautiously, because Secretary of State Seward was opposed to any active employment of federal troops.

The most aggressive general in the Union Army, Philip H. Sheridan, was given the border command and deployed his cavalry corps, plus two infantry corps, at strategic points in Texas. As Marshal Bazaine and the French War Ministry could see at a glance over their maps, his divisions were positioned for invasion the moment word was telegraphed from Washington. Two confidential letters from Grant to Sheridan, as Grant's son later told General Grenville M. Dodge, clearly indicated Grant's intention of getting around the State Department's policy of hands-off-Mexico-for-the-time-being. Grant suggested that the Union arsenals could spare about 40,000 rifles and six batteries of field artillery, and the general in chief wouldn't be at all upset if they found their way into Juarista hands.

During the fall of 1866 Sheridan conducted psychological warfare along the Rio Grande by constantly shifting his forces from one point to another as though getting ready for an offensive across the border. He openly conferred with officials of the Juárez government and once rode to Fort Duncan to make ostentatious inquiries about the best military roads across the border. Tension was further increased when he ordered a pontoon train sent to Brownsville, Texas.

General Sheridan was also quick to report to Washington that the steamer *San Antonio,* flying a French flag, fired shots into an American artillery camp near Brownsville on November 15, 1865, and a short time later drew up a brief for the War Department on "Franco-Mexican violations of neutrality," in which he charged that Maximilian had supplied the Confederate Army with arms, munitions and other supplies, that the imperial forces often fired at American troops across the Rio Grande and that the Confederate General Edmund Kirby Smith had crossed into Mexico with forty wagons loaded with military equipment. Sheridan's letterbooks and dispatch files for 1865-66 were filled with messages from his intelligence agents detailing the movement of French troops and reporting minutely on the Confederate colony established at Córdoba, 60 miles west of Veracruz.

He was hot for action and later wrote in his memoirs that "It required the patience of Job to abide the slow and poky methods of our State Department, and, in truth, it was often very difficult to restrain officers and men from crossing the Rio Grande with hostile purposes." Yet one filibustering attempt turned out disastrously. He authorized the issuance of arms to a band of fifty men who slipped across the border to join the Juarista forces. They were attacked by what was described as a force of former Confederates and Mexican "renegades," and half of them were killed. That ended "all open participation of American sympathizers with the Liberal cause," Sheridan reported, but "the moral support offered by the presence of our forces continued."

Certainly his aggressive attitude worried the French generals in Paris, as well as those commanding the army of occupation. Marshal Marie Edmé Patrice de MacMahon, studying the situation from Paris, delivered the opinion that "it might be worth a fight" if Bazaine were confronted by an army commanded by General Grant, but not the bullet-headed General Sheridan.

During the fall of 1865, Minister Romero in Washington could pride himself on having performed as effectively on behalf of Benito Juárez as those more aristocratic expatriates had in encouraging the intervention. He played skillfully on the resentment in the North against those Confederates who had joined Maximilian and forwarded to the State Department the copy of an interview with one of the lesser Confederate paladins, General Isham Harris, who boasted that "I have selected 640 acres about ten miles from here [Córdoba] where I propose to surround myself with coffee plantations, in the midst of which I will nestle down, constantly inhaling the odors of the rich tropical fruits, and gaudy-colored and fragrant tropical flowers. . . ."

Romero saw to it that the interview was widely republished, arousing considerable resentment in the North that a whipped Rebel could make such an easy transition from cotton to coffee and escape the consequences of defeat. All this encouraged subscriptions to a loan being floated for Juárez by the Mexican Patriots Club in New York, security for which was to be the state of Baja California.

Even those Americans who had a certain sympathy for Maximilian and Carlotta as hapless, pretty little puppets agreed that the Mexican empire could not long endure against the weight of American opposition.

10. "Every Drop of My Blood Is Mexican"

> *No power on earth shall turn me aside from the accomplishment of my task; henceforth every drop of my blood is Mexican . . . you shall see me fight side by side with you for your independence and integrity.*
>
> —Proclamation by Maximilian

Even for Maximilian, and especially for Carlotta, the autumn of 1865 was filled with ominous portents. They had begun to realize that though their agreement with Napoleon had provided for a 30,000-man French army to stay in Mexico until the end of 1867, that support might be withdrawn at any time. In the meantime there had been little progress in recruiting, arming and training a native force to replace it. Worse yet, the guerrillas were swarming in greater numbers and force and on occasion managed to cut the road to Veracruz—the lifeline of the empire.

The problem of the guerrillas and the impossibility of combating them had become an obsession with Carlotta, as they would other rulers in later and equally vexatious times. After studying reports of their activities, probably with greater diligence than Maximilian, she wrote Eugénie: "Your Majesty must consider that no one can foresee whence guerilla bands

Photo by Korty, Vienna

The Hapsburgs. Standing (left to right): Emperor Franz Josef, Archduke Maximilian, Archduchess Charlotte (Carlotta), Archduke Ludwig Victor and Archduke Karl Ludwig. Seated (left to right): Empress Elizabeth with Crown prince Rudolf, Archduchess Gisela, Dowager Duchess Sophie and Archduke Franz Karl.

Maximilian I, Emperor
of Mexico.

Alpenland-Austrian National Library

Carlotta, Empress of
Mexico.

Alpenland-Austrian National Library

Napoleon III. From a painting by Winterhalter.

Benito Juárez. Engraving from a painting by Chappel.

Maximilian receiving a deputation in the throne room of Miramar as he is offered the Mexican crown.

Maximilian and Carlotta (foreground) as they prepare to embark for Mexico.

Maximilian and Carlotta landing in Mexico.

The staged reception for the royal couple after their arrival in Mexico City.

Maximilian, with Generals Mejía and Miramón, at prayer in his cell before his execution.

Maximilian's execution, June 19, 1867.

A rare candid photo of Carlotta, accompanied by her lady-in-waiting and the commander of her castle-retreat at Bouchout in Belgium, made in 1882. Carlotta lived on until 1927.

may spring up. Theirs is a kind of spontaneous generation. As I understand the matter, a man leaves his village with a horse, a weapon and a firm determination to acquire riches by any means except work. He has plenty of audacity and a certain disregard for his own safety. If he gets shot it won't matter, for life is dull anyway and the only thing he cares about is lucrative adventure. Such a fellow as this has little trouble recruiting others of the same kidney. (We have here a shifting population with just the right propensities.)

"They plunder the first hacienda they come to; this achievement constitutes their baptism into the bandit profession. Newspapers make the most of it and lend importance to the band by reporting all its escapades in a given region. The robbers grow bolder and next hold up a stagecoach, carrying off a few rich people who can be held for ransom, and retreating over unknown trails across the sierras into some remote district. Here another band, and sometimes a third, can be found in hiding. Likely as not they all merge, swelling in number from a handful to several thousand."

Carlotta's analysis of the guerrilla problem as one of law and order, attributing it solely to criminal instincts, failed to account for many guerrillas who took to the high chaparral out of political or ideological motivation. There were those who took arms because they hated the idea of a foreigner sitting on a throne fabricated by other foreigners. Yet she was probably right about loot causing much of that "spontaneous generation." Almost half a century later the American novelist Jack London, a Socialist, who was covering a subsequent revolution, wrote that the guerrillas he observed had nothing in mind but plunder. "What peon with any spunk in him," London remarked, in words oddly echoing Carlotta's, "would elect to slave on a hacienda for a slave's reward when, in the ranks of Zapata, Carranza or Villa, he can travel, see the country, ride a horse, carry a rifle, get a peso or so a day, loot when fortune favors, and, if lucky, on occasions kill a fellow creature—this last a particularly delightful event to a people who delight in the bloody spectacles of the bull ring."

Marshal Bazaine and his field commanders, of course, saw the guerrillas as a technical problem, one of a type they had solved in North Africa and elsewhere. But Mexico, it seemed, was different. Elsewhere they had isolated the guerrillas by punishing the people who helped or sheltered them. Here they swarmed in such numbers that no punishment could be devised to fit the crime. Anywhere outside artillery range of a French garrison was guerrilla country.

Bazaine and his officers, with 28,000 troops scattered throughout a subcontinent, never began to cope with the problem, perhaps because they regarded their duty in Mexico as soon to be terminated. They never established a Mexican counterpart of the Arab Bureau, which had combined the functions of civil administration and intelligence gathering. Perhaps that was because the Mexicans refused to be administered, except at gunpoint, and any who passed information to the French were likely to be killed as renegades. Nor did the French command devise any tactics to counter those of the guerrillas. Time after time French detachments were lured into ambushes. Heavily armed columns would march out in pursuit of rebel bands and never hear a shot fired. They were attacked only at their weakest points. It was maddening the way the Mexicans refused to accept battle unless the French were greatly inferior in strength. One town was occupied and evacuated fourteen times before Bazaine, in his headquarters at San Luis Potosí, gave up the place in despair.

His only solution, by early autumn, 1865, was to abandon many of his outposts and smaller garrisons and occupy only the larger towns. There were fewer of the razzias which could be turned into disastrous ambushes. The French army had assumed a defensive posture.

Among the Foreign Legion units stationed in northern Mexico, life had been so pleasant for a time that many legionnaires told their comrades they would take their discharges there and settle down to become Mexican citizens. Now all that had changed. There were a number of desertions, particularly from the units posted close to the American border, though most of those who deserted were either captured by Juaristas, guerrillas or nomadic Indians or simply perished in the desert. And even if they managed to escape across the Rio Grande, there was always the legendary "long arm" of the legion itself. Long afterward the cautionary tale was told in the legion of a young Swiss who deserted in 1865, was captured by Indians but escaped from them, and reached an American settlement. He married an American girl, settled down and raised a family, and became the vice-president of a railroad. In 1889 he took his family abroad to visit the Paris Exposition. Just as they were standing under the Ferris wheel, someone tapped him on the shoulder and accusingly snapped, *"Legionnaire!"* It was his former company commander, who shouted for the gendarmes. He was arrested, sent to Algiers in irons as a member of a legion penal battalion. His family, despite the attempts of the American embassy in Paris to obtain his freedom, never saw him again.

With the tactical situation seemingly deteriorating day by day in the autumn of 1865, Marshal Bazaine decided to adopt the final desperate remedy, to kill those who could not be persuaded. If the Yankees were threatening invasion from the north, it was essential that his own rear areas be cleared of the internal opposition. Bazaine believed there was some legality behind his proposed measures. Juárez, by his lights, was a traitor because he or his subordinates had conspired with the Americans. Furthermore, the rebels had often shot prisoners of war. It was a nasty business, and the time had come to formalize it.

Now his problem was persuading Maximilian to sign the necessary decree, to shake the Austrian princeling out of his liberal-humanitarian attitude, his dreams of winning the people's devotion through benevolence and good works, and make him realize that his empire could be ruled only by force. In the most forceful manner, Bazaine argued before Maximilian and his advisers that "misplaced clemency"—Maximilian had often pardoned those found guilty by French courts-martial—could no longer be afforded. He cited a rumor, quite unfounded, that Juárez had fled to the United States, that therefore those who took arms against the imperial government were not "rebels" but "bandits." The only way the country could be saved from such widespread "banditry" was to allow the French army to condemn those guerrillas it managed to capture.

Maximilian swallowed the military argument, no doubt with anguish. It meant awakening from his dream of being the just and beloved ruler. It revealed that his regime was built on foreign military force, a fact which Maximilian liked to conceal from himself.

Later his defenders would maintain that what the Mexican people called the Black Decree was issued without his agreement, but this apparently was untrue. Bazaine's orderly officer, the Count Émile de Kératry, later claimed that Maximilian himself drew up the proclamation; this also was untrue. On the fairly objective testimony of Maximilian's secretary, José Luis Blasio, "the draft was written by one of the employes of the Ministry of War, on a large sheet of official paper, which was doubled in the middle. On the right was the original draft and on the left were the changes, and on loose sheets some additions, made with a red pencil. The only writing of the Emperor which it bore consisted of the initial 'M,' which he was accustomed to inscribe with a half-flourish on the drafts of all documents submitted for his approval." In denying Bazaine's aide's claim that the Black Decree had been promulgated by Maximilian, Blasio added, "As a matter of fact, Bazaine was summoned to the palace on October 2. When the Emperor read the decree, Bazaine limited himself to asking that the death penalty be applied also to the *haciendados* [large landholders] who were in complicity with the Liberals. This provision comprised Article 10 of the unfortunate decree."

On that day, October 2, 1865, the imperial government issued a manifesto which would serve as a preamble to the Black Decree published the following day. It read:

"Mexicans! The cause which Don Benito Juárez upheld with such constancy and valor has succumbed both to the national will and to those very laws invoked by the rebel chieftain in support of his titles. Today even the banner under which that cause degenerated has been abandoned by its leader who has left the fatherland.*

"The National Government has long shown indulgence and clemency to those recreants who ignored the true facts as well as their chance to join the majority of the Nation in a return to duty. Even so the Government has achieved its purpose; honest men have rallied to our flag and accepted the just and liberal principles of our policy. Disorder is maintained by only a few brigands misled by unpatriotic passions and supported by a de-

---

* This referred to the rumor that Juárez had fled to the United States, which either had been concocted by the French military or was based on false information or possibly false hopes.

moralized rabble, as well as that unbridled soldiery constituting the sad dregs in all civil strife.

"From now on the struggle will continue merely between the honest men of the Nation and those hordes of criminals and bandits. Indulgence must cease, lest it encourage the desperadoes who burn villages, rob and murder peace-loving citizens, persecute the aged, and violate defenseless women.

"The Government, strong in its power, will henceforth show itself inflexible in punishment, for such are the demands made by the precepts of civilization, for the rights of humanity, and every moral canon."

Even the most ignorant peon in the remotest Indian settlement could sense the hollowness of the manifesto; weak governments, not those "strong in power," are "inflexible," and the "rights of humanity" would hardly be affirmed by the Black Decree.

That decree was published the following day, October 3, in the official newspaper, *Diario del Imperio,* beginning: "We, Maximilian, Emperor of Mexico, by the advice of our Ministerial Council and our Council of State, do decree that: I. All persons who are members of armed bands or societies not authorized by law, whether or not of a political nature, and regardless of size, character or denomination of the groups in question, shall be tried by a military court and, if found guilty of merely such membership, shall be condemned to capital punishment and executed within twenty-four hours after passing of sentence."

Heavy fines and imprisonment were prescribed for those who "spread orally or in writing any false or alarming news calculated to disturb the order or who give the hostile bands advice, news or counsel, or voluntarily sell them or procure for them arms, horses, ammunition or provisions," and also for those who "do not give notice of the passage of an armed force in their locality, and those who do not resist bands of guerillas." Thus a whole town or village could be punished simply for not defending itself—how was not explained—from either the Juarista regular forces or the guerrillas.

Article 9 provided that "All male citizens between the ages of eighteen and fifty-five, free from physical disability, are expected to come to the defense of any town threatened by hostile bands; anyone refusing to obey when called to arms shall be punished by a fine of from five to two hundred pesos, or fifteen days to four months of imprisonment. If the authorities deem it necessary to punish an entire community for not having defended itself, a fine ranging from two hundred to two thousand pesos may be imposed, to be paid jointly by all who being aware of this decree disregarded it." As for that old established cottage industry of the backcountry—kidnapping and holding travelers for ransom—it would be punished by death. Amnesty was promised, however, to "all who have belonged or still belong to armed guerilla bands but prefer surrender to the imperial cause."

The decree was published over the signatures of José Vicente Ramírez, Minister of Foreign Affairs; Juan de Dios Pera, Minister of War; Luis Robles Pezuela, Minister of Improvement; Pedro Escudero, Minister of Justice; José María Esteva, Minister of the Interior; Manuel Siliceo, Minister of Education; and Francisco de Paul César, Secretary of the Treasury. Maximilian's signature was not included, but he was regarded as its author. It was the death warrant for uncounted Mexicans—and finally for Maximilian himself.

Almost before the ink was dry on that document it persuaded thousands of Mexicans, who had been indifferent to the regime or had gone along with it with a semblance of fealty, that the time had arrived to rid the country of foreign domination. Mexico, except for the very thin overlay of the aristocracy and the largest of the landowners, was outraged. Nothing could have been designed more effectively to unite the country against the crown. Like most mail-fisted military solutions imposed on civil affairs it did more harm to its promoters than its intended objects. Romero, the Juarista envoy in Washington, could hardly restrain his glee in calling Secretary of State Seward's attention to the decree and noting that Maximilian "condemns to death every man who is not a French soldier, or a traitor."

And the French command proceeded with bullheaded determination to demonstrate that it meant every word and comma of the Black Decree. In a surprise attack, French troops captured two republican generals, Arteaga and Salazar, seven colonels, eight majors, five lieutenants and a number of noncommissioned men. The whole batch of captives was run through a court-martial and sentenced to die before firing squads the next dawn.

That evening General Salazar wrote a letter to his mother on a scrap of paper: "It is seven o'clock at night and General Arteaga, Colonel Villagomez and other chiefs and I have just been condemned to death. I go down to the grave at the age of thirty-three, without a blot on my military career or my name. Do not weep, have courage; for the crime of your son is that he has defended the sacred cause of the independence of his country.

"For this I am going to be shot.

"I leave no money. I have been able to save nothing. But God will aid you and my children who will be proud to bear my name. Bring them and my brothers up in the path of honor. The scaffold does not stain the name of a patriot.

"Goodbye, dear mother. Bless my tomb. Embrace my Uncle Luis for me, and give many kisses to Tecla, Lupe, Isabel, Camelita, Cholita and Manuelito. I bid them all farewell from the depths of my heart.

"I leave to Manuel my silver watch and my four suits. . . . For yourself, receive the last farewell of your obedient son who loves you greatly."

Copies of General Salazar's farewell to his family were run off on clandestine printing presses and secretly but widely circulated. They did almost as much damage to the imperialist cause as the Black Decree itself, striking a chord in all but the most sclerotic aristocratic Mexican hearts. Even Maximilian, in his isolation, sensed the mass reaction, and instead of making a long-planned goodwill tour of the southern state sent Carlotta in his place. But Maximilian still had his illusions, as his secretary, Blasio, would recall. "Maximilian was ingenuously convinced that the decree would result in attracting Riva Palacios and many other leaders like him, who were the honor and glory of the Liberal cause. . . ."

General Vicente Riva Palacios was perhaps the most attractive and chivalrous of all the republican generals—the sort of man Maximilian could identify himself with. Palacios had exchanged almost 400 prisoners, including many Belgians, rather than see them killed in reprisal for the Black Decree. The young American girl Sara Yorke later characterized him as "a patriot and a gentleman . . . with some reputation as a poet and a dramatic author. At the outbreak of the war he organized and equipped a regiment at his own expense and was with General Zaragoza at Puebla. His division was one of the finest in the Mexican service and he conducted his campaigns in strict accordance with recognized usages. He cared for the wounded, exchanged prisoners and, at the last, even went to the length of extending his protection to small detachments of French troops making their way to the Gulf Coast from the shores of the Pacific."

If only a man like General Palacios could see how much they had in common! It had begun to occur to Maximilian that many of his professed enemies were preferable to his professed friends—Hidalgo, for instance, writing him an appeal *from Paris* for a title, for an allowance that would permit him to bank his salary in exchange for "twenty years of work for the fatherland."

Another illusion persisted: the extension of his empire to Central America. When Carlotta and her suite departed on the tour of Yucatán, Maximilian gave her a secret "letter of instructions" which indicated that he still clung to his visions of expanding power and increasing glory. Yucatán was the "center of gravity" for the Central American empire. "Our true orientation," Maximilian stated somewhat grandiosely, "consists in regarding the Empire as the central power in the new continent, while conceding the dominion of the north to the United States, and that of the south to the Brazilian Empire."

A gracious and approving smile fixed on her pale features, Carlotta dutifully toured Yucatán for two weeks and visited Uxmal and other vanished glories of the Aztecs. She returned in a weary, bitterly disillusioned mood, all but convinced that Mexico in its present state was ungovernable.

"Unquestionably this country has a character all its own," she wrote the Empress Eugénie, whom she still regarded as a friend to whom she could express herself candidly. "The talkative Gutiérrez was quite right about that too, except that he approved, and we don't. We fail to see anything of real worth and are determined to bring about a change. The broad

masses here are outrageously dull and ignorant, a state which
the intelligentsia will certainly do nothing to correct. This ex-
plains how the clergy could get its stranglehold over the common people; no one has bothered to educate the poor, they are
left in their stupor, and because they are left in it the Church
has gained control.

"I am prompted to remark, at this point, that Your Majesty
has surely read Marie Antoinette's charming letters edited by
that Monsignor d'Hunolstein? The implication is of course
that everything will some day come to light, whether one becomes famous or not. You never can tell what will happen, and
when uncharitable judgments (such as these) find expression it
is not at all desirable—Your Majesty must know what I am
driving at. In order to make quite certain that the Mexicans
will not discover what I am saying about them, at least not
until a new nation is formed which will agree with me, I urge
upon Your Majesty to destroy all my letters. They are, after all,
just conversations; once the ideas are voiced, my purpose has
been accomplished. . . ."

The native Mexicans being what they were, in Carlotta's
opinion, she may have contemplated several hundred new immigrants from the north with greater favor. They were the ex-
Confederates, many of whom had trekked from lost battlefields
through Texas and across the Rio Grande to offer their services
to the new Mexican empire without reflecting they might be
fighting for another lost cause. What was called the Carlotta
Colony was established for them, and for a time they graced the
salons of the capital. Sara Yorke's mother was a Southerner and
threw her drawing room open to them. "Truly a heterogeneous
set," as the girl remembered her mother's salon, "Confederate
officers, members of the diplomatic corps, newly fledged chamberlains and officials of the palace, and the Marshal's officers—
Frenchmen, Austrians, Belgians and a few Mexicans, each
group bringing its own interests, and, alas, its own animosi-
ties."

A Southern-born archeologist named William M. Anderson
scouted the possibilities of settling his compatriots on Mexican
soil. Arriving in Veracruz shortly after the Confederate surren-

der at Appomattox, he was commissioned by Maximilian to survey the possibilities of locating such a colony in the northern state of Coahuila.

Weeks of traveling over the northern barrens convinced him that the colony should be located farther south in the state of Veracruz, where the soil was richer and the climate more favorable. Even so, he was pessimistic about its prospects. There was a social and cultural gap begween North Americans and Mexicans it would be difficult to bridge: the "difference between Catholic conviction and Protestant impression."

To point up that difference, both religious and philosophical, he cited a graphic example. "For several mornings I had seen lying on the cold, hard pavement of the church a barelegged, shoeless supplicant kneeling before the statue of St. Anthony of Padua. She begs, she implores him to give vigor and vitality to her sick infant. She says, 'You see how he suffers, why don't you cure him? Why don't you go to God and ask him to help me?' She knows that God is everywhere. She knows that God is there on the altar." The contrast between Indian fatalism, their submission to the "Grand court & council of General Mañana," and North American pragmatism would lead to misunderstanding, he believed, but he enthused over the "long rains, rich soil and warm sun" around Córdoba as an ideal place for Confederates to settle.

In his inital enthusiasm for the project of Confederate immigration, Maximilian appointed Matthew Maury, the great hydrographer whose charts he had admired as an officer in the Austrian navy, as his commissioner of immigration. Maury, who had represented the Confederacy abroad and was excluded from the first amnesty granted by the Union, came to Mexico with high hopes that dissident Southerners might find a home there. "From such a wreck," he wrote, "Mexico may gather and transfer to her own borders the very intelligence, skill and labor which made the South what she was in her palmy days—except her bondage." A daydreamer to match Maximilian, he even believed that emancipated blacks would be willing to accompany their former masters to the New Eden in Mexico.

That possibility also attracted such Confederate generals as "Fighting Joe" Shelby, a picturesque hothead who often composed his reports to headquarters in verse, John Bankhead

Magruder, Sterling Price and Alexander W. Terrell. Shelby brought the remnants of his cavalry brigade with him and proposed to hurl them into the fray against the Juaristas. In an audience with Maximilian and Marshal Bazaine he suggested raising a force of 40,000 former Confederate soldiers, whom he was confident would migrate to Mexico. This proposal was gently shunted aside, however, as Maximilian believed it would only worsen relations with the United States.

His plan called for the fire-eaters to settle down around the dusty little town of Córdoba on the road from Veracruz to Mexico City. There Maximilian, "in consideration of the sparseness of the population . . . desiring to give immigrants all possible security for property and liberty," proclaimed in a decree that the Southerners should settle on lands which had been confiscated (under Juárez's Reform Laws) from the church. Neither the Juaristas nor the church, of course, were pleased by granting land both claimed to the ex-Confederates.

Soon those Americans who did not succumb to homesickness and return to the States settled down on their sections of land, 640 acres each, to revive the plantation way of life and raise coffee, sugar, tropical fruits, even cotton in the rich soil and favorable climate of the country above the coastal swamps. They laid out a town which was to be called Carlotta City, with mango trees shading the central square. Generals Simon Buckner, Richard S. Ewell and Isham Harris came down to join the colonizers, but General Robert E. Lee turned down a similar invitation from Matthew Maury, saying he preferred to work for the rehabilitation of the beaten South.

North American journalists began visiting the Carlotta Colony and viewing its progress with a skeptical and unfriendly attitude. One of them described his journey from the nearest railroad station, Paso del Macho, in a wagon driven by a Confederate veteran with a wooden leg. They came to a settlement of tents and unfinished houses lying alongside a tree-shaded brook. His guide explained to the reporter that this was General Price's settlement. The account continued:

" 'And pray,' [the reporter asked], 'what is the name of this rival of Richmond and New Orleans?'

" 'The name of this city,' he said gravely, 'is Carlotta, a compliment to the Empress, whom we all love and admire and for whom we are ready at any moment to shed what remains of Confederate blood in this and the other country.'

"The wagon then stopped before a low, straw-roofed cottage.

" 'Here is General Price's house,' said the driver, 'but as it is not yet finished he lives still under his tent which he has pitched under the orange grove yonder.' "

General Price welcomed the journalist under the misapprehension that he was a prospective colonist. "Ah, my dear fellow, I am glad to see you. Are you coming here to settle and be one of us? . . . Well I am sorry to hear you refuse, on my own account as well as yours. I do not believe that a man of mature years like yourself can do better than settle down in the midst of this magnificent country and turn farmer. I have been here four or five months and all I have seen or heard goes to convince me that this is really the land of promises. Where will you find a richer soil or a healthier climate?"

Convinced that Maximilian's regime would survive external and internal threats, that the Mexican people would accept them in any case, the Confederate veterans worked hard to make something of their project. Within a year, one ex-officer had learned enough Spanish to establish a law office in Córdoba; an ex-governor of Louisiana had established an English-language newspaper in Mexico City; one general had gone into business as a photographer, another as the operator of a sawmill; and General Price was boasting that he could raise better tobacco than the Cubans.

In the capital, however, interest dwindled in the scheme to import large numbers of dissident Southerners to offset what the imperialists regarded as the sloth and ignorance of the native population. Instead of recruiting more Americans for the colony at Córdoba, Matthew Maury was assigned by Maximilian to make a report on the state of public opinion—that old anxiety of the emperor's. In two secret reports made to Maximilian in October and November, 1865, Maury bluntly stated that the Mexicans were becoming totally outraged by the maladministration of the government. Maximilian's ministers were ruining everything with their greed; the clergy was stirring up hatred of the throne and its occupants and proclaiming as martyrs anyone sentenced to death by the French courts-martial. Public security was nonexistent; the postal service was a bad joke.

The only way Maximilian could win respect for himself and his regime, Maury concluded, was to transform himself into a stern martial figure, wear a military uniform at all times, surround himself with "a brilliant general staff," and display the utmost force and energy in putting down the *insurrectos* and building a strong central government.

Maximilian did not resent Maury's candor. Neither could he summon the reserves of inner strength and determination to accept Maury's advice and turn himself into a soldier king.

He was an escapist, and besides, he lacked the capacity to concentrate on anything for long, even his own survival. He was easily bored by affairs of state, quickly disgusted by the venality, corruption and opportunism which surrounded him in the offices at the National Palace and pursued him to Chapultepec with its constant jostling for social position and imperial favor. The French were robbing the country blind, the Mexican upper class was lining its pockets with the leavings, the clergy were conspiring against him without considering that they would suffer much greater penalties under the Juarista alternative, the bureaucracy produced blizzards of official documents but could not keep the civil life of the country running with any degree of efficiency, and his courtiers gossiped endlessly, stuffed themselves at his table, and conducted their intrigues in his corridors.

But Maximilian, knowing how things were, could only shrug, a true son of Biedermeier Vienna, where conditions were always critical but never serious.

And he could escape from the capital to Cuernavaca and busy himself with his true vocation. The builder of Miramar, the renovator of Chapultepec had found himself a new project. Early in the autumn he had visited Cuernavaca, and had fallen in love with the place. "Picture to yourself a broad level valley," he wrote a Viennese friend, "blessed by Heaven, stretching out before one like a golden bowl, surrounded by a variety of mountain ranges rising one beyond the other in the boldest outlines and bathed in the most glorious shades, ranging from the purest rose-red, purple and violet to the deep-

est azure, some jagged and confused, like the legendary coasts of
Sicily, others soaring upwards and thickly wooded like the
green mountains of Switzerland; beyond them the enormous
volcanoes with their snow-clad crests towering up like giants
towards the deep-blue heavens. Imagine this golden bowl filled
at all seasons—or rather all the year around, for there are no
seasons here—with a wealth of tropical vegetation, with its intoxicating fragrance and sweet fruits, and, added to all this, a
climate as lovely as the Italian May, and handsome, friendly,
loyal natives."

He had journeyed south from the capital with an escort of
Austrian hussars on that occasion and been given a warm reception by the townspeople. On the spot he decided that this
would be the ideal place to rusticate, to revive from the despair
and fatalistic lassitude of his capital. Carlotta had grown much
thinner, was pale, and looked ill with anxiety; she had lost so
much weight since midsummer that her collarbones showed,
and she no longer wore gowns with any degree of décolletage.
In Cuernavaca they could isolate themselves from everything
they had learned to detest about the capital and live quietly
with their adopted son, Prince Agustín, and a few dozen servants.

One of the townspeople showed him a run-down, long-
abandoned estate called the Gardens of Borda; a mansion surrounded by formal gardens landscaped in the Italian style with
arcaded walks, terraces, fountains and pergolas. It had been
built in 1716 by a Frenchman named Josèph le Borde, who had
made a vast fortune in Mexican mining. Though it had fallen
into disrepair, Maximilian with his architect's eye saw that it
could be renovated in short order. A corps of artisans was summoned to make the place habitable within days. The gardens
were cleared, the pools drained, new furniture installed and tapestries hung.

Not content with that whirlwind job of renovation, he
bought a site at Acapatzingo, just outside Cuernavaca, and
proceeded to build a small villa in the Pompeian style for Carlotta's use. It did not occur to him that the style was inappro-
priate for an emperor whose throne was being steadily undermined.

Soon Maximilian and Carlotta, with Prince Agustín and part

of the servant corps from Chapultepec, were spending about half their time in Cuernavaca. As Carlotta wrote Eugénie, her husband loved his country retreat "because he can work here at his ease." His working conditions, as described by Blasio, were indeed salubrious. The private quarters were located on the inner patio, and he worked at a desk set up on an outside gallery overlooking the pools and gardens. Carlotta meanwhile would take their adopted son down to the poolside and watch him sail his boats among the water lilies.

By his secretary's account, however, Maximilian did not spend much time brooding over dispatches from the capital. Most of the time at Cuernavaca he spent in the learned company of Herr Professor Otto Bilimek, who had been in charge of the collections at the museum Maximilian had established in the old monastery of Lacroma on the Adriatic. Maximilian had brought him over to found a similar museum in Mexico. During the critical autumn and winter days of 1865-66, he and Bilimek coursed over the countryside chasing butterflies and collecting insects and reptiles.

Bilimek was a tall, corpulent, bearded man with thick spectacles who was in the habit of murmuring to himself, as he impaled a butterfly or drowned a lizard in a specimen bottle, "Ah, the little creatures of the good God." His appearance amused young Blasio, who recalled that "His equipment included an immense yellow umbrella, a cork helmet and a linen duster with capacious pockets. . . . Often on our visits to the haciendas we would see him bobbing about like a gigantic mushroom. . . . Occasionally he would take off his helmet and display to us centipedes, scorpions, flies, grasshoppers and grubs pinned to the lining." Maximilian, as Blasio recalled, "would put in long hours with the professor, perfectly happy."

Certainly Maximilian seemed to have acquired the ability to relax despite all his cares. A group of young bloods in Cuernavaca had organized the Cocks Club, which formed a guard of honor for Maximilian every time he appeared outside the Gardens of Borda. Its members wore a uniform of black trousers, blue blouse, gray felt hat with black plume and a badge representing a small golden cockerel. Maximilian accepted the honorary presidency of this organization and relaxed among the carefree young aristocrats. Then too there was that secret door in the garden wall through which young women slipped, as Blasio later learned from Maximilian's valet, whenever Carlotta was staying on at Chapultepec or spending the night at her Pompeian villa—which just may have been built to allow Maximilian to conduct his extramarital affairs with a certain amount of discretion.

Thus almost on the eve of disaster he could write his Viennese friend Baroness Binzer, "In this happy valley, a few hours from the capital, we dwell in the midst of a luxuriant garden in a pleasant, unpretending *quinta*. The old-fashioned garden is dotted with splendid arbors of dark foliage, covered with ever-blooming tea-roses. Innumerable fountains diffuse their freshness beneath the shady canopies of secular orange and mango trees. On the terrace running the length of our rooms, and shaded by a veranda, hang our fine hammocks, and we lull ourselves in sweet dreams to the song of gaily colored birds. Here at Cuernavaca, for the first time, we lead a real tropical life. . . ."

Perhaps as much out of bravado as contentment he wrote another old Vienna friend, Count Hadik, that he was more than satisfied with the bargain he made. Securing his position in Mexico was spiked with difficulties, but "fighting is my element, and the life of Mexico is worth a struggle."

With enthusiasm that stemmed either from self-deception or the determination to put up a brave front, he explained to Count Hadik, "One finds something which I sought in vain in my earlier life—recognition. On this continent one at least reaps a harvest from one's work which I never knew in Europe —gratitude." He could only pity those who had to live in "old, narrow-minded, outworn Europe." He declared that "Europeans cannot bear things to be better, stronger, and pleasanter on our continent than upon the old one; hence their envy and ill will. . . ."

Carlotta, though she tried not to show it, was dismayed at this moonstruck escapism of her husband's, his refusal to glimpse beyond the borders of their retreat and admit awareness of the gathering storm. Every night, according to Blasio, she insisted that the secretary bring to her apartments the dispatches and reports received that day. "She would listen attentively, as she paced the floor. Concerning some of them she would dictate her opinion; in connection with others she would give positive orders and place her initial or signature at the bottom. This would occupy us until ten or eleven o'clock"—the emperor by then would have been asleep for two or three hours, since he retired every night at eight—"and so it went on for twenty days."

For a critical period Maximilian temporarily, in effect, abdicated in favor of Carlotta while he indulged himself in the pleasures of Cuernavaca. Some sense of the difference in their two rulers seemed to have seeped through their well-guarded privacy. According to one of Matthew Maury's secret reports to the emperor, Carlotta was regarded with a measure of respect by the Mexican people. With her inheritance of Coburg practicality and Bourbon tenacity, she could not bear to watch the drifting, rudderless course the regime was taking. As she wrote Eugénie, everyone was "wrong in thinking that this country is eager for regeneration. Everybody makes a great noise about the idea, both in books and speeches, but in reality they love chaos simply because it is old and ugly. They revel in it because it is so old that it has become national."

The romantic Maximilian, just about then, was striking a heroic attitude and declaring in a speech, "No power on earth shall turn me aside from the accomplishment of my task; henceforth every drop of my blood is Mexican, and if God permits new dangers to menace our beloved country, you shall see me fight side by side with you for your independence and integrity. I may die, but I shall fall at the feet of our glorious flag."

That "glorious flag" was now being fired upon, and more than once hauled down in surrender, at garrisons closer and closer to Mexico City.

11. Broken Promises, Dashed Hopes

The day that the French army sails, the Empire will collapse with a bang.

—COLONEL VAN DER SMISSEN TO THE
BELGIAN MINISTRY OF WAR

IN a last attempt at keeping up a brave pretense, Carlotta wrote Eugénie that it was really quite thrilling to live in Mexico City on the brink of uncertainty. That near-sisterly correspondence would soon come to an end, disrupted by the exigencies of separate national destinies, but Carlotta could pluck up the courage to write Paris that "Life here seems quite like the Middle Ages. One moment we are gay, comfortable and serene, only to realize that at any minute a band of guerillas may fall upon us."

There were moments, she wrote Eugénie, when she felt that they were already under siege at Chapultepec. "Cannon have been installed up here and a system of signals was worked out to keep us in communication with the city. Even so we are constantly on the *qui-vive*. . . . Two nights ago I jumped out of bed on hearing artillery fire. It turned out to be a boisterous celebration in honor of the Virgin of Tacubaya, as if God had picked four o'clock in the morning for the Annunciation! But I suppose people here try to allow for the difference of time between Mexico and Jerusalem. They celebrate all religious occasions at night amid explosions of firecrackers and a din that seems to rip the earth asunder. Daytime festivals are less violent."

Actually the whole foreign community in Mexico, military and civil, was beginning to acquire a stockade mentality. It had been months since the 28,000 French troops, the 6,000 Austrian and the 2,000 Belgian, plus Mexican auxiliaries, had managed to bring off a success in countering the probing tactics of the republicans and their guerrilla allies. Every time they moved they seemed to be surrounded by a dense swarm of the enemy, mounted or on foot, clinging to their flanks, working around their rear. Maximilian kept receiving reports of detachments which had been cut off, most of them slaughtered, a few of them straggling back to safety with tales of torture and other horrors. Marshal Bazaine could find no way of retaliating. Instead, he began concentrating his forces and abandoning a number of outposts, some of them taken over by the Austrian Jäger regiments.

Bazaine had begun the process of extrication. Sooner or later, he knew, orders would come from Paris for an evacuation, and the Treaty of Miramar be damned. He wanted to be ready for an orderly withdrawal without, at the same time, alarming the people he was charged with protecting.

It was a delicate operation, which the French, on the whole, conducted in a masterly style. Occasionally, however, French *élan* (the psychological counterpart of Mexican *machismo*) interfered with the marshal's longheaded calculations. The strictest orders had been given, over Bazaine's signature, that withdrawing units break all contact with the enemy and resist any opportunities for striking back. Among the retreating Foreign Legion formations was the Second Battalion, which treasured the bitter glory of Camerone. It was ordered to withdraw from Monterrey to Parras. When the battalion reached Parras, Major Brian, the commanding officer, learned from a Mexican informant that there was a band of Juaristas quartered in the village of Santa Isabella a few miles away.

Major Brian could not resist the temptation of a surprise attack. Shortly after midnight he led a column of 7 officers and 188 enlisted men in a stealthy advance on Santa Isabella. Shortly before dawn, as they marched through a narrow defile, they were assailed by sheets of musketry from above. Major Brian and 8 of his men were killed in the first five minutes. His successor in command organized counterattacks to drive the Juaristas off the high ground, but every one failed. At the end the whole outfit was killed or captured except for one man who escaped to Parras.

Other dispatches forwarded from the Ministry of War made even more depressing reading for Maximilian. He kept writing Bazaine to urge the necessity of counteraction, asked the marshal to come to Mexico City for a conference, but Bazaine preferred to stay at his field headquarters and supervise the concentration. No reaction came from French HQ when Maximilian forwarded information that a rebel "governing power" had established itself at Tlacotlpan, that a republican force was operating in the vicinity of Veracruz, that a dissident group had taken over La Paz, the capital of Baja California.

The faintest sort of consolation came to Maximilian's regime when the French finally agreed that the time had arrived to organize a Mexican imperial army with the Austrian corps as a nucleus. Napoleon wrote the emperor that such a force—disregarding the fact that the Austrians had not distinguished themselves in battle or shown any of the efficiency of the French troops—would yield "rich results." He urged on Maximilian "the advantages which it would have for the whole world, if Your Majesty were to organize a real army with Austrian troops. When that has been done, I can withdraw the greater part of our troops, which would deprive the Americans of all pretext for their objections. This would make the war in Mexico less unpopular in France, and would give your Government an appearance of stability, which would contribute towards increasing confidence in the future. . . . In such an arrangement I see the best prospect for the consolidation of your throne."

The project of training and equipping an Austro-Mexican army should have been initiated long before, but the French, with the customshouse receipts and other financial matters in mind, wanted to keep all the real power in their own hands. They consented to the idea of an independent, largely native army only when it was much too late. Furthermore, the suggestion that Austrians should form the hard core of a new army was based on the supposition that the Americans would look more kindly on an Austrian-dominated Mexico than on the French version, which was doubtful.

On December 27, 1865, Maximilian decided to unburden himself with Napoleon. The situation was growing critical, he wrote, with insurgent bands prowling within two hours' march of the capital, with the French forces abandoning towns and outposts daily, with the Mexican state treasury exhausted by military costs of 60,000,000 francs annually. He asserted that he had wanted to organize a national army, but Marshal Bazaine had always temporized. Bazaine, in fact, had been an uncertain commander, Maximilian citing the fact that three times Bazaine had evacuated, then reoccupied, and finally abandoned the important northern center of Monterrey.

"I tell Your Majesty frankly this situation is a difficult one for me; I add, as a good and true friend, that it is dangerous both for you and me; for you, in that your glorious reputation suffers by it; for me, since my intentions, which moreover are yours too, cannot be carried into effect. Such military and financial proceedings will be the ruin of Mexico; I cannot govern without order and economy in the finances, with an ever-increasing deficit."

He also pointed out that the loyalist faction's confidence was shaken by French withdrawals, "for everybody knows that if the guerrillas return everyone who has declared for the Empire will be hanged or shot without mercy, and people are naturally careful not to express their sympathy for a Government which is unable to protect its subjects."

He referred to reports in the European newspapers that France was planning to evacuate its forces before it was provided in the Treaty of Miramar, and commented, "I must inform Your Majesty that such a statement would undo in a day the work laboriously built up by three years of exertion, and that the publication of such an intention, together with the refusal of the United States to recognize my Government, would suffice to shatter all the hopes of those well-disposed to me. . . . Nay, more: the honor of the French army itself would be severely compromised. . . . Time is an indispensable aid in the restoration of a nation that has been shattered for half a century, and has 16,000 armed guerrillas in its midst, scattered over almost the whole area of the country. . . ."

That letter had almost as little effect in Paris as other communications from Maximilian to Bazaine's headquarters at San Luis Potosí. He appealed to the marshal to take a look at the situation in the state of Michoacán, which extended westward of the capital to the Pacific coast. "What will be thought of us abroad," he demanded of Bazaine, "when they learn that only fifty miles from the capital there is a whole province that cannot be subdued, with a republican army in it that we cannot defeat?"

Another worry arose in the worsened interallied relations between the Austrians and Belgians on one side and the French forces on the other. Wrangling between them had resulted in the Juarista capture of the port of Bagdad. Maximilian warned Bazaine that the time for "tentative efforts and half measures has gone beyond recall, and so has that for idle mutual recriminations." He charged Bazaine with the responsibility of "regulating the mutual relations and rights of command within the different bodies of troops, all of which are under your exclusive command."

Another vexation was the affair of Colonel Dupin. The latter was a renegade officer who had once been cashiered from the regular army, but had managed to obtain an audience with Napoleon and persuade him that he should be authorized to organize a "counterguerrilla" commando which would retaliate against the guerrillas with "the utmost severity." This counterinsurgency effort had aroused a clamor among the Mexicans, who protested Dupin's cruelty. Maximilian had obtained his recall to France, but now the villainous colonel was reported back in Mexico. Maximilian could only protest to the French minister at a reception at Chapultepec, "I had forbidden Dupin's return, and hope that in future my orders will be carried out. It is the first time that I have been disobeyed since I have been in the country; but I intend to be obeyed and shall take care that I am. Notify the Marshal of this for me."*

Meanwhile, the work of recruiting and organizing a national army was fitfully proceeding. Many of its formations were in the best Chocolate Soldier tradition, with much attention paid

---

* The imperial command was disobeyed. Colonel Dupin was given command of the Veracruz area and was among the last French officers to leave Mexico.

to aiguilettes, braid, epaulettes, sabretaches and color schemes. There was protracted correspondence between Mexico City and Paris over a new decoration for valor in Maximilian's New Army which duplicated the colors of the ribbon of the Legion of Honor and brought outcries of plagiarism from the French.

To the professional soldier's eye of Colonel Van der Smissen, the commander of the Belgian Legion, it was a sullen mob of conscripts led by jumped-up rascals. "One can have no idea in Belgium of the Mexican Army," he wrote the Ministry of War in Brussels, "that is to say, of the five or six thousand bandits that compose it, mule-drivers and bakers' boys suddenly turned colonels. To obtain men, they are taken by force and brought to the barracks between two rows of bayonets. As soon as they were led through a field of sugar cane where they could hide, they deserted. The day that the French army sails, the Empire will collapse with a bang."

The Belgian colonel was exaggerating a trifle and, in fact, later became more optimistic about his Mexican allies. In some of the new Mexican regiments, particularly the "elite" outfit named for Carlotta, there was at least a semblance of morale and discipline. Mostly these were formations taken in hand by French officers who had been allowed to arrange their discharges and enroll in the Mexican army with higher ranks and substantial bonuses.

Maximilian eventually sold his silver plate to help equip the native levies. Early in 1867 they began to assume the appearance, if not acquire the spirit and discipline, of a military organization. The army was built around a force of 15,000 Mexican chasseurs, with other cavalry regiments to be added. One of the first of the mounted regiments was turned over to the command of Colonel Miguel López, who had been in charge of the escort which brought Maximilian and Carlotta from Veracruz to the capital—and who would eventually play a much more sinister role in the imperial drama.

Other units of the Mexican imperial army included three companies of gendarmes, about 1,200 men in all, who were placed under the command of Colonel Émile Tigdal, a Belgian, and a regiment of Red hussars, about 700 Austrians who had taken their discharges in Mexico, under the command of an

Austrian, Colonel Prince Karl von Kevenhuller. Another regular Austrian regiment, commanded by Colonel Baron Franz
Hammerstein, completed the Mexican order of battle.

Just before Maximilian learned the worst from Napoleon, he
was given "categorical assurance" by Marshal Bazaine that the
French would soon launch an all-out counteroffensive against
the swarming insurgents. On January 19, 1866, Bazaine apolo-
gized for his "momentary inactivity" on the grounds that he had
been giving his troops time to rest and refit after the ardors of
pursuing rebel bands in all directions. The tables would shortly
be turned on the enemy. "So soon as the troops have received
all the reinforcements from France and are so far organized as
to be able to undertake a fresh campaign, it is my intention to
dispatch them in every direction at once, and Your Majesty will
then see that it is not the military situation in Mexico which
ought to cause the the greatest anxiety."

Since the marshal had already been warned by the Ministry
of War to prepare for evacuation, he must have known the
only direction his forces would be taking was toward the port of
embarkation.

Maximilian, always eager to clutch at any false hope, was so
reassured by the promise of a vigorous pacification campaign
that he and Carlotta, with their adopted son, journeyed to
Cuernavaca and a long respite in the Gardens of Borda. Once
again he felt able to daydream, to envision the peaceful and
prosperous Mexico that would soon be built on the ruins of
civil war and class hatred. With some of his civil advisers he
busied himself with plans for a national academy of science, a
school for Indian painters who had shown themselves talented
at murals, a wholesale reform of the system of primary education.

He was dreaming of the golden age to be inaugurated under
the reign of Maximilian I and carried out under that of Maximilian II—now busy with his toy boats in the pool—when civil
peace was restored. Even Carlotta had become philosophical
about their present difficulties, as she wrote "Madame and our
good sister," Eugénie, that "It must be admitted that in this
country everything must be started all over again from the very
beginning, for there is nothing but nature in either the physical
or the abstract sense. I am reminded of the Mexican railway;

civilization seems to have begun at several points, but interme-
diate stages and the most important connections are still miss-
ing. There is a need for education in the very fundamentals of
living. Fortunately one finds a general docility which has enabled Mexicans to endure the most barbarous and criminal op-
pression. Because of this we are reconciled to our task and shall
consecrate ourselves to duty in the full knowledge of what we
are doing. Personally I have been shocked by nothing but the
country roads. All the rest struck me as an improvement on
what we actually expected."

For the moment she was certain that "our affairs will work
out nicely, if only Your Majesties will continue to grant us your
support."

Their optimism, of course, had been inflated only by Marshal Bazaine's word that active campaigning against the rebels
would shortly be resumed and by their trust in the pledged
honor of a French officer.

It was punctured, brutally, one sunny afternoon in mid-
February, 1866, when an envoy direct from Paris, Baron Saillard, came riding down the road from Mexico City. He found
Maximilian lying in a hammock on the patio with Prince Agustín sitting on his chest.

The definitive bad news came in the form of a letter from
Napoleon, which Baron Saillard handed Maximilian: "It is not
without pain that I write to Your Majesty, for I am forced to
inform you of the decision at which I have been bound to arrive in view of all the difficulties caused me by the Mexican
question. The impossibility of obtaining fresh subsidies from
the Corps Législatif for the upkeep of the army in Mexico, and
the statement of Your Majesty that you are not in a position to
contribute towards it yourself, force me to set a definitive term
to the French occupation.

"In my opinion, this must be as soon as possible. Meanwhile
I am sending you Baron Saillard, to ascertain Marshal Bazaine's
views and then come to an understanding with Your Majesty,
in order to fix the term for the gradual withdrawal of my
troops, in such a way that it may not happen suddenly, that
public order may not be disturbed, nor the interests of which
we have the protection at heart imperiled."

If Maximilian would take a firm grip on the tiller of state,

"display the requisite energy," and "effect all possible econo-
mies," Napoleon affirmed his belief that "your throne will be
consolidated" and the withdrawal of French troops only "a
momentary cause of weakness." He insisted that "I do not believe—and I repeat this—that Your Majesty's power can be
shattered by a measure which is imposed upon me by the force
of circumstances."

A raging sense of betrayal competed with renewed anxiety at
the temporary court in Cuernavaca. For a day or two Maximilian was so stunned that he could make no reply. He could only
think back to the days at Miramar when Napoleon was urging
the impossibility of his backing out of the Mexican arrangement and had indignantly asked, "What would you think of me
if—after Your Imperial Highness reached Mexico—I were to
declare abruptly that I can no longer keep the pledges to which
I have put my signature?" Maximilian could make bitter reply
now to that once-rhetorical question.

On February 18, he finally composed himself sufficiently to
answer Napoleon but was still so enraged that he suggested that
Napoleon take his troops out immediately. The letter, which
was given to his chief adviser, M. Eloin, for delivery to Paris
immediately, was not a model of discretion. It read:

"In Your Majesty's opinion pressing circumstances warrant
the breach of solemn treaties which you signed with me hardly
two years ago, and you inform me of this change with a bland-
ness which cannot but do you credit.

"I have been too much your friend to wish misfortune upon
the Bonaparte dynasty, either directly or indirectly. For this
reason I propose, with a zeal to equal your own, that you immediately withdraw your armies from the American Continent.
There is no need for stretching the procedure out over a period
of time. As for myself, guided by my honor as a Hapsburg, I
shall try to make arrangements with my fellow-countrymen in a
decent manner, placing my life and services at the disposal of
my new subjects."

When Eloin delivered that note to the Tuileries, Napoleon
flushed, with either shame or rage, and commented, "I have
just received an answer from the Emperor; it is obvious that he
is annoyed. I am not offended at this." Then, showing every
sign of being annoyed, he cited his own sources of information

about Mexico and Maximilian's aptitude for his task. "All the reports which we receive from out there concur in the opinion that the Emperor Maximilian is lacking in energy; he confines himself to drawing up and promulgating decrees, without realizing that they often cannot be carried into effect . . . he loses himself in Utopian schemes so that the practical side suffers."

Eloin journeyed from Paris to Brussels to convey Maximilian's plea for more troops and funds, but Leopold II turned him away emptyhanded.

Maximilian and Carlotta, meanwhile, were listening to the frightened and confused counsel of their ministers. As his secretary observed, "Maximilian could not disguise his discouragement and dejection; his vacillations increased day by day. Among the high dignitaries some were of the opinion that the time had come to take a definite resolution, to proceed with energy and to demonstrate to the world that the Empire could live without the aid of France. Others, who were more sensible, judged that Maximilian should renounce the throne." Both the British minister, Sir Peter Campbell-Scarlett, and the Prussian envoy, Baron von Magnus, advised him to depart for Miramar at the earliest opportunity.

For days Maximilian wavered between the "go" and "stay" positions advocated by his various advisers. His decision, a wobbly stance in keeping with his temperament, was for "stay—for the moment." The several measures he next took were also unlikely to provide the thrust of leadership, the example that might be provided by a soldier king, to accomplish a reversal of events.

Instead, he concerned himself with the bad press he had been receiving in Europe, continued to sojourn at Cuernavaca, and appealed to one of his brother's ministers to bribe editors, if necessary, to change the opinions being expressed on his regime in the Trieste *Zeitung* (even his hometown paper!), the Cologne *Zeitung*, the Vienna *Freie Presse*, and especially the *Times* of London. "There is nothing more important to win than the *Times*," he wrote in the midst of so many greater troubles than journalistic deprecation.

Hours were spent among the tranquil Gardens of Borda planning the establishment of an elaborate "Mexican press bureau," or propaganda agency, in Europe, with one office in

Paris for the French- and English-speaking countries and another in Vienna for the Germanic nations. Maximilian, in fact, was fretting about his European image just about the time that a Belgian delegation, bringing formal notice of the accession of Leopold II, was attacked on the road 16 miles east of Mexico City; Baron Huart, the chief aide of Carlotta's younger brother, the Count of Flanders, was killed, and several companions were wounded.

Another measure he took, one which afforded him sardonic pleasure, was to order Hidalgo, still his envoy in Paris, to return to Mexico immediately for consultations. Hidalgo for many years had slithered away from every opportunity to return to his homeland. Now he received not an invitation but a command. After making every effort to avoid complying, he finally appeared in Mexico, where it was obvious to malicious observers that the self-proclaimed First Patriot was frightened out of his wits. Once Maximilian insisted that Hidalgo accompany him on a ride into the countryside which the latter believed to be swarming with guerrillas. He appeared so heavily armed, it was noted, that he listed visibly to starboard and quaveringly protested when he and the emperor were accompanied by a single groom. Maximilian then informed him that he was being relieved as minister to Paris, with General Almonte as his lucky replacement, and was to be appointed a councilor of state instead. Rather than accept that honor, Hidalgo slipped away without leave and caught the next ship bound for France. He spent the rest of his life in exile complaining of the ingratitude of princes.

From his homeland there came little of comfort or substance except reports that the Austrians delightedly referred to him as Kaiser Max and some of them indicated they wished he ruled from the Hofburg instead of Chapultepec. Naturally this did not endear him to Franz Josef. His jealous older brother, Maximilian felt, was letting him down; not only did Franz Josef refuse to revise the Family Pact and restore him to the succession, but he was reneging on the promises of assistance which had persuaded Maximilian to undertake the Mexican venture.

Emperor Franz Josef had promised to raise additional troops for the Austrian Legion, and several thousand were recruited and sent to Trieste to await shipment overseas, but he hesitated to give the order for embarkation. All along, secretly, he had been playing a double game with Maximilian. While ostensibly supporting his brother's cause, he also instructed his ambassador in Washington to assure President Lincoln that Austria was following a "line of perfect neutrality," that he would not supply his brother with enough troops to encourage any grandiose ambitions.

When the U.S. State Department strongly suggested that it would be unwise to send reinforcements for the Austrian Legion, Franz Josef quickly gave in to the American pressure and reneged on his promise to his brother. And when a Confederate general offered to raise 5,000 veterans to serve in Maximilian's army, the Austrian ambassador in Washington was instructed to turn him down (without consulting Maximilian) because such a gesture would "aggravate the already quite difficult position of that Empire vis-à-vis the United States. . . ."

Maximilian had begun to comprehend the depth and range of his brother's animus. To his younger brother, Archduke Karl Ludwig, Maximilian bitterly commented that "I accept my disappointment as a trial sent by Heaven, and I only hope with my whole heart that a time of disillusionment may not come for others. I am used to it, for my family have never understood me and are therefore unable to understand my work or my views; they will not do so at any rate till the distant future, when it will perhaps be too late."

There was more than a tinge of self-pity in his attitude when unalloyed rage might have been more appropriate. It was true enough that all his sponsors were backing away from him with more haste than dignity. It was also true that he should have expected nothing more or less. Perhaps it was just as well that he didn't know he was being called "Archdupe" Maximilian in London and Washington.

The rulers of France, Austria and Belgium all had urged the Mexican venture on him, had used every means of persuasion to accept the spectral crown. Now that the business was going bankrupt—through lack of support from abroad, as he persuaded himself—his sponsors apparently expected him to cut and run, to become another of those royal remittance men, the bane of moneylenders and tradesmen, who fiddled their lives away in casinos and watering places from the Baltic to the Mediterannean.

In giving his instructions to the new Mexican minister to Paris, the fortunate General Almonte, Maximilian emphasized that if France was determined to leave him in the lurch, if it persisted in its precipitate withdrawal, "Almonte shall give the Emperor Napoleon to understand that His Majesty the Emperor Maximilian will never abandon his great work, but, true to the benefit of Mexico, will remain in the Empire as a good Mexican and share its fate."

A royal education may equip a man with an understanding of history, with a variety of languages, even with the principles of governing, but the isolation of his upbringing will rarely provide him with much insight into human nature. There have been more brave and noble kings than shrewd and knowing ones. Perhaps Maximilian's greatest handicap, aside from a boundless capacity for self-delusion, was his inability to sort out the tricksters and opportunists, his eagerness to favor anyone who amused, charmed, or told him what he wanted to hear.

There was, for instance, the fatal attraction of Father Fischer, which persisted despite what everyone else knew about him. The Jesuit, from all the evidence, was a man who loved intrigue for its own sake, regardless of its object or the people it involved or the suffering it might cause. Young Sara Yorke characterized him as "an obscure adventurer of low degree and of more than shady reputation. . . . Utterly unscrupulous, with everything to gain for himself and his party, with absolutely nothing to lose but a life which he took good care to save by avoiding danger, he insinuated himself into the confidence of Maximilian and became the Mephistopheles of the last act of the Mexican drama."

Why couldn't Maximilian see what was clearly visible to a girl in her teens? In the first place, he was investing considerable hope in Father Fischer's mission to Rome, where the Jesuit was supposed to be assisting the efforts of a special three-man commission appointed by Maximilian to work out his differences with the Vatican. If only a truce could be arranged with the Pope, Maximilian believed, many of Mexico's internal troubles would be eased.

Second, and perhaps as important to a man of his self-indulgent nature, Maximilian was charmed and entertained by the worldly churchman. In the correspondence between Mexico City and Rome, the progress of Father Fischer's mission was detailed, but it contained much else to delight Maximilian, who was not invulnerable to artful flattery.

Probably Maximilian never learned how poorly he was served in Rome by Father Fischer. The latter's first objective was to take over the negotiations with Pius IX and his cardinals by maneuvering around the commission already at work, then to gather all the glory of achieving a new concordat. The commission, headed by Velásquez de Léon, was working patiently with the Curia, trying to make the papal council understand that the church's tenure in Mexico could be established only under special conditions. The Pope and his counselors, however, stubbornly refused to concede any points—particularly Maximilian's demand that all creeds have the freedom to worship in Mexico.

Negotiating with the Vatican under the most favorable circumstances was a slow and laborious process, requiring the utmost in patience, diplomacy and endurance. Father Fischer, however, believed that a man of his dynamic intellect could slash through all the pettifoggery and obtain a quick agreement. Soon he and the commission were embroiled in personalities and complaining about each other to Maximilian; Velásquez de Léon wrote that he couldn't stand the arrogant Jesuit, Father Fischer that the commissioners were a trio of dunderheads.

Father Fischer managed to obtain a private audience with the Pope and reported to Maximilian that Pius IX was contemptuous of the commission. "Eh, the Mexican triumvirate!" he quoted the Pope as saying. "The first is a child, the second a blockhead, and the third is an intriguer. That is what has come to us from Mexico."

Actually, as was apparent to everyone in Rome, no concordat would ever be signed so long as Maximilian refused to yield on almost all the points at issue, particularly the exclusive rights of the church in Mexico.

From that inevitable failure Father Fischer managed to divert Maximilian by supplying him with a running account of Roman gossip and social intrigue. He provided Maximilian with all the available information on Cardinal Antonelli's mistress, on how Cardinel Alfieri was willing to sell himself "body and soul" to become Pius IX's successor. Maximilian was fascinated and began to consider the Jesuit another Talleyrand. "I received your two charming letters of May 11 with heart-felt joy, and read what was in them with the greatest interest, enchanted with the lucid intelligence and just judgment that shine in every line. If I had only six diplomatists like you, our affairs would be in a very different state. The more and oftener you write, the better I shall be pleased." Undoubtedly it was a reflection of Father Fischer's Roman gossip columns that glinted maliciously in Maximilian's complaint, in a letter to Velásquez de Léon, that the real reason no progress was being made in the negotiations was that no one in the Vatican had time for work. "The Cardinals," Maximilian alleged, "were out dancing every carnival night and slept all day to recover; during Lent they weakened themselves into debility by conscience-stricken fasting, and after Easter they spent weeks eating and drinking to make up for their privations."

The Roman mission was a resounding failure, with acrimony issuing from all sides. Father Fischer was ordered by the papal advisers never to show himself at the Vatican again. Mexico was to be cast into the outer darkness just when the church, as well as its contentious imperial defenders, was placed in the greatest danger of a revolutionary upheaval.

To demonstrate that he still considered himself a loyal communicant, Maximilian ordered his representatives in Rome to find an abandoned church, have it reconsecrated and dedicate it to Our Lady of Guadalupe.

There may have been an ironic barb fixed to that project. Maximilian must have known that the Mexican masses, with more than a touch of nostalgia for the old gods, venerated the Madonna of Guadalupe as a goddess superior to God. Whether or not his intent was tinged with sacrilege, it was a dangerous sort of ecclesiastical joke. The Aztecs' descendants, with the enormous patience which had outlasted so many other self-appointed saviors, were waiting to supply the riposte.

12. Adíos, Mama Carlotta

Abdication amounts to pronouncing sentence on oneself . . . this is admissible only in old men and idiots, and is not a thing for a prince thirty-four years of age, full of life and hope in the future.

—CARLOTTA TO MAXIMILIAN

THE bad news arrived in a deluge during the spring months of 1866, and it hardly seemed to be ameliorated whether it came down the roads from Mexico City to the retreat at Cuernavaca by dispatch rider or was sent over to the National Palace by messenger from the Ministry of War. It was all military bulletins, communiqués from French headquarters, alarms from imperial governors in the states; civil affairs seemed to have ceased to exist.

What time he could spare from matters of internal security, Maximilian had to devote to anguishing over government finances. The French were confiscating half the revenues collected by the customshouses, which were the government's sole support. That left him with 17,000,000 francs annually, and the army budget alone was 64,000,000. Not only that, the customshouses were being captured one by one, up and down both coasts, by the Juaristas.

But the military situation was critical enough to keep him from totting up figures and always coming out with minus signs. It had deteriorated so badly that even Napoleon, considering what would happen to his prestige if Maximilian's empire fell in a welter of bloodshed and horror, had second thoughts about rapid evacuation. In mid-May he wrote Marshal Bazaine an astonishing letter that reflected his anxiety over the possibility of a sudden collapse. Before leaving Mexico, the emperor ordered, the French army was to counterattack in all directions, wipe out the Juaristas, and all of Mexico was to be pacified. In other words, Bazaine was to accomplish in a couple of months, against a much stronger enemy, what had not been done in the past four years. That incredible order, which reached Bazaine a month later, when his withdrawal operation had passed the point of no return, testified to the steady decline in Napoleon's physical and mental health.

To the north, particularly, the edifice of French military law and order was crumbling. Juárez had reoccupied Chihuahua. General Escobedo with a large Juarista force was closing in on the imperialist General Tomás Mejía at the supply port of Matamoros. In the Tamaulipas region between Matamoros and Tampico the republican forces were in complete control. News of another disaster arrived in the capital late in June. An imperialist supply column moving out of Matamoros had been attacked by General Escobedo. The worst part of that fiasco wasn't that the supplies had been captured, but that many of the Mexican imperial troops immediately went over to the Juaristas and the Austrians who had accompanied the supply column were abandoned to the slaughter. A few days later General Mejía, regarded as the ablest and most dedicated of the Mexican imperialist commanders, was forced to surrender Matamoros. At another northern garrison a mutiny attempt by the Belgian Legion, no longer dazzled by "our Carlotta," had to be put down.

Never again would Maximilian's blue eyes, so quick to light up at any morsel of hope offered him, be unclouded by worry. He maintained a pretense of royal calm, but in private he was hagridden by doubt and indecision.

Only occasionally did disinterested advice reach him. One rather surprising source was a French-born bureaucrat, who felt he owed Maximilian at least as much loyalty as Napoleon. Leonce Détroyat was the undersecretary of the Mexican navy—surely a bootless occupation, since the navy existed only in Maximilian's imagination—but he was a perceptive man.

Other members of the French colony regarded him with contempt because he was grateful for a better post than he had ever held in France. "The fate of the Empire," he warned Maximilian in a confidential letter, "is at stake at this moment. The veil has been drawn aside. Napoleon's policy which has been equivocal for some time past, is now clear for all eyes to see. It will end in Your Majesty's fall. The Convention of Miramar can no longer be appealed to, the friendship of a brother sovereign can no longer be believed in, there is not a soul who has received a letter from Europe but says: 'The Emperor is about to fall.' Your Majesty may hope to obtain something by struggle and resistance, but I believe that they are in vain; nay, more, that they are dangerous."

Détroyat had nothing to gain from his unsought advice; he was leaving Maximilian's service to return to France, but he emphasized in the letter to his benefactor: "The French troops are bound to retire now at all costs. Bazaine has had a sort of vexatious trusteeship, ill-conceived and executed in the wrong spirit, which led to lamentable results. But now Napoleon says: 'I can no longer fulfil my obligations, I violate them all; I withdraw my troops, demand my money, and abandon you.' "

Détroyat's advice was to issue a proclamation to the Mexicans admitting and apologizing for his failures and to then announce his abdication. Then, wrote Détroyat, if he were Maximilian, "I should unmask my enemies ruthlessly, and, what is more, since there is a God who punishes all evil deeds to all eternity, I should with all respect speak my mind to him [Napoleon] with regard to the final outcome of this ill-fated drama."

Maximilian was deeply impressed by Detroyat's letter; it almost persuaded him to get out when he had a chance. But there were closer and more influential advisers with their pride and self-interest at stake, particularly Carlotta and Father Fischer. The meddlesome cleric, on his way back to Mexico City after the failure of his mission in Rome, stopped off at Vienna to rally family support for Maximilian's continuance on the Mexican throne. Maximilian's mother, the aging Archduchess Sophie, was heard to say during her interview with the good father: "My poor Maxl—how it will gall him to reappear in Europe as a failure." Father Fischer, to bolster Maximilian's

determination, rather freely translated that maternal outcry
and quoted her to Maximilian as saying, "One must bury oneself with the ashes of Mexico rather than admit defeat."

As for Carlotta, she found the thought of abdicating unbearable, the prospect of returning to Europe as an ex-empress
insupportable, the idea of rusticating the rest of her life at Miramar incongruous for a woman just past her twenty-sixth birthday.

She knew her husband well enough to probe at that exposed
nerve, his sense of honor, which had gone out of style even
among monarchs by then. It would be dishonorable, she kept
telling Maximilian, to abandon those Mexicans who wore his
uniform or who had shown their sympathy for his regime; the
vengeance of the republicans would be pitiless. "During these
days of discouragement," as Blasio observed, "the Empress
provided a proof of her energy." Maximilian was encouraged to
renew his pleas to Napoleon for the help the imperial army
would need when it finally confronted the enemy. He asked for
more artillery, for officers skilled in logistics and administration
to back up General Charles Auguste Osmont (his French chief
of the general staff) and Commissary General Jean François
Friant. Napoleon, however, referred the matter to his Cabinet,
which responded with a flat refusal.

There was now only one way to save themselves, Carlotta believed: a dramatic appeal to the "conscience of Europe," surely
a last worst hope with the grasping Leopold II reigning in her
own country, the cautious, dynasty-obsessed Franz Josef in
Vienna, a Hohenzollern in Bismarckian Berlin, and the worn-
out lecher Napoleon III in Paris, not to mention the inimical
Pope Pius IX in Rome.

Whatever may have driven them apart, they were closer now
than they had ever been since their wedding day. For hours
they paced the gardens of Chapultepec together, trying to decide how to save themselves.

Carlotta declared that she must go to Europe and present
their case in the most forceful terms to the people who could
help them. "She argued that questions of such importance
should not be discussed in Mexico with Bazaine," as Blasio related, "or by plenipotentiaries in Paris, or much less by an
exchange of notes. She decided that she would go to Paris in

person to deal with Napoleon. The courageous woman never doubted of her success; she assured Maximilian that the force of her supplications would bring Napoleon to do what was necessary for the salvation of the imperial cause."

"I'll go to Europe for an army corps," she pleaded with her husband. "I'll force my way into the presence of Emperors and Popes. I'll scream the truth into their faces, I'll win you the concordat with the Vatican, or stalk from door to door as a ragged beggar."

Maximilian knew she meant every word of it. She would create a scene in every court in Europe, if necessary, but would such melodrama persuade any of their hardheaded sponsors? Also, perhaps, he was concerned by her vehemence, the glitter in her dark eyes, the psychic tension visible in every feature. He could not help remembering that there had been cases of mental instability among her antecedents. And there were two other factors that made him hesitate. If Carlotta went over to Europe, he would be accused of hiding behind a woman's skirts rather than face his imperial sponsors himself. Furthermore, the royal purse was so slender that the cost of the journey for Carlotta and a respectable entourage was more than could readily be paid.

Détroyat's letter, moreover, had made a deep impression on Maximilian because its selfless goodwill was implicit in every line, and disinterested advice was so hard to come by. He pointed out that by hanging onto their throne, they might only be prolonging the country's agony.

Carlotta decided to marshal all her arguments in a memorandum written for her husband alone, which revealed much of herself and the intensity of her ambition, much also of how she had studied her husband and decided how he could be appealed to. It began with a reference to lamentable recent history, including the abdications of Charles X of France after the July Revolution of 1830 and of her grandfather Louis Philippe in 1848, the former having "made the future of his dynasty impossible," the latter having "condemned his family to a lasting exile." She continued:

"Abdication amounts to pronouncing sentence on oneself, and writing oneself down as incompetent, and this is admissible only in old men and idiots, and is not a thing for a prince thirty-four years of age, full of life and hope in the future. Sovereignty is the most sacred possession existing among men, one does not give up the throne like an assembly surrounded by a body of police. The moment one assumes responsibility for the destiny of a nation, one does it at one's own risk, at one's own danger, and one is never free to give it up.

"I know of no situation in which abdication has been anything but a mistake or a piece of cowardice, it could only be necessary in case of some offense against the interests which one is bound to protect, the prospect of an onerous treaty, or a cession of territory; then it is a subterfuge and an expiation, it could never be anything else. Moreover, a man can resign only when he is in the hands of the enemy, in order to deprive the actions he has been forced to perform of any legal character.

". . . I say that emperors do not give themselves up. So long as there is an emperor here, there will be an empire, even if no more than six feet of earth belong to him. The Empire is nothing but the Emperor. It is not a sufficient objection that he has no money, one will get it if one has credit, but credit can be got only by success, and success is won by effort."

It was unthinkable, she maintained, having a much lower opinion of their chief opponent than Maximilian had, to be driven off the throne by a man like Juárez. "One does not give up one's place to such an opponent as that; one cannot say, as in a gambling-den, that the bank is broken, or the play is played out and the lights are to be extinguished. All this is worthy neither of a prince of the House of Hapsburg, nor of France and its army, which would be called upon to witness this spectacle and to sanction it, for in that case with whom would Marshal Bazaine stay on till next year?"

She briskly concluded: "The Empire is the only salvation for Mexico; everything must be done to save her, since one has pledged oneself to do so by oath and word, and no amount of impossibility discharges one from these. Since the affair is as feasible now as it was before, the Empire must be upheld, it must remain standing, and be defended if necessary against everybody who attacks it. The words 'too late' must not be used here, but 'too soon.'

"I do not by any means ascribe the proposals of the person in question [Détroyat] to discouragement, I only consider that a man must have been in our position, or a similar one, if he is to judge it as it is; not out of an immoderate desire to keep it, but out of the duty of loyalty, patriotism, and honor. One does not abandon one's post before the enemy; why should one abandon a crown?

"To have come forward as the introducer of civilization, as a saviour and regenerator, and then to retire on the plea that there is nothing to civilize, to save, or to regenerate, and to do all this in entire agreement with France, which has always been taken for a country of intellectual power, would amount to admitting that this has been the greatest absurdity under the sun for the one as well as for the other. I hope to be able to argue like this beyond the ocean. They may play with single individuals, but they must not play with nations, for God avenges this."

Aside from its passion and its deadly aim on her husband's psyche, the document which Carlotta presented her husband was notable for several things. In referring to the possibility that his empire might dwindle to "no more than six feet of earth," she was plainly proposing that he give up his life rather than abdicate; more than that, she demanded it—and no doubt it would prey on her mind during its lucid moments during the long years ahead. It was also significant that she referred to Detroyat's warning, without mentioning his name, indicating how seriously Maximilian had taken that appeal.

Otherwise, her memorandum was an unabashed exhibition of feminine willfulness, of contempt for logic and reason. She did not explain how Maximilian could sustain himself against the rising of a whole nation; only that he *must*. The historical analogies she cited, which she had imbibed from nursery days at a court still obsessed by the loss of patrimony when her grandfather abandoned the French throne, had little to do with Maximilian's case. Charles X and Louis Philippe, after all, were ruling over their native land while Maximilian, to most of his subjects, was the "foreign usurper."

A man of Maximilian's character and upbringing, his indoctrination at the Archduchess Sophie's bony knee in the God-given duty of a Hapsburg to rule, no matter what or where, was more likely to be swayed by emotional force than observable facts. The romantic would die for as well as live by his illusions. He would accept the destiny others urged upon him.

So it was decided that Carlotta would leave for Europe and raise a clamor while Maximilian tried to ride out the storm in Mexico City.

In a letter to his "dearest and best of mothers" written just before Carlotta's departure, Maximilian showed that he had swallowed his wife's arguments entirely and also displayed the bitterness he felt at European betrayals.

Carlotta, he wrote the Archduchess Sophie, was carrying his secret instructions, "the main object of which is to call to mind certain promises for the good of Mexico and ask for support in certain points. Words cannot describe how much it costs me to part from her; to know that one's faithful life-companion, the star of one's existence, is so far away, and that at a moment when perhaps the whole of Europe is in a conflagration, is extraordinarily hard; but one must make every sacrifice—even the heaviest—in the fulfillment of one's duty. . . .

"Besides, the time will pass more quickly, and seem more easy to bear, because I shall probably undertake a number of important tours in the country during Carlotta's absence. Since Europe has begun falling away from us on all sides in the basest way, and the world now grown old is quaking in cowardice before North America, the utmost exertion has become doubly necessary here.

"The European sovereigns will bitterly regret one day the unpardonable weakness with which they have bowed before our neighboring republic, through ignorance of its nature; but that does not concern me, I have to think night and day of nothing but how to save my new, but already so dearly beloved country, in so far as my poor strength allows. . . .

"I do not yet know whether Carlotta will be able to make a short flying visit to our beloved Miramar. She cannot, unfortunately, visit Brussels or Vienna at present, for political reasons; moreover her presence would, I think, be awkward in the critical circumstances of the moment. The Austrian government in particular was forced by the political situation to behave to our volunteers at Trieste in a way that makes it impossible for Carlotta to visit Vienna at present. The same case with regards to Brussels. . . ."

Early in July all preparations had been made for Carlotta's departure. The villa at Cuernavaca was closed. A way of financing the journey was arranged; this amounted to a simple case of royal embezzlement. The funds came from the 30,000-peso "inundation tax" which had been collected for the relief of flood victims.

Despite the expense involved, Carlotta was accompanied by a decorative but unduly pretentious suite. It included Don Martín Castillo as her diplomatic adviser; Count del Valle, grand chamberlain; Marqués Neri del Barrio, junior chamberlain; Marquesa Neri del Barrio, lady-in-waiting; Count Charles de Bombelles, commandant of the Palatine Guard at Chapultepec; treasurer Jacob von Kuhacsevich; Frau von Kuhacsevich, lady of the bedchamber; Montalba Poliakowitz, secretary; and Mathilde Doblinger, maid. A few weeks later José Luis Blasio was dispatched to join the party, possibly as Maximilian's most trusted observer, but ostensibly to assist in the secretarial chores. It was hardly the "beggarly" style which Carlotta had promised as a last resort.

During her last days in Mexico, she made one last public appearance in place of her husband. That was on July 6, Maximilian's thirty-fourth birthday. As usual on such occasions, Maximilian announced that he was "indisposed" and Carlotta would receive congratulations on his behalf. She was driven down the road from Chapultepec to the National Palace for the reception, at which she told his well-wishers: "Gentlemen, I am happy to receive your good wishes, in the name of the prince who has consecrated his entire life to you and I assure you that his life and mine have no object other than your welfare."

Austerity now reigned at Chapultepec beside the nominal sovereigns, and there was no other celebration to mark the event; the time for feasting and dancing, gossiping and flirting, and jostling for imperial favor had long passed from the castle; it was now the somber, guarded headquarters of a regime under siege. Iron resolve, stern dedication to the struggle were the mood. It was exemplified by Carlotta. After the birthday ceremony, Blasio observed, "her ladies begged permission to embrace her, in obedience to the affection they felt for her. Her Majesty was not unaware of the sentiment which dictated this demonstration and yielded to it. Sobs and tears accompanied the act. She regarded it as an unpardonable weakness to permit her own emotion to be shown, and retired." Dry-eyed, almost harsh in her manner, she would show her court what empresses were made of.

Two days later the official newspaper, *Diario del Imperio*, announced the coming departure: "Her Majesty the Empress will leave tomorrow to discuss the interests of Mexico and to arrange various international matters. This mission accepted by our sovereign, with true patriotism, is the best proof of abnegation which the Emperor could furnish his new country; especially as the Empress will risk yellow fever, which at present is claiming victims on the coast of Veracruz, and is so dangerous during the rainy season. This notice is given in order that the public may know the real object of Her Majesty's journey."

The next morning at four o'clock a long line of coaches escorted by Austrian cavalry formed in the courtyard of Chapultepec, then rumbled off down the road toward Veracruz. In the coaches were Carlotta, her suite, and a last-minute addition of ten personal servants, made after Carlotta expressed fears that the French would "look down" on her if she were not lavishly attended. Maximilian accompanied her as far as Ayula, twenty miles down the road to the coast. Whatever they said to each other, on parting in the adobe village in the mountains, stayed private.

Maximilian watched the procession of coaches trundle off on the rocky road eastward in a driving rainstorm, then mounted and rode back to Chapultepec, where he was comforted by the presence of his adopted son, Prince Agustín, who was being cared for, among the dust sheets and empty corridors of the summer castle, by his aunt Princess Josefa.

Maximilian and Carlotta had never been separated for more than a few days, and whatever their differences or the degree of their previous and prolonged estrangement, they seemed to have been dissolved in the past several weeks. Some of his feelings about Carlotta were expressed in a letter to his brother Archduke Karl Ludwig, written shortly after Carlotta's departure. "Carlotta's voyage is the heaviest sacrifice I have yet made to my new fatherland, and all the harder since Carlotta must travel through the deadly yellow-fever zone during the worst season. . . . Carlotta with her sure tact will ascertain how far we can still reckon upon the help of sluggish old Europe. If the old continent abandons us entirely, as Austria has already done, we shall at least know for certain that we must help ourselves by our own efforts alone."

The joint career of Maximilian and Carlotta was punctuated by premonitory incidents, filled with portents, like the forebodings of an old gypsy fortune-teller. Those who participated in it or observed it at close hand would often look back on those events as unheeded signals from a fate that could not have been more scrutable. There was a constant rustling of omens, barely audible or visible, warning them to turn back or take heed.

On Carlotta's road to Veracruz and the sea there occurred several cautionary events that should have alerted her entourage to the onset of a mental disturbance. Psychic storm signals began flying, in fact, almost as soon as she parted from Maximilian. It almost seemed as though she could hold herself together only as long as he needed her strength of purpose. Her strongest prop was the necessity of serving as Maximilian's prop.

Undoubtedly Carlotta's mental state was undermined partly by the rigors of the long, jolting journey over mountain roads, the fear of being ambushed at any moment by bandits or guerrillas, the torrential rain which washed out sections of the road, all the desperate circumstances of her mission on behalf of a bankrupt empire. The first stage was to Puebla—a landmark to Carlotta, which she associated with the defeat of the republicans and the welcome that citadel had given them on their way to enthronement in the capital—which her party reached at nine o'clock at night. They had been on the road for fifteen racking hours. A house had been opened for them, where they dined hurriedly and retired for an early start the next morning.

At midnight, shrill-voiced and greatly agitated, Carlotta awakened her servants and demanded to be taken to the house of Señor Esteva, the prefect of Puebla, whose guests she and Maximilian had been when they were given the triumphal reception of a little more than two years before. She could not be dissuaded. Through the downpour she marched with servants bearing torches until they reached Señor Esteva's mansion.

The place was in darkness, but Carlotta clamored outside at the gate until the servants inside were awakened and came out to see the Empress of Mexico standing in the rain and begging to be admitted. Señor Esteva, they told her, was in Veracruz on government business. She still insisted on being admitted, and finally they led her inside.

For half an hour she wandered through the house and with great excitement pointed out the salon where the banquet had been held, where General Brincourt and his brilliant staff had assured her and Maximilian that they were the saviors of Mexico—it almost seemed as though she had to substantiate the memory of their regime's few moments of glory, that the past was as real as the present, that her mind was groping backward for a bearing on the future.

Then, without explanation, she and her companions returned to the house where they were staying overnight. Later Blasio affirmed that "this was the first indication that her mind was disordered"; yet there must have been subtler warnings of a breakdown. Later, he recorded, stories circulated both in Mexico and Europe that at Puebla she had been secretly given a poison called *toloache* by the Indians—an herb said to be capable of producing insanity. It was an intriguing story but Blasio was undoubtedly right when he said such tales were "absurd and unproven."

The next day the roads were worse, if anything, but they reached Orizaba that night. On July 11, between Orizaba and Córdoba, the road degenerated into a river of mud, and time after time her carriage was mired and had to be lifted by members of the escort. Once again Carlotta became agitated. She cried out that "they" were plotting against her, that she was being detained so the steamer for Europe would sail without her. Only with the greatest difficulty was she prevented from mounting a horse and riding off alone to Veracruz.

Near Paso del Macho, the first station on the railroad that would take them into Veracruz, a worse indignity than rutted roads was visited upon the imperial party. A guerrilla band suddenly descended on the road ahead and cut off the caravan. While the empress' escort stood by without firing a shot, the guerrillas drove off their mule teams and horses.

As they rode off, they sang the jeering verses of "Adíos,

Mama Carlotta," a satirical song composed by General Riva Palacios, the Mexican most admired by Maximilian.

Rain-soaked, bedraggled like some touring theatrical company stranded by its manager on a tour of the provinces, Carlotta and her entourage walked through the tropical downpour until they reached the station at Paso del Macho. The comedy of errors continued; the special train supposed to take them into Veracruz hadn't arrived.

Along came one of the ubiquitous Yankee adventurers who had been migrating from the States, not one of the Carlotta Colony but a young Irish-American engineer named Braniff. He was no lover of empires, but he was gallant enough to offer Carlotta a ride down to Veracruz in his high-wheeled open buggy. In that humble conveyance the Empress of Mexico arrived in Veracruz while the rest of her party waited for transportation to take them and the baggage to the Veracruz quays.

Carlotta arrived in Veracruz at 2 P.M. on July 13, her sodden retinue a few hours later. That evening they all went down to the wharves, where a crowd, more curious than admiring, had gathered to watch the embarkation.

With hundreds of spectators looking on, Carlotta suddenly caused a distressingly loud and painful scene. Though she was half French by birth, anything French was now abhorrent to her, representative of a treacherous and boastful race. So she flew into a rage when she learned that the mail steamer waiting to take her to France was the *Empress Eugénie* (though she might have reflected that Eugénie herself was part Scottish and part Spanish). And she was even more upset that the launch which was to take her out to the ship in the harbor was flying the tricolor instead of the Mexican flag.

She would not board the launch, she shouted, until the tricolor was lowered. A tiny international crisis had erupted. The port captain, Tomás Marín, was summoned, but he could hardly order a French boat to haul down its ensign. His only recourse was to send for Commander Cloué of the French navy. Cloué, seeing no reason to prolong the melodrama, shrugged and ordered his launch to raise the Mexican flag.

For the moment Carlotta seemed to be pacified, and her party began boarding the launch.

Just before she stepped onto the launch herself, lingering to thank Commander Cloué for his courtesy, the *Empress Eugénie,* anxious to catch the tide, sounded her siren to signal those ashore that her last passengers were overdue and she couldn't wait much longer to lift her anchor.

Again Carlotta flew into a tantrum and was calmed down only when Commander Cloué, a diplomat if ever the French navy produced one, managed to convince her that no *lèse majesté* was intended by the siren's blast.

Once aboard the *Empress Eugénie,* she seemed to have recovered her self-possession and thanked Commander Cloué for his tact. Her last words before leaving Mexico were directed to him: "I will be back in three months."

A few minutes later, as the ship started steaming out of the roadstead, she still stood at the rail and watched the dark, jungle-covered coastline slip into the background against the evening sky. It was as mysterious and indefinably menacing as it had been two years ago when she first viewed it from the same vantage point. Perhaps she would have agreed with Ambrose Bierce when that professional cynic, just before disappearing into a later Mexican upheaval, said, "To be a gringo in Mexico—ah, that is euthanasia."

III. QUERÉTARO

13. "Put Not Thy Trust in Princes"

They will give her [Carlotta] a dinner, no doubt, but I don't think she will get money or soldiers. . . .

—PROSPER MERIMÉE TO A FRIEND

IF the soon-to-be-completed Atlantic cable had been in working order, Carlotta would never have undertaken her mission to Europe. Cyrus Field's electric cable would have brought news that the whole military, diplomatic and economic structure of western and central Europe had been altered overnight. Ten days before she embarked at Veracruz, in fact, the balance had been tipped against Austria and France, in favor of Prussia, whose star was now ascendant from the Danube to the Channel. Europeans could not know, but many could sense that the long hegemony of the newly integrated German empire was beginning—and little thought could be spared for a bankrupt imperial venture across the Atlantic.

It was not merely that Prussia had defeated Austria in a brisk two-week campaign early in July, 1866; nothing less could be expected, with Prussian superiority in leadership, men and matériel. It was the brutally efficient manner in which the fully mobilized forces of a sovereign power were smashed; it was the speed with which that was accomplished and the question it raised: What nation in Europe could survive if Bismarck willed otherwise? Military experts were inclined to attribute the Prussian victory to technological advances which had been achieved in the past few years—specifically the Neyse "needle gun" with which the Prussian infantry was equipped and the batteries of breech-loading Krupp field guns. With rifled barrels, infantry weapons could now be fired accurately at a range of 500 yards and field artillery at 2,000 to 3,000 yards. The age of musketry, with smoothbores confined to a range of 50 yards, was over. In addition, the Prussians were organized down to the last jackboot and cannon wheel, were mobilized and concentrated through a modern railway net, and had forged a robotlike discipline. Against the gray soldier ants of Prussia the Austrians could muster only their courage, chivalry and brilliant costuming.

In diplomacy, too, the Prussians had maneuvered with the precision of a Uhlan squadron. Bismarck's strategy was simply to insult and humiliate his intended victim into declaring war on him. The undermining of Austria had begun in 1864 with an alliance of one-sided loyalty. It was formed to teach Denmark a lesson over the Schleswig-Holstein affair, of which Lord Palmerston later remarked, "Only three persons really understood the war of Schleswig-Holstein: the Prince Consort, who is dead; a German professor [Nietzsche], who has gone mad; and I, who have forgotten all about it."

It wasn't really so unimportant as to warrant flippancy at No. 10 Downing Street. A small war, yes, but it served as a signal flare. Both Napoleon and Franz Josef, observing the increasing power of Prussia, hoped they could appease Bismarck through friendly gestures. That, in fact, was one flank of Napoleon's foreign policy; friendship on the Rhine to free him for adventures in southern Europe, the Near East, North Africa and Central America. Franz Josef saw his chance to obtain the favor of Bismarck when the uproar over Schleswig-Holstein began. He had long dreamed of a confederation among Austria, Prussia and the German states under the ancient sway of the Holy Roman Empire, with its capital in Vienna, not Berlin. Such calculations only aroused a vast Mephistophelean contempt in Prince Bismarck, who regarded the Austrians as amiable blockheads; such allies were useless in building a modern monolithic empire, and besides, Prussia and most of northern Germany were

Protestant, with a Lutheran rigidity on the question of association with a Catholic monarchy.

Austria was used, then discarded, when Prussia moved against Denmark in 1864. Her army helped the Prussians detach the semi-Germanic provinces of Schleswig and Holstein. Then, with calculated contempt, Bismarck turned aside Franz Josef's demand for a share of the spoils. During the next two years Bismarck parried all of Franz Josef's attempts to amalgamate or even to reach an understanding. Then Austria was trapped into supporting the refusal of the German states of Saxony, Hesse-Kassel and Hanover to join the Prussian-dominated German Confederation in June, 1866. Prussian armies mobilized under their peerless field marshal, Helmuth von Moltke, and demonstrated the new dimension in warfare, his secret weapon being an utterly businesslike conduct of operations. The South German forces were swept aside, and early in July, 221,000 Prussians with 776 field guns confronted Austria's 197,000 men and 770 guns.

The two armies crashed into each other on the Bohemian plain, where the long-ranging Prussian needle guns mowed down the Austrians in multicolored windrows. At the battles of Olmütz, Sadowa and Königgrätz on July 3 and 4, the Austrian army was slaughtered. Its I Corps lost 10,000 men and 279 officers in just twenty minutes of fighting. Franz Josef could only sue for peace. "All that had happened," one historian of the Hapsburg dynasty has written, "was that Austria was finished as a rival to Prussia. Bismarck had achieved his first great object; but now he had another in sight, and for this he needed Austria as a strong and healthy ally . . . he had broadened his horizon, and he was now aiming at nothing less than German unity under a Prussian King. . . . The new enemy was France, already deeply alarmed by the great success of Prussian arms. . . ."

Not merely alarmed, France was terrified. She read the communiqués from Von Moltke's field headquarters in Bohemia as the direst sort of message for Louis Napoleon and his regime. As Marshal Randon, the French Minister of War, remarked, "It is the French Empire, and not the Austrian, that was defeated at Sadowa." All the energies of France, her marshals and generals saw, must be concentrated on building her defenses and keeping the Germans at bay across the Rhine. Hardly a thought could be wasted on frivolous projects undertaken overseas; the expeditionary forces had to be recalled for the protection of metropolitan France; the vainglory of Napoleonism had dissipated in the space of a Parisian summer's night.

Just one month after the terrible news came from the Bohemian battlefields, the steamer *Empress Eugénie* docked at St.-Nazaire and discharged the Empress Carlotta with her entourage and her untimely obsessions about reinforcing the French army in Mexico. For most of the voyage Carlotta had been sullen and withdrawn; there were no more outbursts such as had alarmed her companions at Puebla and Veracruz. For the first time she had been troubled by seasickness, and from Havana had written one of her favorites among the court at Chapultepec: "I am quite well despite a day of *mal de mer* . . . I did not go ashore, since the Emperor would not have wished it, but the principal personages of the town visited me. Most of the dignitaries had walking-sticks which reminded me of Mexico and pleased me. . . ."

On disembarking at St.-Nazaire she learned that the Emperor Napoleon was ailing and despite the crisis which had arisen over the Austrian defeat was spending August at his summer palace of St.-Cloud. She immediately sent him a telegram stating that she was on her way to Paris and must be granted an immediate audience. The last thing Louis Napoleon wanted was an interview with the importunate Carlotta. She must be fended off. He sent her a telegram, which was waiting when she arrived at the station in Nantes. "Your Majesty's wire has just reached me," it read. "Since I returned from Vichy quite ill, I am obliged to stay in bed and therefore cannot see you. But if, as I assume, Your Majesty will first visit Belgium, I shall find time to recover." Napoleon also instructed the prefect of Nantes to make clear to Carlotta that he would be unable to receive her.

Carlotta, however, was determined to carry out her pledge to Maximilian that she would "scream the truth" at Louis Napoleon. The No Trespassing signs had been placed around the summer palace of St.-Cloud but her business was too urgent for noblesse oblige or any other polite nonsense. When she and her suite arrived at the station in Paris, there was no one to meet them, no royal welcome, as the capital sweltered in the August heat. Instructions from St.-Cloud, in fact, had forbidden any ceremony; it was later explained, with false smiles, that Louis Napoleon's greeters had gone to the wrong railroad station.

Forlorn and heat-wilted, Carlotta and her courtiers were conveyed to the Grand Hotel in hacks. The name of the hotel promised grandeur, but it was a run-down place which only depressed Carlotta the more. Later that evening the chief aide-de-camp of Napoleon, General Waubert de Genlis, finally made his appearance at the Grand Hotel.

"How long," he blurted out, "does Your Majesty plan to stay in France?"

Carlotta regarded the question as an insult and refused to answer.

Count Cossé-Brissac, who had accompanied the emperor's aide, smoothed things over by announcing that Empress Eugénie would call on Carlotta the following afternoon.

Carlotta's determination to confront Louis Napoleon was demonstrated the next afternoon when Eugénie came calling with two ladies-in-waiting, Mme. Carette and the Countess of Montebello, Princess of Essling, the granddaughter of the Napoleonic marshal killed at the Battle of Aspern. She was also accompanied by Count Cossé-Brissac and Waubert de Genlis, the emperor's chief aide-de-camp. Eugénie was received with a lavish display of etiquette. At the bottom of the main staircase, she was awaited by Carlotta's gentlemen-in-waiting, Count de Bombelles and Count del Valle, and Marquesa Neri del Barrio. When Eugénie appeared, Carlotta stepped forward, as prescribed, and welcomed her on the first step of the staircase. Then the two empresses embraced and kissed. It was all as formalized as a minuet.

They got down to business privately, in the salon of Carlotta's suite. Eugénie's purpose was to avoid all talk of Mexican state affairs and simultaneously to foreclose any hopes Carlotta had of an audience with Louis Napoleon. She went on and on about how very ill her husband was. Carlotta smiled skeptically, convinced his illness was a subterfuge. (It wasn't entirely; the imperial liver and other organs were in a state of acute disrepair.) Eugénie also kept plying Carlotta with questions about the court at Chapultepec. With "tears rising in her heart," as Eugénie put it, Carlotta fended off the small talk and poured out a description of the Mexican crisis.

When Eugénie finally managed to break away, Carlotta asked when she could return the call. The day after tomorrow, Eugénie replied. "And the Emperor?" Carlotta persisted. "Shall I not be able to see him too?" No, Louis Napoleon was "still unwell." Fearing the latter would slip away to one of his numerous retreats, Carlotta demanded that Louis Napoleon receive her the next day.

"For otherwise," she added, "I shall break in."

Eugénie saw that there was no way of preventing the interview, short of having Carlotta expelled from the country or repulsed by the palace guard, so she offered to send a royal carriage to pick her up the following day and bring her to St.-Cloud. No mention was made of finding room for the "dear sister" from Mexico at the summer palace, though Eugénie could hardly have failed to notice the faded plush draperies and the odor of stopped drains that distinguished the Grand Hotel. The rest of that day at St.-Cloud was marked by the hurried comings and goings of Napoleon's military and diplomatic advisers.

Carlotta spent a fretful and anguished twenty-four hours consulting with Don Martín Castillo, her adviser on foreign affairs, and Count del Valle, her chamberlain. The hopelessness of her mission was apparent to everyone else in a capital dazed and distracted by the reverberation of Prussian kettledrums and thudding jackboots. Prosper Merimée, the gossipy author of *Carmen,* who was Napoleon's court librarian and served as the prototype for General Charles de Gaulle's André Malraux, wrote an English friend, regarding Carlotta's unbidden descent, "They will give her a dinner, no doubt, but I don't think she will get money or soldiers. It wouldn't surprise me if Maximilian abdicated in a few months, after which there will be a republic or, what is more likely, a state of anarchy. This, to my mind, will be followed by lynch law on the part of the Yankees who are hoping to introduce Anglo-Saxon colonization."

Shortly after noon the next day, August 11, Carlotta, with Don Martín Castillo and Count del Valle at her side, climbed into the carriage which had arrived from St.-Cloud. They were driven through the drowsing suburbs, through the heat-dazed countryside and into the vast woods and parkland surrounding the summer palace which had served Napoleon I and his successors. Bittersweet reflections may have occurred to Carlotta that it was the former residence of her grandfather, the dispossessed Louis Philippe; that she might be its chatelaine now instead of a petitioner.

Napoleon and Eugénie awaited her on the steps leading to the vestibule of their private apartments. Eugénie was favorably impressed by the way Carlotta bowed to the tricolor as her open victoria passed the page; at least the poor woman observed some of the outward forms of courtly behavior. Eugénie later described their visitor with a sharp but generous eye. "The Empress Carlotta was then only twenty-six, tall, imposing and elegant, with an oval face which bore marks of great anxiety; fine, large brown eyes and graceful features in every respect. She wore a long, black silk dress, an elegant white hat, and was every inch a queen, physically, intellectually and in outward appearance."

Carlotta was also greeted by the ten-year-old prince imperial, whose fate would be even stranger than Maximilian and Carlotta's heir apparent. Carlotta was encouraged, she said later, by the fact that the prince imperial was wearing the Order of the Mexican Eagle—a gift from Maximilian—on a gold chain around his neck.

But she was discouraged when she saw that she would not be given a private audience with Napoleon, who had had enough experience of feminine hysterics to group stouthearted men around him. Louis Napoleon was surrounded by Marshal Randon, Finance Minister Achille Fould, Foreign Minister Édouard Drouyn de Lhuys, Court Librarian Prosper Merimée, and Empress Eugénie herself. Later Louis Napoleon must have congratulated himself on his foresight; Carlotta kept control of herself on that occasion, but with visible difficulty. It was apparent that they were dealing with a young woman tormented by apparitions of disaster invisible to her auditors, who in their eminently practical way believed that there was a simple solution for their protégés' difficulties—cut and run. They could only ask themselves what demons drove Carlotta into believing Maximilian was duty-bound to hang onto his throne. In their own checkered careers, of course, Napoleon and Eugénie had learned the virtues of nimbleness, opportunism and knowing when to cut your losses, a practical education which circumstance had denied Maximilian and Carlotta.

In her memoirs Eugénie described that painful session in a cool dark reception room on the ground floor of St.-Cloud:

"A little later, for two hours, the unhappy princess, with all the resolution and eloquence born of great misfortunes, told the pitiful tale of trials and difficulties of all sorts against which Maximilian had struggled, a prey to the revolutionary agitations of the country, to open treason and to every possible opposition on the part of ambitious politicians, both native and foreign. . . .

"It was absolutely necessary that the Emperor refuse any further support to Maximilian, or to interfere again in Mexican affairs. He repeated, therefore, that he could give no help, and, moreover, after trying to open the eyes of the Empress Carlotta to the real situation, he urged her at all hazards to induce her husband to give up such a desperate enterprise, such a forlorn hope, and sail back to Europe. Such a response was not at all what the Princess had expected, for she was blinded by illusions.

"She suggested all sorts of plans. One of these was to go even to Rome and beg the help of the Holy Father; another, to make a supreme effort with the Emperor of Austria, and a third, to urge the King of the Belgians to come to their aid. When the poor Empress left, her weary face and fatigued features told of the tears she had forced back. . . .

"When this distressing interview was ended, Empress Carlotta walked unassisted to her carriage, apparently seeing nothing. She declined the hand of the aide-de-camp who wished to help her to her seat and then, falling back upon the cushions, in a despairing attitude, she even forgot, in her sorrow, to salute the flag which bent over her on the castle wall."

Either discretion or the painful memories of that afternoon at St.-Cloud prevented Eugénie from giving more of the details of that confrontation. One matter Carlotta brought up was the systematic looting of the Mexican treasury. At her command, Don Martín Castillo emptied a dispatch box full of documents relating to the drainage of the Mexican internal and external revenue, all of it coursing in a flood of pesos to Paris. Finance Minister Fould tartly informed her that before the intervention was finally concluded, it would cost the French government 300,000,000 francs. "That," retorted Carlotta, "may be what your bankers have extorted from the French public, but where is the balance between those figures and the sum actually forwarded to us? Do you think we don't know whose pockets are stuffed with gold while Mexico must pay the bills?"

Knowing how impressionable her husband was when a beautiful young woman appealed to his sense of chivalry, Eugénie brought that first interview to a close by pretending to swoon. Carlotta was not deceived by that classic gambit. That night, when she wrote Maximilian from her rooms at the Grand Hotel, she also remarked that "I note the Empress has lost much in looks and youthfulness since that day when we last saw her."

But what struck her "most forcibly is the fact that I know more about China than these people do about Mexico, yet they are responsible for one of the most serious crises in which the French flag has ever been embroiled." She referred to the French involvement in Mexico, not the disastrous impact on France of the Prussian victory over Austria; Königgrätz meant nothing to her, compared with the military situation in Chihauhua. "Amid all their pomposity Napoleon and his wife are unable to cope with real issues and it is my conviction that they will not last much longer. The throne of France ages those who occupy it, casting them off before their time. History shows that this nation, like the fickle goddess of fortune, always smiles on new faces."

That first letter home indicated that Carlotta still had a grip on herself, was bolstered by the contempt she felt for Napoleon and Eugénie, hopeful perhaps that her will could prevail against such weak and confused creatures. Later that evening she conferred with the Austrian ambassador, Prince Metternich, who tried to make her see that the menace of Prussia had ruined any hopes that France could invest anything else in Mexico. He urged, however, that she seek a second interview with Napoleon, preferably without his ministers or Eugénie present.

On August 15, Carlotta sent a note to St.-Cloud asking for

that private audience. Back came a brief reply, written by Eugénie, who had taken over management of *L'Affaire Carlotta*, that Napoleon had been prostrated by the ague and couldn't possibly see anyone.

Energized by that cool dismissal from the woman she had formerly addressed as her "dear sister," Carlotta impulsively set out for St.-Cloud in a hired carriage. She was accompanied only by the Marquesa Neri del Barrio, her lady-in-waiting. Shortly before noon she arrived at the gates of St.-Cloud and demanded admittance. Such a furious and unannounced descent, outside the bounds of protocol and etiquette, was not expected even of Carlotta, and it caught the master and mistress of St.-Cloud completely by surprise. Late risers even in critical times, Napoleon was just being dressed by his valet for a ride in the Bois while Eugénie was still in her boudoir being painted, powdered and perfumed to face the exigencies of her day.

The servants managed to delay Carlotta for a few minutes while Napoleon quickly undressed and put on his nightshirt and dressing gown to make good his claim to being aguestricken. Before the stage could properly be set, however, Carlotta had dashed up the grand staircase and found the private apartments on the floor above. She was racing up and down the corridor, banging on doors and calling for Louis Napoleon. She finally found Napoleon and Eugénie waiting for her in a study, slightly out of breath and looking around for their props, like actors who had tumbled onstage just before curtain rise.

This time they listened to a much more disjointed plea, almost a harangue, from their former protégée. She now seemed to have cast herself in the role of their accuser, her eyes wild, her gestures melodramatic, her manner verging on that of lunacy. The burden of her appeal was for Napoleon to confer once more with his ministers before turning her away with a final refusal. Napoleon could only agree—anything to get her out of St.-Cloud and back to her miserable hotel. A glass of iced orange juice was sent for, in hopes that it would calm her down. Instead she sprang back when the glass was offered her as though convinced that it was poisoned.

She fled from the palace with her lady-in-waiting. That evening she had recovered some of her composure; she had to convince Maximilian there was still some hope or he might give up before she could return to his side. Her second letter from the Grand Hotel read:

"Before all else I am in excellent health and let your heart be at ease about this point. Next, it is my conviction that something can be accomplished here since there is an interest in our cause, but among those higher up disinclination and helplessness are great and I know through a positive source, Metternich, that during the past two years the Emperor Napoleon has been sinking physically and mentally. The Empress is not capable of managing the affair—she constitutes no barrier against the ministers and does more damage than good. They have grown old, and both are childish. They burst into tears occasionally, but I don't know if that will lead to anything. I made every conceivable effort and submitted our ultimatum to the Emperor at once. After that I had to start working for those 500,000 piastres which I hoped to send back with the ship, but I soon realized that this was not feasible. Still, it was my duty to try.

"Just the same, I have not played all my cards against the Emperor Napoleon. I visited him only twice and the second time I brought him excerpts from his own promises in order to rankle him secretly. He talked a great deal about Mexico, and yet they seem to have forgotten all about the subject long ago. Incidentally, he cried more the second time than the first. If things succeed here they will certainly do the same in Rome and Washington. . . . I am clinging to you from the depths of my soul."

Three days of mounting tension passed as Carlotta waited to hear from Napoleon on his promise to confer again with his cabinet. On August 18, Minister President Eugène Rouher paid a courtesy call at the Grand Hotel, the real purpose of which, apparently, was to show Carlotta an item in *Le Moniteur* reporting that the Emperor Napoleon had left St.-Cloud on a vacation. Carlotta informed M. Rouher that regardless of journalistic gossip, she firmly expected Napoleon to grant her another audience.

A few hours later a messenger arrived with a note from Napoleon. The imperial family, it seemed, had resumed residence at the Tuileries. The emperor would call on her the following afternoon.

At four o'clock on the afternoon of August 19 Napoleon's carriage rolled up in front of the Grand Hotel, and that exceedingly uncomfortable personage presented himself to Carlotta. The interview was brief; all Napoleon could say was that the French government could no longer support the Mexican intervention.

Carlotta exploded; she shouted denunciations at the little man, whose rouged cheeks took on a purplish tinge when she hurled the final insult at him: "What, after all, should I—the daughter of a Bourbon—have expected from a Bonaparte?"

The emperor departed in haste. Carlotta had become so agitated, calling for servants to pack at once so they wouldn't have to spend another night in this verminous capital, that her personal physician was summoned. Dr. Bouslaveck secretly administered sleeping powders. Though she wanted to leave for Miramar immediately, she was persuaded to rest for several days. Her mind seemed unable to accept the fact of the French rejection; she had really believed that she could persuade them to help her cause, and she had brushed aside the looming Prussian armies as having nothing to do with the promises Napoleon had made to Maximilian in the Treaty of Miramar. On August 22 she wrote her husband again, and it was apparent that several days' rest had not calmed her down:

"In the morning I am leaving for Miramar via Milan, which will prove to you that I have achieved exactly nothing. But there remains the satisfaction of having defeated their arguments, torn down their dishonest pretexts, and in the end having won a moral victory for you.

"Nevertheless, He [apparently she referred to Napoleon] has turned against us, and no power on earth is of any avail, for He has Hell on his side and we have not.

"You must not believe that the opposition comes from outside, for He himself appoints legislative bodies to do his will; nor is this professed anxiety about the United States the real reason for his stubbornness. He wants to commit a long premeditated crime, not through fear or change of heart, or for any motive whatever, but only because He is the reincarnation of villainy on earth and means to destroy what is good. It is because men do not see the perversity of his actions that they adore him.

"Up to the last I interrupted him in order to delay his refusal, but it is obvious that He alone chooses to be unmerciful, for the least of his ministers would have softened. I can assure you of this much, that for me He is the Devil in person; at our last meeting his expression would have made your hair stand on end, and his ugliness was a reflection of his soul. . . . He has never liked you, for He is incapable of loving. Like a viper He fascinated you with tears that were as false as his words, and with deeds that were perfidy. You must be freed from his claws as soon as possible.

"Even while delivering his final no, by which He knew you would be ruined, his conduct was oily. A genteel Mephistopheles, He kissed my hand; but I can recognize pantomime, for I have seen through him twice. . . .

"You probably think I am exaggerating, but conditions here absolutely resemble the Apocalypse, with Babylon on the Seine fitting the picture; it makes hardened skeptics believe in God when they can see the Devil so close at hand. . . .

"As a direct result of my visit the wine has been spilled, for humanity to judge and condemn. I got a peep at the records of the Finance Commission, another putrid affair from start to finish. . . . But you must not believe that I grovel before these people. I just tear off their masks and then thunder at them, without getting vulgar, to be sure. They probably have never in their lives been more mortified.

"I can not understand their willingness to let you abdicate. It seems to me that you ought to hold on, because the day is coming when He will be dethroned and France as well as the whole of Europe will see that their interests are furthered by an empire in Mexico. The Old World is crumbling because He has his finger in every pie; you can smell him in the bloodshed of all the nations struggling for unity. He uses Prim* and Bismarck as his agents and spreads a network of propaganda across the map, laughing at those whom He has victimized. There's no defying him except from the other side of the Atlantic.

"Austria is changing into a Magyar state and will soon collapse. In Italy they have a financial depression, while Spain is ablaze with unrest. You have nothing to hope for in this hemi-

* The Spanish general who had backed out of the original bondholders' intervention in disappointment at not being named the viceroy to Mexico.

sphere where He would destroy you with his hate, for He can hardly bring himself to utter your name. I advise you to dismiss his hirelings and to control your army without French interference, otherwise you will be lost. If you can enlist native sympathy success is still possible, but never again put your trust in the French. . . .

"I shall be overjoyed when you send for me. Don't plan to come to Europe yourself because He will crush you; He wants to own everything from the North Cape to Cape Matapan. Call me back after you have emancipated yourself from him in Mexico. It is quite apparent that my presence here has been the worst blow He has had in years. I must also add that many charming people are taking a real interest in me.

"I embrace you with all my heart. . . ."

The letter was a study in paranoia, though that disorder had not yet been isolated and identified by the pioneer "alienists" of Vienna. It would have been obvious to anyone who read it that Carlotta was on the verge of a mental collapse, if only for her conception of Louis Napoleon, the sick and aging man, the failed gambler, as the devil incarnate. If there was a devil's disciple loose in Europe, certainly he could be seen with the naked eye across the Rhine. In none of her letters did Carlotta touch on the overriding reality of Western Europe those long hot summer days, when everyone else awaited Bismarck's next move with breathless interest. Instead, with manic exultation, she believed that she had devastated the emperor and his government; she could not see, of course, that she was a mere inconvenience and embarrassment in Paris.

Perhaps the crack-up would have come more quickly if her physician and the other members of her suite had not persuaded her to go to Miramar instead of Rome. It seemed to her companions on the long journey across Europe that she regained some of her balance once the party had crossed the frontier into northern Italy. They paused at Lake Como, where she stayed at her father's Villa d'Este. The serenity of the place calmed her, and her letter to Maximilian on August 29 might have been written by another person:

"In this land, so full of memories of happiness and joys, in this land where we have spent the best years of our life, I think of you, unceasingly of you. I have before my eyes your Lake

Como, which you so loved in its calm blue. Nothing is altered except that you are far, far across the ocean, and nearly ten years have passed. . . . Every name, every event emerges once more from some unused nook in my brain, and I rejoice again in our Lombardy as though we had never left it; in these two days I have relived two years which were once precious to us.

"If only you could see the friendliness of these people. Early yesterday morning I went to mass before the tomb of San Carlo and also visited the cathedral which happened to be crowded. People surrounded me in a moment, but it was not curiosity as much as because of an enduring affection which they still harbor. In my bedroom I came upon a youthful portrait of you, put there on purpose, no doubt; it was inscribed Governor General of the Kingdom of Lombardy-Venice.

"And now I hope, my beloved, that you will be pleased with me, for I have striven endlessly to accomplish what you set before me. The moon has come up . . . it is all so indescribably beautiful. . . ."

A few days later she was further uplifted by a civic welcome in Trieste and her homecoming to Miramar, where many members of their retinue were still installed. She walked in the gardens under a mellowing Adriatic sun, and was greatly pleased by a visit from the jovial King Victor Emmanuel.

Strolling in those sunlit groves Maximilian had planted, with the Adriatic sparkling a few hundred yards away, she experienced a moment of prescience about the future of her world, a clarity of vision available to few of her contemporaries. Somehow, whatever shadows were closing around her sanity, she foresaw events that were to be a half century in the making. As she expressed that prevision to Maximilian:

"Europe is due for a series of convulsions which will last many years. Austria is going to lose all her lands. But we, on the American continent, are in the prime of life and need only civilizing influences and strong men to attain a prosperity never known before. Somehow European affairs strike me by contrast as on such a small scale, but one does not perceive this until one has been away, as we have. The glory of the House of Hapsburg crossed the seas with the name of one of its last triumphs, *Novara*. Over here it has been sinking with the sun, but it will rise again on that other shore. Remember the motto of your forefathers was *Plus Ultra*. Charles the Fifth led the way as you have followed. Do not regret this, for God's hand is over us as it was over him."

In mid-September, however, Carlotta's mind appeared to have clouded over again. Her husband's secretary, José Luis Blasio, arrived on September 14 after pausing in France only long enough to have General Almonte, the Mexican minister in Paris, forward a cipher message from Maximilian to Carlotta. A half hour after his arrival at Miramar Blasio was received by Carlotta, whose face "already showed her intense sufferings."

Without preamble she demanded, "Why are you so late? Since you arrived at Saint Nazaire we have lived in the greatest impatience; you should have understood how anxious we were and not delayed a moment in coming to find us."

Blasio explained that except two days of stopovers in Paris and Vienna he had spent all his time since landing at St.-Nazaire on various trains and had come as soon as possible.

"Probably," she snapped, "you are unaware that the cipher telegram sent by Señor Almonte is full of mistakes and incomprehensible."

Blasio told her he had brought the original of the coded telegram and offered to decipher it immediately.

Instead she insisted that one of her retinue decode the message and added, "Are you sure that no one has touched the Emperor's letters that you brought, on your crossing or on your way through France?"

"Señora," he replied, "those letters have not been separated from me for an instant, either on the boat, in hotels, or on trains. They have been constantly in a small portfolio, inside another which was locked, and the key was always in my pocket on the boat. . . . Your Majesty can also see that the seals are intact."

Carlotta said she did not mistrust him but that "you come from America, you are ingenuous and suspect no one. That would not happen if you knew the intrigues of the European courts."

He was so bewildered by her suspicious manner that he brought up the conversation with Kuhacsevich and Dr. Bouslaveck, who nodded gravely and told him that "since her interview with Napoleon the Empress had been suspicious of everyone, and that there was no doubt that she was rapidly becoming insane." In the past few days she spoke of fearing that someone would try to poison her and dined alone in her apartments.

Yet, as young Blasio learned, Carlotta was permitted to go ahead with plans to journey to Rome shortly and make her plea for a concordat to the Pope. Shouldn't somebody do something, advise her husband and family, seek treatment of a specialized kind? The only answer from members of her retinue was a Viennese shrug, which conveys an immeasurable fatalism.

14. A Jesuitical Interregnum

Let me begin by informing Your Majesty that I cannot lend Mexico another silver ecu or another man. . . .

—Napoleon to Maximilian

MAXIMILIAN was one of those men who are most deeply impressed by the last person they have spoken to. He always needed a confidant, someone to test for reactions, someone to provide support for his ego. The lonely eminence of power, of unshared decisions, was not for him. He may have been inculcated since infancy with the belief that he was divinely appointed to rule, but essentially he was a committeeman, and with his charm, his intelligence, his unwillingness to take risks or assume large responsibilities on his own, he would have fitted neatly into a large modern corporation.

Now that Carlotta's presence was removed, temporarily as he assumed, he needed someone else to help him face the realities of decision-making. For most of their short reign, Carlotta had supplied the stiffening element and was in fact his coequal. Her replacement wore a cassock instead of a skirt. Father Fischer had just returned from Rome, his luster undimmed in Maximilian's eyes despite the failure of his mission to convert the Pope to a new transatlantic brand of Catholicism. The ecumenical spirit would have to wait another century for its true flowering.

Father Fischer, for reasons which can be divined, was eager

to become the power behind Maximilian. His principal motive was undoubtedly temporal, the urge to become another Richelieu, even among the tumbling fragments of what was pompously styled the Third Empire (one up on Louis Napoleon). No doubt he would have agreed with the quotation from Milton: "Better to reign in Hell than serve in Heaven."

Maximilian would not listen to those who tried to enlighten him regarding the Jesuit's character; he had his own reasons to be tolerant of charges that his closest associate was, or had been, a libertine. He made Father Fischer his chief of cabinet, and all but abdicated to him. Rumors passed around the capital that Fischer had been offered 30,000 pesos by the French to persuade Maximilian to leave Mexico. Obviously a canard, his enemies replied, because if he had been offered such a bribe, he would have accepted it. There is no evidence, however, that he was corrupted by anything but a taste for power.

For once in his life, having risen from the humblest origins, he had a chance to use his aptitude for intrigue, and he could not bring himself to neglect the opportunity.

Without Father Fischer at his side, constantly pointing him toward his duty to struggle against the revolutionary tide, even as Carlotta had, Maximilian undoubtedly would have fled Mexico and spent the rest of his life pottering around the gardens of Miramar, writing his memoirs, and mapping imaginary voyages on his collection of charts.

For some time after Carlotta left for Europe, Maximilian faced the future serenely in the halls of Chapultepec. The possibility that Carlotta's mental condition might be disintegrating did not trouble him. "When Maximilian heard of Carlotta's vagaries at Puebla and Veracruz," as Blasio noted before his departure to join Carlotta at Miramar, "he attached no importance to them, and set them down to feminine caprice."

He was delighted by the opportunity of sending one of the first cables to be dispatched from America to Europe. Still unaware that on that day, August 15, Carlotta was being told that Napoleon couldn't see her again after her first distressing interview at St.-Cloud, Maximilian cabled Napoleon: "Availing myself of the most glorious scientific triumph of our era, I am sending Your Majesty my sincerest congratulations."

During the next two weeks he was confident that Carlotta would succeed in rousing the ephemeral conscience of Europe and obtaining the money and troops necessary to continue the struggle. By then he had received letters from friends at the court in Vienna detailing the extent of Austrian losses in the war with Prussia, with enclosed newspaper clippings hinting at a national disillusionment with Franz Josef. Maximilian was sorrowed by the evidence of Austria's decline as a first-rank power; it meant that the family estate had been depreciated by that much. He may also have experienced one or two quivers of *Schadenfreude* over his brother's misfortunes. Sibling rivalry was stronger than ever, not at all diminished by Franz Josef's insistence on the Family Pact and his refusal to allow Austrian volunteers to sail for Mexico at the last moment, when they were waiting in Trieste, merely because Washington frowned on the reinforcement.

Maximilian was especially enthralled by accounts of how Franz Josef, returning to Vienna from surrendering to the Prussians, had been jeered by people along the way, and how they had called out "Long live Maximilian!" So Austrians had not forgotten him; he was still a prince for the Biedermeiers. He had always been more popular among the masses, he believed, than his stodgy, legalistic elder brother. You had to realize the Austrians were Germanic, but with Latin and Slavic infusions that made governing with a loose rein advisable. The hope that he might be recalled to his homeland refused to be extinguished.

That hope, of course, made it all the more necessary to hang on in Mexico. A fiasco here would ruin his credibility as a future head of the House of Hapsburg. Somehow he had to bring off a success, or at least contrive the appearance of success, or at the *very* least withdraw with honor and dignity intact.

From his old friend Count de Bombelles, who had accompanied Carlotta as far as Paris, he received an accurate account of how the Prussian victories had changed the French position regarding Mexico, and of how Louis Napoleon's physical and mental deterioration was only an additional complication.

To Bombelles' rather alarming report he replied in a jocular mood: "I am still quite unable to believe that illness and the needle-gun have so far crushed the poor Emperor Napoleon that he is tottering helpless and perplexed towards the abyss. He will recover his accustomed fortitude; and the cool judgment of the Empress, who stands before him like a living conscience, will succeed in reviving in his sick soul the memory of the sacred duty of abiding by his plighted word." News had just arrived of the details of a minor Austrian naval victory in the recent war, which "filled me with the purest and most heart-felt joy. Old memories revive again; the navy, with my splendid officers, my beloved Dalmatian and Istrian sailors, and the wondrous Adriatic, float once more before my mind's eye, and it is only with difficulty that I can control my grief that it was not granted me to give its baptism of fire to the young flag on board the ship that bears my name. . . ."

During that upswing of mood, that rejuvenation of his hopes, the idea of marital glory, if naval fame was to be denied him, was encouraged by Colonel Von der Smissen, the commander of the Belgian Legion.

Colonel Von der Smissen on September 19 made the rather startling proposal that Maximilian organize a division and lead it into battle against General Escobedo, the republican paladin, who was marching south at the head of seven or eight thousand "bandits," as Von der Smissen called them, and proclaiming that he would capture Mexico City. What a glorious opportunity for Maximilian, Von der Smissen urged, to smash Escobedo and rally thousands to the defense of his throne.

"An Austro-Belgian brigade under my command," Colonel Von der Smissen wrote, ignoring the fact that the more numerous Austrians might object to serving under a Belgian, "a Mexican one under that of Colonel López, a brave soldier upon whom Your Majesty can rely, with two battalions of the French Foreign Legion, and Mejía as Chief of the General Staff, would do it. I would beg Your Majesty to allow me to lead the main attack with the Austro-Belgian brigade, and I pledge my word as a man of honour that we should gain a brilliant victory, and that the enemy would lose the whole of his artillery, and at least three thousand prisoners." The 3,000 prisoners he was so confident of capturing would be pressed into service in the imperial army, and "the Conservative party would rally round the throne."

It was more of a fantasy than a workable military plan—

Colonel Miguel López was possibly the *least* reliable Mexican in Maximilian's service; the Belgians and Austrians were too dispirited for any but limited action; the French were not likely to hand over two battalions of the Foreign Legion. But the proposal exhilarated Maximilian in his present mood. It was not carried out, but the concept of Maximilian leading his forces into battle was to lodge itself, fatally, in his imagination.

Toward the end of August Marshal Bazaine returned to the capital, evidently having completed all his arrangements for evacuation by early the following year. The French were abandoning their positions all over the country, contracting their forces and preparing for the march to Veracruz. In August the French forces gave up Guaymas, Mazatlán, Durango, Saltillo and Tuxpan, and the republicans pressed closer and closer to Mexico City and the corridor to the sea.

Marshal Bazaine was urging Maximilian to begin his own preparations for leaving the country, but the question in Bazaine's mind was whether his practical advice could prevail against the counsels of Father Fischer and Empress Carlotta. He wrote Paris that if Maximilian "continues obstinately to remain in the country after our troops have left, I fear that without money the Mexicans will desert him, and then a catastrophe is certain to happen. A few days since I had an audience with His Majesty, when I strongly urged him to consent. . . . I will, of course, do the best I can, so that our country may not suffer in reputation from our withdrawal." Meanwhile the marshal, whose teen-aged wife had just given birth to a son, was also determined that he would not suffer financially from the coming debacle and leave Mexico emptyhanded. He had placed his wedding present from Maximilian, the Buena Vista Palace, up for sale but there was no present demand for real estate, especially the sort that might be declared stolen property by a new government.

During those last days of August, in the midst of all his outward concerns, Maximilian was hugging himself with a secret joy. Not only Marshal Bazaine but Emperor Maximilian was congratulating himself on attaining fatherhood. Unfortunately the birth could not be announced in the *Diario del Imperio* or cabled to Vienna for national rejoicing over the infant

Hapsburg, but on August 30 he proved that the rumors of impotence and sterility were untrue.

The day after Empress Carlotta had written from Lake Como that "I think of you, unceasingly of you," her consort's thoughts were centered on Cuernavaca. There a seventeen-year-old girl named Concepción Sedano y Leguizano, the wife of one of the men who tended the Gardens of Borda, gave birth to a son. She was one of the young women who slipped through the hidden gate in the garden wall and down a passage to Maximilian's private apartment.* The birth of the emperor's illegitimate son was confirmed in the history of the Mexican intervention written by Colonel Paul Blanchot, an officer on the French staff in Mexico City.

The young Mexican girl was only one of his inamoratas, probably not even the favorite, and there is no record that he made any princely provision for her or their son. Undoubtedly, though, he brimmed with secret self-congratulation. Maximilian the man, if not Maximilian the emperor, would be guaranteed continuity.

The news that Napoleon would provide no more assistance also arrived late in August, first in Carlotta's troubling letters, then in one from Napoleon which stated, "It gave us a vast pleasure to welcome the Empress Carlotta, although I found it painful not to be able to fulfil the requests which she addressed to me. It so happens that we are approaching a decisive moment with Mexico, and Your Majesty will have to adopt some sort of heroic resolution since there is no time for further half-measures.

"Let me begin by informing Your Majesty that I cannot lend Mexico another silver *ecu* or another man. This detail being disposed of, there remains the question of what Your Majesty will do. Are you able to maintain yourself through your own resources or will you be forced to abdicate? In the former case I can arrange for my troops to remain with you until 1867, but in the latter [case] I would have to take other steps.

"It seems to me that Your Majesty ought to try a public appeal, explaining the noble ambition that first prompted you to

---

* The property was restored about thirty years ago, and that romantic alleyway of Maximilian's sexual conquests was preserved.

accept the mandate offered by an impressive number of Mexican citizens; next you might announce that insurmountable obstacles now compel you to relinquish your post. If they allow this to happen you may still take advantage of the presence of the French army and propose an election of a new government.

"Your Majesty will understand how unpleasant it is for me to be going into such detail, but we cannot afford to lull ourselves any longer with fallacies. It is essential that the Mexican problem, as far as it touches France, should finally be solved."

The reference to leaving French troops in Mexico "until 1867" was puzzling, also imprecise. Did Napoleon mean the beginning of 1867 or the end of the year? A twelve-month difference in their evacuation, to Maximilian, could mean the difference between disaster and survival. From the pace of Marshal Bazaine's preparations to embark with his divisions, however, it could mean only that Maximilian would be deprived of their protection very early in the coming year.

When he received that letter from Napoleon, he knew how Carlotta had been treated at St.-Cloud; when he allowed for her hysterical overstatements, it was still apparent that Napoleon and Eugénie were weaseling out of their commitments. It must have been especially galling for a Hapsburg, with more than seven centuries of history to attest the legitimacy of his house, to be urged to behave with "heroic resolution" by the member of a tribe of Coriscan opportunists.

Realizing that he still might be able to achieve a slower pace in the French evacuation, Maximilian replied in his suavest manner. If one or two phrases might seem barbed with double meaning, so much the better. He thanked Napoleon for "the manner in which you were good enough to welcome my wife," and added that "In a recent letter she described to me her emotions at the reception Your Majesties accorded her." Napoleon could take that any way he liked.

"In regard to the political portion of your letter," he continued, "my conscience stands in the way of a decisive reply. I am handicapped by my position which requires me to ponder seriously any step upon which would depend the fate of so many loyal adherents. But whatever Providence may hold in store, Your Majesty must be aware of my sentiments and the degree of my attachment. . . ."

Despite the firmness expressed in that letter, Maximilian was whipsawed by doubt and conflicting emotions late in September and early in October. Carlotta had cabled him from Miramar that she expected to return to Mexico in mid-October, and perhaps he felt that he should not make any irrevocable decisions until she had renewed the assault on the Vatican for a concordat and had come back to Chapultepec. He spent many days at the Cuernavaca retreat, usually with Father Fischer, his naturalist friend Dr. Bilimek, and a new addition to his inner circle. The latter was a Hungarian, Dr. Samuel Basch, who had become his personal physician since Dr. Bouslaveck accompanied Carlotta to Europe. During the ensuing months and in his memoirs subsequently published, the Jewish physician was to prove one of the most loyal of Maximilian's companions in the final tragedy. Unfortunately his common sense was not quite balanced by Maximilian's fascination with the intellect of Father Fischer.

On October 18 the state dining room at Chapultepec was to be reopened for a large dinner party. On the eve of that occasion, however, two cablegrams in cipher arrived from Europe. One was from his boyhood friend Count de Bombelles, at Miramar; the other from Don Martín Castillo in Rome.

Both messages related that Carlotta was desperately ill and under the care of a Dr. Riedel of Vienna. They were handed to Maximilian in his study at Chapultepec. Pale and shaken, he came out a few minutes later and asked Dr. Basch to join him.

"I understand that something dreadful has happened to Carlotta," he told Dr. Basch, "but I can't comprehend exactly what. Do you know of a Dr. Riedel?"

"Why, he is the director of an insane asylum."

15. Breakdown

> *Her Majesty the Empress Carlotta was seriously attacked by congestion of the brain on October 2. The stricken empress is being conducted to Miramar.*
>
> —ANNOUNCEMENT BY CARLOTTA'S SUITE

ON the night of September 16, at Miramar, it appeared to her husband's secretary, José Luis Blasio, that Carlotta's eyes were "unusually brilliant." After dinner she watched a fireworks display celebrating a Mexican national holiday and seemed to be delighted by the spectacle. Her unusual vivacity, however, was only evidence of one of the upswings of a manic-depressive personality. Later that night, greatly excited, she announced to her retinue that they must leave for Rome the following morning. Mexico could still be saved! The Pope must be persuaded to withdraw his disapproval, and then they would return to Mexico.

She was dissuaded from embarking immediately only when she was told that there was a cholera epidemic in Trieste and the Greek islands, that she and her party might be quarantined at Venice if they began the journey by sea.

The next morning, however, she was still on fire with her determination to save Mexico in Rome. Instead of going by sea they would travel by post chaise through the Tyrol and down to Rome. Dr. Bouslaveck was certain that the journey was "merely an indication of the new and extravagant ideas which possessed her and which daily indicated that her mind was rapidly approaching complete collapse," as Blasio noted in his journal. But even a mad queen cannot easily be defied. Blasio and Kuhacsevich were detailed to go ahead and arrange for accommodations along the coach route to Rome.

Meanwhile, preparing to depart a day after her advance agents, Carlotta wrote her next to last letter to Maximilian urging him to stand fast: "The Mexicans loved you from the first, as an individual; their flag is your flag, and you are the nation. You must proclaim to all Mexico that you are the Emperor; nobody has any real use for presidents. Nor can you as an emperor's son call yourself president, so don't encourage unnecessary elections. Make them bow to you. A republic is no more than Protestantism; whereas a monarchy is mankind's haven. A monarch is a good shepherd, while presidents are mercenaries; that absolutely expresses the point. If you could get the Mexicans to see it this way all your troubles would be over, and we would receive help from all quarters. As for troops, you will need very few once the rebellion dies down; and then, there you will be, acclaimed before all the world by your own happy subjects."

The journey to Rome was hectic, as Carlotta's mind became feverishly disordered with the obsession that unidentified enemies were trying to poison her. Her advance guard, Blasio and Kuhacsevich, were bewildered when they arrived at Reggio and found a telegram from Brixen waiting for them: The empress had changed her mind and was returning to Miramar. Backtracking, the next day in Mantua they received another telegram telling them that Carlotta had decided to proceed to Rome after all. The cause of the backing and filling as a melodramatic scene which erupted in Brixen, where Carlotta arrived in great fatigue from the coach trip, her mind fibrillating with anxiety. She told her attendants that she was certain she was going to be poisoned at the inn where they stopped for the night, that she must return to Miramar; but they calmed her down, and the next morning she agreed to resume the journey.

At Mantua she was greeted by a 101-gun salute, at Reggio with a lavish banquet arranged by a wealthy Italian count. She finished the journey by train and arrived in Rome on a rainy autumn night. A large crowd was waiting in the station, more out of curiosity than hospitality. Carlotta was escorted to a carriage which was surrounded by a mounted detachment of the papal Swiss Guard. The behavior of the Roman mob frightened her as she was driven to quarters reserved for her at the Grand Hotel in the Corso. "The populace of Rome," one observer wrote, "were distinguished for their ill manners and insolent conduct, and the reception accorded to the papal uniforms was anything but flattering, the gibes and insults levelled at the empress' conveyance, as it made its way with no small difficulty through the seething, shrieking mobs, tending to frighten the occupant considerably. This proved the first time within her experience that she had found herself the object of foreign public ridicule and hatred."

She retreated into the privacy of her quarters at the Grand Hotel, where the whole second floor had been rented. The center salon, with its balconies overlooking the Corso and facing the Church of San Marcos, had been set aside for Carlotta, with her retinue taking rooms adjoining her suite and her servants quartered on the ground floor.

For several days nothing happened. The Vatican, like Napoleon and Eugénie, was treating her with studied inhospitality, not realizing the torment being inflicted on a mind taut with the final effort to maintain its balance. For diversion, she was persuaded to take carriage rides over the hills of Rome in the afternoon. Once they met young Blasio, who had rented a horse, riding along in his *charro* suit. Carlotta smiled for the first time in days and remarked to her companion in the carriage, "These Mexicans can't keep away from a horse. See how quickly Blasio has obtained one, so he can show himself off. How happy is youth, to be able to enjoy everything!"

Finally an emissary from the Vatican made his carefully refrigerated appearance in the person of Giacomo Cardinal Antonelli, a leading member of the Curia and papal secretary of state. Under the scarlet biretta was a bland, baby's-bottom face, shrewd dark eyes and cheeks well larded from rich living at the Pope's table—and a mind teeming with schemes. On his death ten years hence it would be discovered that Vatican finances were short 45,000,000 lire, which were traced to him and his family. Cardinal Antonelli was the leader of the faction which advised Pius IX against any relaxation of the church's prin-

ciples and particularly any *modus vivendi* with that bastard regime in Mexico.

Carlotta received him on the upper landing. They were closeted together for about an hour in her apartments, though the
Cardinal could have delivered his message in ten seconds: Go
back home. "A whole hour went by," she wrote in her diary
that night, "during which he listed for me all my consort's sins
against the Church, adding that there could never be any sort
of concordat."

The Pope's refusal of an audience was suddenly reversed,
however, after the Austrian embassy interceded on Carlotta's
behalf. She was told to present herself at the Vatican on September 27 at eleven o'clock in the morning. Significantly, the
invitation was addressed to "Princess Carlotta." A stately procession was sent from the Vatican to escort her there, including
gilded coaches, papal cuirassiers with lances and guidons, lack-
eys and outriders in the papal livery. The Swiss Guard was
turned out in greeting, with their striped uniforms designed by
Michelangelo, silver helmets, white plumes and halberds for
sidearms.

After trudging for what seemed like miles through a maze of
Vatican corridors, Carlotta and her retinue finally reached the
throne room. Above them sat the Pope on his scarlet and gold
throne, with Cardinal Antonelli and other Vatican officials and
advisers flanking him. "As Carlotta approached the throne,"
Blasio later described the scene, "the Pope arose. She knelt to
kiss his sandal, but he stopped her and extending his right hand
permitted her only to press her lips to the papal ring. He invited her to take a seat on his right. All who accompanied her
filed before His Holiness, knelt and kissed his sandal. He then
blessed us and everyone retired, leaving the Pope and Carlotta
alone."

Her companions wandered through the galleries, the courtyard of St. Damaso, the Pauline and Sistine chapels, waiting for
the audience to end. After about an hour they were rather hastily summoned by Vatican attendants. White-faced, her eyes
glaring, Carlotta was led from the throne room and turned over
to her retinue for the ride back to the Grand Hotel. She was silent, withdrawn. When her companions asked her what happened, she only replied, "You may retire." That night, for

hours, she sat alone in a rocker on her balcony overlooking the Corso and was unapproachable.

Later Blasio and the others learned that an alarming scene had erupted when Carlotta was left with the Pope. Voice rising to a shriek, forgetting that she had come to plead for a truce between church and state, she had cried out that agents of Napoleon and Eugénie were trying to poison her. Members of her own suite had been bribed to administer the poison. She could trust no one but the "Holy Father," to whom she appealed for protection. But the Vatican was no sanctuary for deranged royalty. At seventy-four Pius IX had not been schooled in dealing with a hysterical woman—everything but that. His aides had closed in around him in a defensive cluster of cassocks, purple mantles and white lace, and the Pope scuttled away in their midst. Over his shoulder he flung a parting promise that he would come to call on her at her hotel when she had composed herself.

For two days Carlotta, eying everyone in her retinue with a wild surmise, wondering which had taken bribes from Napoleon to slip poison into her food and drink, refused to speak to anyone. Afterward they reflected that the poor lady should have been bundled off to the railroad station, doped with Dr. Bouslaveck's sleeping powders and returned to the seclusion of Miramar, but they all had been trained to regard the sovereign's person as sacred, untouchable except at her command. Yet, in effect, they had all become the keepers of a madwoman.

The Pope kept his promise and paid his courtesy call on September 29, and perhaps her companions were encouraged by the fact that she behaved calmly and with an appearance of rationality. Whatever her affliction, she seemed to Blasio and the others to have periods of calm alternating with moments of frenzy.

The day following the Pope's visit, September 30, she stayed in seclusion until dusk. For several days now she had refused to touch any food or drink placed before her. Then, suddenly, she summoned her lady-in-waiting Marquesa Neri del Barrio and announced that she wished to be taken to the Vatican. Blasio saw her leave the hotel with Marquesa Neri del Barrio at her side: "She wore deep mourning, a cloak of black velvet, and a small bonnet with black silk ribbons tied under her chin. As she descended the staircase, we could see that her face was haggard, her eyes sunken, and her cheeks blazing—symptoms of the intense fever that had consumed her in recent days."

The Marquesa Neri del Barrio had no idea what Carlotta intended to do but followed obediently while her sovereign went outside and summoned a public carriage on the Corso. First they drove to the Fountain of Trevi, where Carlotta got out and drank water from the fountain in her cupped hands. She indicated she could drink only water from a spring or public fountain without fear of being poisoned. Then she and her attendant returned to the hack, and Carlotta told the driver to take them to the Vatican. Presumably the marquesa tried to argue her out of appearing at the papal seat without invitation, but Carlotta was beyond reason.

Dreadful, unthinkable scenes ensued, as the marquesa later related to other members of the retinue. Carlotta dismissed the coachman and told him not to return for her. She approached the guards at the gate and demanded admittance. They refused until the marquesa convinced them that this wildly gesticulating, all but incoherent female was indeed the Empress of Mexico.

The Pope received her immediately, listened gravely to a reiteration of her claims that agents of Napoleon were trying to kill her, that she would be safe only under papal protection. The Pope patiently tried to explain that the Vatican was not a hostel, a sanctuary or a police station, that no woman had ever slept under the Vatican roof; but that only drove his supplicant to wilder accusations and more piteous pleas.

"Kneeling before the Pope and sobbing, almost shrieking," as Blasio later learned from the Marquesa Neri del Barrio, "she implored him to protect her, saying she would not rise until she had obtained the asylum which she asked. The Pope sought to calm her by speaking to her kindly and gently. He told her that she was mistaken, that no one wanted to assassinate her, and that all of us Mexicans who were with her were faithful and devoted. But he was unable to subdue her terrible nervous excitement. She repeated that no one could compel her to leave the Vatican and that if accommodations were not provided for her she would spend the night in the corridors.

"The struggle went on and the night advanced. The Pope

consulted with some of those about him as to what course to adopt, and sent for Señores del Valle, Castillo, and del Barrio, who hastened to answer his summons. They were apprised of the situation by the Pontiff's secretary, and called the Empress' physician. He stated that she was suffering from a grave attack of mental aberration, that probably she would lose her mind permanently, and indicated that the only way of calming her a trifle would be to permit her to remain for the time being in the Vatican as she desired and keep her away from seeing any of the persons of whom she was suspicious."

To the Pope it must have seemed the culmination of all his troubles with barbaric Mexico, its heathenish variations on revealed doctrine, its amalgamation of the Aztec pantheon with the Roman saints, its contempt for the property and privileges of the Mother Church, its constant rebellion against the dictates of the hierarchy—and now these unprecedented scenes in his throne room and corridors, outcries and lamentations, the seat of papal authority turned into the anteroom of a madhouse. Yet he was stirred by the necessity of demonstrating Christian charity; Carlotta was an empress, though a troublesome daughter of the church, and must be handled delicately.

He placed an apartment at the disposal of Carlotta and two of her women, the Marquesa Neri del Barrio and the empress' maid, Mathilde Doblinger, who were provided with two cots and a candelabrum. All that night Carlotta paced the floor, while the other two women watched. Toward dawn, exhausted, she lay down on one of the cots for an hour or two.

The next morning, October 1, she was persuaded to return to the Grand Hotel in a closed carriage. When she arrived at the hotel, on orders from Dr. Bouslaveck, the other members of the retinue hid themselves to prevent another outburst of accusations. Carlotta looked calmer, more self-controlled, but a few minutes after locking herself in her suite she sent for Frau von Kuhacsevich, the lady of her bedchamber, whom she had known from the earliest days at Miramar, and vehemently told her: "I never would have believed that a person like you, whom I have known for so many years and loaded with favors and to whom I have given my love and confidence, would sell herself to Napoleon's agents so that they might poison me."

The court treasurer's wife threw herself at Carlotta's feet and protested her innocence, but Carlotta would not listen.

"Leave at once," she ordered Frau von Kuhacsevich, "and say to your accomplices that I have discovered their plots and that I know who the traitors are. Tell the Count del Valle, your husband and Dr. Bouslaveck to flee, if they do not want to be arrested at once. You, too. I never want to hear your name."

A manic energy took possession of Carlotta; all that day she busied herself with various projects. Summoning the Marquesa Neri del Barrio, who naturally feared another descent on the Vatican, she ordered a carriage which took them to a nearby public fountain, where Carlotta filled a glass jug of water. She then drove to a public market and bought a small iron stove, a wicker basket of charcoal, various cooking utensils, two live chickens and a basket of eggs. On returning to her hotel, she announced to her maid, Fräulein Doblinger, that from now on she would eat nothing but food that had been prepared before her own eyes. The maid was ordered to kill the chickens, dress, and cook them immediately. From then on the apartment of the Empress Carlotta took on the appearance of a Mexican hovel.

Later in the day she wrote a note to Maximilian, which read, "I am saying goodbye, for God may soon call me to him. But first I must thank you for the joy you always gave me. May you be blessed with eternal happiness."

It was the last word Maximilian would ever receive from his wife.

Later still she summoned Blasio and ordered him to take dictation. In a pleasant rational voice, as he recalled, she dictated while "occasionally I would steal a glance at the Empress' face, upon which a few days of emotion and suffering had wrought so many changes. It was haggard, the cheeks sunken and flushed; her eyes had a wild expression and, when her attention was not fixed, roamed vaguely and uncertainly as though in search of absent figures or faraway scenes." At her orders Blasio wrote out the decree:

"Inasmuch as our Grand Chamberlain, Count del Valle, has taken part in a conspiracy to attempt the life of his sovereign, we have thought well to deprive him, as we do by this, of all his titles, charges and honors, and to command him to leave the court without returning to it for any reason; and to communicate to His Majesty, the Emperor Maximilian, this disposition which I have signed and which is for the information of our officer in charge of the Civil List and the Minister of the Imperial Household."

Then she added: "Write others for the dismissal of Señor del Barrio, Dr. Bouslaveck, Don Martín Castillo, Frau von Kuhacsevich and the others."

She told Blasio that he, too, was dismissed but without prejudice, that he could continue his travels in Europe or return to Mexico, as he pleased. Before kneeling, kissing her hand and saying good-bye, Blasio glanced around the chamber in which the Empress of Mexico was issuing her last official orders, at "a large wooden bed with a silken canopy, which showed no signs of having been occupied for nights. On the night table by the bed was a candlestick, with a half-consumed taper and a small gold watch. There was an armchair at the foot of the bed, in which the Empress took her brief intervals of rest; a wardrobe with mirrors, a dressing table with silver toilet articles and a silver pitcher, some chairs upholstered in brocade, and a table, on which was the charcoal stove used by Mathilde in cooking the Empress' meals. Some hens were tied to the legs of the table, and on it were eggs and the pitcher of water which Charlotta procured for herself."

A distraught and hurried council was held by her retinue. Obviously those closest to her, who had been chosen by her in Mexico City as her most devoted aides and servitors, were the ones who could do the least for her now, since she suspected that they were conspiring at her assassination. Their continued presence seemed to disturb her all the more. There was little they could do but obey her last orders and depart, except for the Marquesa Neri del Barrio and Fräulein Doblinger, who would care for her. Meanwhile her family must be notified and take charge. Telegrams were dispatched to Brussels and Vienna stating that Carlotta had collapsed.

During the next few days, while word was awaited from King Leopold in Brussels, her court disbanded. Count del Valle left for Seville, where he took up residence; the Kuhacseviches departed for their native Vienna, the Marqués del Barrio for Paris, where he was to await his wife.

Telegraphed word came that Carlotta's younger brother, the Count of Flanders, was on his way to take charge of his sister. During the anxious days and nights that followed, the Marquesa Neri del Barrio and Fräulein Doblinger kept constant watch over Carlotta. She could rarely be persuaded to sleep or rest. She paced the floor of her apartment endlessly. A kitten was bought to serve as food taster, and Carlotta would eat nothing until certain that it was not poisoned. Her rooms became squalid with chicken droppings, feathers and blood from the slaughtered hens. The only time Carlotta left her apartment was to take a carriage to the Fountain of Trevi and fill her water jugs.

Before leaving her service, Dr. Bouslaveck issued a communiqué, which was also cabled to Maximilian, stating: "Her Majesty the Empress Carlotta was seriously attacked by a congestion of the brain on October 2. The stricken empress is being conducted to Miramar." Then Dr. Bouslaveck left for Mexico City.

Meanwhile the celebrated alienist and nerve specialist Dr. Riedel of Vienna had been engaged for consultation and agreed to journey to Trieste, where he would await the arrival of his patient.

On October 7, the young Count of Flanders, who had always been Carlotta's favorite in the family, arrived from Vienna and was closeted for hours with his sister. She was soothed by his presence. The Marquesa Neri del Barrio, who was on the verge of collapse herself after watching over Carlotta night and day for a week, was put to bed in an adjoining apartment. The Count of Flanders cooked her meals, sat with her, and persuaded her to accompany him to Miramar as soon as the Marquesa Neri del Barrio felt strong enough to travel. Apparently it was assumed that her maid, Fräulein Doblinger, being of sturdy peasant stock, required no such consideration.

Meanwhile one of Maximilian's special commissioners in Rome, Velásquez de Léon, was cabling him the available details on Carlotta's breakdown, necessarily limited by the fact that no physician qualified to treat mental diseases had as yet examined her. "We could imagine many Mexican calamities," he informed his sovereign, "but it certainly never entered our minds, while we were admiring the courage and heroic valor of Her Majesty that the empress at leaving Your Majesty, enduring the dangers and the fatigues of the bad roads to Vera Cruz in the rainy season in the midst of the yellow fever, crossing the ocean, and coming as a great negociatrix to demand rights for Mexico and the execution of treaties, that she would be so ungraciously received in Paris as to affect Her Majesty's mind so seriously."

Don Martín Castillo, who had proceeded to Paris with José Luis Blasio after his dismissal, cabled Maximilian that Carlotta's condition was irremediable, for the moment, and urged his immediate abdication and departure from Mexico. There was nothing more Maximilian could do for the country; it was his duty to care for his wife. He further informed Maximilian that Austria was sending two frigates, the *Elizabeth* and the *Dandolo,* to Veracruz for the purpose of evacuating the emperor and as many of his European followers as possible.

The difficult process of removing Carlotta from Rome to Miramar, via the port of Ancona, began on October 8. Her brother, Count Philippe, and the two women who had stayed at her side after her suite was broken up took her from the hotel to the railroad station in a closed carriage. A special train had been engaged to take them to Ancona, the Adriatic port from which they would sail to Trieste. Carlotta, apparently reassured by her brother's presence, was unexpectedly docile, and none of the scenes her companions dreaded took place.

They reached Miramar on October 10. For a day or two Carlotta seemed to be tranquilized by the familiar surroundings but was closely observed by her attendants as she wandered through the gardens or walked along the shore. Suddenly she became agitated again. Miramar reminded her of her duty to Maximilian and Mexico. She must journey at once to Vienna and Brussels to urge their respective families to send the troops and money they needed. Hatless and cloakless, despite the autumn chill, she made a number of attempts to escape. Once she asked why Maximilian wasn't at the luncheon table.

Dr. Riedel had arrived from Vienna and examined her. For

days he kept her under close observation, alternating in that duty with Dr. Jilek. New delusions assailed her. She was now convinced that her husband, as well as Napoleon, was plotting to have her poisoned. After days of patient effort Drs. Riedel and Jilek succeeded in persuading her that Maximilian was not plotting against her life.

Early in November she seemed to be recovering somewhat and spoke of having emerged from a "nightmare." A week later she was railing at the servants for planning a "fresh slaughter." Dr. Riedel shook his head and admitted defeat after Carlotta attacked Dr. Jilek and had to be placed under restraint. There was nothing to do, he decided, but return her to her homeland and keep her under constant observation and restraint.

On a mid-November day Carlotta took leave of Miramar forever, Count Philippe and Marquesa Neri del Barrio accompanying her to Brussels. The royal house of Belgium reclaimed its broken daughter—but not without reluctance on the part of her elder brother, King Leopold II, who abhorred the idea of having the seat of his mini-empire, now expanding vigorously into the Congo, cluttered up with a demented sister. No, the castle at Laeken simply wouldn't be suitable for an extended stay.

Carlotta, with her attendants, was banished to the turreted Château de Bouchout, north of Brussels in the province of Brabant, which was suitably enclosed by dense woods and thickets. Bouchout was known in legend as the Castle of the Beauty of the Sleeping Wood and dated back to 1173. Despite the suggestion of a Hans Christian Andersen background, it was a grimly medieval haunt which had once been the demesne of a Lord d'Aremberg, whose career was summed up in his unofficial title of the Butcher of the Ardennes. It had a bloody history and had been fought over, possessed, and repossessed by various ducal families.

Bouchout's five towers and crenellated walls had been restored after years of vacancy in 1832. In recent times the château had served as a museum and been stocked with the relics of the ducal families which had contested for the Belgian provinces for centuries. There Carlotta was incarcerated at the age of twenty-six in a setting that might have been chosen by Edgar Allan Poe for one of his hapless heroines, surrounded by sculptured knights, ancestral portraits of titled thugs, regiments of armor, acres of canvas and tapestry depicting scenes of conquest, walls bracketed with halberds, swords, battle axes, arquebuses and other souvenirs of a bloody past.

Ultimately Carlotta, too, became a museum piece.

16. The Vivandière from Vermont

To speak the truth, I was a soldier with all my soul, and war was my element. What I had seen of it in Europe and America served only to make me more eager to extend my experience. . . .

—PRINCE SALM-SALM, *My Diary in Mexico*

MOBILITY was the first essential of any man who presumed to rule Mexico. Capitals were interchangeable; the seat of power might be a saddle, a throne, a peon's hut or an office in the National Palace. One could not become too fond of one's surroundings because they were likely to be changed at the next turn of events. Juárez had presided over his rump government as a fugitive for the past several years. Now it was Maximilian's turn to put wheels under his throne and wander from place to place.

The gentle Jewish physician from Budapest, Dr. Basch, and others who wished him well would always remember with anguish how often and how close Maximilian came during the several weeks following the news of Carlotta's collapse to giving up and leaving Mexico.

On the evening of October 18, just after Maximilian learned that Carlotta was considered incurably insane, Dr. Basch found him restlessly pacing the roof of Chapultepec. Maximilian had been suffering from a recurrence of malaria, and the physician told him that he ought to stay in bed.

Maximilian disregarded the advice and said abruptly, "Do you think I should abandon Mexico?"

"I think," Dr. Basch carefully replied, "that Your Majesty should not remain in this country."

"Will people think that I return to Europe solely on account of the Empress' illness?"

"Your Majesty," Dr. Basch told him, "has a thousand reasons for doing so; and Europe will realize that from the moment that Napoleon went back on his treaty you were under no obligation to remain in Mexico."

"What will Herzfeld [a newly arrived adviser from Vienna] and Fischer think?"

"Frankly, Herzfeld thinks as I do. As to Fischer, to speak the truth, he does not inspire me with much confidence. I believe that the interests of his [Conservative] party have greater weight with him than the personal interests of Your Majesty."

For two days after that Maximilian lay ill with grief over Carlotta and the malarial fever. In the sickroom he made up his mind—but not finally—that steps toward abdication must be taken immediately. Maximilian, when faced with the necessity of making a decision, clung to the tentative, abhorred the definite. The weight of the advice he was receiving at the moment seemed to tip the scales against Father Fischer and the Mexican Conservatives, who were pleading he must not abandon them.

So Maximilian would proceed tentatively toward abdication. He would go to Orizaba, as it was announced in the official newspaper, to recover from the malaria in a gentler climate. Orizaba, however, was well down the corridor to the sea, between Puebla and Veracruz, almost within sight of the two Austrian frigates *Elizabeth* and *Dandolo* which his brother had sent to bring him back to Europe and which were anchored off Isla de los Sacrificios. For a man of his temperament it was the ideal spot to teeter on the fulcrum of indecision; within a day he could flee on one of the frigates, if the situation fell apart suddenly, or within two days he could be back in Chapultepec.

On October 21 he and his entourage, including a number of haggard and despondent Mexican politicians, set out from Chapultepec under the protection of a squadron of 400 Austrian hussars commanded by Count von Kevenhuller and a rather shabby group of Mexican gendarmes whose recent conduct had not endeared them to the populace of Mexico City.

A few miles down the road, ironically, the cavalcade passed General Édouard de Curières de Castelnau, the Emperor Napoleon's personal aide-de-camp, who had just arrived with orders to work out plans for the French withdrawal, to persuade Maximilian to abdicate and to set up some interim form of government. Maximilian refused to stop to talk with the plenipotentiary from Paris. Whatever he did, it would be without any counseling from the French.

Along the way he decided (temporarily) to announce his abdication ten days hence, on October 31, and sail immediately thereafter for Europe and dispatched orders to Marshal Bazaine revoking the Black Decree and all other harsh measures against the Mexican people. He also wrote a letter to the Iturbide family in Paris saying that Prince Agustín would be leaving the country shortly, in the care of his aunt Princess Josefa, and would be returned to them. There was no future for a Maximilian II and not much, it appeared, for Maximilian I.

Not until much later was it remarked upon that Father Fischer had slipped away from the others and gone ahead to Orizaba, supposedly to make arrangements for Maximilian's stay there. Actually that assiduous plotter was arranging to change Maximilian's mind about leaving Mexico. With a furious display of energy, he rounded up as many supporters of the regime as possible in and around Orizaba and imported others from Mexico City. The Conservatives, the clerical party, everyone who had life or property to lose by Maximilian's departure was rallied to a last-ditch effort. The emperor must be convinced, within the coming weeks, that the empire could prevail even after the last French troops left early in 1867. But first there must be a visible demonstration of "the people's" affection and trust at Orizaba to cancel or delay his plans to ship out on the last day of the month. It could fairly be said that through the exertions of one man, Father Fischer, the situation was to be turned around and an orderly transition, such as General Castelnau had come to arrange, was prevented.

When Maximilian arrived in Orizaba, he was stunned by his

reception: thundering cheers, flowers strewn, dark-eyed beauties waving from balconies. Maximilian was always deeply affected by such demonstrations, unaware that this, like all the others, had been promoted behind the scenes. To Maximilian this was the best possible evidence that the people wanted him, that he hadn't been a failure; it was a reenactment of his triumphal progress to Mexico City and enthronement, though on a more modest scale.

Father Fischer's charade had begun its work by the time Maximilian and his entourage were installed at the mansion of Señor Bringas. Already his malaria was losing its grip, and his spirits were uplifted. The impassioned cries of hundreds—or was it thousands?—who gathered in the streets to welcome him still echoed in his ears: *"Viva Maximiliano! Viva el Emperador!"*

Now he began wavering on the subject of an October 31 departure. Dr. Bouslaveck and José Luis Blasio were hurrying from Europe; wouldn't it be the decent thing to wait for their arrival? Meanwhile, his Cabinet, which had not met for weeks, and his Council of State suddenly and rather mysteriously assembled in Orizaba.

A tug of war began now between the Mexican contingent, with Father Fischer as their front man, and the foreigners in his entourage, whose spokesman was Stefan Herzfeld. The latter had served with Maximilian as an ensign on the *Novara*, had been a councilor of state in Vienna, and several months before had come to Mexico as an adviser. Herzfeld, seeing things with a fresh and clear vision, knew that Maximilian was doomed if he stayed. Everyone not ruled by self-interest, even including the French, was urging abdication. The people of Mexico themselves either were indifferent, if they were apolitical, or wanted all foreigners to leave. Mexico had become a death trap.

All this Stefan Herzfeld urged upon Maximilian, but the emperor was intoxicated by the memory of those cheering Orizabans and reinforcements brought from elsewhere under the stage management of Father Fischer. Again he had fallen under the fascination of the Jesuit, whose methods of persuasion were subtle and eloquent and psychologically accurate.

Dr. Basch studied those methods with an appalled interest in the intimate sessions between himself, Father Fischer, Herzfeld and Maximilian in the gardens of the Bringas mansion. He noted that the Jesuit would usually avoid giving a direct answer or would reply with eloquent shrugs, eye rollings, grimaces of distaste or encouragement.

"Shall I abdicate?" Maximilian would ask in his agony of indecision.

Father Fischer would sigh.

"Shall I leave without abdicating?"

Father Fischer would shrug, as if to indicate that Maximilian still hadn't asked the right question.

Father Fischer, Dr. Basch observed, had a habit of studying the ceiling whenever he didn't like the turn of the conversation. An artful actor, he gave the impression that his sole aim was to serve Maximilian's best interests, of course, but also to preserve Maximilian's honor. Like Carlotta, the Jesuit knew that was Maximilian's tender spot.

He also realized that Maximilian fancied himself an intellectual games player, liked to toy with audacious (if impractical) stratagems. Once, with a knowing smile, he suggested, "Why not abdicate in favor of Napoleon?"

"In favor of Napoleon!" Maximilian roared with delight. "The idea is positively Machiavellian!"

For the moment Father Fischer's game was simply to postpone the departure, to keep Maximilian vacillating, while he mustered the pressures against abdication. He listened calmly while Herzfeld pleaded that there was no time to lose, that they must stick to the scheduled departure; the French would have all they could do to withdraw down the corridor to Veracruz without fighting costly rearguard actions, and who was to replace the French? Already their baggage, the furnishings of Chapultepec, the state papers were being forwarded to the Austrian frigates off Veracruz. Suavely, knowing how it would offend his main opponent, Father Fischer suggested that since Herzfeld was in such a rush to board the *Dandolo*, why not send him on in charge of the freight? When Herzfeld flared up at this insult to his honor, Father Fischer smoothly replied, "There is no thought of abandoning the journey altogether. The matter will merely be postponed. As soon as Mexican conditions improve, Your Majesty naturally will hasten to the

Empress' side." Herzfeld, however, declined the honor of being the party's baggagemaster.

For little more than a month Maximilian and the remnants of his regime were poised at Orizaba. On the royal side of his nature the elements of Father Fischer's flattery, the pleading of the Mexican Conservatives, the dregs of his ambition to be a great ruler, his indoctrination as a Hapsburg (*Plus Ultra*) all made a persuasive argument for a last stand; on the human side, there was his duty to Carlotta, the arguments of his oldest and most trusted friends from the old country, his own inclination toward the quiet contemplative life. The man of action, as he sometimes fancied himself, and the dreamer struggled for possession of his psyche.

He listened almost tearfully when Dr. Teodosio Lares, the president of his Council of State, pleaded with him to stay for the sake of the "people" and cannily, emotionally, recalled the night in Dolores on Independence Day when Maximilian had pledged his services to them. The British minister, Sir Peter Campbell-Scarlett, who was also sojourning among the rose gardens of Orizaba, had always displayed a friendly attitude toward Maximilian and now added his influence against abdication. Formerly Sir Peter had advised it; now he believed that when the French were gone, Maximilian would have an excellent chance to win the adherence of the Mexican masses. Just how Sir Peter came to that startlingly wrongheaded conclusion is still a mystery, except that British diplomacy has occasionally been marked by woolly-mindedness when monarchial considerations arise.

By the time Dr. Bouslaveck arrived early in November with the considered opinion that Carlotta's case was hopeless, followed a few days later by José Luis Blasio, the issue of go or stay was still balanced on a knife-edge. It was apparent to Blasio, however, that Father Fischer's influence over his sovereign was in the ascendant. Before Blasio went in to see Maximilian, Father Fischer warned him not to mention Carlotta. Maximilian, as Blasio recalled, "asked me a multitude of questions about my journey, without saying a word about the Empress. He added that within a few days he would decide whether to remain in Mexico or return to Europe, but regardless of what might happen to the Empire, I should always be with him." He noted that Maximilian had aged in the past several months, no longer laughed or joked, and "his head, which before had been so proud and erect, was bowed as though by the weight of his worries and sufferings."

In the end, characteristically, Maximilian left the decision to others. After three more weeks of palaver, he summoned a Council of State on November 25 at the Bringas mansion. He told his councilors, in effect, that he would leave it to them to decide which of two propositions was correct: "I. The Empire should continue to subsist. II. The Emperor should resign, if at this price he believed that the peace, independence and the interests of Mexico created by the erection of the throne would be guaranteed." The second proposal, of course, was as ridiculous as the first; it suggested that the imperial idea—not to mention the privileges it restored to the aristocratic class— could endure without the emperor.

For four or five days the council debated with Maximilian in absentia. Armed with butterfly nets, he and Drs. Bilimek and Basch spent those days botanizing, collecting flowers and capturing butterflies, in the fields around Orizaba.

Down in Veracruz, during those crucial days, preparations were confidently being made for Maximilian's departure. The citizenry, always Juarista, was storing fireworks to celebrate the event. The Austrian frigates were being loaded with the imperial baggage and other possessions. On November 29, the U.S. frigate *Susquehanna* sailed into Veracruz with the new American minister, Lewis Campbell, and General William T. Sherman, who was to make a survey of the military and political situation for his government, aboard. To General Sherman's knowing eye, it was evident that Maximilian was on the run. "Everything indicated the purpose of the French to withdraw," he reported, "and also that the Emperor Maximilian would precede them, for the Austrian frigate *Dandolo* was in port, and an Austrian bark [*sic*] on which were received, according to the report of our Consul, as many as eleven hundred packages of private furniture to be transferred to Miramar. . . ."

Those "packages" also interested Colonel Blanchot, the commander of the French garrison, who was something of a collector himself. Blanchot reported that Maximilian, through a

certain Austrian colonel, had gathered up a viceregal treasure
to console himself with: ivory and porcelain from China, Spanish antiques, laces, ornaments, paintings, tapestries, crystal and
other *objets d'art* dating back to the Spanish conquest.

Despite all those expectations, on December 1, Maximilian
announced that he would heed a higher call to duty than his
own "domestic misfortunes." His proclamation continued:
"Our state and ministerial council . . . are of the opinion that
the welfare of Mexico demands that we should continue to retain power. We believe that we should accede to their desires
and have at the same time announced to them our intention of
convoking a national congress to which all parties may have access on the broadest and most liberal bases. This congress will
decide whether or not the Empire should continue, and if the
decision is in the affirmative it will promulgate the laws which
are vital to the consolidation of its political institutions. . . .
In the meantime, Mexicans, counting upon all of you, without
exclusion of any political color, we shall strengthen ourselves to
continue with valor and constancy the task of regeneration that
has been confided to your fellow citizen."

The same day, in an attempt at man-to-man diplomacy, he
wrote President Andrew Johnson, enclosing a copy of his proclamation and pleading that his only objective was to "prevent
further bloodshed and to put an end to the war." Writing in
English, with frequent misspellings, he informed the American
President:

"I have accordingly not hesitated to appeal to the good sense
of the whole people of Mexico calling upon them to elect freely
and without obstacle whatsoever a national Congress, based on
the principle of universal suffrage, who is to decide on the future form of the Government. Should that body determine upon
any other form than the monarchical, I am ready to deliver the
power which I hold, into the hands of that body and to retire
from the headship of a government which I have accepted only
because I was made to understand that such was the wish and
will of a majority of the people of Mexico: a position which certainly offers no other inducement except the hope of being enabled to accomplish the happiness and welfare of Mexico.
. . . I have appealed, as Your Excellency will perceive from the
content of the documents to the several chiefs of the republican

army to lay down their arms until the assemblage of the Deputies and the decision of the principal question; the main object
of the present letter is to ask Your Excellency's good interference and influence. . . . To this decision none will subject
with greater cheerfullness, nor bow to their selection with more
sincere gratification than myself. . . ."

Maximilian was positively euphoric as he contemplated a
promise from his Ministerial Council to raise 30,000 fresh
troops and provide him with an annual budget of 15,000,000
pesos once the French loosened their grip on the internal revenues. He did not ask himself why his supporters had waited
until that late and critical hour to supply him with the money
and troops he needed.

His naïveté in accepting those pledges so disenchanted Stefan
Herzfeld that his old friend announced that he was leaving for
Vienna on one of the Austrian warships. That defection undoubtedly shook Maximilian, but just as his council was predic-
tably deciding that he should stay on the throne there came
similar pressure from the Hofburg, to which Maximilian was
more sensitive than to Herzfeld's influence. It was conveyed in a
letter from his mother which revealed that Vienna had been
hearing reports the French government was spreading rumors
that Carlotta was feigning madness to force Maximilian's abdication and thus remove from the French the onus for that measure.

His mother wrote that the Family sanctioned in advance any
decision Maximilian might make to stay in Mexico.

"Your poor Charlotte," she related, "wrote me such a pretty,
loving, quite rational letter in which she expresses great joy, as
she also seems to have done about the Christmas presents from
Papa and me. . . . I can now *fully* approve the fact that, in
spite of your natural desire to hasten to Charlotte, you have
stayed in Mexico; for you have thus avoided the *appearance* of
having been got rid of by intrigue (to which you would in any
case never have lent yourself, since you told both me and
Herzfeld that, in case of necessity, you were determined to
place your abdication in the hands of the nation); and since it
is your great love, sympathy, and gratitude, besides dread of the
anarchy that will follow, that keeps you in your new country, I
can only rejoice in it, and hope profoundly that the rich people

in the country will make your remaining there possible. Today's papers say that Campbell and Sherman, who were sent by the United States, did not find such great sympathy for Juárez as they expected in Mexico, but rather a number of parties, all of them hostile to each other. . . .

"Gustav Saxe-Weimar dined with us yesterday, and when I spoke to him, he at once said, with a true-hearted eagerness which delighted me deeply: 'I must tell Your Imperial Highness that I find the Emperor Max admirable; I am also convinced that he will maintain himself in Mexico; I have wagered a large sum that he will still be there in May!'

"On December 26 Papa and I for the first time asked our four grandchildren (quite *en famille*) to a Christmas-tree. Gisela and Rudolf had been rejoicing for a long time beforehand at spending Christmas with their little cousins, of whom they are enormously fond. . . . The Emperor, who can be so charming with little children, rocked fat Otto [son of Archduke Karl] in a sledge, which they can pull along, and in which Rudolf eagerly gave the little ones a ride. Franzi [Archduke Franz Ferdinand, who was to be assassinated at Sarajevo] chose the better part; he sat down on one of the sofas beside Sisi and chattered and played with her. Beauty is a magnet for little boys as much as for big men. . . .

"After luncheon the big clock struck—the one with *your* works from Olmütz—and it seemed to me like a greeting from you, chiming in the family circle from afar. Tears came to my eyes. . . . And yet I am bound to want you to stay in Mexico now as long as this is possible, and can be done with honour."

A curious combination of maternal concern and overriding dynastic necessity, the message was clear enough to Maximilian. He would be welcome to share the *Gemütlich* family circle in the Hofburg and play with fat Otto and the other Hapsburg cherubs, but only after his duty was done.

Another letter from Europe that bolstered his concurrence with the council's decision came from M. Eloin, the Belgian who had formerly headed his Civil Cabinet and was now traveling in Europe. The French, M. Eloin, wrote, wanted Maximilian to abdicate before their army was evacuated so they could say it had not been defeated; it was withdrawn because Maximilian had quit on them. M. Eloin was also certain that Maximilian could appeal successfully to the Mexican people once the French bayonets had been taken out of their backs. In his travels through Austria, he added, he found much sentiment against Franz Josef and a corresponding enthusiasm for Maximilian. It was important, Eloin instructed him, to avoid doing anything to mar his chances of succeeding his older brother.

So they were calling him Kaiser Max in Vienna? So his own people wanted him back? Things were looking up. It was also encouraging that the "national assembly" convened in accordance with his proclamation of December 1 voted unanimously that Maximilian should stay on the throne. (Not so encouraging: that body, supposedly representing the whole spectrum of political conviction, was packed with diehards who had been fighting against progress since Santa Anna's times.)

Once again, when the time called for the most vigorous activity, Maximilian lapsed into a sleepwalking state. He dawdled in Orizaba and Puebla until after the new year while every passing day became more precious with the approaching departure of the French expeditionary force. He pleaded ill health when various people, including the French minister and General Castelnau, tried to obtain interviews and discuss the most pressing concerns.

When he finally agreed to receive Castelnau, it was not to discuss the means of an orderly withdrawal of all the forces of foreign intervention, but to gloat over Napoleon's envoy. He had firmly decided against abdication, he told Castelnau, and nothing could persuade him that he should abandon Mexico. Utterly bemused by Maximilian's self-confidence, his eagerness to be duped, General Castelnau listened in silence while Maximilian displayed a telegram from Marshal Bazaine offering the French army's support until the moment it evacuated the country. Castlenau did not attempt to argue.

"I've squashed him," Maximilian exulted to his aides as the French general withdrew.

Castelnau was not "squashed," merely dumbfounded by Maximilian's foolhardiness. In his published papers, he revealed that he considered Maximilian lacking most of the virtues a ruler of Mexico needed. "He is a Utopian dreamer who remains constantly shut up . . . never mixing in the life of his people whom he does not know. . . . He has no understanding of affairs and no initiative, but he has already acquired from the Mexicans a kind of cunning which makes him conceal his thoughts so that it is very difficult to get a decision or a definite answer out of him." The emperor wanted to "appear a strong man in politics and diplomacy, but always reasoned from his imagination. A perfect 'gentleman,' gracious and good, he exhibits a dilettantism and an emotional instability which prevents him from enjoying himself in any serious work. He is often in the clouds and only comes down to earth to bother with frivolities."

On January 3, 1867, with the dilettante in him still holding the upper hand, Maximilian returned to the vicinity of his capital and established himself at the hacienda of La Teja. In one month the French army would be leaving, yet he took only the most desultory interest in the recruiting and organizing of the army which was supposed to defend his interests. Generals Leonardo Márquez and Miguel Miramón had returned from Europe to command divisions in that army, along with the abler and determined General Mejía. He ignored reports that General Leonardo Márquez, who had been placed in command of the forces around Mexico City, was creating much dissension by his methods, which included virtually kidnapping men into his ranks and imposing a heavy tax on the residents for their protection.

Nor was he greatly affected when relations with the French command worsened. A quarrel had broken out between Lares, the president of his Council of State, and Marshal Bazaine. Lares had summoned Bazaine to a conference with the council, but the latter abruptly declined, explaining, "You appear to accuse the French army of want of energy—have not I a much greater right to exclaim against the arbitrary acts and deeds of violence [he referred to Márquez's recruiting methods] which have been daily committed from some weeks past, and does not our presence in Mexico appear to render the flag of France an accomplice in these proceedings? For this reason, Sir, and because the wording of your letter betrays a feeling of mistrust undoubtedly based upon calumnies which affect our honor, I consider it necessary to state to you that I do not wish to have any further communications with your ministry."

Foolishly, on reading that letter, Maximilian bestirred himself to reply on Lares' behalf or to allow Father Fischer, rather, to make the reply in terms that could only further embitter Marshal Bazaine: "His Majesty the Emperor instructs me to return to you the accompanying letter since he cannot permit you to address such communications to his ministers as you have chosen to send. Since you have adopted such methods, I am commanded to inform your excellency that for the future His Majesty can hold no direct communications with you."

That haughty reply was a terrible mistake, not only because it was an uncharacteristic expression of ingratitude but because Maximilian needed Bazaine's sympathy up to the moment the last red-legged French infantryman marched through the eastern gate of the capital. Because it was untypical, if not because it was unwise, it may justly be attributed to the sinister influence of Father Fischer, who wanted a rupture between Maximilian and the French, who feared that Bazaine still might persuade Maximilian to leave with or before the French troops.

No doubt as a result of that letter, Maximilian's forces were deprived of French arms and ammunition they might otherwise have been given. This was indicated by an indignant letter which Captain J. J. Kendall, a British resident of the capital, later published in the *Times* of London: "I cannot but condemn the conduct of Marshal Bazaine during the latter portion of his sojourn in the country. He doubtless had instructions to do what he could to induce Maximilian to abdicate, but he overstepped all bounds, not only of diplomacy and of the laws of nations, and also of good conduct upon the part of an officer and a gentleman, to say nothing of the dignity of a Marshal of France. Several pieces of cannon that he could not take with him were spiked at the gates of Mexico City; an immense quantity of surplus small arms and ammunition were thrown into the Vega Canal."

Thus the Emperor Maximilian and the man who had conquered Mexico for him would part without a word.

Already the bulk of the French army was marching down the road to Veracruz and its transports. The last units would leave Mexico City on February 5 with Marshal Bazaine at their head. Maximilian would have preferred to stay out in the suburbs, ignoring that departure, except for a disturbing incident at the hacienda La Teja. One night late in January two men were surprised by his guards as they lurked in the garden of the hacienda. They were all too ready to confess that they were thieves. Undoubtedly, Maximilian was informed, they were Liberal agents assigned to kill or kidnap him. It was decided then that Maximilian should reoccupy the National Palace.

On February 5, with Marshal Bazaine riding at their head, the last regiments of the French expeditionary force, with a last unfurling of their banners and a last flourish of their drums, marched out of the capital. Among them was Captain Paul Laurent of the Chasseurs d'Afrique, who reflected that the Mexicans liked the French so much better than the Austrian troops which had just moved into the city. "Bizarre that they should prefer us Frenchmen who have done them so much evil. But our careless gaiety is more in tune with the Mexican character than is the haughty Austrian calm." A different view of that leave-taking was that of a newcomer to Maximilian's forces, the Prussian Prince Salm-Salm, who from a balcony of the Hotel Iturbide watched the French march out. "The departure of the French," he observed in his diary, "was a happy event for everybody, for they had made themselves hated by all parties. . . . They despised the Mexicans with a French arrogance and insulted the inhabitants of the city every day. Gentlemen on the sidewalks who did not get out of the way fast enough were kicked from it in the street; ladies who ventured to go out were insulted by their low importunity. . . . When the troops passed our hotel the French ladies waved their handkerchiefs and went into ecstasies. 'What a brilliant army! Let them only return to la belle France and they will march against Berlin and take it à la bayonet!' I did not regard their talk, but only wished to be in Berlin to meet them there."

Whatever the feelings of the people they formerly "protected," the French conducted a masterly operation of withdrawal, moving by echelon back to the port of embarkation in an orderly fashion that cost them no casualties, perhaps mainly because the republican forces were only too glad to see them leave in disciplined haste. They brought off the evacuation, in fact, more efficiently than their original landings. Marching columns had to be extracted from all over the hostile country and arrive in Veracruz on schedule. There thirty army transports and seven chartered steamers awaited them in the roadstead.

Between February 18 and March 11 the considerable logistics feat of embarking 169 staff officers, 1,264 line officers and 27,600 troops, plus 35 horses, was accomplished. A little fewer than 3,000 of these were Austrians and Belgians returning to their homelands after receiving a bounty to reenlist in Maximilian's army and being released from that obligation.*

Maximilian had watched the march-past of the last battalions of the French army with mixed feelings, mainly those of resentment. As a sign of his displeasure with Marshal Bazaine, he had ordered all the doors and windows of the National Palace shuttered. Even the guards stayed inside. But Maximilian himself watched the departure of the rear guard, standing behind the high parapet on the roof of the palace. He was wrapped in a gray cloak with a wide-brimmed felt hat concealing his face.

When he saw the last ranks of the last battalion disappear down the Calle de la Moneda, he turned to his companions and with evident relief said: "At last we are free!"

Free to confront an estimated 60,000 republican forces with several thousand troops of dubious loyalty.

During the last days of the imperial occupation of Mexico City, what remained of the capital's society was enlivened by the presence of Prince Salm-Salm and his American wife. A handsome couple with a keen sense of drama and an appetite for high adventure, they had come to Mexico City to offer the Prince's well-honed sword to the imperialist cause, although many of his former comrades in the Union Army up north had joined the Juaristas. Two more spectacular personalities could hardly be imagined; their joint career reads like something concocted by Ouida or Anthony Hope.

Prince Félix Constantin Alexander Johann Nepomuk Salm-Salm was a tall, handsome, swaggering fellow with black hair, prominent brown eyes and waxed mustachios. There was a touch of the hyperthyroid in the way his eyes popped, in the intense pleasure with which he flung himself into every avail-

---

* The Carlotta Colony also joined the exodus from Mexico, except for a few individual members. Some of the ex-Confederates went farther south to Yucatán, to Venezuela or Brazil, but most returned to the States to face the rigors of Reconstruction.

able arena of combat. The younger son of the ruling prince of Westphalia, he was educated at a Berlin cadet school. Later, having acquired the tastes of a field marshal, he was posted to Vienna, where he lived so extravagantly and gambled so recklessly that he was forced to flee from Europe to escape his creditors.

America was then the refuge of the bankrupt and bereft. It also offered a war in which there was a great demand for professional soldiers, with the highest premium going to those with European service. On the voyage over he upgraded his rank in the Prussian army and bluffed his way into a colonelcy in the Union Army. His first assignment was to the staff of Major General Louis Blenker's division, which was composed mainly of German-Americans and conducted a disastrous campaign in western Virginia. Whether or not this could be charged to Salm's work as Blenker's chief of staff, the division actually got lost in the mountains and had to be rescued by another division with officers who could read maps.

At this low-water mark in his career, Prince Félix met a young woman of twenty-two named Agnes Leclerq. She had come to Washington as a bareback rider with a circus, and such was the topsy-turvy condition of wartime society in the capital that no one was greatly surprised by a romance involving a Union colonel and a circus performer. She was always reticent about her early life, but the available evidence indicates that she was born Agnes Elizabeth Leclerq Joy in Swanton, Vermont. One of eight children, she had run away from her impoverished family in her early teens to become an equestrienne. She looked smashing in pink tights. Though not a great beauty, her sexual magnetism comes across even in a murky surviving daguerreotype: dark sultry eyes, ripe mouth, dimpled chin, a mass of dark-blond hair and a supple figure.

She first fell in love with Salm's monocle, as she later confessed, then with the man himself, the dashing cavalier who could write, "To speak the truth, I was a soldier with all my soul, and war was my element. What I had seen of it in Europe and America served only to make me more eager to extend my experience. . . ."

Shortly after they met in a military camp outside the capital, with Prince Félix clicking heels and kissing hands until Agnes was giddy with adoration, they were married in a Washington cathedral.

When Blenker's luckless division was disbanded, Princess Agnes used her formidable charm on the governor of New York and persuaded him to appoint her husband as commanding officer of the Eighth New York Volunteers, II Corps, Army of the Potomac. They spent the winter of 1862-63 at the Army's headquarters at Falmouth, just after the disaster at Fredericksburg. The new army commander, Major General Joseph Hooker, revived the morale of his senior officers by throwing parties every night under a dozen hospital tents joined together, with a profusion of Chinese lanterns and catering by Delmonico's of New York. "The headquarters of the Army of the Potomac," wrote Charles Francis Adams, Jr., then a somewhat austere cavalry captain, "was a place to which no self-respecting man liked to go, and no decent woman would go. It was a combination of barroom and brothel."

Princess Agnes thrived in that raffish atmosphere, however, and was "the toast of the officers," it was said, "and the talk of the men." She was not dismayed by a small scandal she created when President and Mrs. Lincoln came down to Falmouth in April, 1863. Presented to President Lincoln at a reception, bold little Agnes stood on tiptoe, pulled down the President's face, and kissed him lingeringly on his bearded cheek while Mrs. Lincoln glowered and other matrons whimpered for smelling salts.

The incident inspired one of Lincoln's more outrageous puns. A few nights later the Lincolns were dining with General Daniel Sickles. The latter, whose reputation was anything but saintly, was greatly surprised when Lincoln leaned over and remarked, "Sickles, I never knew you were such a pious man until I came down this week to see the army."

Sickles mumbled that he didn't "merit such a reputation."

"Oh, yes," President Lincoln insisted, "they tell me you are the greatest Psalmist in the army. They say you are more than a Psalmist—they say you are a Salm-Salmist."

Prince Félix's career, under his wife's astute management, prospered to the end of the war. His regiment was sent to join Sherman's Army of the Tennessee and he handled it well at Chattanooga and Nashville. Princess Agnes had no intention of

being left behind, not when her husband's troopers were calling her the Soldier Princess and cheering every time she rode
into view. She had dresses made for her with a tuniclike bodice
and a Red Cross insignia affixed to an armband, and hastened
to join the regiment in Alabama. Somehow she smuggled herself onto a military train along with a black-and-tan terrier
named Jimmy, who unwillingly became one of the most celebrated canines in military history, with Confederate, Mexican
and finally French shot and shell fired over his reluctant head.
Since she could ride better than any officer, she had no difficulty
in staying with the regiment for the rest of the war—a vivan-
dière, or camp follower, of the romantic tradition.

Viewed in a cold retrospective light, the couple may seem a
trifle ridiculous—a debt-dodging Shakespearean ruffian of the
ancient Pistol breed and an adventuress with a bold smile and
an opportunistic eye, with nostrils flaring for the chance to play
a melodramatic role. True enough, but they were as brave and
loyal as they were glory-struck. If you hired the prince's sword,
you also engaged the whole man. If you won the fealty of the
princess from Vermont, you had a tigress on your side.

After the Civil War ended with Prince Félix a brigadier general and in command of the Sixty-eighth as well as the Eighth
New York Volunteers, he was appointed the military governor
of Atlanta. Ruling a conquered city, presiding over the local
Reconstruction were not the sort of work that accorded with
Salm's hyperactive disposition. In any case, he had no great
sympathy, as an aristocrat, for the Union's postwar program.
There was a war going on in Mexico, and he could not shut his
ears to the echoing trumpets, nor could Agnes easily surrender
the role of the Soldier Princess. In her memoir she recollected
that she fought with her husband for six hours before he
yielded to her demands that she accompany him to Mexico
City. Soon after arrival in Mexico, Prince Félix wangled an invitation to dine with Maximilian through the Prussian Minister, Baron von Magnus, and was posted to the Belgian corps,
with which he served in covering the withdrawal operations of
the French army. Later, reunited with Agnes and Jimmy in
Mexico City, he watched the French depart and began angling
for a command of his own. Father Fischer might have been the
best possibility in that regard, but Prince Félix couldn't stand

his fellow German. "About his morals," the prince later wrote, "very queer reports were in circulation, and it was well known that he, though a priest, had many children in different parts of the country." Finally he swallowed his objections to the Jesuit's character, went to Father Fischer, and asked him to obtain Maximilian's permission to raise a mounted regiment. "The oily priest promised. I went every day to see him, and he continued his promises, but my affairs did not make any progress at all." A volunteer of Salm-Salm's stripe was not so easily discouraged.

On February 10, the imperialist forces also began to evacuate the capital, five days after the French left. The Republican armies, having cleared the north and south, were beginning to converge on Mexico City in four different columns. One column, under Porfirio Díaz, would detach itself from the concentric movement to threaten the capture of Mexico City and Puebla and thus block any chances of Maximilian's fighting his way back down the corridor to the sea.

If there were any military strategists around imperial headquarters, their endeavors did not make themselves apparent. The imperial decision was to concentrate at one of the remaining strongholds, the walled city of Querétaro, and confront the rebels there, when the only sensible solution would have been to fall back down the road to Veracruz. Outnumbered as they were, the imperialists, in heading for Querétaro, then rendering themselves immobile, were only sinking themselves into a death trap; they might have outmaneuvered the enemy, live today to fight another day, but they couldn't outfight the armies being concentrated against them.

So the hopeless march to Querétaro began, with the vanguard leaving February 10, Maximilian and the bulk of his forces three days later. All foreign troops, he ordered, were to be left behind in Mexico City. To take them, his flimsy reasoning ran, would indicate he didn't entirely trust his Mexican forces. The Austrian hussars begged to accompany him, but he would promise only to send for them if the situation at Querétaro became unmanageable.

Prince Salm-Salm found a way to circumvent that order. He persuaded one of the Mexican commanders, General Santiago Vidaurri, to take him along as a member of his staff and disguised himself as a Mexican officer. "Salm jumped nearly out of his skin for pleasure," as his wife wrote in her diary.

Princess Agnes naturally assumed that she and Jimmy would go along with him, but for once Prince Félix ruled against any camp following. "He refused in the most determined manner," she recorded. "I cried and screamed so as to be heard two blocks off; and Jimmy, who felt for his mistress, howled and barked; but Salm stole away and took a street where he could not hear me. I believed I hated him at that moment, and felt very unhappy, for I knew he would come to grief, having never any luck without me."

A Vermont girl of Princess Agnes' mettle would not take treatment like that with a few snuffles into a cambric hankie; soon she and Jimmy were involving themselves in adventures more hair-raising than her fleet-footed husband's.

Maximilian literally stole out of his capital at dawn on February 13. "We traversed the streets without the knowledge of most of the citizens," his secretary Blasio noted, "and only a few early risers saw the Emperor's party pass." The city which he had entered in triumph less than three years before slept through his departure, mainly indifferent to whether he would ever reappear.

Just outside the northern gate of the city they found a brigade of infantry—including the Empress Carlotta's Regiment commanded by the soon-to-be-infamous Colonel Miguel López —waiting to escort the emperor on the march to Querétaro. Twelve miles out of the capital the column of infantry, which now also included the mounted Municipal Guard, was attacked by a guerrilla band. After an hour of skirmishing—"I stayed close to Maximilian," Blasio confessed, "believing that the safest place, although bullets continually snapped about us like whiplashes"—the guerrillas were driven off in the direction of Cuautitlán. When the imperialist column reached Cuautitlán, they found a captured comrade hanging head down from a tree in the plaza, his whole body hacked by the guerrillas' machetes.

Obviously the 170-mile march to Querétaro was not going to be a frolic. Maximilian's brush with death, however, seemed to have lightened his spirits. He was gay and talkative at dinner that night. "Evidently," Blasio thought, "this life of action and danger had the effect of distracting him from the gloomy thoughts that had been tormenting him. . . . The Emperor congratulated me on the manner in which I had comported myself under my baptism of fire. Someone jestingly said that my bravery was due to the effect of the champagne of the curé of Tlalnepantla [with whom the Emperor's party had breakfasted en route], and he was not altogether wrong."

A day or two later, on the march, Maximilian discovered Prince Salm-Salm and a number of Austrian hussars who had also disobeyed his orders under their sombrero and serape disguises; a fellow Teuton could hardly have failed to notice cobalt eyes and fair complexions under the brims of the steeple hats.

"Zounds!" Maximilian exclaimed. "Salm, how did you get here?"

Salm-Salm explained himself.

Maximilian shrugged and remarked that it would be good to have someone around with whom he could speak German.

Up the line rebel activity became more strenuous. If Maximilian's military training had been more thorough, he would have realized that he was marching his forces into an untenable position with guerrillas cutting all the roads and preventing him from being supplied or reinforced. In the defile outside the village of San Miguel Calpulaplan, the imperialist column was attacked by a republican force which had seized the high ground. For more than an hour Maximilian and his party, including Dr. Basch, Blasio and various servants (but not Father Fischer, who had discreetly chosen to stay at Chapultepec with the rear echelon), were under heavy fire from the fusiliers on the heights. His nonchalance was impressive. "The Emperor," Salm-Salm recorded, "was always in the middle of the fight, and distinguished himself by his coolness. I was close to His Majesty when I heard someone blubbering. I looked around, and saw that it came from the poor Hungarian cook. A spent ball had passed through his upper lip and knocked out some of his teeth. They must have been strong teeth, for the bullet remained in the mouth, and the cook, who did not like the taste of lead, spit it out together with his ivories. By this his tasting faculties were spoiled for some time."

It took most of the morning for Maximilian's commanders to organize the counterattack, work around the rear of the enemy on the high ground, and clear the road through the defile. If things were that bad on the road, in a countryside evidently swarming with regular and irregular republican forces, what would they find at Querétaro?

17. The Condemned Men of Querétaro

> *Not only the rationality of millenniums—also their
> madness breaks out in us. Dangerous it is to be an
> heir.*
>
> —FRIEDRICH WILHELM NIETZSCHE,
> *Thus Spake Zarathustra*

WHAT awaited Maximilian at Querétaro was yet another round
of dainty ceremony, the last in a life filled with the emptiness of
ritual. He entered his last stronghold on the morning of February 19 after halting a mile from the outskirts to change from his
dusty cloak to a general's uniform with the Grand Cross of the
Mexican Eagle hanging around his neck. A triumphal welcome
had been arranged by Generals Márquez, Miramón and Mejía,
who had preceded him with 8,000 troops. The generals had
been diligent, and it seemed that every one of the city's 30,000
or more citizens had been turned out to line the streets from
China Hill to the Casino Español, where he would be quartered with his retainers. The people dutifully cheered; flowers
were thrown; sloe-eyed beauties clapped their little hands on
the balconies. There were long speeches in the main salon of
the casino by various military and civil dignitaries, then a procession to the cathedral for the celebration of a *Te Deum*. A re-

ception took up the afternoon hours which might better have
been spent bolstering the city's defenses.

By nightfall Maximilian, who was still racked by malarial
headaches, was too weary to attend the banquet in his honor,
which was just as well for his peace of mind. An exchange over
the wine revealed a deadly rivalry between General Márquez,
chief of staff, and General Miramón, chief of infantry. The
quarrel was personal and to some extent professional. According to the information received at imperial headquarters,
three republican columns where approaching the citadel, Escobedo with 12,000 troops, Corona with 8,000 and Riva Palacios
with 7,000.

General Miramón contended that the proper course was to
assume the tactical offensive: to use Querétaro as a springboard
and attack each approaching enemy force in turn with their
9,000 to 10,000 imperial troops. The enemy might be beaten
piecemeal, but the imperial forces could never endure a siege
by all three columns. This strategy offered at least the semblance of a hope of success. But Márquez, as the general in
chief, insisted that they must assume the defensive. When the
time of testing came, he took care to be elsewhere while the
theory was being tried in the crucible of battle.

Maximilian stood aloof from the dispute over strategy,
believing that all he had to offer in the fighting ahead was a heroic example. As he surveyed this last capital of his, this last bit
of territory he could claim to rule, Maximilian was rather
pleased by its aspect. A military strategist would have shud-
dered—the place was enclosed by hills on which enemy artillery
could be emplaced. Maximilian saw it with an esthetic eye—
poet, architect and dreamer to the end. Querétaro was (and is)
a beautiful old city of domes and towers and red-tiled roofs; it
might have been transplanted from Moorish Spain. Located on
a high fertile plain surrounded by low hills, its climate was salubrious for anything but an extended siege. One of the more
prominent features of the landscape, which Maximilian could
see from his windows, was the Cerro de las Campanas, the Hill
of the Bells.

During his first days in Querétaro Maximilian settled into
the routine which he had followed since youth, up before
dawn, to bed not long after the light faded on the hills. "After

the Emperor finished dictating letters," Blasio later recalled, "we would go about the city, often on foot. Maximilian, in civilian clothes, would stop to watch passing soldiers, mingle with the people or, as he was always smoking, ask a light from a passer-by or offer one to some gentleman. Other days he would ride, in *charro* costume, or in a plain blue uniform. Afterwards he would return to the Casino for breakfast and until dinner was served receive visits from the generals or the authorities. In accord with his old habit, there were always guests for dinner. He would retire at nine, at the conclusion of an hour of billiards."

Quite gracefully, as always, he had fallen back on the role of spectator.

Often at dinner, Blasio said, he and his guests would "talk at length about the past, so full of hope and splendor. . . ."

Meanwhile, day after day, the enemy forces were closing and strengthening their ring around the city. The imperialist officers passed their off-duty time at the Theater Iturbide, where a company was presenting Spanish comedies, or the bullfights at the arena near the Alameda. General Miramón, Prince Salm-Salm and other officers kept urging an attack on the enemy wherever he was weakest, but Chief of Staff Márquez opposed any such activity. Finally Maximilian decided to send a message to Mexico City with instructions that the forces still available there, mostly Austrians and Mexicans, be launched in an attack on the rear of the besieging forces. Salm-Salm was riding with the emperor on March 2 when an answering dispatch was received from the capital.

"Now look at these blackguards," Maximilian exclaimed after reading it, referring to his ministers in Mexico City. "These fellows are afraid and won't send me any troops. They say the capital is in danger. They are only afraid for themselves."

The enemy was so close now that the gunpowder breath of his cannon could be felt in the city, and Maximilian moved his headquarters behind the stouter walls of the Spanish-colonial Convent of the Cross. The republicans had begun to cut off the water and other supplies by March 6. That day Maximilian and his staff rode out along the city's defenses and conferred with his commanders. Again Miramón and others urged an attack but were overruled by Márquez.

Five days later the republicans broke the aquaduct which had supplied most of the city's water. On March 13 they had emplaced artillery on China Hill and the Hill of the Bells and opened up with a daylong bombardment. Maximilian refused to take shelter behind the fortresslike walls of his convent headquarters, but stood out in the Plaza de la Cruz. He was a member of the last generation of military leadership which held that a king or general must expose himself to enemy fire, both to prove his courage and to show the troops he was willing to shed his own blood. On such chivalric occasions a polite charade generally took place. His officers would beg the leader to take cover, pointing out his inestimable value as the heart, soul and mind of the cause, and the leader would dramatically refuse.

So it was in the Plaza de la Cruz. "All remonstrances," Prince Salm-Salm reported, "proved as useless as those made by a deputation of generals the day before, who besought him not to expose himself so much. Bold Mejía said, in his plain language, 'Consider, Your Majesty, if you are killed all of us will fight against each other for the presidency,' but he [Maximilian] said the place where he stood was the right place for him."

On March 14 the enemy's troop movements indicated a general attack would be made on Querétaro's defenses. A large body of republican cavalry advanced against the southern flank, between the Casa Blanca and the Alameda. This was repulsed by Mejía's mounted forces. On the La Cruz sector enemy infantry managed to capture a cemetery and chapel but were finally driven back by repeated counterattacks. The strongest thrust was directed at capturing the bridge across the Río Blanco, which divided Querétaro from its northern suburb of San Luis.

Here the star performer was Prince Salm-Salm, who for days had been fuming over the supinity of his superiors. He had just taken command of a battalion of chasseurs (cazadores, as the Mexicans called them) when their commanding officer was wounded. They made quite a change from the Union brigade he had commanded at the end of the Civil War. "The wild fellows," he wrote, "were always fighting among themselves, and I had to do all in my power to prevent bloodshed and murder; but as soon as they were led against the enemy, they were like one man. . . . Even the very buglers, boys between fourteen and sixteen, stole sometimes outside the lines, armed with a gun and a box full of cartridges, to hunt down the *Chinacos* (Liberals) on their own hook."

Across the Río Blanco a Parrot gun was raking the imperialist positions, and Prince Salm-Salm finally received an order from the brigade commander to take it and establish a bridgehead on the republicans' side of the river. Raising his saber, shouting orders in Spanish, German and English, he and the wild-eyed chasseurs "rode forth like a pack of hounds waiting for the signal." *Furor Teutonicus* fused with *Furor Mexicanus,* and a reckless charge against the republican positions ensued. It ran into a red-hot shower of canister fired over the sights of the Parrot gun, but the chasseurs plunged on and closed in with the gun crew and its defenders. "All the artillerymen belonging to the rifled cannon were bayoneted or killed with the stocks of the guns used like clubs. The conquered piece was sent back to the bridge whilst the battalion Celaya fired on the Liberals in the *meson,* who soon saved themselves, and fled through the gardens up the hill. The infantry we saw before us fled panic-struck into the houses, of which they locked the doors; but I advanced into the street to dislodge them, and the doors were opened by well-applied shots."

The republicans had been smartly repulsed on all fronts and had suffered heavily in their first general attack on the city's defenses. Maximilian's forces, however, had lost 630 men in killed and wounded. They took between 700 and 800 prisoners, most of whom were pressed into the imperial service.

It was a victory, but no occasion for celebration. Maximilian's staff officers figured the city could hold out for about another month. Prince Salm-Salm kept urging that they take the offensive. "To permit the enemy to shut us up in a place situated so unfavorably as Querétaro," he later wrote, "seemed to me not only ridiculous but fatal. Moreover, it was not in accordance with the intentions of the Emperor, with those of Márquez either, which, at least, might be concluded from the circumstances: Márquez left all the haciendas round Querétaro perfectly untouched, whilst the securing of their superabundance, in every kind of provision, would have been his first aim if he intended to sustain a siege. How richly those haciendas were provided was experienced by the army of the enemy, which was mostly fed by them."

In any case, General Márquez, it seems, did not intend to share the fate of those besieged at Querétaro.

On March 21 a council of war decided that General Vidaurri's cavalry, 1,200 men, would break through the siege lines and ride back to Mexico City with Maximilian's plenipotentiary accompanying them. The latter would round up all the men, money and supplies available and return to the besieged citadel within two weeks. Maximilian decided that General Miramón should perform this function, but General Márquez objected on the grounds, as Blasio related, that "Miramón's youthful valor and temerity would cause the project to fail." Márquez proposed that he go instead.

Maximilian should have been suspicious of Márquez's eagerness to act as his messenger. Certainly the place of the chief of staff was with his combat forces, not to go haring off on a supposed rescue mission. However, as Prince Salm-Salm observed, "The Emperor was perfectly infatuated by Márquez. Though a man of good sense, his character was too noble and too pure to suspect the honesty of others."

So Maximilian yielded to Márquez, elevated him to the rank of lieutenant general, and sent him with Vidaurri's brigade over the roads north to the capital. With him also went a letter to Father Fischer instructing him to facilitate Márquez's job of rounding up all the available troops, foreign and Mexican, and reinforcing and resupplying Querétaro as soon as possible. "What worries me most," Maximilian concluded his letter to the Jesuit, "is the conduct of the feeble old wigs in the capital, who are probably engaged in open treason out of sheer funk and inanity."

Before Márquez left, according to Salm-Salm, he pledged himself to carry out his mandate. "He was expressly forbidden to undertake any *coup de main* or other expedition, but was bound to return as soon as possible. Before all the generals assembled, Márquez gave his word of honor to return to Querétaro within a fortnight, *coute que coute!*"

Leonardo Márquez, his protestations of loyalty to the imperialist cause and the foolish trust placed in them, epitomized much that was wrong with Maximilian's intermittent conduct of his government. The latter had often been warned about Márquez but persisted in entrusting him with the highest

responsibilities. On arrival in Mexico City Márquez repaid that
trust by illegally levying a 500,000-peso "loan" on the foreign
colony. He heard that Díaz was marching to besiege Puebla,
broke his pledge to return to Querétaro, and marched off to
confront Díaz with 4,000 troops he had rounded up in the capital. At San Lorenzo he was hurled back by the republicans.
Most of his troops were killed or captured, but Márquez surrounded himself with the 400 Austrian and Belgian troopers
who formed his bodyguard and rode to safety.

Márquez had deserted his army in the field, he had betrayed
his comrades at Querétaro, but he managed then and later to
save his own skin. When he returned to the capital, he was
shunned as a coward and a traitor. Subsequently, when the republicans took Mexico City, the man who had earned the title
the Tiger of Tacubaya by executing a number of physicians
and medical students for having cared for the republican
wounded, concealed himself in an unoccupied grave in one of
the city's cemeteries until he could make his escape.

In Querétaro Maximilian waited anxiously for word from
Márquez. Ammunition and other supplies were running low.
By April 3, two days before Márquez had pledged himself to return, even Maximilian began to wonder aloud if Márquez had
let him down. Then he would hastily add, "No no, it is impossible!"

No general attacks had been launched by the enemy, but he
was being reinforced almost daily. The republican forces now
totaled about 40,000 against Maximilian's approximately 8,000
—5-to-1 odds that could not be long sustained.

Meanwhile, he was learning how tightly bottled up Querétaro was, with every road, river, hill and suburban rooftop
posted with watchers quick to land on anyone who tried to escape through the siege lines. The republicans had also begun to
entrench themselves, to push sapping operations, to conduct a
formal, bitter-end siege.

Several times Maximilian sent couriers with messages to Márquez in Mexico City demanding to know when he would arrive.
Each time the courier was captured, hanged, and strung up
over the republican trenches with a huge placard around his
neck reading THE EMPEROR'S COURIER.

Even the emperor's table, in which he had always taken a

gourmet's pride, had begun to suffer from the privations of the siege, just as his sensitive and compassionate spirit suffered from the loss of friends and comrades as a result of enemy action—sometimes with shocking swiftness.

The nuns at the convent baked his bread, any surplus stocks of which he distributed to his officers. Blasio told of one April morning when the emperor was breakfasting and a favorite of his, Colonel Loaeza, appeared in the corridor to collect his ration of fresh bread. The menu that morning was preserved fish and bread. "I offered him some bread and fish and a glass of wine," Blasio recalled. "Loaeza, who was a jovial fellow, referred to his breakfast as 'the feast of Belshazzar.' Heavy firing was going on, and Loaeza announced his intention of proceeding to the roof to see what the music was all about.

"Because of his gayety he had numerous friends among those about the Emperor and among the officers who, by reason of his stature and his always wearing big boots and full uniform, called him 'Napoleon the Little.' He had scarcely reached the roof when we heard a cry, and a few moments later two soldiers came, carrying him in their arms. A shell had exploded at his feet and shattered both his legs. Hearing his groans, the Emperor came. Dr. Basch amputated his legs and later he was carried on a cot to the house where he lived with his young wife and an infant son."

A day later Colonel Loaeza died.

Maximilian himself missed death by inches a few days later when he watched the artillery dueling from the tower of the convent. A shell exploded so close to him that he was showered with fragments of masonry.

That close brush with death, that picture of himself sharing the perils of the siege with his soldiers, that now obsessive concept of leading his cause in person, uplifted his spirits. He wrote one of the officials of his household at Miramar quite cheerfully of his experiences under siege:

"My old comrades in the navy would be surprised if they knew me as the head of a veritable army. The admiral has gone into retirement, and I am an active commander-in-chief, booted and spurred and wearing an enormous sombrero. . . . I am discharging my new duties vigorously and it gives me great pleasure to direct military operations, particularly with young and enthusiastic troops. Just as at other times I used to make tours of inspection both by night and day, so I now make a point of visiting the advance posts and surprising the men in the trenches at all hours of the night. At such moments as these the enemy has not enough bullets or mortars for me and my staff: we have become in effect a human target."

He added that he was sending a fragment of the cannonball which narrowly missed him on the convent tower "as a souvenir for our museum at Miramar."

By mid-April the defenders of Querétaro knew there was no hope that Márquez would march to their relief. During the next several weeks, desperate sorties and stratagems were tried and each time failed. Prince Salm-Salm attempted a breakout with his *cazadores,* but they were quickly discouraged by the growing enemy trench system. On April 27 a more massive attempt to break the siege lines occurred. The previous day all the church bells in Querétaro were rung, to give the impression that glorious news had arrived, and reports were circulated that Márquez was on his way to attack the republican forces in the rear. Then Miramón directed an infantry assault along the northern sector and the road to Mexico City. His troops succeeded in breaking through the first line of trenches and taking the forward slopes of Cemetery Hill, captured 500 prisoners and 21 artillery pieces in the first hour of fighting. They all were so excited that they forgot the purpose of the attack: to open up an escape route for Maximilian and the whole garrison. All the emperor's belongings had been packed, and his escort had been saddled, since early that morning. Several hours too late Miramón managed to get a second assault under way, but by then the enemy commanders had crowned the hillcrest with artillery. Except for the bag of prisoners and cannon, the attack of April 27 had been wasted.

Horse and mule began appearing on the menu, and soon enough dog and cat, trampled fodder and tree bark. The Mexican generals began bickering among themselves; the newly risen Ramón Méndez whispered reports that Miramón intended to "sell out" Maximilian and the garrison. The rumor even reached Maximilian one night, and he called Prince Salm-Salm to the convent to alert the Austrian hussars against an attempt on his person, but the night passed without incident.

There was a Judas in the camp, but it was not General Miramón. Perhaps already Colonel Miguel López, who had been a
favorite of Carlotta's, who had been liberally honored with
rank and decorations, and for whose son Maximilian had stood
as godfather, had taken the first steps toward playing that un-
lovely role, with a golden handshake and a generalship in the
republican army as his promised reward. Prince Salm-Salm, in
retrospect, thought so. Later he would recall that one day early
in May he was writing a dispatch in Maximilian's room at the
convent with the emperor's pet King Charles spaniel, Baby, sitting in his lap. "López entered and whispered something to the
Emperor in a corner. Little Baby, friendly with almost everybody, now jumped from my lap and attacked the legs of the
colonel with inconceivable fury and would not be calmed. The
Emperor reminded me later of this occurrence." The prince
was convinced that Baby was trying to tell them something.

On May 5—the Cinco de Mayo, commemorating the republican victory over the French at Puebla—the imperialist forces
expected a general attack up and down the line from the republicans. Every day there had been a heavy bombardment of the
city. The whole garrison stood to arms that day, but nothing
happened. That night the enemy positions erupted with fireworks, musketry and artillery fire, but it was more of a holiday
celebration than an assault on the city. The republicans illuminated their camps on the surrounding hills, fired thousands of
multicolored rockets, and apparently every gun at their disposal. A number of drunken republican soldiers launched an
unofficial assault on the bridge over the Río Blanco, but they
were easily repulsed.

The heavy bombardments continued daily through the first
two weeks of May, and the imperial commissariat announced
on May 11 that there were provisions enough for only a few
more days. Something had to be done within the week, or the
garrison's resistance would simply collapse. Already there were
an alarming number of desertions, even from the hitherto fan-
atically loyal Empress Carlotta Regiment.

A Hamlet to the bitter end, Maximilian was unable to tell his
generals what to do. At most he could make a choice of the solutions they presented him. Early on the morning of May 14 a
critical council of war was convened at the convent. The gen-

erals proposed an all-out attack. If that failed, they would "evacuate" the city after destroying their artillery. Obviously that course would be gallant but suicidal. An attack all along the line would certainly fail because of the enemy's 5-to-1 superiority. After it failed, the enemy would hardly allow an "evacuation" of the survivors after giving them time to spike their guns; he would demand their unconditional surrender and, if it were not forthcoming, would charge in and destroy the city.

Maximilian listened to the discussions of this proposed course, occasionally ducking out to tell Prince Salm-Salm, who was installed in another cell of the convent, what the generals were saying and asking the prince's opinion. Salm-Salm was smart enough to know that the only possibility of success lay in attacking in one sector, hoping for a breakthrough, then pouring the whole garrison through.

Possibly through Salm-Salm's indirect influence a wiser plan was adopted. "It was resolved to break through the lines of the enemy with the whole of our little army," Salm-Salm recorded, *"which was still possible at any point we chose.* It is true the enemy had encircled us closely with his lines, but his whole army was employed occupying them, without keeping any reserve at his disposal."

A more definitive account of the final desperate stratagem devised by the imperialist garrison of Querétaro was provided by José Blasio, who attended it as Maximilian's secretary. Perhaps, if it had been given a chance, it would have worked, at least to the extent of freeing Maximilian and several thousand of his troops from the besieged city. The question, Blasio related, was where to break out and where to reconcentrate afterward. "What road should we take and where should we go, after leaving the city? With insufficient and demoralized troops it was impossible to make for Mexico City. At the first encounter with the republicans we would undoubtedly have been cut to pieces.

"Our only hope lay in gaining the mountains, a few miles from Querétaro where the people belonged to Mejía, body and soul. There, with the aid of the valiant Indian supporters of Mejía [a full-blooded Indian himself] and safe from any treason, Maximilian and those who were loyal to him might await developments. The final plans of the evacuation provided that Maximilian's escort should be formed by Prince Salm-Salm, with the forces of Colonel Campos and the Austrian Hussars; a battalion of the Mexican Chasseurs, the Fourth Cavalry, and a squadron of the Empress' Regiment headed by Colonel López." The time of the attempted breakout would be May 15 at 3 A.M. To guard against treachery, the exact place would be decided at the last moment and confided only to the ranking commanders at the selected spot.

Later there would be much speculation, and a certain amount of hugger-mugger, involving Maximilian's "vanished treasure." The truth was that it did not exist. As of May 14, 1867, the entire financial resources of the empire consisted of 5,000 pesos remaining from what had been levied on the citizens of Querétaro for the privilege of serving as the last outpost of that empire and having their homes smashed by artillery fire. Maximilian ordered Blasio to divide the gold among various aides, including Salm-Salm, Dr. Basch and Blasio himself, and the silver among the servants. The gold pieces had already been distributed when Colonel López appeared to demand his share. "Angrily and violently," Blasio said, López protested when he learned that his name had not been on the emperor's list of beneficiaries. Grudgingly he finally accepted the 100 silver pesos remaining. Salm-Salm, who witnessed the squalid scene, remarked that López was oddly excited at receiving his share in pieces of silver and "resented it as an apparent mark of distrust, which was not in the least intended, as nobody distrusted him."

A final council of war, as it turned out, doomed whatever chances Maximilian had of escaping the trap of Querétaro. Such councils were generally fatal, the device of a confused or divided command without a single strong and decisive voice. The command system of modern armies would not be renovated until after the results of the Franco-Prussian War had been digested and the flaws in the committee system exposed.

May 14, hours before the scheduled breakout, passed with little apparent activity in the enemy's positions above the city. Querétaro, however, was bustling with preparations for the crucial operation.

The final conference of the imperialist generals was called for 10 P.M., at which it would be decided where the assault on the enemy line would take place five hours later. General Mejía, whose Indian followers constituted an important factor in the plan, opened the proceedings by asking that the breakout be postponed for another twenty-four hours. An armory at which his amateur gunsmiths were repairing 2,000 rifles with which the Indians in the hills above Querétaro would be equipped had been working desperately, but so far only 1,200 of the weapons had been restored to usable condition. In another day the job could be finished. The council decided to grant him the delay.

When Maximilian informed Prince Salm-Salm of the decision, the latter commented, "Your Majesty, I must confess that I am as little satisfied with delay as I can approve the reasons of the generals."

"Well, one day more or less, will be no matter," Maximilian said with a shrug. "Take care that the hussars and the bodyguard remain saddled." The night passed quietly. Occasionally there was an exchange of shots between outposts.

There was a muted rustle of activity in the bastion called La Cruz, where Colonel López commanded. Certain arrangements with the enemy had been concluded, and now the time had come to the end the siege of Querétaro not in a blaze of glory and bloodshed, but quietly, sensibly, through informal negotiation. López had been promised 2,000 ounces of gold if he would betray the garrison, let the republican shock troops into the city through his position. The enemy general in chief, Mariano Escobedo, had also promised that the emperor would be allowed to slip away and escape before the cleanup operations began. Now López stealthily left his headquarters—with only his second-in-command, Lieutenant Colonel Jablonski, a Mexican-born Pole, knowing what he was up to—and made his way to the hillocks occupied by the enemy.

Prince Salm-Salm was restless that night, angry over the postponement, and was splitting a bottle of champagne with a companion in a cell down the corridor from the emperor's room. Shortly after midnight he lay down on his field bed without undressing, placing his revolver under his pillow and his saber within reaching distance.

About five o'clock, while it was still dark out, he was awakened by scurrying footsteps.

Suddenly Colonel López bounded into the room and shouted to the half-awake Salm-Salm, "Quick, save the life of the Emperor. The enemy has broken through at La Cruz. The convent is surrounded."

Outside, in the gray half-light of the courtyard, Salm-Salm could see the tall shakos of the *Supremos Podres*, the shock-troop regiment of the republican army. They were swarming everywhere. Buckling on his saber and revolver, Salm-Salm hurried down the corridor to Maximilian's room. The emperor had already dressed and said calmly—no longer capable of being surprised by anything that happened to him in Mexico—"Salm, we are betrayed. Go down and let the hussars and the bodyguard march out. We will go to the *cerro* [apparently he referred to the Hill of the Bells] and see how we can arrange the matter."

The *Supremos Podres* were already thronging through the corridors but in their excitement evidently did not recognize the emperor with a greatcoat thrown over his uniform. With Salm-Salm, Blasio, Dr. Basch and others, he dashed across the plaza to the inn where their horses were saddled and waiting. There weren't enough mounts for everyone, however, so Maximilian announced they would all proceed on foot. They were crossing the plaza and heading westward, toward the strong imperialist position on the Hill of the Bells, when they were confronted by a body of enemy soldiers. With them were the *Supremos Podres'* commander, the young Colonel José Rincón-Gallardo, two of whose female relatives had been ladies-in-waiting at Chapultepec—and, surprisingly to Maximilian and his companions, Colonel Miguel López. The latter's treachery was thus made manifest.

Even more surprisingly, Colonel Rincón-Gallardo took a long searching look at the emperor, obviously recognized him, lifted his hand, and ordered his soldiers, "Let them pass." Maximilian and his companions went on their way. "It was obvious," Salm-Salm later wrote, "that it was not intended to capture the Emperor, but to give him time to escape." This made sense; the republicans would only find Maximilian an embarrassment and had no intention of making a martyr out of him, if they could avoid it, and thus supply the reactionary elements with an inspiration in the years ahead. "The whole proceeding was so astonishing and striking, that I looked up inquiringly to the face of the Emperor. He understood my look, and said, 'You see, it never does any harm to do good. It is true, you find amongst twenty people nineteen ungrateful; but still, now and then, one grateful. I have just now had an instance of it. The officer who let us pass has a sister, who was frequently with the Empress, and who has done much good to her. Do good, Salm, whenever you have an opportunity.'" Thus spake the coffeehouse philosopher, even in the midst of danger. But he was deluded: It was politics, not personal gratitude, that was giving him a last chance to escape.

On their way out of the city they again were confronted by the enemy when a battalion headed by mounted officers suddenly marched around a corner. Again Maximilian and his companions were carefully ignored.

Instead of fleeing the best way he could, making his way into the mountains and finding shelter with Mejía's followers, Maximilian was determined on the formality of resistance. The Hapsburg indoctrination, the prescribed ritual for behaving like a king and dying like a gentleman, had taken full possession of him.

Dawn was coming up behind the ridgeline as he and his followers trudged across the plain at the foot of the Hill of the Bells. They climbed the fortified heights and found that they were not nearly so strongly held as they had believed. Desertions had already sapped the outposts; down in the city General Méndez had gone into hiding, and General Miramón had been wounded and taken prisoner. General Mejía had escaped the republican net and came riding up to join the emperor on the hilltop. It was held by about 100 troops and 4 artillery pieces.

Full daylight now illuminated the scene with a merciless clarity. Republican batteries were beginning to take ranging shots on the Hill of the Bells and kicking up dust on the lower slopes. Wheeling into a line of columns, the enemy infantry, regiment after regiment, was maneuvering for the ground assault. A clamor of church bells rose from the city to signal the republican triumph with a secular joy.

Maximilian busied himself with rummaging through his

leather portfolio and handing Blasio private papers to be burned immediately. A little bonfire of inconsequential secrets testified to the end of his empire.

When that task was finished, observing the thousands of enemy soldiers converging on the hill with such a flattering exhibition of overkill, he suggested to General Mejía, "Let us get on our horses and try to get through this chain of men who are hemming us in. If we cannot get out at least we can die in the attempt."

General Mejía shook his head. "There is nothing to do but surrender."

For a moment or two it appeared that reinforcements might be on their way from the city. They saw a phalanx of cavalry in scarlet tunics galloping out of the westernmost suburb and heading for the Hill of the Bells. With tears in his eyes, Maximilian called out to Salm-Salm, "Look, Salm, there come my faithful hussars." A republican battalion, with the turncoat López at their head, blocked the Austrians' path. López ordered them to surrender, and they did.

Maximilian shook his head and murmured to Salm-Salm, "Now for a lucky bullet."

The troops still on the Hill of the Bells, seeing the insuperable odds against them, were dropping their rifles, raising their hands and going down the hill to surrender to the oncoming republicans.

At about 6:30 A.M., May 16, 1867, the seventy-two-day siege of Querétaro and the three-year reign of Maximilian came to an end. A white flag, fashioned from a lance and a bed sheet taken from the tent of the commanding officer on the hilltop bastion, was carried down the hill as the firing ceased. Republican officers came up the slope and escorted Maximilian and his companions to the bottom where General Escobedo, the enemy commander, was waiting to accept Maximilian's sword.

The republicans, with their Mexican sense of the fitness of a solemn occasion, brought forward a horse for Maximilian to ride back to the center of the city. Along the way Maximilian was appalled when two enemy horsemen quarreled over a piece of loot and one shot the other through the chest; it almost seemed that in that commonplace incident, of a sort he had been spared from witnessing by his princely isolation, he glimpsed the true horror of the civil war for which he was partly responsible. There were other moments of theater before Maximilian was returned to the Convent of the Cross. One enemy officer approached, embaced him and cried out in dramatic tones, "I greet you not as Emperor, but as Archduke of Austria." Another, farther along the way, rushed up to Maximilian, shoved his pistol in the emperor's face and might have shot him if the guards had not intervened.

Before General Escobedo left his presence, Maximilian asked that his men be spared, that all foreigners who had served in his cause be permitted to return to their homelands, that "If more blood must be spilled, take only mine." The enemy commander nodded and replied that all of them would be treated as prisoners of war. Maximilian also asked that he be allowed to send a note to General Riva Palacios, the humane, poetry-writing soldier who was somewhere in the city. Maximilian had always admired him, and on December 15, 1865—as Riva Palacios probably knew—had officially made Palacios an exception to the Black Decree.* The contents of the note were never revealed, but possibly they were responsible for Maximilian's quite decent treatment in the enemy's hands.

Maximilian was ushered back into his old cell at the convent —now a cell in a different sense—and found it had been looted in his brief absence. It was stripped of everything except his camp bed, the mattress of which had been slashed by someone (the first of many) looking for "Maximilian's treasure." Prince Salm-Salm claimed that the emperor's silver basin and pitcher had been taken by Colonel López and were found in his room at the convent.

He lay on his ruined bed, suffering from an attack of the stomach trouble that had been plaguing him as a result of the restricted diet under siege but all that day, flat on his back, held informal court for his captors. Many were only curious yokels who had never seen an emperor in the flesh, but he was also visited by a number of republican generals and Colonel Rincón-Gallardo, who, according to both Salm-Salm and Bla-

---

* Maximilian had directed Marshal Bazaine: "In the event Riva Palacios should be captured . . . he should be brought to Mexico City. This exception is for special reasons, and is the only one the Emperor intends to make to the Decree of 3rd October. . . . Your excellency will give positive instructions that if he is taken, Riva Palacios should not be put to death."

sio, gave him some of the details of how Querétaro was betrayed. He did not hesitate to name Colonel Miguel López as the traitor and added, "Men like him serve when they are needed, but afterward one kicks them out the door." That, roughly, was to be Miguel López's fate.

At dusk General Mejía, the best and most faithful of the professionals serving him, as much an Indian as Juárez, was allowed to visit him. "I am ready for anything," Maximilian told the broad-faced, impassive Mejía. "I am finished."

The Emperor Maximilian may have been finished with the world, might have welcomed the news that he would be shot the following dawn, but he had become a *cause célèbre* in Europe and North America, and a Hapsburg prince could not be disposed of so summarily. During the thirty-five days that followed the capture of Querétaro, that small city would become the background for a thrilling spectacle, a circus of newspaper headlines and diplomatic notes, as viewed from the world beyond. Strenuous efforts—some of them combining melodrama and farce, all of them made in recognition of the fact it was a hopeless case—were to be undertaken on his behalf. Maximilian had signed his own death warrant when he issued the Black Decree which condemned so many republicans to the firing squad. He knew it, so did his would-be saviors, but an immense effort was mounted to obtain clemency for him.

Before an extravaganza of revolutionary justice could be staged, there were mopping-up operations in Querétaro. On May 16 republican headquarters posted notices in the streets that imperialist officers, many of whom had gone into hiding, were given twenty-four hours to surrender themselves. The sole holdout against this order was the stubborn General Méndez, who was captured two days later, thanks to his own nasty temper. A few days before the siege ended Méndez had quarreled with a hunchbacked tailor and struck him in the face with his riding whip. The day the city fell the tailor happened to see Méndez slinking along one of the back alleys; he followed the general and subsequently told republican headquarters where he could be found. Méndez was sentenced to be shot and asked to be given a final interview with Maximilian, who told him on parting, "You go in the vanguard, General. We shall soon follow you on the same road."

Maximilian, along with Salm-Salm, Basch, Blasio and other companions in misfortune, were moved from the Convent of the Cross to the Convent of Santa Teresita several squares to the west. They were marched there on foot after the nuns had been dispossessed. "The uncertain fate before us made us all serious," Salm-Salm noted with commendable understatement. "We were escorted by a formidable force. One battalion marched at the head, another brought up the rear. . . . When we arrived at the entrance of Santa Teresita, many women passed through the lines of the guard, and gave the prisoners oranges and cigars."

The emperor and his fellow prisoners, including a number of his generals, lived on donations of food from the populace; the empire had become a small collection of charity cases. "Otherwise," Blasio noted, "we would have starved, for our jailers did not concern themselves with whether we had anything to eat or not." Maximilian himself was crowded into one room of the convent with Dr. Basch and two of his servants.

Five days later the prisoners were transferred to the Capuchin convent, Maximilian himself being confined to the pantheon, or burial vault, under the structure. In the daytime he was allowed to escape from that dank underground chamber— and the morbid thoughts it must have aroused in a man in his position—and permitted to stroll with his companions under the orange trees in the patio. Under those balmier surroundings, Blasio later related, his spirits revived, and so did the daydreamer. He had begun to convince himself that the Mexicans could not be so unseemly as to execute a bona fide prince, that he and his friends would be allowed to return to Europe. "You shall go with me, first to London," he told Blasio. "We'll stay there a year, have my papers brought from Miramar and write a history of my reign. Then we shall go to Naples, and rent a house in one of the beautiful suburbs which surround the city, with a view of the landscape and the sea. On my yacht *Ondina*, with Basch, old Bilimek and four servants we'll make little voyages to the Greek archipelago, to Athens, to the coast of Turkey. Later I shall spend the rest of my life in the midst of the Adriatic, on my island La Croma. . . ."

The details of how he would get out of the republicans' clutches he left to others; reality had always been an unwelcome visitor. There had always been servitors to take care of his needs—why not now when his life needed saving? There was such a volunteer servitor eager to be of assistance. For weeks now the Princess Salm-Salm had been dancing with impatience in the wings, waiting for a cue to come onstage and participate in the struggle. It was too late to save the empire—a project she did not regard as beyond her capabilities—but not, perhaps, to save the emperor. Here, finally, was the role Agnes Leclerq, Vermont starveling, bareback rider, adventuress, had been waiting for all her twenty-three years.

After her husband left with the imperialist forces for Querétaro, she was the guest of an American couple, Mr. and Mrs. Fred Hube, at their home in Tacubaya near Mexico City. Inactivity, even in such luxurious surroundings, made her restless. For three consecutive nights, she confided to her diary, she dreamed that the prince was dying and calling out for her. Fatalists are usually superstitious, and Princess Agnes believed in dreams and portents, especially when they served her purpose.

She conceived a plan which was not only humane but would provide her with a starring role. The imperialist forces, according to her scenario, would surrender Mexico City to General Porfirio Díaz, in return for which Díaz would guarantee the lives and freedom of Maximilian and his followers. Making a dramatic appearance at Chapultepec, she persuaded the imperialist officers headquartered at the summer castle to give her a pass through the lines to interview Díaz.

General Díaz was not enthusiastic over her proposal, suspected that the bustling Americana, who behaved in a presumptuous manner unlike that of any proper Mexican lady, was interested only in facilitating the escape of Maximilian and his friends. He politely brushed her off, but finally agreed that she might carry her plan to President Juárez at the administrative capital in San Luis Potosí. With her little black-and-tan Jimmy trotting at her side, she prepared for the dangerous journey north, rounding up an ancient yellow fiacre, four ill-matched mules and a driver. She also armed herself with a seven-shot revolver. Luckily for them, the bandits operating on the highroad north did not attempt to interrupt her journey.

President Juárez was more sympathetic than the stiff-backed, cold-eyed Díaz and even allowed Jimmy to jump up on the sofa when he granted her an interview at the government palace in San Luis Potosí. She could understand how he had won the trust of the Mexican people, with his "very dark-complexioned Indian face, which was not disfigured but, on the contrary, made more interesting by a very large scar across it. He had very black piercing eyes, and gave one the impression of being a man who reflects much, and deliberates long and carefully before acting."

Juárez was not greatly interested in her proposal because he knew Querétaro was about to fall, and told Princess Agnes he would have to think about it. While he was pondering, she learned that Querétaro had just been captured. She pleaded with Juárez for a pass through the republican outposts, and when he put her off, she simply took off for Querétaro on her own.

At Querétaro she pleaded successfully with General Escobedo to be allowed to visit her husband and the other prisoners at the Capuchin convent. The reunion between the Salm-Salms took place in his cell. At first she was dismayed by his appearance, the loss of his "military chic," including that fascinating monocle; he had not shaved or changed his collar for several days, and he "looked altogether as if he had emerged from a dustbin." She was so affected, she wrote, that "I wept and almost fainted in his arms." The discipline was fairly permissive, apparently, because she was then presented to Maximilian, who, though prone on his cot and suffering from dysentery and malaria, managed a kiss of the hand. Somewhat more dryly, Prince Salm-Salm reported on that reunion that "Her news was by no means comforting, for she said it was intended to shoot us all. She had a long conversation with the Emperor, in which she gave him much information, especially in reference to the treason of Márquez, which mortified the Emperor far more than that of López. It was the general opinion that Márquez marched towards Puebla, instead of Querétaro, with the intention of joining Santa Anna." Santa Anna had recently returned to Mexico in hopes of acting as a power broker between the various factions.

Princess Agnes arranged an interview between General Escobedo and Maximilian, at which the Salm-Salms were also present. Maximilian suggested that he would be willing to abdicate —certainly the hollowest of formalities under the circumstances—and order the surrender of any imperialist forces still fighting if his officers would be permitted their freedom. Escobedo replied that he could only transmit the offer to his superiors in San Luis Potosí.

Using all her formidable charm, Princess Agnes also persuaded General Escobedo and Colonel Miguel Palacios, who commanded the battalion charged with guarding the prisoners at the Capuchin convent, to move the ailing emperor from the dank vault in the cellars to a cell on the second floor.

That day, May 24, the prisoners heard a well-founded report that they would be placed on trial for their lives. While Maximilian's few remaining possessions were being moved up from the pantheon to his new quarters, he and Prince Salm-Salm strolled in the patio. The latter happened to pick up a crown of thorns, which had fallen from the head of a wooden image of Christ. Maximilian, with a bitter smile, took the ring of thorns from the prince, saying "Let me have it. It suits well my position." He then handed the crown of thorns to his valet, Grill, and ordered him to hang it on the wall of his new quarters.

Later that day Prince Salm-Salm learned from Colonel Palacios that there was little chance Maximilian and his leading generals would leave Querétaro alive. "In the course of the conversation I remarked that the Mexican government would do well to take an example from the North American government in their treatment of the rebels of the South, on which Palacios replied, 'The North Americans are our born hereditary enemies. We will neither have anything to do with them or with you; we can exist without any of you.' "

Something obviously would have to be done in a hurry, or Maximilian would be facing a firing squad one approaching dawn. It was decided that Princess Agnes should be dispatched to San Luis Potosí to make another plea before President Juárez; meanwhile, plans must be made for an escape in case her appeal failed. The emperor balked at first, still touchy about his outmoded honor. "The Emperor was first horrified at the idea of 'running away,' but I attacked his prejudice with all the reasons and arguments I could muster. I proved to him that he had done more than sufficient for his 'military honor,' and that it was a duty he owed the world to preserve his life . . . he might still be of very good service to humanity."

Through a republican officer whom Salm-Salm bribed with wine, cigars and money, six horses and six revolvers were bought and held in readiness for an escape. On the question of disguise, Maximilian proved almost as difficult as on the point of honor; he loved his golden beard too much to sacrifice it even to save his life. Maximilian refused to cut it off, Salm-Salm related, but consented to tie it back around his neck with black thread and to wear spectacles.

Meanwhile, in the two weeks since the fall of Querétaro, a considerable effort was being made to persuade Juárez to spare the lives of Maximilian and the other prisoners. Baron von Magnus, the Prussian minister, was hastening to San Luis Potosí to deliver his appeal in person. Other European nations, including France, Austria, Belgium and Great Britain, were urging the United States—which supposedly had the most influence over the Juárez government, having made its success possible through military and diplomatic means—to intercede in the most vigorous way possible. The American efforts left something to be desired. President Johnson did direct the American minister in Mexico City to deliver to Juárez's Minister of Foreign Affairs a note reading: "My Government instructs me to make known to President Juárez its desire that [Maximilian] . . . receive the humane treatment accorded by civilized nations to prisoners of war." Subsequently, General Sheridan, having decided that Maximilian the man was a brave fellow and worth saving, hired a steamer and sent one of his scouts with an appeal of clemency for the emperor.

Juárez and his advisers, however, were no more affected by the American appeals, couched in diplomatic terms, than the personal one so passionately delivered by Princess Agnes. If Juárez would not grant a pardon, she begged, at least he could order a delay in the proceedings. "Trembling in every limb and sobbing," she related in her diary, "I fell down on my knees, and pleaded with words that came from my heart, but which I cannot remember. The president tried to raise me, but I held his knees convulsively; I said I would not leave before he granted his [Maximilian's] life. I saw that the president was moved; he had tears in his eyes, but he answered me in a low, sad voice: 'I am grieved, madam, to see you thus upon your knees before me; but if all the kings and queens of Europe were at your side, I could not spare his life. It is not I who take it away; it is my people and the law, and if I did not do their will, the people would take his life as well as my own.' "

Such celebrated and liberal personages as Victor Hugo and Giuseppe Garibaldi also appealed to President Juárez for clemency on Maximilian's behalf, but he was unmoved. Domestic political considerations would have to take precedence over foreign relations and propaganda; he knew that a revolution may inadvertently eat its young, but it is duty-bound to consume its enemies.

Princess Agnes could only return to Querétaro with Juárez's promise that Maximilian would not be summoned before a drumhead court and executed immediately. There would be the dignity of a trial, the conclusion of which inevitably would be the death sentence.

Back in Querétaro her return over the dangerous mountain roads was awaited with mounting anxiety. The escape plot was not going well; the officer who had been "reached" by Prince Salm-Salm was now insisting it was impossible without the complicity of Colonel Palacios, the commander of the guard battalion.

They knew she had returned on the morning of May 31 when her little dog, Jimmy, suddenly came frisking into the emperor's cell in search of his master, who was seated at Maximilian's bedside. "There," said Maximilian, "our guardian angel is coming!" Princess Agnes' report on her disappointing interview with Juárez convinced Maximilian that there could be no more delay in hatching the escape plot. After fleeing Querétaro, Maximilian and a few selected companions, including the Salm-Salms, would ride up into the Sierra Gorda, and from there to the coastal town of Tuspan and on to the vicinity of Veracruz. He dictated an order, which was to be smuggled out to the commander of any Austrian warship lying off Veracruz: "The Austrian ships in Veracruz are to be instructed carefully where they are to cruise. Signals during night and flags in the daytime. Besides this, to send small boats frequently on shore. It would be good to enter into communication with English and Spanish vessels."

For the purposes of bribing Colonel Palacios and any others necessary to the scheme, Maximilian collected the 5,000 pesos in gold which he had distributed among his retinue the day before his capture and had written a bill of exchange drawn upon the House of Hapsburg for 100,000 pesos.

The escape attempt was set for the night of June 2. That meant Princess Agnes had to arrange to see Colonel Palacios alone that night and persuade him to join the conspiracy. She would ask the young colonel to escort her to the house of Señora Pepita Vicientis, where she was staying, after visiting her husband. Everything now depended on Princess Agnes and her powers of persuasion—and as events proved she was prepared to give her all.

That evening she requested Colonel Palacios' escort to her lodgings, and he gallantly complied. There were still traces of chivalry clinging to the surface conventions of war; it was not too remarkable for the wife of an imprisoned enemy to be accorded gracious treatment by his jailer.

The young colonel, Princess Agnes observed, was "an Indian without any education, who could scarcely read or write." His young wife had just given birth to their first child. Such circumstances should have given her pause. Where but in a revolutionary army, in a cause such as Juárez's, could a son of the peasantry rise to a colonelcy? Young men like Palacios had made Juárez's eventual success possible, just as he had enabled them to rise in the world.

Princess Agnes invited him into the parlor of Señora Vicentis' home and got down to business. She persuaded him to admit that he felt the "greatest sympathy" for the Emperor Maximilian. Then she told him that she had a proposal to make, but he must swear "by the head of his wife and child" that if he rejected it he would not tell anyone about it. Palacios agreed. Maximilian, she said, would be executed if something were not done. Palacios could save him if he would "only consent to turn his back and close his eyes for ten minutes." Allowing Maximilian to escape would be in the best interests of Mexico; otherwise, more European interventions might follow. She then offered him the 5,000 pesos and the bill of exchange for 100,000 pesos to arrange the matter.

Urged to take the money, because she knew the bargain had to be sealed immediately, Palacios backed away, protesting that he couldn't decide to take such a step without more time to consider the matter.

What happened next was not described in Princess Agnes' account, but in the colonel's.

Desperate at the possibility that Palacios might slip out of her clutches, knowing that he was their only remaining hope, she offered herself—her supple equestrienne's body—as an additional inducement. She began to fling off her clothing. One glimpse of her splendidly curved torso, under the dim lamplight of the Vicentis parlor, was enough for the colonel. He recoiled in a frenzy of revolutionary puritanism which Princess Agnes, with her memories of amoral wartime Washington, could not have anticipated. The attempted seduction was a tactical mistake.

The colonel was so horrified—not by the offer of a bribe, which was understandable, but by the sight of Princess Agnes' alabaster skin—that he exclaimed that his honor was being compromised.

He told her that "if she did not open the door at once," as he later deposed, "he would jump out of the window and into the street."

There was nothing for Princess Agnes to do but pull her clothes back on and open the door for him.

The colonel, forgetting his promise, sped to General Escobedo's headquarters and told the commanding general just what had happened. The next morning Escobedo summoned Princess Agnes and observed that "the air in Querétaro did not seem to agree with her." He informed her that she would be removed to San Luis Potosí under escort.

She was so enraged that when a republican captain approached to take her arm, she sprang back and drew out her revolver, crying, "Captain, touch me with one finger and you are a dead man." Despite her protests, she was removed to San Luis

Potosí and kept under surveillance. Querétaro was much quieter and much less interesting when she was gone.

A few days later the republican authorities moved briskly to bring Emperor Maximilian and his two leading generals, Miramón and Mejía, to justice before a military tribunal. All three were notified that they would be tried under President Juárez's decree of January 25, 1862, which prescribed the death penalty for anyone who took arms against Mexican independence or associated himself with a foreign intervention. Their jury would consist of a lieutenant colonel and six captains.

On June 11, two days before the court-martial was to be convened, Maximilian and the others were transferred back to the Teresita convent, which could be more securely guarded. The whole battalion of *Supremos Podres* was assigned to patrol the streets outside, and Maximilian was watched by one officer or another night and day. Prince Salm-Salm observed that the *Supremos* were supposed to be an "elite corps," but that while their officers were decked out in gold-braided uniforms with "kid gloves of the most delicate shades," the men in the ranks were merely a hungry rabble who "importuned us always . . . even the sentinels, who held in one hand their musket, stretched out the other for alms. When we dined they surrounded our tables like hungry dogs, and I have actually seen one of them quarrel with a dog for a small piece of bread thrown to the latter."

Maximilian's attitude toward the proceedings was one of princely hauteur. He would not attend the trial, of which he was the designated star attraction, he decided. To his captors he announced that his illness—and he was still weak from dysentery and malaria, as a military physician determined—would preclude his attendance. Instead of interesting himself in the judicial proceedings, he reverted to daydreams. Long after escape had become impossible, with soldiers thronging the street outside the Teresita convent, he talked with Salm-Salm of his plans to build a new home on the Adriatic island of Lacroma, which he owned, and spending the rest of his life in idyllic seaside retirement. His serenity in those days owed as much to the self-protective habit of escapism, which he had so long cultivated, as to an undeniable, fatalistic courage.

On June 13 the military tribunal was convened and immediately found Generals Miramón and Mejía guilty as charged. The rest of that day in the courtroom, which was the Theater Iturbide, with the judge and jury seated on stage chewing piñon nuts, was given over to Maximilian's trial. The emperor was represented by able counsel, including an American attorney Frederic Hall and three Mexican lawyers, who argued at length that Maximilian did not usurp the throne, but had been summoned by a legitimate Mexican political party, the Conservatives, and that the way had been cleared for him by the French army rather than any actions of his own. It was also pointed out that the Black Decree and other imperial edicts were matched in severity by those issued by the republicans.

Late in the afternoon the case was submitted to the jury, which retired for its deliberations to a lavatory backstage. Three of the captains voted for the death penalty, three for life banishment, but Lieutenant Colonel Platón Sánchez brusquely informed them the verdict was a "foregone conclusion" and broke the tie by voting for death.

The verdict was transmitted to Maximilian late that day: He and Generals Miramón and Mejía would face a firing squad the morning of June 16. That night he wrote Carlotta, not knowing whether she would ever be sane enough to comprehend his last words: "If God should allow you to regain your health, so that you may read these lines, you will learn how cruelly fate has dealt me blow after blow without respite since the day of your departure. Disaster has dogged my steps, breaking all my hopes! Death seems a happy solution. I shall go to my end as a soldier, a sovereign defeated but not dishonored. Then, if your own distress becomes too great to bear, and God calls you to join me soon, I shall bless the hand which has been so heavy upon us. . . ."

The next day, too, he was busy writing letters of farewell to his family and friends and disposing of the few personal effects still in his possession.

On June 16 he awakened before dawn and waited for the escort to come and take him to the wall. Hours passed and the dreaded stamp of the escort's boots in the corridor outside his cell still was not heard. All that day he waited in a torment that can easily be imagined. It wasn't until sundown that an officer appeared at his door and announced that the execution had been postponed until June 19, on telegraphed orders from administrative headquarters at San Luis Potosí.

In that temporary capital of the republic, President Juárez had ordered the execution postponed in order to consider the renewed appeals of Baron von Magnus and other members of the diplomatic corps who had appeared in San Luis Potosí to plead for Maximilian's life. Princess Agnes also entered another dramatic plea, as well as the wife of General Miramón, who brought a half dozen of their children, including a two-month-old infant in her arms, to appeal to Juárez's sense of compassion. On that subject, however, his mind was closed; the reprieve had been granted only out of diplomatic considerations. Later that year, in his address at the opening session of the Mexican Congress, the president explained: "The execution at Querétaro was necessitated by the gravest motives of justice, combined with the imperious necessity of securing peace in the future and putting an end to the internal convulsions and all the calamities inflicted by the war on our society. The application of the law to those in the first rank among those most guilty had permitted the use of great clemency towards all the others." Maximilian's death was demanded not as a concession to the Aztec tradition of human sacrifice—though it may have been considered that by Juárez's less enlightened followers —but as a serviceable warning against any future attempts at foreign intervention.

In Querétaro some of the emperor's circle believed that the reprieve offered hope that he would be pardoned, and one of the optimists, Prince Salm-Salm, broke out a bottle of wine to celebrate. Maximilian, a realist for once, was convinced that it was all over but the messy business of dying. His last gesture, on June 18, was to send a telegram to President Juárez pleading that Generals Mejía and Miramón, "who suffered all the tortures and bitterness of death, the day before last, might be spared and that I might be the only victim." There was no answer from San Luis Potosí, no hope of a further reprieve.

Maximilian slept soundly, as always, the night of June 18-19. It almost seemed that he viewed his imminent death as merely one final round of ceremony. Awaking at three o'clock, he and his comrades knelt before a Mexican priest, who conducted a low mass in the cell and gave them his blessings.

Some of those present wept when he took off his wedding ring and handed it to Dr. Basch and gave his rosary and scapular to the priest.

"Are you ready, gentlemen?" he called down the corridor to Miramón and Mejía in no less cheerful a tone than he would summon his aides for a morning ride. "I am already prepared."

Shortly after dawn the peremptory stamp of boots was heard in the corridors of the Capuchin convent; the executioners had come.

Head high and shoulders back, the soldier king at last, Maximilian descended the staircase. His step was firm. He was dressed in his military uniform with the Order of the Golden Fleece draped around his neck.

The courtyard was flooded with early sunlight, and Maximilian breathed deeply of the cool dry morning air.

"Ah, what a glorious day," he told his companions. "I have always wanted to die on such a day!"

Outside in the street an open carriage surrounded by guards awaited with Generals Miramón and Mejía already installed. Maximilian walked toward it at a stately pace, accompanied by Dr. Basch and two of his servants, the valet, Grill, and the Hungarian cook, Tudos. Suddenly Dr. Basch broke away from the procession, saying, "I cannot take another step." Weeping, covering his face with his hands, he returned to the convent. The final retinue of Maximilian I was composed of his cook, his valet and a firing squad.

A moment later the carriage rolled away in the midst of its cavalry escort. Doors and windows along the way were closed as a sign of mourning for what was about to take place. There was a distressing scene on a street corner when General Mejía's young wife, with her newborn son in her arms, broke through the cordon, tried to cling to the carriage, and was hauled away by the soldiers. The cavalcade proceeded through the silent streets, through the western suburb to the Hill of the Bells, where Maximilian had been captured and which the republicans considered a fitting execution site.

Near the top of the hill was a low adobe wall, where Maximilian and the two generals were led immediately. It was 7 A.M. The niceties of his last public appearance occupied the emperor's mind in its last conscious moments. He insisted that Miramón, "as a brave soldier" and former president, should have the place of honor in the middle. The gesture, like so many others, was misdirected. If there was a "place of honor" on such a doleful occasion, it belonged to the most competent, loyal and dedicated of his generals, Tomás Mejía. The latter, in fact, objected to the shuffling, saying, "The Saviour died, they tell us, between two thieves, and they say that the one on His right was repentant, while the other was not. I am not a thief, Your Majesty, and I am not unrepentant, for I am truly sorry for whatever sins I have committed. But if I stand on the left hand of Your Majesty—" Maximilian placed his arm around Mejía's shoulder and replied, "What difference does it make where we stand? We are all going the same road." No doubt the reference to Christ's passion pleased Maximilian, who had placed a crown of thorns on the wall of his cell and brooded over the significance of Judas-López's treachery, in the recesses of a romantic and mystical imagination. The parallels, to him, were not coincidental but inescapable.

One final gesture: Maximilian distributed the few coins left in his pocket to the members of the firing squad, saying, "Aim well, *muchachos,* aim right here." He pointed to his heart.

The officer in charge of the execution asked him if he had any last words. Maximilian, of course, did. He looked out over the slope of the Hill of the Bells, over the sprawling republican camp at the bottom, at the bright June sun, at the white birds wheeling against the horizon (not *zopilotes,* God be thanked!), at the red-tiled roofs and treelined avenues of Querétaro below, at this strange, beloved and bewildering country for which (involuntarily but without resentment) he was giving his life. Then he said in a clear steady voice, "I die in a just cause. I forgive all, and pray that all may forgive me. May my blood flow for the good of this land. Viva Mexico!"

The officer's sword flashed in a downward arc; the rifles cracked in unison, and the three men fell back against the adobe wall. The two generals died instantly. Maximilian, luckless to the end, was still alive and had to be finished off with a *coup de grâce.*

A few minutes later all the church bells in Querétaro pealed in triumph, but it was a sorry celebration greeted in silence by the townspeople. The real executioners of Maximilian were far away, as a republican colonel remarked several hours later when the emperor's body was being embalmed in the chapel of the Capuchin convent.

"Behold," he said, pointing to the riddled corpse, "that is the work of France."

18. *Exeunt Omnes*

*Maximilian had conquered self . . . where he had
stood posterity will henceforth see only the noble son
of the Hapsburgs, the well-bred gentleman who,
aware of his failure, was ready to stand by it and to
pay the extreme penalty of his errors.*

—SARA YORKE STEVENSON

THE work of France? If so, the guilt over the execution of Maximilian was carefully concealed. That spring of 1867 Paris was
brilliant with the festivities attending the great Universal Exhibition. The Prussian threat momentarily forgotten, France was
congratulating herself on her continuing contributions to civilization. When the news of Maximilian's death arrived on June
30, a prize-awarding ceremony was under way at the exposition
hall, with Napoleon, Eugénie, the prince imperial, the Sultan
of Turkey and the Prince of Wales on the platform.

"Hardly had the twelve-hundred-piece orchestra struck up
the anthem by Rossini," as Albert Guerard related, "when an
aide handed the Emperor a telegram. The sovereign remained
passive, went on with the show, gave a speech on peace, progress and good will. But the Austrian ambassador and his staff
quietly withdrew."

Actually Napoleon and Eugénie had learned the night before
of Maximilian's execution, unofficially, through a telegraphed
résumé of reports in the Belgian press, but had decided to try to

keep the news from the public until after the climactic events of the Universal Exposition. Conscience-stricken, Eugénie had almost fainted on reading the bulletins.

At the prize-giving ceremony the next day the stall reserved for the Count and Countess of Flanders, Empress Carlotta's brother and sister-in-law, was empty; they had hastened back to Belgium. Once the ceremony was over and news spread of Maximilian's death, the visiting royalties fled from Paris as though an outbreak of the plague had been reported.

Napoleon and Eugénie could assure themselves and their confidants that, really, Maximilian's execution was his own fault; he should have taken repeated counsel from the French and left Mexico before it was too late. That disavowal of responsibility was least acceptable to their own people. Thousands of French soldiers had been killed or wounded or died of tropical diseases as pawns in the imperial chess game, and the news of Maximilian's death—one more among so many others mourned—seemed to fix a black seal on the whole debacle.

"There remain now no sovereigns in Paris," a leading newspaper in the capital remarked the day after the news had been confirmed, "except the Emperor Napoleon and the specter of Maximilian at his elbow."

Nor did Adolphe Thiers, Napoleon's most implacable political enemy, remain silent on the matter. Rising from his seat in the Chamber of Deputies, M. Thiers inveighed against Napoleon as the man responsible for the tragedy. "He will never recover from this curse," Thiers declared. "This outrage will overwhelm him with the contempt of France."

A mass keening had also arisen from the thousands of Frenchmen who had invested in Mexican loans which would never be paid by the republicans. Their sorrow was given a sharper edge by revelations that none of the wealthy Mexican expatriates, who had urged the loans, had invested any of their own money in such a dubious enterprise.

Much as the regime tried to smother speculation about the tragedy at Querétaro, there was a morbid interest in the whole affair which was reflected in the thirty-odd canvases depicting Maximilian's death and placed on exhibition at the Salon of 1868. One by Edouard Manet was so graphically accusatory that the police forbade its exhibition and confiscated all reproductions.

The rising Radical politician Georges Clemenceau, the Tiger of France, as he was to be subsequently known, was scornful of such sentimentality and demanded, "How the devil could you suppose that you should pity the Maximilians and Carlottas? My God! They are always charming, these people, I agree beforehand. For five thousand years it has always been so. They have the formula of all the virtues and the secret of all the graces. His wife is mad, you say. Nothing more just. This almost makes me believe in Providence. Was it not her ambitions that incited the fool? I regret that she *has* lost her reason and cannot realize that she killed her husband and that a people are avenging themselves."

Even the Mexicans were more compassionate than that. They saw him for a deluded gringo who had no business appearing in their country under the auspices of still another country, but the manner of his death deeply touched their sensibilities. He was a fool, yes, but he went out like a man. They would have agreed perhaps with the memorial of young Sara Yorke, who saw it all clearly, whose sympathies were with the Mexican people, and who later wrote that in his last weeks on earth "Maximilian had conquered self. Now the ambitious Austrian prince, the weak tool of intriguing politicians, the upholders of religious and political retrogression, disappears; and where he had stood posterity will henceforth see only the noble son of the Hapsburgs, the well-bred gentleman who, aware of his failure, was ready to stand by it and to pay the extreme penalty of his errors. Before the figure of Maximilian of Austria, from the time he took command of his little army and resolved to stand for better or worse by those who had remained faithful to his fallen fortunes, all true-hearted men must bow with respect. From that time forth his words and his acts were noble; and in his attitude at this supreme moment, his incapacity as a chief executive, his moral and intellectual limitations as a man, are overlooked. We forget that he was no leader when we see how well he could die."

Juárez and his military forces completed the process of victory within a month after Maximilian's execution, with Juárez entering Mexico City on July 15. With all the work of reconstruction ahead of him, President Juárez still had to concern himself with the elaborate details of returning his late rival to his homeland. Maximilian dead was almost as much a nuisance to Juárez as Maximilian alive. A Latin-American sense of propriety about death, even that of an enemy, demanded strict attention to mortuarial detail. Maximilian's body had been crudely embalmed with chloride of zinc in Querétaro. His brow had been shattered by one of the firing squad's bullets, and his eyes had to be replaced with artificial ones. No blue false eyes were available, so the black ones of a statue of the Virgin in one of the local churches were removed and placed in Maximilian's sockets. The body was then placed in a zinc-lined cedar coffin, with a small window in the lid, and for some weeks was on exhibition in one of the Querétaro churches. "For the first two or three weeks," noted Maximilian's American lawyer, Frederic Hall, with an almost professional interest, "the body looked tolerably well, but a month's time darkened it, and it soon gave increasing evidence that the work of preservation had been badly done."

By then the Austrian government was making increasingly acidulous inquiries about the imperial corpse and just how long the Mexicans intended to keep it. Juárez then ordered it brought to Mexico City for as scientific a job of preservation as could be done. Three Mexican doctors were assigned the task, with the chapel of the San Andrés Hospital as their workroom. According to a local historian, the "physicians adopted a method of desiccation, similar to that employed by the ancient Egyptians. The fluids of the body were drained off until it was sufficiently dry to enable it to be wrapped in bandages and varnished. In order to do this more easily, and also to facilitate the replacing of the dead Emperor's garments, it was necessary to suspend it from the ceiling by ropes for several days. . . ."

Months after Maximilian's corpse had been shipped home, it still haunted Juárez politically. On the first anniversary of the execution, June 19, 1868, Maximilian's former followers gathered at the San Andrés chapel for a memorial service at which the Italian Jesuit Father Mario Cavalieri delivered a fiery oration denouncing the Juárez government while praising Maximilian. Ten days later Juárez ordered the chapel torn down.

"Seizing on the fact that the Emperor's corpse had been suspended while it was undergoing the second embalming process," the Mexican historian recorded, "the Imperialists made of this incident a political epigram, which ran to the effect that although the 'Puros,' as the Liberals were called, had sought to catch Maximilian while he was alive and hang him, they had succeeded in this only after he was dead. The chapel became known as the 'Chapel of the Martyr,' and was converted into a focus whence the Imperialists radiated discontent and disapproval of the Liberals and the Juárez government."

Late in August, 1867, the Austrian government began negotiating seriously for the return of Maximilian's body. The Austrian Admiral Wilhelm von Tegetthoff arrived on a warship, which anchored off Veracruz, and proceeded to the capital. He bombarded the Mexicans with appeals for release of the body, but they would not do so until November 9. Early the next morning Tegetthoff started back to Veracruz with the mummified corpse, accompanied by Maximilian's physician, Dr. Basch, his cook, Tudos, a number of Austrians who had been prisoners of war, and an escort of 100 Mexican cavalrymen. The frigate *Novara,* which had brought Maximilian to Mexico, arrived in the Veracruz roadstead and took him back to his homeland.

The *Novara* arrived off Trieste on January 16, 1868, and the body was brought ashore in a launch draped in black velvet. The catafalque was placed in the center of the deck, with both Mexican and Austrian flags displayed. Trieste was in mourning. A few hours later a special train conveyed the coffin to Vienna, where it arrived on the snowy evening of January 17. José Blasio was among those who watched the snow-covered coffin carried through the gates of the Hofburg. "It was received at the entrance to the palace by the Archduchess Sophie and Maximilian's brothers," he wrote. "The Archduchess threw herself sobbing upon the coffin. On viewing through the glass the pallid, serene face of her favorite son, she knelt, and for several moments nothing could be heard but her broken sobs."

The body lay in state in a chapel of the Hofburg for a day, during which hundreds of Viennese came to view it, with 200 candles in ornate silver candelabra guttering over the bier. A state funeral was held on January 20 at the Church of the Capuchins. It was almost exclusively an Austrian affair; none of those who had sponsored his fatal involvement in Mexico, except those who were members of his family, were present. Nor was Mexico represented, except unofficially by the faithful Blasio. All those grandees who had urged the intervention, profited from it, and took great care to spare themselves from the consequences of its collapse—most of them living in Europe now off the proceeds of the speculation—absented themselves from the funeral.

Briefly Napoleon and Eugénie had considered attending the funeral. Napoleon backed away from the idea when it appeared that there might be demonstrations against him in Vienna, where the Biedermeiers were declaring him Maximilian's murderer. More delicate considerations weighed upon Eugénie. She told the Austrian ambassador, Prince Metternich, that "It will be the most painful thing in the world to me to find myself face to face with a brother and a mother to whose grief I have contributed by my insistence upon the expedition to Mexico. If I had already known the Emperor, the Empress and the Archduchess Sophie, I should long ago have hastened to them in order to give proof of my sentiments, of which they ought to be in no doubt. But since I do not know them, I am afraid of appearing too cold or too tragic."

Their attendance, at any rate, was ruled out when Archduchess Sophie let it be known that she "did not feel able to meet the Emperor and Empress of the French for the present."

Instead, it was decided that Napoleon and Eugénie would deliver their condolences to Franz Josef and Elizabeth at a rather hurried and furtive meeting in Salzburg, which at least was on Austrian soil. On August 18, 1867, while Maximilian's body was still in the hands of his enemies, the four sovereigns met in the ancient Alpine city. Napoleon was greatly relieved to find no bitterness in Franz Josef's attitude; sending "Maxl" to Mexico had been a joint venture, after all. "Everything," Napoleon declared, "must draw us nearer to each other." Particularly the Prussians. After an exchange of regrets over what had happened to Maximilian, they got down to business and discussed Germany, the Turkish problem and other less personal matters.

Maximilian was entombed in the Hapsburg crypt beneath

the Church of the Capuchins beside another tragic princeling, l'Aiglon, son of Napoleon I and his mother's dearest friend.

To anyone with the slightest tendency toward superstition, there seemed to be a curse on almost everyone involved in the Mexican intervention. Even the Mexican people were not spared. Juárez was a great and able national leader, but he died of heart failure in 1872 before the work of reconstruction could be completed. All the while Díaz, who claimed his military exploits had not been sufficiently recognized by President Juárez, had been scheming to take over. On Juárez's death, he assumed growingly dictatorial powers and turned the presidency into a tyranny that endured for almost forty years, until another revolution sent him into luxurious exile in Paris. His regime was so brutal, his writ was enforced so harshly by the rurales and other oppressive internal security forces that during the mock elections his ticket was known among the masses as "Díaz and Death." The Mexican people would have been better off with Maximilian enthroned at Chapultepec, with his vague but undeniable liberalism, his good intentions, even his amiable inefficiency, but his subjects could never have been reconciled to a foreign ruler, no matter how benevolent.

Among the other Mexicans involved in Maximilian's affairs, General Leonardo Márquez, labeled a "traitor" for having abandoned Querétaro, managed to flee to Cuba, where he established himself as a pawnbroker in Havana. Not until twenty-seven years later, when he was seventy-five, did he consider it safe to return to his native land. He died in 1913, at the age of ninety-three, while visiting in Havana.

Others, on both sides, also met a shabby fate. The widow of General Miramón lost her sanity shortly after her husband's execution and, like her queen across the water, had to be kept under restraint for the rest of her life. Lieutenant Colonel Platón Sánchez, who cast the deciding ballot for the executions, was killed by his own men. Even blacker was the fate of Colonel Miguel López, whose luck turned against him almost from the moment he led the enemy's shock troops through the defenses of Querétaro.

When López returned to his home in Mexico City, his young wife slammed the door in his face. Nor did he receive the 2,000 ounces of gold he had been promised for his treachery, nor any other reward. A New York newspaper correspondent reported in July, 1867, that when López approached Colonel Rincón-Gallardo and asked him to recommend that he be given high rank in the republican army, Rincón-Gallardo replied, "Colonel López, if I recommend you to any position, it will be to a position on a tree with a rope around your neck." Later that year López published a pamphlet in defense of his honor.

He claimed that Maximilian himself had asked him to negotiate with the enemy. "He ordered that I should go there [republican headquarters] in the deepest secrecy, and ask permission for him to leave the city. . . . I acted accordingly. . . . To gain time (after the enemy troops entered the city) and to give warning to the Emperor was my only thought. . . . I do not know why he lingered so long before leaving, but his delay kept me in great anxiety, and to give him time to escape, I had to remain by the side of the conquerors and to divert their attention." López thus attempted to picture Maximilian as a coward bent on saving himself, which even his worst enemies could not believe of Maximilian. The pamphlet was derided, and López became an outcast among his own people and with no means of escaping from their midst. A few years later he was bitten by a rabid dog and died in a hydrophobic agony.

Possibly a greater villain in the closing phases of the melodrama, Father Augustin Fischer, continued to demonstrate his highly developed powers of self-preservation. Obscurity was the better part of discretion, now that his days as a road-company Talleyrand were over, and he wriggled into the clerical shallows of Mexican life and spent his last years in charge of the San Cosme parish in the capital.

Then there was the ironic fate of Maximilian's illegitimate son, Sedano y Leguizano, half Mexican, one-quarter Hapsburg, one-quarter Wittelsbach, and quite as confused a man as his lineage would suggest. His mother died shortly after Maximilian's execution, and Sedano, through a mysterious source of funds, was taken to Paris to be educated. No sign of recognition, of course, came from the Hofburg.

Sedano was befriended by a wealthy Mexican expatriate and provided with a good education. He grew up to be a thoroughly spoiled rascal and assumed aristocratic airs. Not only did he take pride in being called the "imperial bastard," but he grew a beard exactly like his father's. After his patron gave him up as a bad job, he distinguished himself as the worst credit risk in Paris, was involved in various swindles, and finally as middle age began to creep up on him, he became a traveling salesman.

When World War I broke out, Sedano was an aging adventurer stranded and penniless in Spain. Exactly the type the German espionage network in Spain was looking for. Its Barcelona branch recruited him to gather military information in France and forward it to a "drop" in Switzerland. One thing Sedano proved to have inherited from Maximilian: a fatal ineptitude. The German spy masters had instructed him to write his messages in secret ink between the lines of an innocuous letter. He did not bother with composing an imaginary letter but simply wrote out his messages in secret ink. French counterespionage did not have to be brilliant to suspect letters on which nothing, apparently, was written; they applied a chemical reagent to the supposedly blank pages and came up with proof of Sedano's guilt. He was arrested just as he dropped one of his letters in a postbox on the Boulevard des Italiens in 1917. A secret court-martial condemned him to death. On October 10, 1917, like his father, but for less honorable reasons, Sedano faced a firing squad. A small pleased smile was noted on his face when the officer in charge of the firing squad read out the order, beginning "Sedano, son of the Emperor Maximilian of Mexico. . . ." He was fifty-one years old when he died as a traitor to France.

Retribution was slower, but just as inexorable, in dealing with the French who had managed the intrigue, engineered the intervention and then abandoned it with the air of a speculator sensibly cutting his losses on a bad investment. Jecker, whose crooked bond issue started the whole thing, was made to regret the French citizenship wangled for him by the late Duc de Morny. After the collapse of the Second Empire, during a period of anarchy and violent but temporary upheaval in Paris, the communards hastened to arrest Jecker and shot him on May 26, 1871.

For Napoleon and Eugénie, their experiment in overseas empire building had more disastrous consequences than they could have imagined. Like a trail of gunpowder, it led directly to the disastrous confrontation with Prussia. With their best troops in Mexico, they had been unable to help Austria when she was invaded by Prussia. Bismarck thus succeeded in isolating France from her only possible ally. Through the famous Ems telegram, the seriously ailing Napoleon was tricked into declaring war on Prussia, whose armies quickly succeeded in grinding the unprepared French to rubble in a series of swift relentless campaigns. Napoleon himself was captured with 100,000 of his troops at Sedan; Eugénie fled to exile in England, which was overstocked with dispossessed French royalty.

Napoleon was subsequently released by the Prussians and died prosaically enough while undergoing surgery in London. But Eugénie lived on and on, establishing herself, the prince imperial and her retinue in the replica of a court in the Kent countryside, even publishing a periodical (*The Lantern,* with the temporarily expatriated Ambrose Bierce as its editor) to defend the Second Empire from those conducting a hostile postmortem on its dubious glories. Her son exchanged his title for that of a subaltern in the British army and went off to fight the Zulus, whose assegais terminated a promising military career just as promptly as the Mexican firing squad wrote off Maximilian's. But the Dowager Eugénie survived World War I and had the satisfaction of watching the Germans, the grandsons of the Bismarck generation, humiliated at Versailles.

Marshal Bazaine did not escape the falling debris of the Second Empire. He had holed up in the fortress of Metz with an army which he finally surrendered to the Prussians. A subsequent government, dissatisfied with his performance at Metz, brought him before a court-martial which convicted him as so many of his drumhead courts had convicted and sentenced to death those who dared to oppose the French army in Mexico. Bazaine was confined to an island prison off the French coast but escaped with the help of his wife, a smuggled rope and a small boat and lived out his years as an impoverished exile in Madrid.

Maximilian's death also cast a long, sorrowful shadow over the House of Hapsburg. The matriarchy of Archduchess Sophie had come to an end, as her strong-minded elder son decided that he could rule without his mother's advice. She was crushed by the news of Maximilian's execution, her sorrow undoubtedly deepened by a sense of guilt over her part in that final tragedy. Blasio visited her at the Hofburg, and she broke down and wept several times during that interview. "As she dried her eyes she may have recalled her responsibility in the death of her son," Blasio wrote, "when in the letter from her which he received at Orizaba she almost compelled him to sustain the Empire to the end, instead of leaving Mexico with the French. . . . My audience lasted for an hour, and although I started to leave now and again the Archduchess would detain me to ask new questions or to hear me repeat some of the details I had given her before. . . ."

Personal tragedy also afflicted Franz Josef, who had been so disturbed by and jealous of his younger brother's meretricious popularity with the Austrians. Crown Prince Rudolf, with his temperamental resemblance to the slain uncle, was a suicide. His nephew Franz Ferdinand was assassinated at Sarajevo, unwittingly contributing to the outbreak of World War I. Even his beautiful, innocent and impulsive wife, Empress Elizabeth, did not escape whatever furies may have been pursuing the members of his house. On September 10, 1898, as she strolled along a street in Geneva, the Italian anarchist Luigi Lucheni drove a sharpened file into her heart; she insisted on walking to the ferry at a nearby quay and died on its deck as it crossed the lake.

Franz Josef himself lived until 1916, halfway through World War I, but long enough to glimpse the coming downfall of the House of Hapsburg, which had established itself in the eleventh century on the Hill of the Hawks and was subtly diminished by the volley which felled one of its sons on the Hill of the Bells far from its original eminence.

That venturesome and redoubtable trio the Salm-Salms and their dog careened on through more bloody and historic scenes in their joint pursuit of martial adventure. The prince was finally released by the Mexican republicans on condition that he confine his saber swinging to other nations and with the princess and Jimmy returned to his family's Westphalian seat. For a time they were pursued by the moneylenders to whom he was in debt and who had been misinformed that Salm-Salm had acquired part of that ephemeral trove known to rainbow chasers as Maximilian's treasure. They visited Vienna for an audience with Franz Josef, who by then was getting bored by the frequently importunate appearance of Maximilian's former followers, and his creditors there had him clapped in jail. His friends scraped together $2,500 and obtained his release. He and Princess Agnes and possibly Jimmy thereafter traveled under aliases because his creditors were far-flung and diligent. Seeking haven in Switzerland, under the name of Von Stein, they settled down in rooms overlooking Lake Constance while they wrote their books on the Mexican adventure.

Prince Félix, or Herr von Stein, continued to be a bad credit risk. As Princess Agnes explained to her own satisfaction, if not those of bailiffs lying in wait for him, "Félix was a Prince and even if he had wished to economize, for which, however, he had little talent, in consequence of his education, he could not live so quietly and retiredly as prudence would have advised, for propriety required from him more than from other officers of his grade."

Actually the prince was merely another unemployed mercenary, who was keeping his sword polished. The Prussians had no use for an ex-American colonel, Field Marshal von Moltke having defined the American Civil War as unscientific, "a collision between two mobs." Finally, through the influence of Baron von Magnus, who had returned to Germany from his Mexican post, Prince Félix was grudgingly commissioned a major in the Fourth (Queen Augusta) Guards Regiment with headquarters at Coblenz. Thus he was in the forefront when Prussia and France went to war in 1870; Princess Agnes clamored for permission to follow him by storming Marshal von Moltke's headquarters, and Jimmy was left in care of their cook because he had acquired an understandable distaste for the sound of heavy artillery. She served as an army nurse before and after Prince Félix was killed leading his battalion into action at Gravelotte, leaving her with only a final note written just before the battle: "If I should be killed, I beg your pardon for every trouble I ever made you. I always loved you and I take only this love with me in my grave. Kiss little Jimmy."

Princess Agnes was only thirty when her husband was killed. After working eighteen hours a day in the Prussian field hospitals, she was awarded the Prussian Medal of Honor and given an onyx brooch by the Empress Augusta. With her spirit she could not retire respectably into Victorian widowhood. For a time she wandered around Europe with Jimmy, whose "beautiful head," she boasted in her memoirs, "has been caressed by three emperors." There were no more adventures, martial or otherwise; the world had entered a long period of relative peace. An inheritance from one of her relatives in America, plus a $1,200-a-year pension awarded her by Franz Josef, allowed her to live in comfort. On a visit to Rome she appealed to the Pope to allow her to become a nun, but he gently demurred on the grounds that she "didn't have the vocation." In 1876 she married Charles Heneage, secretary of the British legation in Berlin, but they separated soon afterward.

She did not return to the United States until 1899, when she brought back the standards of the Eighth and Sixty-eighth New York Volunteers, which she presented to their survivors at a ceremony moist with sentiment. Journalists covering the occasion observed that she still had a trim figure and a dashing manner, that her bosom was emblazoned with decorations awarded her by Maximilian, Franz Josef and the German emperor. A dozen years later she died in Karlsruhe, Germany, the most glamorous camp follower of the last wars in which a pretense of chivalry was maintained.

Empress Carlotta outlived them all, endured alternating periods of sanity and insanity for exactly sixty years after Maximilian's death. Clemenceau's curse was more than fulfilled. She was carefully and constantly insulated from the world at the Château of Bouchout, partly because her brother wanted no more publicity about "Mad Carlotta"—despite which she was the consolation of Sunday supplement editors any time they had a page of white space to be filled—and partly because any loud noises brought on seizures. She lived in a stone castle with all the doorknobs removed; the servants were her keepers.

Her sister-in-law, Queen Marie-Henriette, as kindly as Leopold II was brutal, made the care of Carlotta her responsibility and spent as much time as possible with her at Bouchout. Soon after Maximilian's death she was restored to physical health, and Queen Marie-Henriette wrote a friend, "You cannot imagine how beautiful she is now, never so beautiful before."

It was said that she did not realize that Maximilian had been killed until years later, but the evidence of José Blasio indicates otherwise. A few weeks after Maximilian's funeral he received a photograph of the late emperor, inscribed by Carlotta in one of her lucid periods, "To Don José Luis Blasio . . . Pray for the repose of the soul of His Majesty, Ferdinand Maximilian Joseph, Emperor of Mexico," followed by a Biblical verse in Latin and Spanish.*

Believing she would be able to receive him, Blasio hastened to Brussels but was told that she might suffer a setback if she saw someone so closely connected with events in Mexico. He went out to Bouchout and stood at the gates one afternoon. "I caught a glimpse of three ladies, walking under the old trees of the park, all dressed in mourning. On nearing the grating I recognized by her graceful figure the Empress Carlotta between the other two ladies. She was strolling along slowly, dressed and groomed with extreme elegance and care. Her gentle and kind face was profoundly sad. Her large eyes, so black and beautiful, appeared even larger and more beautiful under their purple lids. But they stared vacantly, as though questioning her destiny. As the three ladies neared me, they turned and went slowly away among the trees. I left Brussels the next day. . . ."

She spent much of her time at Bouchout conducting a frequently demented correspondence, which people on the other end had difficulty in deciding whether to answer, particularly those in which she referred to Maximilian as Lord of the Earth and Sovereign of the Universe. At times she seemed to realize her husband was dead, at others believed that he was the ruler of the world.

There were periods when she refused to speak to anyone, and others when she talked endlessly to herself in French, German, Spanish or Italian. One disjointed conversation reported by her biographer the Countess Reinach-Foussemagne: "Pay no attention, Monsieur. One talks nonsense. Yes, Monsieur, one is insane. The madness is always alive. You are in the presence of a lunatic. A great marriage, Monsieur. One would have you know that one had a husband, a husband who was an emperor. And then the madness. It was what happened that caused the

---

* Blasio suffered the fate of most followers of lost causes. Intelligent and capable as he was, he never found a career worthy of his talents in republican Mexico, except for producing a candid and clear-sighted memoir *Maximilian: Emperor of Mexico* (translated and edited by Robert H. Murray). In 1923 he died in poverty in a suburb of Mexico City.

madness, Monsieur . . . Napoleon . . . *Canaille* . . . wretch
. . . Blücher came in time to save the situation, but for Mexico
there was nothing, nothing. If only Napoleon had helped!"

In 1875 her other sister-in-law, Empress Elizabeth of Austria,
became obsessed with the idea that Carlotta could be scientifi-
cally restored to sanity. She had been reading or hearing of the
experiments of Louis Pasteur, by which he hoped to prevent ra-
bies by vaccination. Why, she wondered, couldn't human madness be traced to a virus and similarly cured by an inoculation?
She began reading everything she could find on the subject and
consulting with the alienists of Vienna, the pioneers of modern
psychiatry. And she was determined to break through the barriers around Bouchout and see her sister-in-law. Despite the opposition of Franz Josef and the more strenuous objections of
King Leopold II, she journeyed to Brussels in June, accompanied by the court physician.

Finally she gained admittance to the château and was led to a
gloomy salon with draped windows, which had been converted
into Carlotta's throne room. Elizabeth was appalled by Carlotta's condition; the latter was in one of her periods of withdrawal from reality.

Carlotta sat on her mock throne, wearing a tinsel crown,
toying with a bowl filled with fake jewels.

Elizabeth tried to reach her. "Louis Napoleon is gone," she
told Carlotta, "and you have nothing more to fear."

"Love makes time pass," Carlotta whispered, continuing to
play with her baubles.

"And Eugénie is no longer Empress of France," Elizabeth
said. "She is simply Madame Bonaparte."

"Time makes love pass," Carlotta murmured.

It was hopeless; Carlotta was beyond reach.

Elizabeth turned sadly and started to leave, without asking
permission to withdraw.

"Madame," Carlotta said sharply, "do you not know that I
am an empress and the daughter of a king?"

With that reality, Carlotta never lost touch. No fears or apparitions could cloud her mind to the extent that her memories of
having ruled Mexico were vaporized.

Three years later there was a fire at the château, and her
guardians could not locate Carlotta. It broke out at night and

the fire brigade from the nearest town was slow in coming. Flames were shooting out of the windows when Carlotta was sighted on the parapet of the highest tower, leaning over and shouting at the flames, "That is forbidden! That is forbidden!"

When her rescuers reached her, shivering in a nightgown, she protested at being brought down from the tower, crying, "We cannot abdicate, we cannot abandon our post!"

The years passed, her contemporaries died, history unreeled slowly but forebodingly as the European nations prepared for a climactic collision on the fields of her native Flanders, and Carlotta remained the recluse of Bouchout. Her beauty faded. Occasionally a persistent newspaper photographer would snap a picture of her, wizened now, her oval face lined, her once-lovely profile sharpened like a blade, as she was taken for an airing in her carriage.

"It is better to go by one blow," she said once in a moment of rueful clarity, "than little by little."

Perhaps she envied Maximilian then, with his quick death before a firing squad.

Her dissolute brother—known as Cleopold by his less respectful subjects because his mistress was Cleo Merande, who kept him under her dainty thumb—died in 1909 and was succeeded by her nephew King Albert, a much more creditable sovereign who proved his worth during the coming war.

No doubt she was protected from a scandalous eruption of headlines when a London fishmonger named William Brightwell claimed that though he was the adopted son of a Cockney shopkeeper, his real name was Rudolph Franz Maximilian Hapsburg, if only his mother would acknowledge him. Brightwell asserted that he was born to Carlotta the hectic night she spent in the Vatican, and because of her breakdown, his birth was concealed. His diligence in promoting this claim was notable and continued for years. On Carlotta's death he was to claim a share of the estate, as well as a proprietary interest in a number of Maximilian-Carlotta relics believed to have been lost in a shipwreck while being transported from Mexico by the fleeing Díaz supporters in 1911. His claims came to nothing but at least enlivened a career in the fish market.

She was in her seventies, still physically hale, when World War I broke out and fulfilled her prophecy that the copper-plated twilight of the world she knew—the world that propelled her and Maximilian into the Mexican folly—would darken into the blackest night. Far over the horizon she could hear the rumble of artillery; then the field-gray legions of imperial Germany overran Belgium. A Prussian officer drove up to the gates of the Château of Bouchout late in 1914 and posted a notice which read: "This castle, the property of the Belgian Crown, is occupied by Her Majesty, the Empress of Mexico—sister-in-law of our revered ally, the Emperor of Austria. German soldiers are ordered to pass by without singing, and to leave this place untouched."

As she had predicted, many of the principal dynasties were destroyed; the Hapsburgs, the Romanovs, the Hohenzollerns, the Ottomans all vanished into the archives. Historical process had destroyed those who she believed had betrayed her and Maximilian. Whether she rejoiced in this retribution was the secret of those who maintained her in seclusion.

She outlived everyone connected with the Mexican intervention, even her adopted son, Prince Agustín Iturbide, who had been educated in Europe, migrated to the United States, and ended up as Professor Iturbide teaching French and Spanish on the faculty of Georgetown University in Washington, D.C.

For Carlotta death waited until January 16, 1927, when she was eighty-six years old and only a legend in the modern world in which airplanes flew over the boulevards and highroads she had once traveled, in desperate pursuit of a chimerical destiny that would allow her to rule over the lives of millions, in horse-drawn carriages.

Shortly after New Year's, 1927, she came down with influenza, which some days later developed into pneumonia. Willful to the end, she resisted the pneumonia for days before succumbing. Then, finally, she was allowed to go home to Laeken, for burial in the family crypt in the Church of Notre Dame. Only a corporal's guard of survivors of the Belgian Legion, who had gone to Mexico to fight for "our Carlotta," could be mustered to bear her coffin through the woods of Laeken to the crypt. In death, against their wishes, Maximilian and Carlotta were separated, still subject to the dynastic rules which had brought them together in the first place.

*   *   *

Yes, it was a notable scheme which placed an Austrian prince and a Belgian princess on the Mexican throne as debt collectors. Yet it was strikingly unprofitable to all concerned except its craftiest figure, the Balzacian Duc de Morny, who had the sense to take a quick profit and die in his own bed. On the debit side, which did not interest so practical a man, there were thousands of deaths and many more thousands to mourn them, Mexican, French, Belgian, Austrian. It was an unbearable price to pay for a few moments of false imperial grandeur.

Notes on Sources

THE complete listing of many sources indicated below under their author's surname may be found in the Selected Bibliography, which follows.

1. *"A Gathering of Dupes and Rogues"*

The Duc de Morny did not leave many clues to his plots and coups on paper, nor did he believe posterity deserved an explanation for his actions, most of which were self-explanatory. His career, however, has been traced with considerable perception in Maristan Chapman's 1932 biography, *Imperial Brother.*

Talleyrand's advice to his grandson was quoted by Chapman, 70-71.

English newspaper account of Morny's military career, London *Times,* January 16, 1852.

His early career in politics and sugar refining, *ibid.*

First exchange between Morny and Louis Napoleon, Chapman, 169.

Description of Louis Napoleon as "mother-worshipper," Chapman, 204.

President Lincoln's instructions to his Mexico City ambassador, Hudson Strode's *Timeless Mexico,* 162.

2. *A Prince for Herr Biedermeier*

Quotation from Varnhagen von Ense, *Golden Ages of the Great Cities,* edited by Sir Ernest Barker, 247.

Franz Schuselka's observations on his fellow Viennese, Edward Crankshaw's *The Fall of the House of Hapsburg,* 23.

Description of nineteenth-century Vienna, *Golden Ages of the Great Cities,* 248, 252.

L'Aiglon's career is studied at length in André Castelot's *King of Rome*, Hildegarde Hawthorne's *Phantom King; The Story of Napoleon's Son*, and Octave Aubry's *The King of Rome*.

Gossip concerning Archduchess Sophie's relations with l'Aiglon is related in Castelot, 250-51, and Aubry, 217, 231.

Description of Maximilian as a youth, Count Egon Caesar Corti, *Maximilian and Charlotte of Mexico*, Vol. I, 42-43. This is an indispensable source, based mainly on Maximilian's papers in the Austrian State Archives.

Franz Josef's rebuff of Maximilian, Corti, Vol. I, 45.

Maximilian's report on his Vatican visit is quoted in Bertita Harding's *Golden Fleece*, 94.

His description of Napoleon III, Empress Eugénie, their court and their capital is quoted by Corti, Vol. I, 48-49.

His report to Franz Josef on the visit to Brussels, *ibid.*, 62-66.

Princess Charlotte's childhood letter to Queen Victoria is quoted in H. Montgomery Hyde's sterling *Mexican Empire*, 61.

Maximilian's haggling with his prospective father-in-law is described in a letter to Franz Josef, quoted by Corti, Vol. I, 68-69.

Maximilian's letter to his mother on the situation in northern Italy, *ibid.*, 83.

Maximilian to Leopold I on Austrian corruption, dated April 21, 1860, Austrian State Archives.

Carlotta's longing for activity described by Corti, Vol. I, 92.

3. The Invasion of America

Quotation from Philip Guedalla, *The Second Empire*, 307.

Hildalgo's argument for an invasion of Mexico is contained in his *Notes Secretes*, which may be found in the Austrian State Archives.

Captain Louis Noir includes his address to the Zouave company leaving for Mexico in his *Campaign of Mexico*, 17-19.

Sara Yorke's description of her voyage from France to Mexico at the beginning of the intervention is included in her *Maximilian in Mexico*, *passim*, which was published under her married name of Stevenson.

Maximilian's letter to Count Rechberg on Napoleon's purposes, Corti, Vol. I, 158.

Marshal Bazaine's early career is studied in Philip Guedalla's *The Two Marshals*, *passim*.

Bazaine's duties with the Bureau Arabe are described in Guedalla's *The Two Marshals*, *passim*.

Captain Noir's account of the victory at Puebla, his *Campaign of Mexico*, 70-74.

The action at Camerone is described in Charles Mercer's *Legion of Strangers*, 83-88.

Notes on Sources

THE complete listing of many sources indicated below under their author's surname may be found in the Selected Bibliography, which follows.

1. "A Gathering of Dupes and Rogues"

The Duc de Morny did not leave many clues to his plots and coups on paper, nor did he believe posterity deserved an explanation for his actions, most of which were self-explanatory. His career, however, has been traced with considerable perception in Maristan Chapman's 1932 biography, *Imperial Brother*.

Talleyrand's advice to his grandson was quoted by Chapman, 70-71.

English newspaper account of Morny's military career, London *Times*, January 16, 1852.

His early career in politics and sugar refining, *ibid*.

First exchange between Morny and Louis Napoleon, Chapman, 169.

Description of Louis Napoleon as "mother-worshipper," Chapman, 204.

President Lincoln's instructions to his Mexico City ambassador, Hudson Strode's *Timeless Mexico*, 162.

2. A Prince for Herr Biedermeier

Quotation from Varnhagen von Ense, *Golden Ages of the Great Cities*, edited by Sir Ernest Barker, 247.

Franz Schuselka's observations on his fellow Viennese, Edward Crankshaw's *The Fall of the House of Hapsburg*, 23.

Description of nineteenth-century Vienna, *Golden Ages of the Great Cities*, 248, 252.

Princess Salm-Salm's description of travel by Mexican mail coach, *Ten Years of My Life*, 77.

Carlotta's story of the Veracruz-Mexico City journey was related in a letter to Eugénie, June 18, 1864, Austrian State Archives.

José Luis Blasio's account of the Mexico City reception, *Maximilian: Memoirs of His Private Secretary*, 3-4.

6. The Building of Miramar West

Description of Bazaine's ball for Maximilian and Carlotta, Stevenson, *Maximilian in Mexico*, 132-33.

Kuhacsevich on Maximilian's passion for building, Corti, Vol. II, 429-30.

Maximilian's travelogue to his brother, letter to Archduke Karl, July 26, 1864, Austrian State Archives.

Comment on the *Reglamento de la Corte* as "out of place" by Guedalla, *The Two Marshals*, 119.

Countess Paula Kollonitz's strictures on conditions in Mexico were delivered in her *The Court of Mexico, passim*. Several years after her return to Europe, she married M. Eloin, the Belgian who served as chief of Maximilian's Cabinet.

Blasio's appeal for clemency is described in his memoir, 4-5.

Bazaine's criticism of Maximilian's failure to take hold of the governmental reins is quoted by Guedalla, *The Two Marshals*, 121-22.

Maximilian's surprise descent on the capital's bakeries is related by Blasio, 57.

Maximilian on the necessity to "build from the ground up," letter to Gutiérrez, October 30, 1864, Austrian State Archives.

7. An Ill-Will Embassy from Rome

Carlotta's denunciation of the papal nuncio was part of a letter to Eugénie, December 27, 1864, Austrian State Archives.

Her description of the interview with the Pope's emissary, *ibid.*

Her account of the "strained situation" between throne and hierarchy, letter to Eugénie, January 7, 1865, Austrian State Archives.

Gutiérrez de Estrada's involvement in the hierarchy's campaign against Maximilian is discussed by Corti, Vol. II, 456-57.

Maximilian's comment on the need for a parchment factory was recorded by Blasio, 27.

Feasting at Chapultepec was detailed by Blasio, 8.

"Gorging and swilling" by his guests noted by Maximilian in a letter to Archduke Karl, February 24, 1865, Austrian State Archives.

Carlotta's account of her dancing parties was given Eugénie in a letter quoted by Harding, *Phantom Crown*, 166.

Sara Yorke's sizing up of the contrasting characters of Maximilian and Carlotta, Stevenson, 224-25.

Maximilian's exultation over living "among a free people" was conveyed in a letter to Dr. Jilek, February 10, 1865, Austrian State Archives.

Carlotta's concern over troop withdrawals, letter to Eugénie, February 3, 1865, Austrian State Archives.

Bazaine to his sister, quoted by Guedalla, *The Two Marshals*, 126.

Carlotta quoted on the massacre at Tacámbro by Blasio, 47.

Belgian deputy's letter on the massacre appeared in *Het Nederduitsche Bond* (Amsterdam), June 14, 1865.

Napoleon to Maximilian on Mexican finances, April 16, 1865, copy in Austrian State Archives.

Maxamilian's note conveying Buena Vista Palace to Marshal Bazaine quoted by Blasio, 30.

Jerome David's denunciation of the Monroe Doctrine quoted by Angela Stuart, "Maximilian's Phantom Empire," *Mankind* (December, 1969).

Frau von Kuhacsevich's letter to Miramar describing fear and tension at Chapultepec, undated, Austrian State Archives.

8. Uneasy Lie the Heads . . .

Maximilian's discussion of the country's mood with his secretary, Blasio, 50-51.

Description of Maximilian's daily routine, Blasio, 32-40.

His canoe trip to Texcoco and tour of the countryside, *ibid.*, 51-53.

General Douay's long interview with Maximilian and Carlotta is related in Corti, Vol. II, 519-24.

Carlotta's reaction to Douay's departure from the capital was relayed to Eugénie, July 26, 1865, Austrian State Archives.

Carlotta's "Today I am aging" letter to her grandmother, September 29, 1865, quoted by Niles, 186-87.

Blasio's inquiry into the reason Maximilian and Carlotta slept in separate rooms is recorded in his memoir, 16-17, 75-77.

9. The View from Abroad

Duc de Morny's obituary was published in *Revue des Deux Mondes*, Vol. 17 (1865), 768.

Jules Favre's speech is quoted by Stevenson, 163.

Napoleon's expression of disillusion over the Mexican venture to Marshal Bazaine may be found in Paul Gaulot's *The Expedition to Mexico*, Vol. II, 211.

Account of the Romero banquet, Niles, 105-7.

President Lincoln's note to Napoleon is given by Tyrner-Tyrnauer, *Lincoln and the Emperors*, 47-48.

Sheridan's maneuvers on the Mexican border are described in the author's *Sheridan the Inevitable*, 280-83; Grant's intentions regarding Mexico were reported in Grenville M. Dodge's *Personal Recollections*, 95.

General Isham Harris interview, quoted by Niles, 190-91.

10. *"Every Drop of My Blood Is Mexican"*

Carlotta's complaint about the "spontaneous generation" of guerrilla bands is quoted by Harding, *Phantom Crown*, 192.

Jack London's discussion of the same subject, the author's *Jack London: A Biography*, 360.

Escape and capture of the Swiss legionnaire is related by Mercer, *Legion of Strangers*, 91-92.

Claim that Maximilian drew up the Black Decree, Count Émile de Kératry's *The Emperor Maximilian: His Rise and Fall, passim*. Blasio denied the charge in his memoir, 60.

The preamble to the Black Decree is quoted by Blasio, 61.

General Salazar's last letter to his mother is recorded by Niles, 195-96.

Sara Yorke's characterization of General Palacios is contained in her *Maximilian in Mexico, passim*.

Maximilian's secret letter of instructions to Carlotta before she left for Yucatán, Corti, Vol. II, 547.

The history of the Carlotta Colony is recorded in such memoirs as John N. Edwards' *Shelby's Expedition to Mexico*, J. J. Kendall's *Mexico Under Maximilian*, and Alexander W. Terrell's *From Texas to Mexico and the Court of Maximilian*.

William M. Anderson's reflections on the Mexican character, his memoir *An American in Mexico*, 50-51.

Newspaper article on Carlotta Colony quoted by Niles, 211-12.

Matthew Maury's two reports to Maximilian on the state of Mexican public opinion, October 15 and November 19, 1865, cited by Corti, Vol. II, 539-40.

Maximilian's hymn to the beauties of Cuernavaca, letter to Baroness Binzer, February 3, 1866, Austrian State Archives.

Blasio's profile of Dr. Bilimek, his memoir, 70.

Maximilian on his Cuernavaca retreat, letter to Baroness Binzer, *op. cit.*; his letter to Count Hadik on "recognition" he had received in Mexico, quoted by Corti, Vol. II, 572.

11. *Broken Promises, Dashed Hopes*

The military disaster at Santa Isabella is recounted by Mercer, *Legion of Strangers*, 93.

Napoleon urges organization of Mexican army, letter to Maximilian quoted by Corti, Vol. II, 555.

Maximilian protests French withdrawals, letter to Napoleon, December 27, 1865, Austrian State Archives.

Carlotta to Eugénie on need for French support, quoted by Harding, *Phantom Crown*, 197.

Napoleon's announcement of French evacuation, letter to Maximilian, January 15, 1866, Austrian State Archives.

Maximilian's discouragement, described by Blasio, 80.

His complaint that his family does not understand him, letter to Archduke Karl, February 23, 1866, Austrian States Archives.

His instructions to General Almonte, letter of April 4, 1866, Austrian State Archives.

Pope's opinion of Maximilian's commissioners in Rome was transmitted by Father Fischer in a letter dated January 8, 1866, Austrian State Archives. Maximilian's reply to Fischer, May 27, 1866, Austrian State Archives.

Maximilian's complaint about the dancing cardinals, letter to Velásquez de León, quoted by Corti, Vol. II, 623.

12. *Adíos, Mama Carlotta*

Napoleon's surprising order for Marshal Bazaine to counterattack before leaving Mexico, quoted by Gaulot, Vol. II, 311.

Detroyat's warning letter to Maximilian was dated July 6, 1866, and was quoted by Corti, Vol. II, 634.

Carlotta's campaign to stiffen Maximilian's backbone was observed by Blasio, 81. Her memorandum to Maximilian on the necessity to stand fast was quoted by Corti, Vol. II, 638-40.

Maximilian to his mother on Carlotta's trip to Europe, letter dated July 5, 1866, Austrian State Archives.

Celebration of Maximilian's thirty-fourth birthday described by Blasio, 82.

Official reasons given for Carlotta's voyage were published in the *Diario del Imperio* (Mexico City), July 8, 1866. Maximilian's letter to his brother on the same subject, quoted by Corti, Vol. II, 643.

Rumors that Carlotta was poisoned in Puebla were reported by Blasio, 84.

Incidents surrounding Carlotta's trip to Veracruz and her departure for Europe were gathered from members of her entourage by Blasio, *passim*.

13. *"Put Not Thy Faith in Princes"*

Description of Austrian defeat by the Prussians was gleaned from Michael Howard's *The Franco-Prussian War, passim,* and Edward Crankshaw's *The Fall of the House of Hapsburg,* 216-22.

Results of Franco-Prussian War summarized by Crankshaw, 227-28.

Carlotta's letter to Chapultepec from Havana, quoted by Harding, *Phantom Crown*, 233-34.

Prosper Merimée's prediction Carlotta's mission would fail was included in his *Letters to M. Panizzi, 1850-1870*, 229.

Carlotta's letter to Maximilian describing her interviews with Napoleon and Eugénie, August 16, 1866, quoted by Corti, Vol. II, 681.

Carlotta's scene at St.-Cloud described by Percy F. Martin, *Maximilian in Mexico*, 242.

Carlotta's letter to Maximilian from Lake Como, August 26, 1866, quoted by Corti, Vol. II, 690-91.

Her predictions of European disaster, letter to Maximilian, September 9, 1866, *ibid.*, 699-700.

Carlotta's concern over cipher telegram, related by Blasio, 91-93.

14. A Jesuitical Interregnum

Rumors regarding Father Fischer were brought up by Stevenson, *passim*.

Maximilian's unconcern regarding reports on Carlotta's mental condition was noted by Blasio, 85.

Maximilian's jocular reply to Bombelles on Napoleon's declining health, September 20, 1866, Corti, Vol. II, 723-24.

Colonel Von der Smissen's proposal to attack the Mexican army reported advancing on the capital, letter to Maximilian, September 19, 1866, *ibid.*, 725.

Bazaine's fear of an approaching catastrophe, letter to French War Ministry, quoted by Martin, 267.

Maximilian's sardonic thanks to Napoleon, letter dated October 8, 1866, Austrian State Archives.

Dr. Basch's account of giving Maximilian the tragic news about Carlotta, his memoir *Memories of Mexico*, 124-25.

15. Breakdown

Details of Carlotta's departure from Miramar for Rome were related by Blasio, 94.

Her frightening reception in Rome was described by Martin, 244.

Cardinal Antonelli's manipulation of Vatican funds, *ibid.*, 245.

Carlotta's first meeting with the Pope, Blasio, 100. He gathered details of the scene that erupted, after Carlotta was left alone with the Pope and his advisers, from members of the papal entourage.

Her second appearance at the Vatican was also detailed by Blasio, this time from the account of her lady-in-waiting, as well as his firsthand observation of her conduct following the breakdown, 102-7.

Velásquez de Léon's cable to Maximilian on Carlotta's condition, quoted by Martin, 252.

Carlotta's actions following her return to Miramar, Corti, Vol. II, 715-16.

16. The Vivandière from Vermont

Maximilian's conversation with his physician regarding abdication, Basch, *passim.*

His reception at Orizaba and the contest between Herzfeld and Father Fischer, *ibid.*

Maximilian's state of mind during the decision-making at Orizaba, Blasio, 114.

General Sherman's comment on situation at Veracruz, quoted by Niles, 237.

Maximilian's appeal to President Johnson for understanding, quoted by Tyrner-Tyrnauer, *Lincoln and the Emperors,* 147-48.

Archduchess Sophie's stand-fast letter to Maximilian, quoted by Corti, Vol. II, 770-71.

General Castelnau's reflections on Maximilian's character were published by *La Revue de Paris* (August, 1927), 593-94.

Marshal Bazaine's dispute with Teodosio Lares, Martin, 290.

Captain Kendall quoted his letter to the *Times* of London in his memoir, *Mexico Under Maximilian,* 344.

Prince Salm-Salm's description of the French departure from Mexico City, *My Diary in Mexico,* Vol. I, 16-18. This work includes his wife's lively account of her own experiences in Mexico and later in the Franco-Prussian War.

Princess Salm-Salm's Civil War experiences, *ibid., passim.*

Maximilian's departure from his capital for Querétaro was described by Blasio, 129-31.

His meeting with Salm-Salm on the road to Querétaro, Salm-Salm, Vol. I, 25.

Maximilian under fire near San Miguel Calpulaplan, *ibid.,* 30.

17. The Condemned Men of Querétaro

Maximilian's daily routine at Querétaro, Blasio, 137.

His denunciation of his ministers in the capital, Salm-Salm, Vol. I, 49.

His generals' pleas against exposing himself to enemy fire, *ibid.,* 61.

Fighting spirit of the Mexican chasseurs, *ibid.,* 62-64.

Danger of being bottled up in Querétaro, analyzed by Salm-Salm, Vol. I, 73.

Decision of March 21 council of war, reported by Blasio, 146-47.

General Márquez's pledge not to become involved in any other project than relief of Querétaro, Salm-Salm, Vol. I, 90-91.

Márquez's defeat by General Díaz, Charles Smart's *Viva Juarez!,* 377.

Colonel Loaeza's death, described by Blasio, 156.

Maximilian's letter home on his close brush with death, quoted by Hyde, 265-66. In that letter, Maximilian rather ungratefully wrote that he was "entirely surrounded by Mexicans . . . throughout this campaign." Apparently he sought to picture himself to his old friends and courtiers at Miramar as the leader of an entirely Mexican force to prove how he had gained the Mexicans' loyalty. This would bolster his contention that "Europe has deserted me," but it ignored the vital presence in Querétaro of Prince Salm-Salm, the Austrian hussars, and a number of deserters from the French Foreign Legion who chose his service over the legion.

Maximilian's dog attacks Colonel López, Salm-Salm, Vol. I, 178.

Deliberations of May 14 council of war were recounted by Salm-Salm, Vol. I, 185, and Blasio, 158-59.

Betrayal of Querétaro, Colonel López's treachery and Maximilian's flight to avoid capture, Salm-Salm, Vol. I, 190-94, and Blasio, 161-65.

Maximilian's exemption of General Riva Palacios from the Black Decree, Martin, 339.

Maximilian in captivity, Salm-Salm, Vol. I, 215, and Blasio, 169.

His plans for his life after the hoped-for release from Mexican custody, Blasio, 173.

Princess Salm-Salm's whirlwind activity before and after the fall of Querétaro were described by herself in Salm-Salm, Vol. II, *passim.*

Plans for escape attempt, Salm-Salm, Vol. I, 232.

Princess Agnes' pleas before Juárez, Salm-Salm, Vol. II, *passim.*

Arrangements for escape to coast near Veracruz, *ibid.,* Vol. I, 244.

Princess Agnes' thwarted attempt to bribe Colonel Palacios (no relation to General Riva Palacios) was related in various sources: Salm-Salm, Vol. II, 66-71; Harding, *Phantom Crown,* 316-17; Smart, 379; and Corti, Vol. II, 812-13.

The princess' forced departure from Querétaro, Salm-Salm, Vol. I, 265.

Maximilian's last letter to Carlotta, quoted by Harding, *Phantom Crown,* 323.

Juárez's explanation of the execution before the Mexican Congress, quoted by Smart, 381.

Maximilian's last words before the firing squad, gathered from those present, Blasio, 226.

Republican colonel's accusation of France as Maximilian's real executioner, quoted by Salm-Salm, Vol. I, 311.

18. Exeunt Omnes

Albert Guerard quoted on events at Universal Exhibition, Smart, 381.

Paris newspaper quoted on flight of royalties, *Le Matin,* July 1, 1867.

Clemenceau's comment on pitying Maximilian and Carlotta, quoted by Angela Stuart, *Mankind* article, *op. cit.*

Maximilian's body placed on exhibition, Frederic Hall's *Mexico and Maximilian, passim.* Hall, an American, was one of Maximilian's lawyers.

Mexican historian on attempt to make Maximilian a martyr, Don José María Marroqui, *Streets of Mexico, passim.*

Arrival of Maximilian's body in Vienna and his funeral, described by Blasio, 186.

Empress Eugénie to Prince Metternich on fear of meeting the Hapsburgs, quoted by Corti, Vol. II, 829.

Colonel Rincón-Gallardo quoted on Colonel López, New York *Herald,* July 10, 1867. López's pamphlet in defense of his actions at Querétaro was included in Salm-Salm, Vol. II, 192-96.

Career of the "imperial bastard," Maximilian's illegitimate son, Hyde, *Mexican Empire,* 313-15. Details of his arrest as a spy and his execution by the French, Major Émile Massard's *Les Espions de Paris,* 204-8.

Archduchess Sophie's guilt and sorrow after Maximilian's death were described by Blasio, 185.

Adventures of Prince Félix and Princess Agnes after their deportation from Mexico, Salm-Salm, Vol. II, *passim.*

Countess Reinach-Foussemagne's account of Carlotta's rambling conversation, quoted by Niles, 336.

Elizabeth of Austria's visit to Bouchout, Harding, *The Golden Fleece,* 254-57. Incident of fire at castle, *ibid.,* 268.

Selected Bibliography

ANDERSON, WILLIAM M., *An American in Maximilian's Mexico*, Ramón Ruiz, ed. San Marino, Calif., 1959.

AUBRY, OCTAVE, *The King of Rome*, trans. by Elizabeth Abbott. Philadelphia, 1932.

BAREA, LISA, *Vienna*. New York, 1966.

BARKER, SIR ERNEST, ed., *Golden Ages of the Great Cities*. London, 1952.

BASCH, DR. SAMUEL, *Memories of Mexico*. Leipzig, 1870.

BEALS, CARLETON, *Porfirio Díaz*. Philadelphia, 1932.

BLANCHOT, COLONEL, *The French Intervention in Mexico*. Paris, 1911.

BLASIO, JOSÉ LUIS, *Maximilian: Memoirs of His Private Secretary*. New Haven, 1934.

CASTELOT, ANDRÉ, *King of Rome*. New York, 1960.

CHAPMAN, MARISTAN, *Imperial Brother: The Life of the Duc de Morny*. New York, 1931.

CORTI, COUNT EGON CAESAR, *Maximilian and Carlotta of Mexico*. New York, 1928. 2 vols.

CRANKSHAW, EDWARD, *The Fall of the House of Hapsburg*. New York, 1964.

DAWSON, DANIEL, *The Mexican Adventure*. London, 1935.

DETROYAT, LEONCE, *The French Intervention in Mexico*. Paris, 1868.

DODGE, GRENVILLE M., *Personal Recollections*. Council Bluffs, Iowa, 1914.

EDWARDS, JOHN N., *Shelby's Expedition to Mexico*. Kansas City, 1872.

GAULOT, PAUL, *The Expedition to Mexico*. Paris, 1869.

GUEDALLA, PHILIP, *The Second Empire*. New York, 1922.

———, *The Two Marshals*. London, 1943.

HALL, FREDERIC, *Mexico and Maximilian*. New York, 1867.

HARDING, BERTITA, *The Golden Fleece*. Indianapolis, 1938.

———, *Phantom Crown*. Indianapolis, 1934.

HAWTHORNE, HILDEGARDE, *Phantom King: The Story of Napoleon's Son*. New York, 1937.

HOWARD, MICHAEL, *The Franco-Prussian War*. New York, 1961.

HYDE, H. MONTGOMERY, *Mexican Empire*. London, 1946.

KENDALL, J. J., *Mexico Under Maximilian*. London, 1871.

KÉRATRY, COUNT ÉMILE DE, *The Rise and Fall of Maximilian*. London, 1869.

KOLLONITZ, COUNTESS PAULA, *The Court of Mexico*. London, 1868.

MARROQUI, DON JOSÉ MARÍA, *Streets of Mexico*. Mexico City, 1911.

MARTIN, PERCY F., *Maximilian in Mexico*. London, 1913.

MAXIMILIAN, EMPEROR, *Recollections of My Life*. London, 1868. 3 vols.

———, *On the Wing*. London, 1868.

MERCER, CHARLES, *Legion of Strangers*. New York, 1964.

MERIMÉE, PROSPER, *Letters to M. Panizzi, 1850-1870*. Paris, 1881.

NAUROY, CHARLES, *Secrets of the Bonapartes*. Paris, 1889.

NILES, BLAIR, *Passengers to Mexico*. New York, 1943.

NOIR, LOUIS, *Campaign of Mexico*. Paris, 1867. 2 vols.

O'CONNOR, RICHARD, *Sheridan the Inevitable*. Indianapolis, 1953.

OLLIVIER, ÉMILE, *The Liberal Empire*. Paris, 1875.

SALM-SALM, PRINCE FÉLIX, *My Diary in Mexico*, including Princess Agnes' diary, London, 1871. 2 vols.

SMART, CHARLES ALLEN, *Viva Juarez!* Philadelphia, 1863.

STEVENSON, SARA YORKE, *Maximilian in Mexico*. New York, 1899.

STRODE, HUDSON, *Timeless Mexico*. New York, 1942.

TAYLOR, JOHN M., *Maximilian and Carlotta*. New York, 1894.

TERRELL, ALEXANDER W., *From Texas to Mexico and the Court of Maximilian*. Dallas, 1933.

TYRNER-TYRNAUER, A. R., *Lincoln and the Emperors*. New York, 1962.

WHITE, JAMES, *The Republic of Mexico Restored*. Mexico City, 1867.

WYDENBRUCK, NORAH, *My Two Worlds*. London, 1956.

Acknowledgments

The author is deeply indebted to a number of librarians and archivists, especially the staffs of the Guildhall Library, London, and Trinity College Library, Dublin; Robert Woodward, head of the Bangor (Maine) Public Library for obtaining rare books; Lise Kruse of the Athenaeum of Boston; the Manuscript Division of the Library of Congress, which has a duplicate on microfilm of many of Maximilian's Mexican papers; Dr. Walter Wieser of the National Library, Vienna; and Hofrat Gebhard Rath and Dr. Rudolf Neck of the Austrian State Archives.

Index